T0323244

THE
ANNALS

of the American Academy of
Political and Social Science

VOLUME 686 | NOVEMBER 2019

Entitlement Reform

SPECIAL EDITORS:

Robert A. Moffitt
Johns Hopkins University

James P. Ziliak
University of Kentucky

Los Angeles | London | New Delhi
Singapore | Washington DC | Melbourne

The American Academy of Political and Social Science

202 S. 36th Street, Annenberg School for Communication, University of Pennsylvania,
Philadelphia, PA 19104-3806; (215) 746-6500; (215) 573-2667 (fax); www.aapss.org

---

Origin and Purpose. The Academy was organized December 14, 1889, to promote the progress of political and social science, especially through publications and meetings. The Academy does not take sides in controverted questions, but seeks to gather and present reliable information to assist the public in forming an intelligent and accurate judgment.

Meetings. The Academy occasionally holds a meeting in the spring extending over two days.

Publications. THE ANNALS of The American Academy of Political and Social Science is the bimonthly publication of the Academy. Each issue contains articles on some prominent social or political problem, written at the invitation of the editors. These volumes constitute important reference works on the topics with which they deal, and they are extensively cited by authorities throughout the United States and abroad.

Subscriptions. THE ANNALS of The American Academy of Political and Social Science (ISSN 0002-7162) (J295) is published bimonthly—in January, March, May, July, September, and November—by SAGE Publishing, 2455 Teller Road, Thousand Oaks, CA 91320. Periodicals postage paid at Thousand Oaks, California, and at additional mailing offices. POSTMASTER: Send address changes to The Annals of The American Academy of Political and Social Science, c/o SAGE Publishing, 2455 Teller Road, Thousand Oaks, CA 91320. Institutions may subscribe to THE ANNALS at the annual rate: $1257 (clothbound, $1419). Individuals may subscribe to the ANNALS at the annual rate: $134 (clothbound, $197). Single issues of THE ANNALS may be obtained by individuals for $41 each (clothbound, $58). Single issues of THE ANNALS have proven to be excellent supplementary texts for classroom use. Direct inquiries regarding adoptions to THE ANNALS c/o SAGE Publishing (address below).

All correspondence concerning membership in the Academy, dues renewals, inquiries about membership status, and/or purchase of single issues of THE ANNALS should be sent to THE ANNALS c/o SAGE Publishing, 2455 Teller Road, Thousand Oaks, CA 91320. Telephone: (800) 818-SAGE (7243) and (805) 499-0721; Fax/Order line: (805) 375-1700; e-mail: journals@sagepub.com. *Please note that orders under $30 must be prepaid.* For all customers outside the Americas, please visit http://www.sagepub.co.uk/customerCare.nav for information.

Printed on acid-free paper

THE ANNALS

© 2019 by The American Academy of Political and Social Science

Editorial Office: 202 S. 36th Street, Philadelphia, PA 19104-3806
For information about individual and institutional subscriptions address:
SAGE Publishing
2455 Teller Road
Thousand Oaks, CA 91320

For SAGE Publishing: Peter Geraghty (Production) and Mimi Nguyen (Marketing)

From India and South Asia, write to:
SAGE PUBLICATIONS INDIA Pvt Ltd
B-42 Panchsheel Enclave, P.O. Box 4109
New Delhi 110 017
INDIA

From Europe, the Middle East, and Africa, write to:
SAGE PUBLICATIONS LTD
1 Oliver's Yard, 55 City Road
London EC1Y 1SP
UNITED KINGDOM

International Standard Serial Number ISSN 0002-7162
ISBN 978-1-0718-0487-2 (Vol. 686, 2019) paper
ISBN 978-1-0718-0489-6 (Vol. 686, 2019) cloth
Manufactured in the United States of America. First printing, November 2019

Information about membership rates, institutional subscriptions, and back issue prices may be found on the facing page.

Advertising. Current rates and specifications may be obtained by writing to The Annals Advertising and Promotion Manager at the Thousand Oaks office (address above). Acceptance of advertising in this journal in no way implies endorsement of the advertised product or service by SAGE or the journal's affiliated society(ies) or the journal editor(s). No endorsement is intended or implied. SAGE reserves the right to reject any advertising it deems as inappropriate for this journal.

Claims. Claims for undelivered copies must be made no later than six months following month of publication. The publisher will supply replacement issues when losses have been sustained in transit and when the reserve stock will permit.

Change of Address. Six weeks' advance notice must be given when notifying of change of address. Please send the old address label along with the new address to the SAGE office address above to ensure proper identification. Please specify the name of the journal.

THE ANNALS
of the American Academy of Political and Social Science

VOLUME 686 | NOVEMBER 2019

IN THIS ISSUE:

Entitlement Reform

Special Editors: ROBERT A. MOFFITT and JAMES P. ZILIAK

Reflections

FORTHCOMING

Fatal Police Shootings: Patterns, Policy, and Prevention
Special Editor: LAWRENCE W. SHERMAN

Labor Market Uncertainties for Youth and Young Adults
Special Editors: W. J. YEUNG, Y. YANG, and ARNE KALLEBERG

Introduction

Entitlements: Options for Reforming the Social Safety Net in the United States

A combination of demographic aging and diversification, volatile business cycle conditions, stagnant real wages, declining employment, and policy choices have increased the need to examine the adequacy of the U.S. social safety net. Is it accomplishing what it is designed to do? Can it weather a fiscal storm? Current "entitlement" programs are in almost all cases providing important assistance to U.S. families and are improving families' well-being, but they face significant challenges that will require the attention of policy-makers around the country. Some programs may need a structural revamping, while others could do with incremental modifications. Because U.S. entitlement programs address complex social issues, they are themselves complex systems; it follows, then, that meaningful reform must be thoughtful and nuanced, eschewing political expediency. Further, federal support is needed for even more high-quality research that will provide evidence on the types of reforms that will achieve the goals of the programs.

Keywords: social insurance; means-tested transfers; welfare; safety net

By
ROBERT A. MOFFITT
and
JAMES P. ZILIAK

A perfect storm of demographic aging, a deep and protracted recession, secular decline in employment and real wages, and public policy choices at the federal and state levels have resulted in substantial fiscal

Robert A. Moffitt is the Krieger-Eisenhower Professor of Economics in the Department of Economics at Johns Hopkins University.

James P. Ziliak is the Carol Martin Gatton Endowed Chair in Microeconomics in the Department of Economics at the University of Kentucky.

NOTE: We are grateful to the Peter G. Peterson Foundation for financial support that made this volume possible. The articles benefited greatly from the comments of participants at an authors' conference, especially Melissa Kearney, Bradley Hardy, Elaine Maag, Aaron Yelowitz, Karen Dynan, Angela Rachidi, and Jeremie Greer. All opinions and conclusions are solely those of the authors and do not necessarily reflect the views of any sponsoring agency.

Correspondence: jziliak@uky.edu

DOI: 10.1177/0002716219884546

pressure on the national debt, with possible consequences for the design and financial future of the U.S. social safety net. The federal deficit was $779 billion by fiscal year 2018 and is projected to rise rapidly over the next few years (U.S. Department of Treasury 2018). The United States spends 18.7 percent of its GDP on social expenditures as defined by the OECD, slightly less than the OECD average of 20.1 percent but far above the 12.8 percent it spent in 1980.[1]

Public discussion of possible reforms of U.S. entitlement programs is consequently more important than ever. Some have argued that we are spending too much and that many who are not in need, or who could receive help instead from their own earnings or private sources, are receiving support from the government and that major structural reform is needed to reduce expenditures. Others think that many of our programs are inefficient and that the same, or even superior, services could be provided at lower cost, sometimes arguing for major structural reform and, at other times, arguing for smaller incremental reforms. Yet others believe that many families in need are struggling and are still not receiving benefits that should be provided by a wealthy country like the United States and that major expansions are needed to support those families. Still others think that the nation's entitlement programs are doing quite well at the present time, although many incremental reforms could improve their functioning or their coverage, without major structural reform. Incremental reforms generally include changes to program eligibility, funding, and generosity, such as imposing work requirements for beneficiaries, replacing matching grants or direct provision with block grants to states, and capping the amount or duration of benefit receipt. Fundamental reforms are more sweeping in reach, including, for example, proposals to restructure insurance markets to offer "Medicare for All," or for wholesale replacement of most means-tested transfer programs with a guaranteed universal basic income.

In this volume, we bring together leading scholars to assess the options, opportunities, and challenges for reform of the major programs in the U.S. entitlement system and to bring to bear the available research evidence on the potential effectiveness of those reforms. The articles aim to bridge the oftentimes wide gulf between policy and evidence by assessing the efficacy of major proposals to reform entitlements in light of the best causal research evidence, as well as to strike out on new territory to offer a number of innovative solutions to the challenge of providing economic security to a growing and rapidly diversifying population. The articles should serve to inform evidence-based policymaking at both the federal and subnational levels of government. The volume is distinct in the breadth of programs covered—eleven major programs, including programs providing both social insurance and means-tested transfers—and the simultaneous attention to institutional details, research evidence, and policy reforms. The articles are written to be widely accessible to the policy, advocacy, and research communities and to serve as a pedagogical resource at the graduate and undergraduate college and university levels.

In the remainder of this Introduction, we set the stage for the contributions in the volume by offering a brief survey of the programs covered and their trends in spending. We do not discuss in detail the reasons for spending trends, as these are covered in the respective articles. We also provide a glimpse at some of the under-lying demographic headwinds facing the United States and how these will shape the level of financial need and subsequent policy discussions. Next, we summarize the proposals offered in each of the eleven articles, along with the two supplementary reflections. We conclude with a discussion of what we see as the lessons for entitlement reform to be drawn from the contributions to the volume.

Social Insurance and Means-Tested Transfer Programs in the United States

The safety net in the United States consists of both social insurance and means-tested transfers. Social insurance programs typically provide benefits to families or individuals who have a history of significant employment or who have reached old age, while means-tested transfers provide benefits to those with limited incomes and assets and often have no explicit link to employment or age. The programs together are colloquially referred to as "entitlements," but in fact many programs in the safety net offer no explicit entitlement of support in the event of loss of income.

The major social insurance programs are Social Security retirement and survivor benefits, Social Security Disability Insurance (SSDI), Medicare, unemployment insurance (UI), and workers compensation. The key means-tested programs are Medicaid, the Supplemental Nutrition Assistance Program (SNAP), the Earned Income Tax Credit (EITC), Supplemental Security Income (SSI), subsidized housing assistance, the Temporary Assistance for Needy Families (TANF) program, the Additional Child Tax Credit (ACTC), and the Child Care and Development Fund (CCDF). This volume covers all these programs with the exception of workers compensation (although spending on this program is sizable, there is comparatively limited evidence on the program and hence little analysis of it, and the scope of federal oversight is minimal). This list is by no means exhaustive, but it does encompass the overwhelming majority of public outlay that is designed to support individual and family well-being.

Trends in expenditures on social insurance

Figure 1 depicts trends in spending from 1979 to 2017 on the four social insurance programs addressed by the authors in the volume, with inflation-adjusted spending in billions of 2012 dollars shown in panel A and as a share of gross domestic product (GDP) in panel B.[2] We begin with 1979, as that year roughly corresponds with the dawn of much of the subsequent widening inequality and upheaval in U.S. labor markets from the two deepest recessions since the Great Depressions of the 1930s.

Social Security provides income support for retired workers, their spouses, and children, as well as surviving dependents. Funding for the program comes from the payroll tax assessed on labor-market earnings, with the rate fixed at 12.4 percent (paid equally by the employer and employee) since 1990 but with the

FIGURE 1
Trends in Spending on Social Insurance Programs

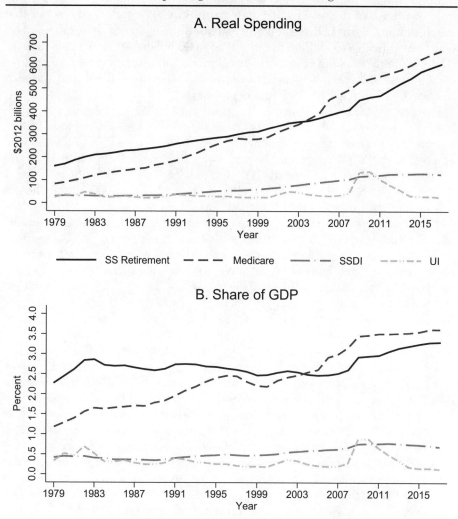

SOURCE: Authors' calculations. Social Security (SS) Retirement is from Table 4.A5 of the 2018 Social Security Annual Statistical Supplement; Medicare is from the National Health Expenditures by type of service and source of funds CY 1960–2017, https://www.cms.gov/ research-statistics-data-and-systems/statistics-trends-and-reports/nationalhealthexpenddata/ nationalhealthaccountshistorical.html; SSDI is payments to disabled workers in Table 4.A6 of 2018 Social Security Annual Statistical Supplement; UI is from https://oui.doleta.gov/unemploy/ hb394/hndbkrpt.asp; GDP is from https://www.bea.gov/national/xls/gdplev.xlsx, and the Personal Consumption Expenditure Deflator (PCE) for 2012 base year is from https://www.govinfo.gov/ content/pkg/ERP-2019/pdf/ERP-2019-table5.pdf.

(capped) taxable wage base increased with inflation each year. The retired worker component makes up the largest and growing share of total benefits paid, rising from two-thirds of the total in 1979 to four-fifths in 2017, and it is this series that we present in Figure 1. Real spending increased nearly fourfold over the past 38 years, rising from $160 billion to more than $600 billion. Spending as a share of GDP was fairly stable over much of the period, but, coinciding with the retirement of the Baby Boom generation around 2007, there has been a sizable increase to 3.3 percent of GDP in recent years.

Even more striking in Figure 1 is the growth in Medicare. The program, which is funded by a combination of a 2.9 percent tax on all wage earnings and general income tax revenues, provides health insurance to those ages 65 and older as well as most on the SSDI program. Medicare spending was $83 billion in 1979 and accounted for under 1 percent of GDP, and today it is larger than the retirement component of Social Security with real spending of $666 billion in 2017 (though still smaller than overall expenditure on Social Security inclusive of dependent and survivors benefits). SSDI partially replaces labor market earnings for workers who have paid into the Social Security system and have become disabled to a degree that they are unable to engage in gainful employment. Funding for SSDI comes from the same payroll tax revenues collected for Social Security. Growth in expenditures on SSDI has likewise been dramatic, falling in between Medicare and Social Security in terms of rate of change. In 1979, total real spending was $30 billion, and it reached a peak of $130 billion in 2015, before subsiding in recent years. While growth has been rapid, as a share of GDP (0.7 percent in 2017), it is much smaller than either Social Security or Medicare.

UI provides partial wage replacement to workers temporarily laid off or actively seeking employment. The program is distinct from the other three social insurance programs in that it is operated at the state level but with federal oversight. Funding comes from a tax on employers, known as an experience-rated tax inasmuch as the rate varies with the level and frequency of worker displacement, and the fraction of wages that are replaced varies considerably across states. Although the amplitudes are suppressed because of the scale in Figure 1, of the social insurance programs UI is the most countercyclical, with benefits rising in recessions and falling in expansions. The very large increase in the years surrounding the Great Recession was a result of both a dramatic increase in unemployment and of emergency provisions enacted by Congress to temporarily increase the cap on receipt from the normal 26 weeks to upward of 99 weeks. Today, however, UI accounts for its lowest share of GDP at 0.14 percent.

Trends in expenditures on means-tested transfers

Means-tested transfers in the United States, like social insurance, include both cash and in-kind assistance, and some programs, such as TANF, provide both forms. Unlike social insurance, however, means-tested transfers have no dedicated funding stream, and all are paid out of general tax revenues. In Figure 2 we present trends in real spending, both overall and as a share of GDP, in the major cash and near-cash transfer programs.

FIGURE 2
Trends in Spending on Cash and Near-Cash Means-Tested Transfer Programs

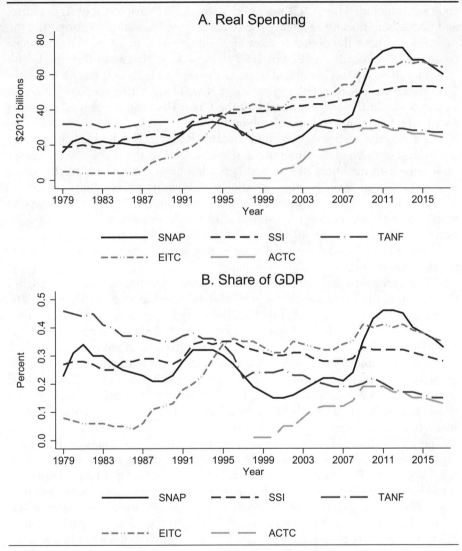

SOURCE: Authors' calculations. SNAP is from https://fns-prod.azureedge.net/sites/default/files/resource-files/SNAPsummary-8.pdf; SSI is from Table 7.A4 of the 2018 Social Security Statistical Supplement. In early 1980s SSI is from Table No. 589 of the 1988 Statistical Abstract of the United States and earlier year from p. 353 of https://www.census.gov/library/publications/1987/compendia/statab/108ed.html; TANF is from https://www.acf.hhs.gov/ofa/resource/tanf-financial-data-fy-2017; the EITC and ACTC are from the Brookings/Urban Tax Policy Center for 1979–2015, and for 2016 and 2017 see Table 1 of the Statistics of Income (SOI) from https://www.irs.gov/statistics/soi-tax-stats-individual-income-tax-returns; GDP is from https://www.bea.gov/national/xls/gdplev.xlsx; and the PCE for 2012 base year is from https://www.govinfo.gov/content/pkg/ERP-2019/pdf/ERP-2019-table5.pdf.

SNAP, which provides assistance to purchase food for home preparation, is technically an in-kind program, though it functions more as a near-cash program and thus is included here. It is operated by the U.S. Department of Agriculture, and, while benefits and eligibility standards are set federally, states operate the program and have the option to alter eligibility. Similar to UI, SNAP is strongly countercyclical, but from 1979 to 1999 there was no change in the trend, with spending about $20 billion in real terms at the peak of both business cycles. After 2000 there was strong secular growth in SNAP, along with a marked antirecessionary spike in the years surrounding the Great Recession, with real spending rising threefold to more than $60 billion by 2017.

SSI serves the aged poor, the blind, and the disabled. The disabled component is the largest share of the program and, unlike SSDI, there is no work history requirement to qualify. Although SSI is funded by general revenues, it is operated by the Social Security Administration with benefits and eligibility set nationally, with a state option to supplement benefits. From 1979 to 1990, there was modest growth in spending on SSI; but after the Supreme Court issued its decision in *Sullivan v. Zebley* (493 U.S. 521 [1990]) that ruled unconstitutional how children were assessed for gainful activity, real spending accelerated, and today appropriations are in excess of $50 billion.

TANF serves low-income families with dependent children under age 18, but that is one of the few constants in program operations over time. Prior to 1997, the program was known as Aid to Families with Dependent Children (AFDC) and was funded by a federal-state matching grant. TANF emerged out of the 1996 Welfare Reform Act, with funding set as a fixed (in nominal dollars) $16.5 billion block grant to states and with a state "maintenance of effort" requirement set at 75 percent of prior spending levels under AFDC. As Figure 2 shows, real combined federal and state spending has declined over the 1979 to 2017 period, which makes it unique in the U.S. social safety net, and has translated into a marked fall as a share of GDP from 0.46 percent to 0.15 percent.

The EITC and ACTC stand out among means-tested cash transfers with their explicit tie to paid employment. Unlike most tax credits in the United States, if the EITC or ACTC result in negative tax liability, then that residual amount gets refunded to taxpayers when they file their annual individual income tax returns.[3] The EITC is available in limited amounts to childless workers, while the ACTC is available only to families with dependent children, and in two-parent households both parents are typically required to be in paid employment to claim the ACTC. Spending on the EITC was initially modest after its introduction in 1975 and then grew briskly after a series of expansions with the 1986, 1990, and 1993 budget bills. Today the program is the largest cash transfer in terms of expenditure at $64 billion in 2012 dollars. The ACTC was established in 1997 but did not ramp up until a couple of expansions in the early 2000s. Currently the program is on par with TANF in terms of overall expenditure.

Figure 3 depicts trends in expenditures on in-kind means-tested transfer programs. Medicaid provides health insurance coverage to low-income and low-asset individuals and families across the age spectrum. Funding is from a federal-state matching grant, using the same formula as employed in the former AFDC

FIGURE 3
Trends in Spending on Noncash Means-Tested Transfer Programs

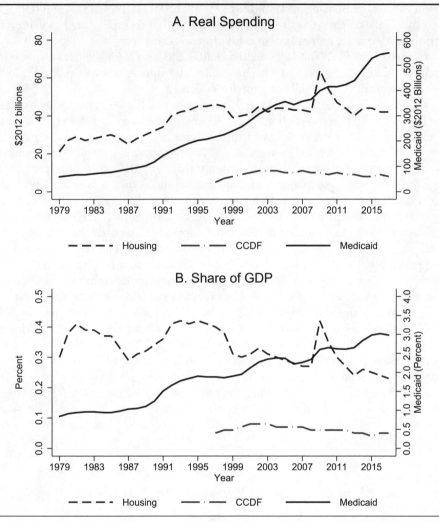

SOURCE: Authors' calculations. Medicaid is from the National Health Expenditures by type of service and source of funds CY 1960–2017, https://www.cms.gov/research-statistics-data-and-systems/statistics-trends-and-reports/nationalhealthexpenddata/nationalhealthaccountshistorical.html; CCDF is from Table 9.4 of https://greenbook-waysandmeans.house.gov/sites/greenbook.waysandmeans.house.gov/files/Chapter%209%20Child%20Care%20-%20Additional%20Tables%20and%20Figures.pdf; and data for FY2017 CCDF is from https://www.acf.hhs.gov/occ/resource/ccdf-expenditures-overview-for-fy-2017-all-appropriation-years; Housing assistance comes from Congressional Research Service (CRS) reports as part of the Green Book for 1979–2002, 2008–2015. The other years are constructed from OMB Budget outlays found at https://www.whitehouse.gov/omb/supplemental-materials/ "Public Budget Database" Outlays.xls. GDP is from https://www.bea.gov/national/xls/gdplev.xlsx, and the PCE for 2012 base year is from https://www.govinfo.gov/content/pkg/ERP-2019/pdf/ERP-2019-table5.pdf.

program. There is substantial federal oversight on the program, but states have significant leeway affecting program eligibility and coverage. Because Medicaid spending dwarfs housing and child care, we placed it on its own scale on the right axis of Figure 3. There, we see that growth in Medicaid spending has even out-stripped Medicare, increasing nine-fold in real terms from $59 billion in 1979 to $549 billion in 2017. The large increase after 2013 coincides with the rollout of the Affordable Care Act, which gave states the option to expand Medicaid to populations not traditionally eligible for coverage.

Housing assistance primarily is delivered in one of three forms: as government managed public housing, as housing vouchers for use in private housing markets, and as tax credits to developers of low-income housing units. Spending on the program was fairly stable throughout the 1980s, followed by a sizable expansion in the 1990s, and then subsequent stability through 2017 with the exception of the large temporary expansion of assistance to homeowners during the Great Recession. As a consequence, housing assistance has declined as a share of GDP from 0.30 percent in 2000 to 0.23 percent in 2017. Finally, CCDF provides finan-cial assistance to low-income families that supports child care costs for children under age 13 to permit the custodial parent to work or attend schooling or train-ing programs. Funding is via a block grant to states and territories, and the ben-efits are delivered either as vouchers or direct payments to providers. Figure 3 shows that real spending increased in the first decade, but real spending has subsequently slipped to about $8 billion in 2017, or about 0.05 percent of GDP.

Combined, these eleven programs cost $2.4 trillion in nominal 2017 dollars and accounted for 12.3 percent of the nation's GDP. As Figures 1 through 3 demonstrate, however, there is substantial variation in spending trends across the spectrum of social insurance and mean-tested transfer programs, which suggests that the financial stakes underlying the need for reform are also quite heteroge-neous. The articles in this volume confront this heterogeneity and illuminate where and how high-impact reforms might be made to improve the overall effec-tiveness of the safety net.

The Changing Demographic Landscape

To understand some of the reasons underlying the trends in spending on the safety net, and how they may shape the future obligations facing the programs, we briefly survey the demographic landscape facing the nation over the 1979 to 2017 period. The data come from the Annual Social and Economic Supplement to the Current Population Survey, the source of official statistics on income, pov-erty, and health insurance coverage in the United States.[4]

We begin in Figure 4 with a breakdown of the age structure in the United States into children under age 18, adults ages 18 to 64, and seniors ages 65 and older. Each line is normalized with respect to their 1979 values and multiplied by 100 percent. The adult share of the population has been stable at about 60 percent over the past four decades, and thus the demographic shift is occurring between

FIGURE 4
Trends in Age Structure of U.S. Population Relative to 1979

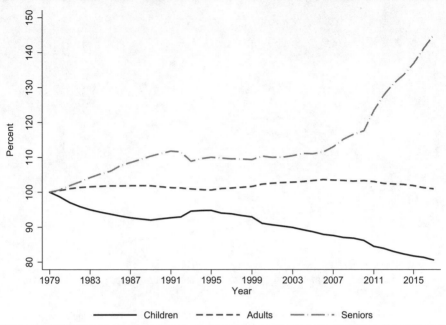

SOURCE: Authors' calculations, based on Current Population Survey Annual Social and Economic Supplement 1980–2018.

the young and the old. There has been a steady decline in the share of the population under age 18 that stabilized in the early to mid-1990s and then resumed in the late 1990s. The decline in child share has been met with a steady increase in the share over age 65 that accelerated rapidly after 2007 with the oldest of the Baby Boom population reaching retirement. The result has been convergence in population shares between children and seniors, with the U.S. Census Bureau projecting that seniors will overtake children by 2030. This has obvious implications for future obligations on the safety net. Clearly Social Security and Medicare will continue to absorb more of national income, but so too will Medicaid because under the current configuration Medicaid covers nursing home care for seniors. At the same time, child-focused programs will abate under current program rules, including EITC, ACTC, CCDF, TANF, and likely SNAP. Given historic trends in health care price inflation, the increase in costs of Medicare and Medicaid are likely to far outpace the reduction in spending on child programs.

In Figure 5, we aggregate persons up into their respective households and compute the share of household heads who report being married and the share unmarried, and, as in Figure 4, we report each series relative to its respective 1979 values. In 1979, just over 60 percent of households were headed by a married person, and just under 40 percent were unmarried. By 2017, the share

FIGURE 5
Trends in Marital Status of Household Heads Relative to 1979

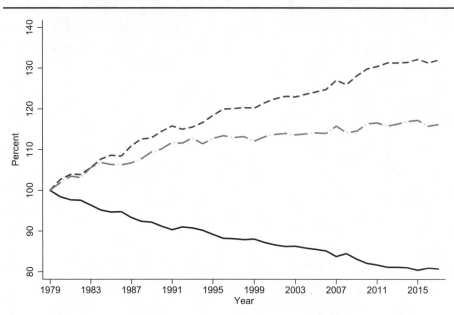

SOURCE: Authors' calculations, based on Current Population Survey Annual Social and Economic Supplement 1980–2018.

married fell by 20 percent, and the share unmarried increased more than 30 percent so that by 2017, there were slightly more households headed by an unmarried person. Some of the latter could be cohabiting with a partner, and thus the figure overstates the share of couple-less households. However, the decline in marriage has multiple ripple effects throughout the safety net. First, all else equal, married households have higher incomes and wealth and, thus, are less likely to encounter means-tested transfers compared to unmarried or cohabiting households. Figure 5 also shows the share of households headed by an unmarried female relative to 1979, who face the highest ex ante risk of poverty and use of transfers if there are children present. That group's share increased just under 20 percent. Second, even though retirement benefits are an increasing share of Social Security outlays, 20 percent are still paid to spouses and dependents, with the bulk of the latter paid to spouses. Cohabiting partners do not have a claim on Social Security benefits, and thus the decline in marriage will likely result in a tapering off of benefit payments.

Another factor correlated with incomes and wealth is race and ethnicity. Research shows a yawning gap in wealth holdings between white and nonwhite households, which means that on average, white households are better able to tap into savings in the event of a temporary loss of income in lieu of transfer

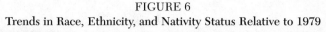

FIGURE 6
Trends in Race, Ethnicity, and Nativity Status Relative to 1979

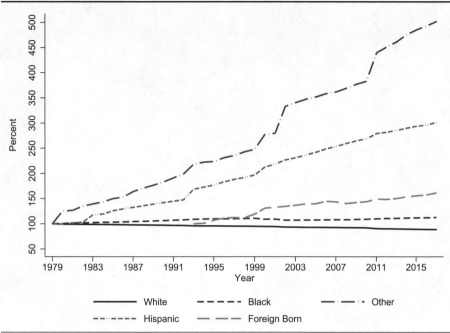

SOURCE: Authors' calculations, based on Current Population Survey Annual Social and Economic Supplement 1980–2018.

programs. On average, whites also have higher savings heading into retirement, which puts less strain on programs geared toward retirees. At the same time, they have higher life expectancy than nonwhites and, thus, have longer spells on programs like Social Security and Medicare. Whites also earn more in the labor market than blacks and Hispanics, which is due to a combination of factors linked to differences in human capital attainment (itself linked to differences in wealth and marriage rates across race and ethnicity) as well as implicit and explicit discrimination in labor markets. Figure 6 shows trends relative to their respective 1979 values in race and Hispanic ethnicity, as well as the share of foreign born. The latter group is generally precluded from participating in means-tested transfer programs in the United States unless they meet certain residency requirements or refugee status. The share of the population reporting as white alone has steadily declined over time from 86 to 77 percent, and because the black share of the population has been roughly constant at 13 percent, most of this decline is being replaced by the 500 percent increase in "other" race, the latter of which is mostly made up of persons of Asian descent. Hispanics of any race have tripled since 1979 to 18 percent of the population. The share of foreign born, which was not collected until the 1994 survey (1993 calendar year), has also grown more than 50 percent from 9 to 14 percent.

FIGURE 7
Trends in Poverty Status of Persons

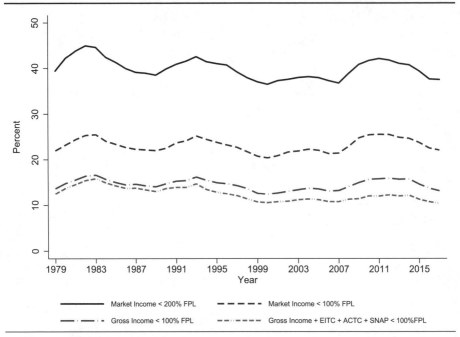

SOURCE: Authors' calculations, based on Current Population Survey Annual Social and Economic Supplement 1980–2018.

Underlying the need for assistance from most of the programs in the safety net is economic status, and the barometer most closely wedded to program eligibility is poverty status of the household. Figure 7 presents four measures of poverty status: (1) the fraction of persons residing in households with market incomes less than twice the household-specific poverty threshold, where market income is income from private sources, excluding government cash or in-kind assistance; (2) the fraction of persons in households with market incomes under the poverty line; (3) the fraction of persons in households with gross incomes (market plus government cash transfers) less than the poverty line; and (4) the fraction of persons in households with gross incomes plus SNAP and refundable EITC and ACTC credits less than the poverty line.[5] There are several noteworthy remarks on Figure 7. The first is that in a typical year, four out of every ten persons in the country have private market incomes placing them in near poverty. The fact that programs such as Social Security, Medicare, Medicaid, SSDI, UI, SNAP, housing assistance, EITC, and ACTC reach families well above the poverty line, that 40 percent of the population is at risk, and that this has changed little over the past 40 years, suggests that the latent demand for assistance is unlikely to abate going forward. The next factor of note from the figure is that gross income poverty is about 40 percent lower in an average year than market income poverty. Most of this comes from the Social Security programs because benefit levels in programs like TANF are generally quite low and only reduce the depth of poverty and not the rate. The next takeaway is how effective the safety net is at reducing the amplitude of poverty rates over the business cycle. This is most evident comparing market income poverty to the gross income poverty inclusive of SNAP and the tax credits. The latter three programs smoothed out much of the increase in poverty during the Great Recession, which reflects both the built-in stabilizing component of the programs as well as the fact that Congress took direct action to increase their generosity during the recession. A common complaint from conservative commentators is that the War on Poverty has failed. However, Figure 7 makes clear that the safety net has succeeded in reducing both the level of poverty and its volatility over the business cycle.[6] More can be done to improve the economic security offered by the safety net, and this is the aim of the articles in the volume.

Summaries of Articles

The articles in the volume are organized into one of the two groups: social insurance or means-tested transfer programs, and within each group by size of the program in terms of FY2017 expenditure.

Social insurance programs

Social Security. Gary Burtless opens the volume with an overview of Social Security, a brief summary of its effects, and potential options for reform. The program was begun during the Great Depression and is credited with being the most effective antipoverty program in the social safety net, lifting millions of the elderly out of hardship, especially after benefit expansions in the early 1970s. The biggest challenge facing the program is the financial solvency of the trust fund, which is projected to be depleted around 2035, just after the youngest of the Baby Boom generation reaches age 70. The insolvency problem is entirely the result of payments to early contributors to the program in the 1940s to the 1960s who were paid benefits far in excess of their own contributions by using tax revenues from then-current workers, thereby depleting the trust fund. Burtless notes that some have argued that this historical imbalance should be financed out of general revenues rather than out of current workers' taxes or current or future beneficiaries' tax payments. But most proposals have instead aimed to address the shortfall with some combination of tax increases or benefit cuts. The last major overhaul of the program was by the Greenspan Commission in 1983, which set in motion several increases in the payroll tax rate and the automatic increase in the taxable wage base. However, as noted previously, the tax rate has been unchanged since 1990 and the wage base has not been adjusted in response to the rising inequality in the upper tail of the earnings distribution, meaning the tax is more regressive. Consequently, the long-run insolvency problem has resurfaced.

Burtless makes the case that incremental reform of Social Security is preferred over fundamental reform options such as partial privatization in the form of 401(k)-type plans. He notes that the program has widespread voter approval, is effective at reducing hardship among those most in need, functions well as an insurance program, and is operated at very low cost per beneficiary. Shoring up the financing of the program is most readily achieved, Burtless argues, by raising the wage base subject to taxation rather than cutting benefits, and he cites voter approval for this approach. He notes that one-fourth of the income shortfall could be eliminated by raising the wage base to 90 percent of total earnings. Cutting benefits is not only politically impractical but could also undo the gains in economic security among seniors. However, he makes a case that the age at which full retirement benefits can be received could be gradually increased from the current age of 67 for workers born after 1959 by tying it to increases in life expectancy, while simultaneously improving access to SSI benefits and increasing the benefits of the lowest wage workers to protect them from the benefit reductions that would arise from such an increase in the full retirement age.

Medicare. Amitabh Chandra and Craig Garthwaite next tackle the challenges raised by the skyrocketing growth of Medicare. Medicare was begun in 1965 as part of President Johnson's War on Poverty and initially only offered basic coverage for hospital services (known as Part A) and physician services (Part B), but then was expanded in the 1970s with the addition of Part C (Medicare Advantage), which offered the option of enrolling in privately provided managed care plans, and then again in 2004 with the Part D option of a subsidized prescription drug plan. Program expenditures have grown rapidly, as we noted above, yet still face major challenges from projected growth of the older population, from a continued high rate (13 percent) of the population without health insurance, and from high health care costs of those who are insured. The authors note that while Medicare is effective overall, it has several fundamental problems, including a lack of incentives for cost-effectiveness in covered treatments; a fragmented fee-for-service payment system that causes significant inefficiencies; the use of government-set administrative prices for health care, which may not well reflect true market prices; a lack of use of market forces for care provision; and, perhaps surprisingly, limited financial protection for individuals covered by only the basic fee-for-service plan and not by Medicare Advantage (MA) or Medigap plans. The authors note that a number of pay-for-performance schemes have been tested to address some of these problems but without success.

Chandra and Garthwaite argue that cost reduction per se should not be the overall goal, instead, they make the case that we should aim to build a health program that has good insurance value for individuals and families by efficiently providing adequate coverage at reasonable cost. The authors set out eight specific guiding principles that follow from this general goal, which they believe should underlie any structural reform to the Medicare program. These principles lead them to propose a number of important reforms. The authors propose a substantial expansion of the MA program, which they view as having the best incentives for providing good coverage with efficient management of costs and because they believe that the program balances access and coverage with long-term innovation in new therapeutics, prevention, and care-delivery models. They suggest that the MA program is best at managing costs, that it is the best vehicle for premium support policies, and that it provides a superior approach to managing costs compared to accountable care organizations. However, they recommend some modifications of the reimbursement and risk-adjustment rules in the MA program. They also propose a number of reforms to address the high cost of prescription drugs, proposing that new pricing pressures be introduced to constrain physician-administered drug prices under the Part B program, that reinsurance plans be scaled back under the Part D program so that that a greater share of the responsibility be shouldered by the private firms that are responsible for negotiating prices, to replace coinsurance in Part D with flat copayments, and to limit protected classes of drugs under Part D. Finally, the authors consider Medicare for All plans and whether they are likely to succeed at both increasing coverage and reducing spending growth, concluding that while coverage increases are almost surely likely to result, reductions in spending growth would face many challenges if the basic structure and poor incentives for cost control in the current system were left unchanged.

Disability Insurance. Nicole Maestas examines the silent epidemic of the growth of the SSDI program. The establishment of Social Security was a watershed moment for federal involvement in providing income assistance, and while some called for inclusion of disability insurance (DI) at that time, it took another two decades before DI was added to Social Security. Workers compensation programs emerged at the state level in the early decades of the twentieth century, but these were limited to disability from workplace accident or injury. There was no government-sponsored program for general disability that affected the ability to engage in gainful employment. The reasons underlying the initial reluctance to include DI remain today—how to simultaneously determine when an individual has lost the capacity for work, minimize the incentive to withdraw from the labor force, and control program costs. The experience of the SSDI program over the last six decades is that the United States has not effectively managed these trade-offs, resulting in explosive program growth coupled with a failure of recipients to return to the labor force after their initial withdrawal from the onset of disability. Changes in the composition of the SSDI caseload toward a greater percent of recipients with some work capacity but with diminished employment opportunities also requires changes in the program structure, which have not been adequately addressed. Numerous program features to increase work among recipients have been tested over the years, with almost uniform lack of success.

Maestas proposes to reverse these trends with two reforms to the current SSDI program. First, she notes that the system used to determine whether the skills of those not deemed totally disabled are transferable to other occupations within the applicant's functional capacity range is dated and does not reflect the current functional demand of jobs. That system is also too coarse in its reliance on fixed age ranges to determine disability and is limited by determining functional capacity solely by physical strength. Maestas proposes that this system be updated and replaced by a more individualized assessment system that assesses both physical and mental capacity and uses a regularly updated database of job requirements given those functional limitations. Maestas' other major proposal is to create a parallel system of partial disability benefits. Currently the system is aimed at serving only those with severe and total disabilities and, because the disability determination process can last several years, most applicants withdraw from the labor force to improve their chances of a severe disability diagnosis even if their disability is only partial. Skills atrophy while they remain out of the labor force, even though many of those individuals retain capacity to engage in gainful employment. Partial disability benefits, which could be more reliably assessed with the new individualized assessment system, and which would be paid as a progressive function of earnings to provide work incentives, would allow the individual to receive some assistance while still remaining in the labor force. Medicare, which is the standard health insurance program for those on SSDI, would also be made available to these participants to both align incentives correctly and to permit regular access to care. The new work-incentive system, Maestas argues, could effectively replace the complex and confusing set of work-promotion features in the current program.

Unemployment Insurance. Till von Wachter addresses the issues and challenges facing the UI system. The demand for UI emerged out of the economic turmoil following the 1929 stock market crash, and as often happens in the United States, several states first introduced variants of UI that were then followed by full federalization—for UI, that occurred with the 1935 Social Security Act, the same legislation authorizing the Social Security retirement program. As a federal-state system, many have long voiced concern that there is too much heterogeneity across states in terms of benefit generosity and eligibility, especially as it pertains to part-time, seasonal, or gig economy work; that the system is not responsive enough to mass layoffs resulting from macroeconomic shocks; and that the system repeatedly faces funding shortfalls because of inadequate state trust funds. A common concern levied against increased benefit generosity and duration is that it only results in longer spells on UI and not in improved matches between workers and firms (i.e., better jobs more appropriate to a worker's skills). This means that any reform to UI must trade off the redistributive insurance aspect of the program against the efficiency cost of reduced work incentives. Finally, a recent concern is that many states, partly for financial concerns, have been reducing the duration of benefits provided to the unemployed in their states.

von Wachter takes a broad look at the strengths and weaknesses of the current UI system. Based on that assessment, and the latest research on UI, he offers a number of potential reforms of the UI system. He proposes that the federal government impose a mandatory minimum wage replacement rate and minimum duration of benefits to guard against political expediency at the state level, where there are incentives to cut benefits in the face of funding shortfalls, which typically occur during recessions when need for assistance is greatest. He also proposes that the current emergency unemployment compensation system, which requires an act of Congress to implement, be replaced with a system of automatic triggers to improve the built-in stabilizer aspect of UI in the event of economic downturns. He proposes that the challenge of underfunded trust funds be addressed by expanding the wage base subject to the UI experience-rated tax and by requiring that states hold minimal reserves, much like the Federal Reserve requires of banks in terms of deposits held in reserve to meet unexpected withdrawals. He recommends that more uniform standards be set across states for benefit eligibility, bringing more part-time and seasonal workers into the system. von Wachter also argues for the establishment of a national data collection system to both improve program operations and to expand research opportunities to build up the evidence base on UI effectiveness. Finally, he discusses a number of proposals for innovation in the system, which would warrant further examination and study in the future.

Means-tested transfer programs

Medicaid. Janet Currie and Valentina Duque provide a sweeping overview of the Medicaid program and an expansive review of the research evidence on program effectiveness. As they highlight in their article, Medicaid serves four distinct populations—low-income children and their caregivers, the elderly, the disabled, and nondisabled, nonelderly adults—with the first two groups part of the original program rollout in 1965, with the disabled added in the early 1970s with the introduction of SSI, and with nondisabled adults added in 2014 as part of the Affordable Care Act. The evidence reviewed suggests that Medicaid has been effective at improving child and parent (mother) well-being, with little evidence of deleterious effects on labor-market behavior; that the elderly are provided comparable nursing home care as non-Medicaid nursing home residents (although finding a bed is more difficult for Medicaid recipients); and that nondisabled adults have greater insurance coverage and improved financial security because of the program. The evidence base on the disabled for other outcomes is too limited to draw many firm conclusions. Even though the evidence weighs strongly toward the view that Medicaid is effective in meeting program goals, millions of Americans still lack health insurance, particularly in states that have not expanded Medicaid coverage of nondisabled, nonelderly adults. Many lower-income families have incomes too high for Medicaid but are not eligible or find options for other coverage too expensive. Cost is on an unsustainable path (see Figure 3), and many covered by Medicaid still lack access to some types of care, such as specialists.

Currie and Duque discuss several reforms to Medicaid, recognizing that any single reform to the program is likely to have limited effects given the heterogeneity of the populations served. Medicaid Managed Care (MMC) has been promoted as a way to address both the cost and access issues, with mixed success: it has improved access in some cases and worsened it in others; and in general, it has not lowered costs, largely because governments are not adept at negotiating with third-party insurers. A major driver of costs is the increased need for long-term care in nursing homes, which is funded by Medicaid once an individual has "spent down" their assets. The authors propose removing long-term care from Medicaid and creating a new plan in Medicare not unlike the creation 15 years ago of the Medicare Part D prescription drug plan. Finally, the authors discuss the merits of several other alternative reforms to Medicaid that have been proposed, including replacing it with a Medicare for All program.

Earned Income Tax Credit. Hilary Hoynes explores possible reforms to the EITC in her article. She also discusses the CTC and ACTC, but because the evidence base is minimal on the child credit, she refrains from detailed reform plans for the program. The EITC was established to incentivize work over welfare and to address the fundamental regressivity in the payroll tax paid into Social Security. The Nixon administration had proposed a variant of Friedman's negative income tax that would have provided income assistance to both the working and nonworking poor. That plan failed in the Senate, and instead, the programs that ultimately emerged were SSI for the nonworking disabled poor and the EITC for the working poor. There have been scores of academic articles written on the EITC, and the evidence is clear that the credit boosts employment, especially among single mothers; that it is effective at lifting families out of poverty; and that it improves child well-being in the short and long run.

Despite the credit's success, Hoynes considers several incremental reforms to the EITC. The first addresses the problem that the credit has been held fixed in inflation-adjusted terms since 1996 except for families with three or more children, who received a higher credit starting in 2009. Because real wages have been flat over the last 20 years, she proposes that the credit be adjusted to account for wage stagnation and rising inequality. A related proposal is to increase the relative credit generosity to both childless and one-child families, for low-earning childless workers only receive a credit equivalent to their Social Security liability (that population also includes former inmates who receive little other assistance). The credit for one-child families is also artificially low vis-à-vis the two-child credit, and Hoynes recommends increasing the maximum credit for this group as well. She also proposes reforms to program operations. For example, a common complaint is that too much of the benefit check is extracted by paid tax preparers, and noncompliance rates (i.e., overclaiming) are higher among paid preparers and the self-employed. Hoynes proposes expanding free filing of returns by the IRS and the use of third-party reporting of self-employment earnings to reduce underreporting of income. In terms of structural reforms, she recommends attention be given to coverage of nonworkers, to means of increasing take-up among nonfilers, and to further research on the efficacy of delivering the credit throughout the calendar year rather than as a lump sum. Intrayear receipt was once a program option but was dropped in 2010 because of low take-up. Recent pilot studies point to improved ways of delivering the credit throughout the year and, in Hoynes's view, are worthy of further exploration.

Supplemental Nutrition Assistance Program. Diane Schanzenbach focuses on SNAP in her contribution. Started as the Food Stamp Program in 1964, and renamed SNAP with the 2008 Farm Bill, the program is unique among developed countries, which rarely offer in-kind assistance in the form of food subsidies. During its peak after the Great Recession, nearly one in six Americans received food assistance from SNAP. Schanzenbach reviews the evidence on the effects of SNAP, which shows the program to effectively mitigate food insecurity, to reduce poverty—especially deep poverty—to smooth consumption in the event of income loss, to function as an economy-wide automatic stabilizer, and to have long-term positive health effects for adults exposed to the program during childhood. She finds that current research suggests that any work disincentive effects that may exist are small in magnitude.

Schanzenbach explores several reforms to SNAP to build on the positive impact of the program on family well-being. The maximum SNAP benefit is determined by the so-called Thrifty Food Plan, the least generous of the U.S. Department of Agriculture's (USDA's) four food plans. It is fixed across the continental United States and thus does not account for geographic differences in food costs. Schanzenbach proposes raising the maximum benefit guarantee to increase the food purchasing power of low-income households, perhaps tying the benefit to the second lowest food plan instead of the lowest, which would result in about a 30 percent increase in benefits. Because children often lack access to breakfast and lunch during the summer when school is not in session, she proposes providing a temporary (summer-long) boost to the monthly SNAP benefit for households with school-age children as well as temporary additional benefits to families with children. To address the problem that many families run out of their SNAP entitlements before the end of the month, she recommends additional research into twice-a-month transfers. To attempt to improve dietary quality, she proposes "bonus dollars" for purchases of healthy fruits, vegetables, and whole grains after a demonstration project revealed positive effects of such a program on diets of SNAP households. Schanzenbach also discusses alternative methods of increasing work among recipients, possible elimination of the gross income test, and approaches to reducing fraud and error (though the rate is quite low). Similar to von Wachter's proposal for UI, Schanzenbach proposes an automatic trigger to boost SNAP benefits during economic downturns to improve the built-in stabilizer component of SNAP. She also discusses proposed reforms related to converting the program to block grant form, changing it to a commodities-based Women, Infants, and Children (WIC)–style program, and cashing it out, finding that none of these reforms is likely to improve the effectiveness of the program.

Supplemental Security Income. Mary Daly and Mark Duggan address the issues confronting the SSI program. Like the EITC, the SSI program was created in the early 1970s as an outcome of the debate over a negative income tax, which it resembles (although only covering the disabled population). It covers the poor elderly, the blind, and the disabled, and replaced a patchwork of state programs that existed prior to that time. Program costs and caseloads have grown dramatically since that time as well as changing in character, with disabled adults and children growing as a proportion of the caseload and the poor elderly proportion declining. Similar to SSDI, one of the main challenges facing SSI is that effects on work; for once an individual joins the program, he or she is likely to remain on in perpetuity and to disengage from the labor force (or, in the case of children, never engage). Unlike many of the other programs considered in this volume, the evidence base of SSI is comparatively thin. As the authors review, there is some evidence that the program reduces work and saving among adults nearing retirement, and parents replace lost child SSI benefits with higher earnings, but children who lose benefits at the age of 18 redetermination stage end up with lower incomes because labor supply does not respond to fill in missing benefits.

Recognizing that the evidence base needs further development, Daly and Duggan propose several reforms to SSI to improve outcomes for the elderly poor and for disabled children and adults. For the elderly poor, they note that individuals who have accumulated insufficient work credits over their lifetimes to qualify for Social Security will remain poor if all they receive is SSI because the federal benefit still leaves them in poverty. They propose an increase in the maximum benefit to increase the effectiveness of the antipoverty component of the program for that group. They also propose updating and tying the liquid asset limit for program eligibility, which has been fixed in nominal dollars at $3,000 since 1989 (they likewise think this is a good idea for other populations in the program, where the asset limit is $2,000). This would also raise the fraction of eligible elderly poor who are not currently receiving benefits because assets surpass the low limits. For nonelderly disabled adults, Daly and Duggan suggest that work incentives could be improved by reducing the implicit tax rate on earnings (currently benefits are cut $0.50 for every $1 earned) and expanding earnings deductions; that the incentive to leave SSI could be improved by guaranteed Medicaid coverage for a grace period if they leave; and, similar to Maestas, that the creation of a partial disability SSI benefit would eliminate the "all-or-nothing" character of the current program. The authors also suggest upfront assistance to reduce the skill atrophy that comes from long waits for an acceptance decision; a better alignment of initial-stage with later-stage medical termination to reduce the high rates of acceptance only after long waits on appeals; and more consideration of early-stage interventions to encourage return to work based on the nature of the individual level of impairment, possibly made with the involvement of health insurers. For disabled children, they propose that consideration be given to tying child SSI benefit receipt to school attendance or other human capital investment activities, encouraging Medicaid managed care plans to provide more tailored treatments to SSI children (especially for those with mental impairments, who constitute the majority of the caseload), reducing the severity of the asset test to encourage parents to save, and further efforts to harmonize decisions of medical examiners and administrative law judges (whose decisions currently often diverge).

Housing assistance. Rob Collinson, Ingrid Gould Ellen, and Jens Ludwig address housing assistance in their contribution. Housing assistance in the United States is unique in its level of decentralization—while the programs are federally supervised and funded, administration is devolved to the roughly three thousand local housing agencies across the nation. This means that there is vast heterogeneity in the amounts and quality of housing available across locales.

Research has shown that residents in public housing or with housing vouchers have more stable and less crowded housing than similar persons without housing aid, and some research shows that educational outcomes and long-term earning potential are greater for low-income children growing up in subsidized housing than low-income children without housing benefits. The Moving to Opportunity demonstration experiment showed that housing vouchers redeemed in low-poverty neighborhoods improved children's long-term education and earnings provided that the move took place while the child was a preteen. There is some evidence that adult labor supply is reduced by public housing and vouchers.

Collinson, Ellen, and Ludwig structure their reform proposals around three key challenges facing housing assistance programs. First, the programs are not an entitlement, and housing agencies receive a fixed annual appropriation. However, housing burden as a share of income among low-income families has accelerated in recent decades and, thus, demand for aid far outstrips agency budgets. As a consequence, most areas have waiting lists for assistance that are often years long, and many have closed their lists altogether. They suggest that one budget-neutral reform would be to reduce the generosity of current vouchers or make them time-limited while spreading them out more widely to reduce the all-or-nothing dimension of the program. Second, they note that housing conditions vary widely across the country, with very tight markets in most major urban centers, especially on the coasts, and relatively slack markets in less densely populated communities, especially in between the coasts. However, current programs like the Low-Income Housing Tax Credit provide the same supply-side subsidy regardless of the characteristics of the housing market. A more flexible program would expand building credits in tight markets and limit the use of the credits in slack markets. The third key challenge identified by the authors is that most voucher holders do not use their vouchers to move to neighborhoods with significantly lower poverty levels. Most recipients redeem their voucher in high-poverty neighborhoods, in part because the voucher goes further with lower rents and because landlords often do not accept vouchers in low-poverty areas. They suggest that the voucher amount could be increased for high-rent areas to induce more holders to select into low-poverty tracts and commensurately lowered in low-rent areas. In addition to these three key proposals, the authors propose a change to the rent subsidy formula that would provide incentives for voucher holders to economize on the rents they pay, discuss possible ways to increase work incentives, and propose offering more mobility counseling and housing search assistance to voucher holders who are seeking rental units. At several points in their article, the authors also discuss current proposals for housing assistance that have been made in Congress or by other political figures, including operating subsidies through the tax code, and assess their merits.

Temporary Assistance for Needy Families. Ron Haskins and Matt Weidinger explore options to improve the TANF program. TANF is a vastly more decentralized program than its predecessor AFDC because it is a block grant program and because federal regulation is dramatically reduced. As a result, there is substantial heterogeneity across states and over time in how the block grant is allocated between cash and in-kind assistance, and how work requirements, earnings dis-regards, time limits, asset limits, benefit levels, and benefit sanctions are designed and enforced. Most of the causal research on the program has used variation in state rules in the five years before and after implementation of TANF. A consist-ent result is that the move from AFDC to TANF reduced participation in the program and boosted average employment and earnings among never-married mothers. The authors show that poverty rates have fallen greatly since 1996 wel-fare reform and say that most observers believe that decline to have resulted from some combination of a strong economy, changes in other poverty-reducing programs like the EITC, and welfare reform.

The reform proposals put forth by Haskins and Weidinger address what they see as the two key issues facing the program: the failure to engage a sufficient number of recipients in work activities and problems with the way TANF funds are spent. The first issue they see is that states have been able to satisfy the strict legal work participation requirements without engaging significant shares of the caseload in work activities. To address this issue, the authors propose to trans-form the work requirement programs to a more outcomes-based system that focuses on long-term employment and earnings outcomes to ensure that state efforts are focused on placing recipients on job ladders and not on one-off dead-end jobs, as well as closing loopholes in the system like those that allow states to claim credit for third-party spending (e.g., food bank spending) toward reducing the target work rate they must satisfy and modifying the other caseload reduction credit rules. More generally, they propose that states be required to engage all work-eligible individuals in work-related activities within 24 months of first receipt. The second issue identified by the authors is problems with state spend-ing, with many states spending an increasing share of funds on noncore activities (that is, unrelated to the core purposes of work and basic assistance) and with some states, in addition, devoting TANF funds to non-TANF purposes. Congress gave states great leeway in designing their TANF programs, including what mix of cash and in-kind assistance to offer. Under the AFDC program, the typical state spent 75 percent of its funds on cash assistance and 25 percent on in-kind assistance such as child care or transportation vouchers. Under TANF, that share has reversed, with only 25 percent going toward cash and work supports and, in some states, 10 percent or less of spending. Haskins and Weidinger propose that a floor be placed on the fraction of federal and state funds devoted to core activi-ties like cash assistance, work supports, and related supportive services, with that floor being at least 25 percent. States also may spend TANF nonassistance mon-ies on a broad spectrum of the population, not just the poor, so they propose that TANF be redirected back to those most in need, such as families with incomes under twice the poverty line. The authors also mention a number of programs recently advanced by the National Academy of Sciences (National Academies of Sciences, Engineering, and Medicine [NASEM] 2019), which were calculated to reduce poverty as well as to increase employment. Haskins and Weidinger pro-pose reforming the current TANF "contingency fund" so that it is more focused on increased needs in the event of a national recession. The authors also propose making TANF performance indicators more uniform than it is currently across states, conducting high-quality research studies to determine what works, and devoting additional attention to reducing marriage penalties in the program.

Child care. V. Joseph Hotz and Matthew Wiswall survey the landscape of child care policy and its effects in their article. They note that child care policy is important because of growing evidence that high-quality care has important short-term and long-term impacts on children's cognitive and noncognitive development and economic success, because of its role in supporting female employment including that of low-income women (consistent with the general movement toward a work-based safety net), and because of the significant antipoverty effects of child care. The authors also emphasize the tensions between the goals of increasing maternal employment and the goal of providing high enough quality care to have significant positive effects on children. Their review of the extensive research on child care includes describing a growing body of evidence pointing to the importance of early childhood interventions for both beneficial short-run outcomes through childhood and long-term outcomes into adulthood. Results from demonstration projects show positive long-run effects from intensive, wraparound child care provision on improved health and test scores in childhood; and higher education attainment, employment, earnings, and reduced criminal activity in adulthood. Similar findings have been identified from nonexperimental evaluations of Head Start and from statewide expansions of pre-K and kindergarten. Research on the labor-market effects of child care subsidies points toward higher employment rates among parents in response to subsidized care. They also survey research on the effects of child care regulatory policy, notably minimum quality and licensing standards. The evidence here is mixed, with some studies finding that more stringent care requirements reduce (1) hours of care, (2) employment of mothers, and (3) the number of child-care suppliers; while other studies find no effects, positive or negative.

Hotz and Wiswall direct their reform attention on the merits of expanded direct provision of child care, expanded child care subsidies and credits, and improved information to parents about the quality of different child care providers. For expanded direct provision of care, the authors consider making Head Start eligible to all children under age five living in low-income families and estimate its incremental cost to be between $10 and $25 billion. They compare this to a universal child care program that covered all children under five, finding it to cost almost ten times more, and argue that it would have little additional employment effect or effect on child development. As for expanded child care subsidies and credits, such as either expanded subsidies through the CCDF or converting the Child and Dependent Care Tax Credit (CDCTC) to be refundable for low-income families, Hotz and Wiswall think the available evidence suggests that these policies would result in substantially reduced out-of-pocket child care costs and higher employment of mothers. However, in part using recent calculations from a report on child care reforms by the National Academy of Sciences (NASEM 2019), they find that a CDCTC credit that was made refundable, more progressive, and more targeted on low-income families would have much larger effects on poverty and maternal employment than a CCDF expansion. However, its impact on child development would depend on whether parents used the subsidies to purchase high-quality care, and the authors discuss the possibility of restricting subsidies to higher-quality care, finding them likely to be administratively burdensome and likely to unduly restrict the child care choices of low-income parents. Finally, the authors see promise in existing quality rating systems but find them to be inadequate in their current form to correctly assess quality or to get information to parents. Hotz and Wiswall propose that the federal government invest in a new system that provides more and better information on child care quality ratings at the state and local levels, coupled with information on the differential effects of alternative care choices on child development. They propose that more research be conducted on methods for assessing quality and on how to convey that information to parents in a way that increases their awareness of the importance of child care choices on their childrens' development.

Reflections on Entitlements in the United States and the Path Ahead for Reform

The volume closes with two reflections on the various proposals presented herein, which also include assessments on what should be prioritized in addressing entitlement reform.

Robert Doar and Angela Rachidi compliment the authors of the volume in recognizing the complexity of the issues surrounding entitlement programs and for demonstrating the many ways in which the safety net works well, including its provision of some support to almost all poor families and its success in raising almost all full-time working families out of poverty and its major gains in reducing material hardship. But the authors believe that most of the articles in the volume take the view that current benefits are inadequate and are consequently too focused on expanding the safety net programs, when they should consider reforms that would make the programs reinforce to a much greater extent the values of work, family, and the role of community and local autonomy that should be the goals of the system. Doar and Rachidi support the proposed partial disability reforms and reforms to Medicaid for SSI recipients for that program, the proposed new disability assessment system for the SSDI program, and the increased outcomes-based approach for work requirements in the TANF system. But they believe that the articles on SNAP, housing assistance, and Medicaid downplay their roles in discouraging work and that the article on the EITC downplays its role in discouraging marriage. The authors also prefer a Medicaid system that gives more control to states and encourages them to better control costs; a more state regulatory approach to ensuring child care quality; a change in housing assistance toward a modest time-limited approach; and, more generally, approaches that give more flexibility to states such as through block grants. Doar and Rachidi would also prefer a SNAP program that puts more restriction on the items that can be purchased to increase the nutritional impact of the program.

The authors conclude by arguing that a rethinking of the proper role and function of the safety net is needed, including an emphasis on preventing the problems that cause poverty and poor social functioning in the first place.

Karen Dynan provides a discussion of the broader economic and financial context that should be understood when considering entitlement reform, especially since financial pressures on government expenditures are likely to intensify in the coming years. She describes the problem of growing federal debt, which is projected to rise to 144 percent of GDP by 2049 compared to its 35 percent level in 2007, and why low interest rates are not a solution to such an extreme increase; the slow rates of economic growth that the United States has experienced over recent decades, largely a result of declining employment rates among men and women, and why this is contributing to the fiscal challenges facing the country; the possibility that low interest rates will make fighting recessions more difficult and that recessions in the future may be more severe, last longer, and be associated with weaker and more fragile recoveries; the growth in income inequality that is unlikely to be reversed in the short run that impedes individuals from reaching their full potential; and the continuing struggles that many U.S. families face that prevent them from accumulating wealth, thereby hampering economic and social mobility. Dynan draws six important implications from these trends in the larger context. She argues that the financing of the Social Security system must be fixed and that the fix should be progressive, that the growth in government health care spending must be curbed, and that programs that benefit poor children and their parents should not be cut. She also recommends changes in safety net programs to provide stronger incentives (or smaller disincentives) to work but that replacing the system with a universal basic income would not be desirable. Finally, Dynan recommends that any reshaping of the safety net system take into account the important role that the system plays as an automatic stabilizer, especially in light of the rising limitations on government policy to fight recessions.

Conclusion

The articles in this volume provide a rich set of material on how U.S. entitlements are currently performing and what potential reforms are available that will satisfy the goals of the system, which are to improve the well-being of U.S. families both in the short run and the long run and to do so efficiently, at reasonable cost, and with due consideration given to work incentives and economic success. The articles in this volume provide four important lessons about U.S. entitlement reform.

First, the available evidence shows that the current programs are in almost all cases providing important assistance to U.S. families and are improving their well-being. Assistance in the form of health insurance; cash to assist the disabled; support for the elderly and the unemployed; and assistance in the form of food, housing, and child care are reducing poverty rates, improving health and other outcomes for adults and children, and, in several cases, increasing work and earnings. The programs are often large and expensive, but they are achieving major goals that they are intended to achieve.

Second, however, the programs face important and significant challenges to achieving additional success that need the attention of policy-makers around the country. The articles identify both major structural reforms as well as modest incremental reforms that are needed to address those issues. In some cases, notably health care, costs are rising at possibly unsustainable rates and the authors identify ways to deliver the same or better service at lower cost. In other cases, the programs are not serving all eligible families and families in need, and the authors offer reforms to provide assistance to more of those families. In several programs, the structure of the program imposes barriers or disincentives to work and are failing to promote employment and human capital accumulation, and several authors propose changes in rules and structure to address that important issue. Some of the reforms would be expensive but some would be more modest in cost, and some would actually save money. The reforms discussed in the articles provide a rich menu of alternatives for policy-makers to consider.

Third, the articles demonstrate that entitlement programs in the United States, and their rules and issues, are complex. As a result, the reforms are necessarily also often complex. Simple sound-bite reforms that gloss over the complexities are unlikely to achieve the goals of reform. Expert guidance, such as that provided by the authors of this volume, with major consideration given to the strongest evidence on the effects of those reforms, needs to be brought to bear. Policy design is never a simple matter and must be carefully studied, and the articles in this volume demonstrate how those design issues can lead to reforms that can result in major improvements in their operation and provision of assistance to U.S. families.

Finally, the articles illustrate, as is often the case, how much we do not know about what reforms would succeed and which ones would not. Continued, and increased, federal support is needed for research that will provide strong evidence on the types of reforms that will achieve the goals of the programs and to identify what reforms will work and which will not. Support for that research will lead to the identification of more reform possibilities and will serve to widen the already large and rich menus of alternatives for reform of U.S. entitlement programs.

Notes

1. See https://stats.oecd.org.

2. Nominal spending is deflated using the personal consumption expenditure deflator with 2012 base year.

3. The ACTC is part of the Child Tax Credit (CTC), which also gives a credit to families with children below an income cutoff, although the cutoff is very high and hence goes to many non-low-income families. The CTC is also not fully refundable. Currently, CTC spending is about equal to ACTC spending.

4. The Current Population Survey (CPS) Annual Social and Economic Supplement (ASEC) is a stratified random sample of household addresses, with fifty to sixty thousand households interviewed in a typical year until the 2001 survey year, when an additional thirty thousand households were added to improve

state-level estimates of the State Children's Health Insurance Program. All statistics presented are weighted to be representative of the U.S. population using the ASEC supplement weight.

5. All the income sources are self-reported on the CPS ASEC except for the EITC and ACTC. For these, we construct tax units and use the National Bureau of Economic Research's (NBER's) TAXSIM calculator, version 27, to simulate the dollar value of the EITC and ACTC.

6. The Supplemental Poverty Measure constructed by the Census Bureau, which incorporates additional near-cash benefits as well as making a number of other adjustments to thresholds and resources, shows poverty rates that decline even more. See https://www.census.gov/content/dam/Census/library/publications/2018/demo/p60-265.pdf.

References

National Academies of Sciences, Engineering, and Medicine. 2019. *A roadmap to reducing child poverty*, eds. Greg Duncan and Suzanne Le Menestrel. Washington, DC: The National Academies Press.

U.S. Department of Treasury. 2018. *FY2018 financial report of the United States Government*. Washington, DC: U.S. Department of Treasury. Available from https://fiscal.treasury.gov/files/reports-statements/financial-report/2018/03282019-FR(Final).pdf.

Social Insurance

Fixing Social Security: Major Reform or Minor Repairs?

By
GARY BURTLESS

Without congressional action, the Social Security reserve fund will be exhausted by 2035. When that occurs, benefit payments must be cut by one-fifth. To avoid that outcome, Congress must agree on a reform plan that boosts revenues, cuts pensions, or does both. The choice of a reform strategy should depend on voters' support for the goals of the Old-Age, Survivors, and Disability Insurance (OASDI) program and evidence about the program's effectiveness in achieving those goals. This article explains the aims of the Old-Age and Survivors Insurance (OASI) program, briefly describes how the program attempts to achieve those aims, and considers evidence on whether the goals have been achieved and at what cost. It then considers alternative reforms that address OASI's main problem, namely, the long-term shortfall in program revenues compared with pension commitments. It concludes by identifying the reforms that seem best suited to achieving OASI's core aims while conforming to voter preferences.

Keywords: entitlements; aging; Social Security; pension policy

Social Security is the largest and, along with Medicare, the most popular entitlement program in the United States. Known formally as Old-Age, Survivors, and Disability Insurance (OASDI), the program collects contributions from an overwhelming majority of U.S. employers and workers and pays out retirement, disability, and survivor benefits to about 63 million children and adults, roughly one-fifth of the population. Nine out of ten Americans older than 65 collect a monthly check from the program.

Though the popularity of the program has proved to be enduring, its financial outlook has

Gary Burtless has been a researcher and senior fellow in the Economic Studies Program at Brookings Institution since 1981. He does research on issues connected with social insurance and pension policy, aging, labor economics, income distribution, and the behavioral effects of government tax and transfer policy.

Correspondence: gburtless@brookings.edu

DOI: 10.1177/0002716219872161

grown increasingly bleak. A major overhaul of Social Security in 1983 boosted the payroll tax that finances the program, slowed the growth of future benefit payouts, and for the first time imposed federal income taxes on the benefits that many families receive. The revenue raised by the new tax was dedicated to paying for a portion of the program's cost. The 1983 reforms generated large and growing surpluses, with payroll and dedicated income tax revenues comfortably exceeding the annual benefit and administrative costs of the program. The reserves of the system, invested in U.S. government securities, began to produce a sizable stream of interest income, supplementing the dedicated taxes flowing into the OASDI trust funds. By 2009, the combined trust funds held reserves equal to almost 18 percent of gross domestic product (GDP), the equivalent of almost four years of annual benefit payments.

Measured as a share of GDP or in comparison to annual benefit outlays, 2009 represented the high-water mark of the OASDI trust funds. At the end of that year, the combined trust funds held $2.54 trillion, or 3.62 times the following year's benefit payments. The Great Recession in combination with the slow but inexorable effects of adverse demographic trends raised the annual cost of the system relative to its income stream. Though the combined trust funds continued to grow, they increased much more slowly than benefit outlays. By the end of 2018, the trust funds held $2.89 trillion, or just 2.76 times predicted benefit payments in 2019. In 2008, the first wave of the Baby Boom generation reached age 62, earning the right to claim a Social Security retirement check. By 2026, the youngest members of the large Baby Boom will reach 62, swelling the ranks of adults eligible to claim a pension. In 2000, there were about 3.4 Social Security–covered workers contributing to OASDI for every beneficiary collecting benefits. By 2018, the ratio fell to 2.8; and in 2030, it is expected to fall to 2.4 (Board of Trustees OASDI 2019, Table IV.B3). The surge in pensioners compared with active workers has produced a shortfall in the tax revenues needed to pay for benefits. The growing gap between tax receipts and outgo means the program's reserve fund will soon shrink and eventually be exhausted. Both the OASDI trustees and the Congressional Budget Office (CBO) expect reserves to be depleted sometime between 2030 and 2035. When reserves fall to zero, benefit payments will be limited to the annual amount of tax income flowing into the program's coffers. Under current law and the OASDI trustees' intermediate projections of future income and outgo, benefit payments to pensioners must be cut by about 20 percent below their scheduled level starting in 2035, the year when the trustees expect the reserve fund to hit zero.

In the remainder of the article, I outline the basic goals of the Social Security retired-worker and survivors insurance program, briefly describe how the program tries to achieve those aims, and consider evidence on whether the program's main goals are being achieved. Some of the program's successes are clear. Compared with their situation in past generations, the elderly now enjoy higher living standards. Their average consumption is much closer to that of Americans in families headed by a working-age person. Social Security has contributed to this progress. What is less certain is how much past progress would be put in jeopardy if future benefits are scaled back. Finally, I consider the implications of this evidence for Social Security reform.

Goals, Benefits, and Financing

The aim of the OASDI program is to insure workers against the risks of invalidity and early death and provide old-age pensions to insured workers who are at least 62 years old and to their dependent spouses if the spouse is also at least 62. In addition, the program provides benefits to the surviving spouses of deceased workers if the survivor is at least 60.[1] Since Disability Insurance (DI) is covered elsewhere in the volume, I focus on Old-Age and Survivors Insurance (OASI). Survivors insurance benefits are of great value to young workers with child dependents. In the event of a worker's death, the worker's dependent children can receive monthly benefits until reaching age 18 (or age 19 if the child is still in high school). The Social Security actuary estimates that for an insured worker earning the average wage who has a spouse and two young children, the face value of the insurance is over $725,000 (Center on Budget and Policy Priorities 2018). Survivors insurance benefits are also valuable to older insured workers married to a partner who had substantially lower earnings during his or her career. The survivor's benefit is valuable in this case because the surviving spouse can inherit the full monthly benefit received by the deceased, higher-earning worker. The inherited survivor benefit is likely to be more generous than the retired-worker benefit available to the lower-earning surviving spouse.[2] Note, however, that survivors who are younger than the full retirement age (FRA) can have their benefits reduced if they have labor earnings above a certain limit.

At the end of 2018, the number of retired-worker beneficiaries dwarfed the number of survivor beneficiaries. Almost 90 percent of OASI beneficiaries were retired workers and their dependents rather than survivors (Table 1). Workers who have accumulated enough earnings credits can collect retired-worker pensions starting at age 62. In 2019, a worker who earns at least $5,440 will receive four earnings credits toward pension eligibility. Accumulating 40 earnings credits entitles a worker to a retired-worker pension. Crucially, the monthly pensions are payable for the worker's remaining life. Pensioners with dependent children can collect auxiliary benefits for those children until they reach age 18. The spouses of retired workers may collect spousal benefits, typically equal to one-half the retired worker's benefit at the FRA, though the amount is reduced if the spouse claims the benefit before reaching the FRA.

The benefits paid to retired workers and to aged survivors have a number of key features. First, they are calculated based on the covered earnings record of the insured worker. Workers with higher lifetime earnings qualify for higher basic monthly pensions. Second, the formula for determining monthly benefits is redistributive in favor of eligible workers who have the lowest lifetime earnings. The ratio of the monthly pension amount to the worker's average monthly wage is commonly referred to as the replacement rate. The progressivity of the basic

TABLE 1

Contributing Workers and OASI Beneficiaries, 1980–2017 (millions of persons)

	1980	1990	2000	2010	2017
Workers contributing to OASI	112.7	133.0	154.8	157.2	173.6
Beneficiaries					
Retired workers	19.6	24.8	28.5	34.6	42.4
Spouses of retired workers	3.0	3.1	2.8	2.3	2.4
Surviving spouses of deceased workers	4.4	5.1	4.9	4.3	4.0
Children of deceased or retired workers	3.2	2.2	2.3	2.5	2.6
All OASI beneficiaries	30.9	35.6	38.7	43.8	51.5
Memo: Ratio of OASI beneficiaries to contributors	3.6	3.7	4.0	3.6	3.4

SOURCE: Social Security Administration (SSA), Annual Statistical Supplement (2018); Board of Trustees OASDI (2018).

benefit formula means that Social Security replacement rates are generally higher in the case of low-wage workers and lower in the case of high-wage workers. Third, the calculation of a worker's basic retirement pension is based on her or his earnings in the 35 years of highest wage-indexed earnings during the worker's career up through retirement.[3] Fourth, the basic pension amount is adjusted depending on the age when a worker first claims a benefit. Workers who claim at the FRA receive the full basic pension; workers who claim at a younger age receive a reduced pension; workers who claim later (up to age 70) receive a larger pension.[4] The adjustment in benefits to reflect a worker's initial claiming age is intended to compensate workers for the fact that any delay in claiming results in a smaller number of months collecting a pension. Finally, benefits in force are adjusted, usually once a year, to reflect changes in consumer prices that have occurred in the months since the last benefit adjustment. This means that after a worker's pension begins, it is regularly adjusted to keep its purchasing power constant.

Two key features of the benefit formula are illustrated in Figure 1, which shows Social Security Administration (SSA) estimates of retired-worker replacement rates for ten representative workers who differ with respect to their lifetime earnings profiles and the age at which they first claim a retired-worker benefit. Although the calculations are based on the stylized earnings profiles of specific representative workers, the earnings profiles are based on the observed earnings records of a 1 percent sample of workers who claimed benefits between 2012 and 2017 (Clingman, Burkhalter, and Chaplain 2018). The specific earnings patterns reflect those of workers at the 12th, 25th, 56th, 82nd, and top percentiles of lifetime average earnings in those years. Benefits are calculated for each representative worker under the benefit formula for workers born in 1952. The two lines in the chart correspond to the calculated replacement rates for workers first claiming benefits at two different ages, 62 (the earliest possible claiming age) and 66

FIGURE 1
Gross Social Security Replacement Rates for Workers Born in 1952, by Lifetime
Earnings Percentile and Age at Benefit Claiming

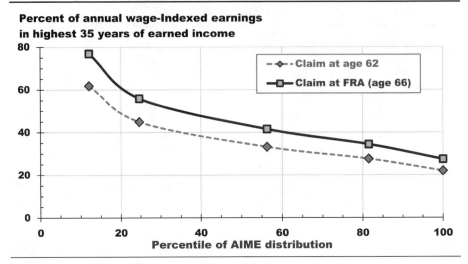

SOURCE: Clingman, Burkhalter, and Chaplain (2018).
NOTE: AIME = average indexed monthly earnings.

(the FRA for workers born in 1952). For a given earnings profile, benefits are
always higher for workers who claim benefits at a later age. Workers claiming
benefits at age 66 receive a pension that is 25 percent larger than the one
received by a worker with the same earnings profile who claims at 62. The basic
benefit formula is tilted heavily in favor of the poorly paid. Workers in the top
earnings group who claim benefits at the FRA receive a benefit that replaces 27
percent of their average indexed monthly earnings (AIME). Workers in the bottom wage group who claim a pension at the same age have a replacement rate of
77 percent. Note that a high replacement rate does not necessarily translate into
a comfortable standard of living. If workers earn very low wages during their best
35 years of covered employment or if they did not work during a large share of
those years, the resulting pension can be small.

The SSA figures understate the percentage of net earnings that is replaced by
Social Security benefits, because the calculations do not account for taxes paid on
preretirement wage income and postretirement pension income. If we adjust for
taxes on preretirement and postretirement income, net replacement rates will be
higher, especially for workers with modest or low lifetime earnings. Pension
income is typically more lightly taxed than preretirement earnings. A significant
tax on preretirement earnings is the payroll tax that pays for OASDI pensions and
Medicare Part A insurance. Since 1990, the tax rate on most workers' wage earnings has been 7.65 percent. An identical payroll tax rate is imposed on employers.
In 2019, the 7.65 percent total payroll tax consisted of a 5.3 percent tax for OASI,

a 0.9 percent tax for DI, and a 1.45 percent tax for Medicare Part A.[5] Importantly, there is a cap on the annual earnings that are subject to the OASDI payroll tax (though not the Medicare tax). In 2019, the cap was $132,900, an amount that is raised each year in line with increases in the economy-wide average annual wage. About 6 percent of earners have annual earnings that exceed the taxable cap. The long-term rise in earnings inequality has meant that a growing percentage of earned income is above the taxable cap and hence is not taxed.

Workers' pensions are calculated on the earnings that are taxed by OASDI rather than on their total earnings. If the replacement rates in Figure 1 were calculated on the basis of earners' total earnings rather than their OASDI-taxed earnings, the replacement rates of earners in the top 5 percent of the lifetime earnings distribution would be lower than those displayed on the right of the chart. When Congress raises the cap on taxable earnings, it has always included the extra covered earnings in the basic benefit formula, meaning the maximum possible benefit payment rises along with the cap. The increase in benefits is modest, however, because the basic pension formula provides only a small upward adjustment in benefits for workers at the top of the covered wage distribution.[6] Raising the cap is therefore advantageous for Social Security's finances but very disadvantageous for highly paid contributors. They and their employers will pay higher OASDI taxes, but when the future additions to their OASDI pensions are suitably discounted, the extra benefits will be worth substantially less than the additional taxes they had to pay. If very high earners wanted to obtain better life and disability insurance or a fatter retirement check, they have cheaper alternatives than to pay OASDI taxes on a larger share of their earnings.

To see this, consider the real rates of return that workers obtain on their contributions and those of their employers. SSA analysts have estimated lifetime earnings profiles for a number of representative workers, as noted above. Based on these profiles, they have calculated the level and timing of expected OASDI contributions and benefit payments for these same representative workers, including benefits expected to be paid to dependents and survivors. Analysts performed the calculations for workers born in a variety of years from 1920 through 2004 and in a variety of family circumstances. With this information in hand, it is straightforward to estimate the real rate of return that each of the representative workers or worker couples obtains on their contributions. Figure 2 shows the results of these calculations for married couples when each spouse earns the same wage throughout their careers. The five lines in the chart reflect results for worker couples with wages in different positions of the lifetime earnings distribution. As in Figure 1, the earnings patterns reflect those of workers at the 12th, 25th, 56th, 82nd, and top percentiles of lifetime earnings, who are designated "very low," "low," "medium," "high," and "top" in Figure 2. For workers born in more recent years, the SSA analysts had to predict what future payroll tax rates and benefits would be. The results in the chart are based on the assumption that future payroll tax rates will remain unchanged while future benefits will be trimmed as needed once the OASDI trust funds are depleted.

The chart shows that workers' returns on their contributions will be lower for later birth cohorts compared with earlier ones. The main reason is that more

FIGURE 2
Real Internal Rate of Return on OASDI Contributions for Married-Couple Workers, by
Lifetime Earnings Levels and Year of Birth

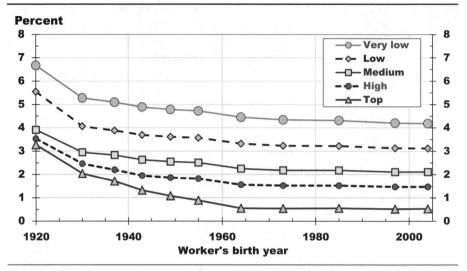

SOURCE: Clingman, Burkhalter, and Chaplain (2019).

recent cohorts have paid a high OASDI payroll tax through their entire careers, while earlier cohorts paid lower tax rates in their early careers. The basic trend is the same for each of the five earnings profiles examined. Within a given birth cohort, couples who earn higher wages can expect to obtain lower returns on their OASDI contributions. Among worker couples born in 1964, for example, those earning the top taxable wage every year in their career can expect to obtain a real return of just 0.55 percent. In comparison, those earning the medium wage can expect a return of 2.25 percent, while couples earning very low wages will receive a return of almost 4.5 percent. For purposes of comparison, since 1926 the average return on large company U.S. stocks has been a bit more than 7 percent, the real return on long government bonds has averaged 2.6 percent, and the return on short-term U.S. Treasury bills has averaged 0.5 percent, approximately the same return that top lifetime earners can expect on their OASDI contributions.[7]

From the inception of Social Security up through 1983, Social Security benefits were tax free under the federal income tax. When the system was reformed in 1983 to restore solvency, Congress made part of the annual benefit taxable for middle- and high-income recipients. Up to half the benefits became taxable, and the extra income tax revenue was deposited in the OASDI trust funds where it is used to finance benefits and administration. Ten years later, Congress raised the income tax assessed on higher-income beneficiaries by including up to 85 percent of benefits in taxable income. The extra revenues from this addition to taxable income are deposited in the Medicare Part A trust fund. These changes increased the progressivity of OASDI, both through the inclusion of benefits in taxable income in a progressive tax system and through inclusion of a progressively *larger* percentage of benefits as taxpayers move up the income scale. This change represents a method for means testing Social Security based on pensioners' retirement incomes. Retirees with little taxable income besides Social Security receive their full benefit without any reduction. High-income taxpayers pay 85 percent of their marginal income tax rate on all the benefits they receive. The top statutory federal marginal tax rate in 2019 is 37 percent. Taxpayers facing this rate thus lose 31.45 percent of their pensions to federal taxes, and almost 60 percent of the resulting tax revenue flows back into the OASDI trust funds.

The taxation of OASDI benefits has little impact on the predicted replacement rates and expected real returns facing low-wage contributors, but it has a sizable impact on replacement rates and returns received by high-earnings contributors. The rates of return shown in Figure 2 are calculated based on contributors' gross or pretax OASDI benefits. Because high-income retirees can expect to pay federal taxes on most of their benefits, their after-tax returns will be lower than the returns displayed in the figure. In contrast, low-income retirees receive their benefits tax free.

Revenues from the income tax on pensioners' benefits account for a growing share of trust fund income (Table 2). The share will continue to increase because Congress did not index the income thresholds for including pensions in taxable incomes. Steady inflation will mean a growing percentage of pensioners must include benefits in their taxable incomes. In addition, the number of pensioners is increasing relative to the number of workers. Before 1984, benefits were exclusively financed with a somewhat regressive payroll tax. That tax financed pensions computed under a very progressive formula, but the pensions were not subject to a means test. That is, pensioners could collect all their scheduled benefits, regardless of whether they were rich or poor. The absence of a means test meant that Social Security did not deter employers from offering pensions to their workers. Nor did it discourage workers from saving more for retirement, either on their own or through an employer's pension plan. Withdrawals from employer pension plans were taxable, but the withdrawals did not result in any reduction in a retired worker's Social Security entitlement. When Congress decided to include part of Social Security benefits in taxable income, it indirectly subjected benefits to a means test. Low-income retirees do not pay income taxes, so the net value of their benefits was unaffected. Retirees with higher incomes, either from past savings or from a company retirement plan, were now forced to pay income taxes on their Social Security benefits. Under a progressive income tax, the tax is heavier as retirees' non–Social Security income rises. The change in the tax status of Social Security benefits has made the system more progressive, but it may discourage workers from saving for retirement and may deter employers from making workplace pensions more generous. After all, any measure that eventually boosts a retiree's private income may result in higher income taxes on the retiree's Social Security pension.

Of course, a common criticism of Social Security is that its very existence deters workers from saving for retirement. If workers were fully confident the

TABLE 2
OASI Taxable Payroll and Operations of the OASI Trust Fund, 1980–2017
(billions of 2017 dollars)

Item	1980	1990	2000	2010	2017
Taxable payroll	$3,268	$4,298	$5,696	$5,969	$6,959
OASI income					
Payroll tax receipts	294	485	602	614	707
Income taxes on OASI benefits	. . .	9	17	25	36
Transfers from U.S. Treasury	2	−1	0	2	0
Net interest on OASI Trust Fund	5	30	82	122	83
OASI outgo					
Benefit payments	298	407	503	651	799
Program administration	3	3	3	4	4
OASI Trust Fund operations					
Change in OASI Trust Fund	−5	108	189	104	19
Reserves in Trust Fund, end of year	65	391	1,329	2,737	2,820
Memo: OASI benefit payments as % of U.S. personal income	4.5%	4.5%	4.1%	4.6%	4.7%

NOTE: Current dollar amounts are converted to 2017 values using CPI-U-RS deflator.
SOURCE: SSA, Annual Statistical Supplement (2018); Board of Trustees OASDI (2018); National Income and Product Accounts (December 2018).

program will continue to exist and pay good pensions, they might see little need to accumulate a retirement nest egg. However, the replacement-rate schedule in Figure 1 implies that middle-income workers who elect to rely solely on Social Security to pay for retirement will face a sizable drop in income and living standards when they retire. Assuming the pension is tax free while the preretirement wage is subject to a 7.65 percent payroll tax plus an average income tax rate of 15 percent, the worker earning the median lifetime wage would expect to see her after-tax income fall by about 45 percent when she stops working and claims a pension at the FRA. The net income loss is even greater for workers who claim Social Security before the FRA as well as for lifetime earners further up the earnings distribution. The size of the income drop is big enough so that far-sighted workers have reason to supplement their Social Security pension with other sources of retirement income, including a workplace pension, personal savings, or an owner-occupied home.

One way to see the exceptional generosity of OASI benefits received by early generations of contributors is to calculate the internal rates of return obtained by those and later generations on their contributions to the program. Calculations by Leimer (2007) show that the real return obtained by generations born before 1900 was 18.4 percent per year. A return this high allows investors to double their money in a bit more than four years. In contrast, the predicted return for the generation born in 1945 is expected to be just 2.7 percent. This annual return requires investors to wait 26 years to see their money double. An 18.4 percent per year real return is far above the historical real return earned on the trust fund reserves, which are invested in Treasury securities. Indeed, the return is far higher than the long-run real return earned on U.S. equities. It is therefore clear that early generations of contributors received generous net transfers, whereas more recent ones will obtain returns approximating those on a conservative investment portfolio. Generations born after 1945 will receive even lower returns depending on how the solvency crisis in Social Security is resolved.

A couple of reform plans were considered by Leimer (2007), who performed his analysis when the insolvency of the program was already foreseen. Under one plan he considered, benefit payouts would gradually be trimmed to preserve the current tax rate. (A similar assumption is used to calculate the returns displayed in Figure 2.) Under a second reform plan, the payroll tax rate would be gradually raised so that scheduled benefits can be paid in full. Either reform will reduce workers' real returns below the level Leimer predicts for the workers born in 1945, but the decline in returns will be much faster if benefits are cut and the tax rate is held at today's level. If instead the tax rate is increased to protect scheduled benefits, more of the burden of restoring Social Security solvency will be pushed onto younger birth cohorts. Older generations will collect all the scheduled benefits promised to them, but younger workers will face rising payroll tax burdens throughout their careers.

The current law governing Social Security already contains a mechanism for dealing with a funding shortfall. When the trust fund is depleted, the program will stop paying scheduled benefits and cut pensions to a "payable" level, specifically, to the amount that can be financed with current dedicated taxes flowing into the program. Under the current OASDI trustees' forecast, this will result in a 20 percent across-the-board cut in benefits around 2035, when the combined OASDI trust funds will be depleted. Nothing in this outlook is new or surprising, except to voters who do not read annual trustees reports and news items that mention the reports. Since 1991, the OASDI trustees have published twenty-nine annual reports, each containing a prediction of the year when the combined trust funds will be depleted. The estimates have ranged between 2029 and 2042, with a mean and median forecast of 2036 (top line in Figure 3). The main difference between 1991 and 2019 is that the predicted year of trust fund depletion is nowadays much closer at hand, mainly because the passage of time has brought us 29 years nearer to the expected depletion date. All of the ingredients that will produce trust fund exhaustion were known in the mid-1980s: slow future growth in the working-age population because of the drop in birth rates after 1964; the rapid growth in the pension-eligible population starting around 2010; the steady rise in life expectancy, which increases the percentage of workers' lives spent past the pensionable age; and painfully slow improvement in workers' average productivity and wages.

FIGURE 3
OASDI Trustees' Predictions of Trust Fund Depletion, 1982–2018

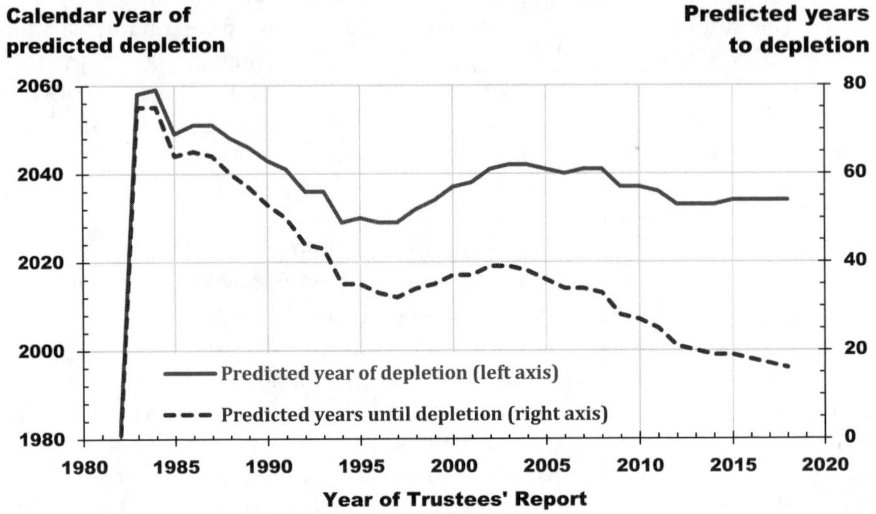

SOURCE: Board of Trustees OASDI (2019), Table VI.B1.

Effectiveness and Redistributional Effects

The main goal of OASI is to protect insured workers and their eligible dependents against outsize income loss in old age or in the event of a worker's death. A closely related goal is to keep retired workers as well as child and aged survivors of insured workers out of poverty. Historical statistics confirm the program has been successful in reducing income poverty in the population past 65. The best-known measure of poverty is based on the U.S. Department of Health and Human Services' (HHS's) official poverty guidelines. Using this benchmark, the elderly have seen spectacular and sustained improvements in well-being in the past six decades. The gains have been both absolute and relative. The elderly have enjoyed faster gains than other age groups in the population. The percentage of the aged with cash incomes below the official poverty line fell from 35 percent in 1959 to 15 percent in 1979, to 9.7 percent in 1999, and to 9.2 percent in 2017 (U.S. Census Bureau 2019). The poverty rate of nonaged adults, initially much lower than that of the elderly, has declined much less. In fact, all of the progress of this group occurred in the 1960s. Beginning in the early 1970s, the poverty rate of 18- to 64-year-olds has trended upward. Since 2003, the poverty rate of nonelderly adults has been higher than that of the elderly. By 2017, it was 2.0 percentage points above the old-age poverty rate. Children under 18 have fared worse than either nonaged adults or the elderly. In 2017, the child poverty rate was 7.9 percentage points higher than that of the aged. With respect to extreme poverty—money income below one-half the official poverty line—the elderly have also fared well compared with other age groups. In 2017 just 3.2 percent of the aged population had income below half the poverty line compared with a 6.2 percent rate in the nonelderly population.

Much of the progress in reducing old-age poverty is traceable to Social Security. Analysts have long known that Social Security accounts for a large percentage of the income received by the elderly, especially aged adults who have low incomes. If Social Security benefits were subtracted from their household incomes, many of the elderly would be poor. For example, Short (2012) calculated the Census Bureau's new supplemental poverty rate with and without inclusion of families' Social Security benefits, leaving unchanged income from all other sources. When Social Security pensions were excluded from household income, the 2011 poverty rate in the population 65 and older was 54.1 percent. When Short included Social Security in household income, the old-age poverty rate fell to just 15.1 percent. For the total population, including the nonaged, the comparable poverty rates were 24.4 percent with Social Security excluded and 16.1 percent when Social Security was included (Short 2012, 15).

Englehardt and Gruber (2006) examined the impact of Social Security benefit changes on the incomes of Americans born between 1880 and 1935. They concluded that Social Security benefit increases between 1967 and 2007 caused virtually all of the 17-percentage-point drop in old-age poverty between the two years. The economists' findings are significant in shedding light on the overall impact of the program on beneficiaries, net of its effects on their labor supply and investment income. Benefit increases may cause pensioners to work or save less, reducing their non–Social Security income and partially offsetting the direct impact of benefits on household income. Englehardt and Gruber's findings suggest the legislated benefit increases produced relatively small offsets.

Social Security has not only boosted incomes at the bottom of the old-age distribution, it has improved the relative income positions of the elderly compared with the nonelderly. Since the late 1970s the share of aged adults who are near the bottom of the income distribution has fallen sharply while the shares in the middle and at the top three quintiles have increased. Figure 4 shows estimates of the percentage of Americans 65 and over who have incomes that placed them in each fifth of the overall income distribution. The estimates are derived from CBO (2018) data on the distribution of household-size-adjusted incomes in 1979 and 2015. CBO uses three income definitions, and the chart is based on the most comprehensive one. That definition measures households' post-tax, post-transfer income from both money and in-kind income sources. In 1979, the aged population was overrepresented in the two bottom income quintiles. By 2015, the elderly were overrepresented in the top two quintiles. The share of the elderly in the bottom one-fifth of the distribution fell from 29 percent in 1979 to just 12 percent in 2015. The percentage in the top quintile increased, though not as spectacularly as the share in the bottom quintile fell.

A great deal of evidence shows that Social Security has improved the relative position of the aged and lifted the incomes of the low-income elderly. It is less

FIGURE 4

Percent of Aged Population in Each One-Fifth of the Overall Distribution of After-Tax, After-Transfer Income, 1979 and 2015

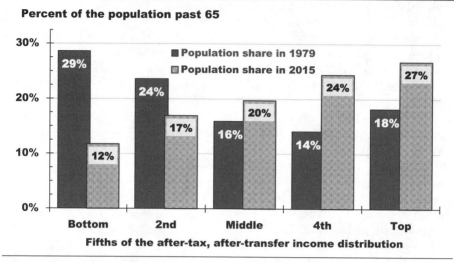

SOURCE: CBO (2018) and author's estimates.

clear whether the program redistributes income from the most affluent in a given generation to the less affluent in that generation. Most benefits paid by the system are to retired workers and their aged or widowed spouses. Their benefits are paid as life annuities. Annuities offer valuable protection to people worried about depleting their assets in old age, but they have less value to people with short life expectancy. It has long been known that people with higher incomes on average live longer than people with low incomes. The redistributive tilt in Social Security's benefit formula may simply compensate low-wage workers for their shorter expected lifespan. The benefit schedule in Figure 1 provides low-wage workers with higher monthly benefits per dollar of contribution than it gives to workers who earn high wages. However, if the high-wage contributors expect to live longer than low-wage contributors, they can also expect to collect retirement benefits for a greater number of months.

Most research suggests Social Security is redistributive in the intended direction within a given generation. Notwithstanding the fact that affluent members of the generation live longer than the less affluent in the same generation, they pay more in contributions per dollar of benefits received than do low-income contributors. This is partly because Social Security insures workers against early death and disability as well for old-age retirement benefits, and the risks of early death and disability are greater for low-wage contributors (Leimer 1999). However, there is increasing evidence the life expectancy advantage enjoyed by high-income Americans is growing (Waldron 2007; Bosworth, Burtless, and Zhang 2016). Recent gains in life expectancy have been small or negligible for people with low Social Security–covered earnings and much faster among people with high earnings. This trend has important implications for proposals to restore Social Security solvency by raising the FRA or increasing the earliest benefit claiming age.

One reason Social Security appears to play such a large role in old-age poverty reduction is that it is well reported in household surveys. Many other sources of income important to the elderly are less accurately reported. Underreported income sources include means-tested benefits, such as Supplemental Security Income (SSI), interest and dividend income, workplace pensions, and withdrawals from workplace retirement plans (Meyer, Mok, and Sullivan 2015; Bee and Mitchell 2017). If these items were accurately reported in surveys, Social Security would feature somewhat less prominently in the incomes of the aged. Bee and Mitchell (2017) compared income reports in the Census Bureau's Current Population Survey (CPS) with reports of the same five income items reported in SSA and Internal Revenue Service (IRS) administrative records. In 2012, survey respondents older than 65 failed to report more than a quarter of their SSI benefits, one-third of their interest and dividend income, and over half their workplace pensions and retirement savings plan withdrawals. The most important missing items were workplace pensions and withdrawals from workplace retirement plans, including IRAs.[8] While income underreporting is significant at the top and bottom of the old-age income distribution, Bee and Mitchell find that its biggest proportional impact is on estimated incomes in the middle of the distribution. They find that the median cash income of aged family units increased 30 percent when incorrect survey responses for 2012 were replaced with more accurate SSA and IRS information. Further, they find that income underreporting, especially of private pension and retirement plan withdrawals, has worsened over time, causing income gains among the aged to be understated in household surveys.

In one respect, the underreporting problem in household surveys represents good news. When we perform analysis using better information about the distribution of old-age income, we learn that the nation's retirement programs, including especially SSI and workplace retirement plans, perform better than we thought based on household surveys. For example, Bee and Mitchell (2017) find that actual SSI benefits received by aged families in the bottom one-tenth of the income distribution are more than two and a half times the level reported in the Census Bureau's Current Population Survey. The finding suggests SSI is both better targeted and more generous to aged families at the bottom of the distribution than indicated in household surveys. Unfortunately, the average income received by aged Americans at the bottom of the distribution remains distressingly low. In principle, SSI should protect most of the elderly who do not receive Social Security or receive very meager benefits. However, the program provides a maximum monthly benefit of just 74 percent of the official poverty line to single persons and just 82 percent of the poverty line to aged married couples. Even when Supplemental Nutrition Assistance Program (SNAP) benefits are added to these allotments, the incomes of many aged remain below the poverty threshold. Furthermore, many indigent elderly are kept off SSI because they fail the program's asset test limits, currently \$2,000 for a single person and \$3,000 for a married couple. If SSI asset limits had been increased to reflect price inflation since the program's creation in 1974, they would now be about four times higher, and more of the low-income elderly would be entitled to benefits.

The SSI program aims to boost the incomes of the indigent elderly, whether or not they receive Social Security. The generous tax preference for workplace retirement programs and individual retirement accounts (IRAs) is intended to encourage workers and their employers to set aside some of their pay for retirement savings. This tax preference primarily benefits middle-income and especially high-income workers, for whom the tax preference is most valuable. The private retirement system is now larger than Social Security. In 2015, taxable payouts from the private retirement system were \$1.42 trillion, or about 65 percent greater than benefit payments from OASDI (Burtless and Koepcke 2018). How are benefits from the private retirement system distributed across the population? Not surprisingly, they are much more unequally distributed than Social Security. Benefit recipients in the top fifth of the old-age income distribution receive more private retirement income than recipients in the other four quintiles combined (Bee and Mitchell 2017). Many small employers, especially employers of low-wage workers, do not offer a workplace retirement plan (Dushi, Iams, and Lichtenstein 2015). Furthermore, participation in many workplace plans is voluntary. Workers may elect not to contribute to the plan or may choose to make only small contributions. A good reason to participate is to obtain the tax preference for contributions. The tax preference is less valuable to low-income workers, who face low marginal income tax rates on their earnings, Finally, the schedule of Social Security replacement rates, displayed in Figure 1, suggests that well-informed low-wage employees may see no compelling need to supplement their Social Security pensions with withdrawals from a retirement plan.

While low-wage workers may not want a supplement to their Social Security retirement check, there is a stronger case that median-wage workers will need one. Their scheduled Social Security benefits do not provide a high net replacement rate, and future replacement rates will decline if the threat of insolvency induces lawmakers to scale back future benefits. How likely is it that middle-wage workers will end up with an adequate nest egg? The survey evidence on pension coverage is not very reliable, but the best evidence suggests the percentage of employees covered by a workplace retirement plan has not changed very much in the past four decades. Probably the best evidence about current coverage comes from survey data supplemented with tax information on survey respondents' plan enrollment and contributions (Dushi, Iams, and Lichtenstein 2015). These data suggest that in 2012, about 75 percent of 21- to 64-year-old employees in the private sector were offered enrollment in a workplace retirement plan, and 61 percent of private employees were actually enrolled in an offered plan. Coverage and participation rates are much higher in public employment. Outside the public sector, there is a good chance workers will be employed in an establishment that does not have a workplace retirement plan. If workers are employed in a private establishment with a plan, about one in five will decline to enroll.

While available statistics suggest Social Security helps to equalize the incomes of aged and nonaged Americans, they do not tell us how much the program has lifted old-age income net its possible impacts on labor income in old age and on workers' preretirement savings. Social Security can depress work effort after 62 for a couple of reasons. First, by providing a reliable source of income in addition to labor earnings, the program reduces the need for an older person to work. Second, pensioners who are younger than the FRA face an earnings test if their annual earnings are above an exempt amount ($17,640 in 2019). Every $1 of earnings above that threshold reduces the pensioner's annual benefit by $0.50. The reduction is only temporary, since the worker's monthly payment will eventually be permanently increased to offset the short-term benefit cut. However, many workers may interpret the cut as a 50-percentage-point increase in the marginal tax rate on earnings, and some will limit their annual earnings so they do not exceed the exempt amount.

Most economists who have studied old-age labor supply agree that both these channels of effect reduce work effort and earnings on average.[9] Employment rates of the population past 65 certainly declined in the first half century after Social Security was introduced, but employment rates also fell in the decades before the first benefit payment. What is hard to know is how much old-age labor supply would have fallen in the absence of Social Security. Much of the research on the program's work incentives is based on episodes when benefits were raised or lowered or when the earnings test was changed. For example, real Social Security benefits were increased about one-fifth between 1969 and 1973, and benefits were later cut sharply for workers born in 1917 and later years (sometimes called "notch babies") compared with workers born before 1917. Burtless (1986) examined responses to the first episode, and Krueger and Pischke (1992) examined the second. Both studies found comparatively modest impacts on the work behavior of older men. The 20 percent benefit increase in 1969–1973 speeded up male retirements by about two months, equivalent to a 2-percentage-point decline in the male labor force participation rate at ages 62 and 65. Krueger and Pischke (1992) found a very small impact of the cut in benefits to men born in and after 1917. They interpreted their results to imply that overall improvements in Social Security benefit levels over the 1970s could account for less than one-sixth of the drop in old-age male labor force participation during that decade. Later analysis by Blau and Goodstein (2010) confirmed this basic finding. They conclude that Social Security changes explain at most 16 percent of the decline in male participation rates from the 1960s through the 1980s.

A few researchers find bigger effects of benefit changes on work behavior. In a recent study, Gelber, Isen, and Song (2017) used SSA earnings and benefit records to reexamine work responses to the benefit cut imposed on workers born in 1917 and later years. Since the researchers have access to administrative data on 724,000 men and women, they are able to directly measure the earnings difference between people born just before and just after the date of birth for which the benefit cut became effective. The modest earnings increase for workers born immediately after January 1, 1917, led the authors to conclude that the long-term increase in average OASI benefit levels can explain almost three-fifths of the 15-percentage-point drop in the old-age employment rate between 1950 and 1985. I am skeptical that a modest, short-term response to a poorly understood policy change can have this interpretation. At any rate, old-age employment and labor force participation rates reversed direction and began climbing after the early 1990s. Part of the reversal was due to Social Security policy changes that eliminated work disincentives in the benefit formula and that gradually raised the FRA starting in 2000.

The debate over whether and how much Social Security reduces private saving is voluminous and still unresolved. In a review of the literature in 1998, the CBO found a wide range of estimates of the impact of Social Security on saving (CBO 1998). The value of a worker's accumulation of future Social Security benefits can be discounted to the present and compared to other kinds of wealth accumulated by workers—equity in a home, private retirement savings, and so on. How much does $100 in additional Social Security wealth reduce workers' private wealth accumulation? When CBO analysts threw out the least plausible empirical estimates of this effect, they were left with a range of estimates from as low as $0—no effect at all—up through –$50 (CBO 1998, 30). A crucial point is that means-testing Social Security based on beneficiaries' current incomes can reduce the marginal payoff to saving for old age, either in a personal savings account or a workplace retirement plan. On the other hand, formula changes that reduce the expected value of future Social Security retirement benefits may increase the necessity or attractiveness of accumulating a retirement nest egg. If workers have no retirement savings outside of Social Security, they may face a dauntingly large drop in income after they retire. One option is to set aside savings in a way that escapes federal taxation, for example, in a home or a Roth IRA. The flows of income from these saving vehicles are not subject to the income tax and do not affect how much Social Security income is included in taxable income.

Any reduction in private saving caused by Social Security could in principle be offset if the program itself accumulated enough saving in its reserve fund. The annual saving within OASI could partly or fully offset the drop in private saving caused by the program. As is well known, however, during most of its history the program financed current benefit payments on a pay-as-you-go basis, that is, largely out of current taxes. It did not accumulate a large enough reserve to cover more than a small fraction of the accruing cost of future benefit claims. Early generations of workers paid modest annual contributions for relatively few years and received outsized benefits compared with the taxes they paid. As the number of beneficiaries rose and their pension entitlements increased, Congress regularly hiked the payroll tax to cover growing annual outlays. Between 1960 and 1997, the reserves in the OASI trust fund never surpassed two years of annual benefit outlays, far too little to cover the future benefits promised to current pensioners and insured workers.

Major Reform or Minor Tweaks?

The OASI program is the main pillar of old-age income security for an over-whelming majority of low- and middle-income families. Without the retirement income it provides, a large percentage of these families would be at risk of living in poverty or in much-reduced circumstances when breadwinners' earnings cease in retirement. Even under optimistic assumptions about workers' ability to boost personal saving and delay retirement, a sizable cut in benefits in the next two decades will increase old-age poverty and inflict hardship on the low- and middle-income elderly. On humanitarian grounds, lawmakers need to preserve OASI or create something very similar to it to ensure income protection for the low- and middle-income elderly. To do that, they must devise at least a short-term fix for its looming insolvency. Optionally, they might also phase in new old-age insurance arrangements for middle- and high-income retirees.

The case for preserving something like the current system, at least for low- and average-wage workers, is compelling. The available evidence suggests Social Security enjoys broad voter approval, is effective in providing support to the most vulnerable workers (assuming they become insured), offers good insurance at modest cost to low- and middle-income contributors, and is administered at stag-geringly low expense. On average, current contributors pay reasonable premiums for the insurance they obtain. OASI's projected funding shortfall does not arise because today's average workers pay too little for the protection they receive. Rather, it is the result of the program's generous treatment of early contributors to the system, nearly all of whom are now deceased. If current workers' contribu-tions had been placed in a reserve where they earned a modest real return until the funds were used to pay pensions to retired workers and eligible dependents, the OASI program would be solvent. Most of the funds in the "missing reserve" were instead used to make benefit payments to earlier contributors. A good case can be made for gradually filling the missing reserve with debt securities of the U.S. government. In that way, the burden of paying for the debt would be shifted from OASI payroll taxpayers to federal taxpayers more generally. A related pro-posal was offered by Diamond and Orszag (2005), who recommend imposing earmarked taxes to pay off the legacy debt accumulated in the early decades of Social Security. Among their suggested taxes was a levy on labor income above the current OASDI taxable earnings limit. Their proposed tax rate would start at 3 percent and then gradually increase over time.

The conventional debate over fixing Social Security's funding imbalance focuses on short- and long-run cuts in benefit entitlements and short- and long-run measures to boost revenue. Measures that increase revenues allow the cur-rent benefit package to be preserved. Measures that cut current and future benefits would help to keep the future payroll tax rate low. As already noted, the longer tax hikes or benefit cuts are delayed, the larger the burden on younger and future workers. They would be forced to accept either higher taxes throughout their careers or smaller benefit entitlements when they reach retirement than would be the case if solvency measures went into effect immediately.

When he calculated the rates of return successive generations will receive on their Social Security contributions, Leimer (2007) was aware the promised benefit package could not be financed out of reserves plus future tax revenues. To calculate younger generations' rates of return on their contributions, he considered two reform plans. Under one plan, benefit payouts would gradually be trimmed to preserve the current tax rate. (A similar assumption is used to calculate the returns displayed in Figure 2.) Under the second plan, the payroll tax was gradually raised so that promised benefits could be paid in full. Either reform reduces current workers' returns below the level Leimer calculated for workers born in 1945. However, the decline in returns would be much faster if benefits are cut and the tax rate is held at today's level. If instead the tax rate is increased to protect scheduled benefits, most of the burden of restoring Social Security solvency would be pushed onto today's younger workers. Older generations would collect all the scheduled benefits currently promised to them, but younger workers would face rising payroll tax burdens throughout their careers.

The 2019 trustees report estimated that the 75-year shortfall in funding for the combined OASI and DI programs amounts to 2.78 percent of taxable payroll. This way of expressing the long-range imbalance is convenient, because it allows us to see how much the payroll tax rate must rise to eliminate the 75-year funding shortfall. The combined employer and employee OASDI tax rate is currently 12.4 percent. A 2.78 percent tax hike imposed immediately and for the entire 75-year projection period would eliminate the shortfall. Instead of paying 6.2 percent of their earnings for OASDI, covered workers would pay 7.62 percent. Employers would face the same payroll tax hike. The tax increase could be phased in gradually, lessening the shock but requiring the ultimate tax hike to be bigger. Alternatively, current tax rates could be preserved but scheduled benefits cut to keep the program solvent for the next 75 years. If pensions are cut immediately and proportionately for all current and future beneficiaries, this would require a benefit cut of about 17 percent.[10] If instead the benefit cut were limited to beneficiaries who become initially eligible for pensions in 2019 or later years, the required benefit cut would be about 21 percent (Arnone and Murphy 2019, 7).

For the past quarter century, most policy discussions about Social Security reform have focused on steps to reduce the long-term funding imbalance to keep the program solvent. We have plenty of information with which to judge the likely effects of specific reforms, both on long-term solvency and on tax burdens and benefits of future workers and retirees. If forced to devise a plan that eliminates most of Social Security's funding gap, Congress has the necessary evidence at hand. Some of the estimates are mentioned below. In recent years, a growing number of politicians, especially on the Left, have proposed expanding rather than shrinking Social Security's commitments, especially on behalf of low-wage workers, aged widows, and the very long-lived. Furthermore, many advocates now urge indexation of OASDI benefits to a consumer price index that is more favorable to beneficiaries than the index we currently use. Unless these benefit improvements are offset by benefit cuts for identifiable groups of beneficiaries, they will require additional revenue beyond what is needed to close the current funding gap.

Public opinion polling shows the majority of Americans, even those under 35, support Social Security tax increases rather than benefit cuts to restore long-term solvency (Walker, Reno, and Bethell 2014). There are at least two ways to increase payroll taxes. Congress can boost the tax rate on covered earnings above the current rate, or it can lift the cap on taxable earnings. Big majorities of poll respondents support either of these steps in preference to cutting benefits. SSA's chief actuary predicts that removing the taxable earnings cap while continuing to provide benefit credits for all taxed earnings would eliminate two-thirds of Social Security's 75-year funding gap. If instead the earnings cap were eliminated and *no* benefit credits were provided for taxed earnings above the current cap, the actuary predicts that 83 percent of the funding gap would be eliminated. Both these reforms, but especially the second, would result in a major shift in the funding basis of the program. An overwhelming share of the burden of eliminating the funding shortfall would fall on the shoulders of current and future workers in the top 6 percent of the earnings distribution. That top 6 percent of workers would face a 12.4-percentage-point increase in the marginal tax rate on their earned income. Many would devote considerable time, energy, and ingenuity to converting earned income into forms of income, such as capital gains and noncash compensation, that are lightly taxed or untaxed.

At the same time, completely eliminating the earnings cap might pose a long-term political challenge. If benefit credits were provided for earnings above the current cap, some high-income pensioners would qualify for very large, perhaps scandalously large, pensions. If benefit credits on the extra earnings were withheld or were provided at a very low rate, the program could lose key support among a small but politically influential minority of voters, specifically, high-earnings contributors.

Still, the motive behind lifting the taxable wage cap is understandable. Earnings and income inequality have increased sharply in recent decades, and a number of analyses show top income recipients have seen their average tax burdens fall. A much less controversial policy shift would be for Congress to raise the taxable earnings cap so that 90 percent (rather than 100 percent) of earnings in Social Security–covered employment is taxed. Only 83 percent of all earnings is currently taxed. About 90 percent was taxed back in the early 1980s, when Congress last overhauled Social Security. The percentage of earnings under the cap fell as inequality rose. Even if full benefit credits were awarded for all taxed earnings above the old cap, this reform would eliminate more than one-quarter of the 75-year funding shortfall.[11] On grounds of equity, popular acceptance, and political feasibility, it seems like a sensible first step toward reform.

A proposal popular among conservatives is to raise the FRA. This would not affect workers' eligibility for retirement benefits at 62 or any later age, but it would reduce the OASI benefits payable at each age from 62 onward. The 1983 Social Security Amendments gradually increased the FRA from 65 (for workers born before 1938) to 67 (for workers born in 1960 and later years). One idea is to raise the FRA in line with changing life expectancy. For example, the FRA could automatically be adjusted to maintain a constant ratio of life expectancy at the FRA to potential work years (say, the FRA minus 20, where 20 is the expected age at which a working career begins). This reform has no immediate effect on benefits, because the FRA would not rise above its current path for almost a decade. In the long run, however, it would gradually reduce Social Security replacement rates and eliminate one-fifth of the 75-year funding shortfall.

There are three advantages of this kind of reform. First, it seems roughly equitable, since part of Social Security's funding problem is traceable to rising longevity. Second, the reform does not affect disability benefits, so disabled workers would be held harmless. Third, a higher FRA gives middle-age and older workers a highly visible and slowly rising target age for leaving the workforce. There is considerable evidence that workers are responsive to this signal. As the FRA increased from 65 to 66, the percentage of new retired-worker claims filed by 66-year-olds increased, and the percentage filed by 65-year-olds fell below the percentage filed by 66-year-olds. A notable disadvantage of the FRA adjustment is that it imposes proportionately similar benefit cuts on all workers, regardless of the age at which they claim a pension. This may seem unfair if workers with low lifetime earnings, who typically claim pensions at 62, have seen little improvement in their life expectancy, while high-wage workers, who more commonly file for benefits later, enjoy outsize life expectancy gains. For low-wage workers who have seen little improvement in life spans, a higher FRA simply reduces the lifetime benefits they receive. In contrast, high-wage workers receive a partial compensation for the higher FRA. Their improved lifespans mean they get to collect benefits longer.

The perceived unfairness of raising the FRA for short-lived and less healthy workers has pushed policy-makers toward other strategies for slowing the growth of future benefits. One simple way is to revise the basic benefit formula (see note 6). Congress could cut replacement rates for workers with high lifetime earnings while boosting replacement rates for workers whose lifetime wages are low. One problem with this fix is that some of the benefit improvements would flow to pensioners who are members of high- and middle-income families, for example, secondary earners who worked only a limited number of years or retirees who earned most of their wages outside of Social Security–covered jobs. To avoid giving extra benefits to affluent pensioners, many reform plans focus on boosting pensions to workers who earn low annual wages for a lengthy minimum period, such as 30 years. Retirees who meet this test would be guaranteed a higher minimum benefit than the one provided under the current formula. For example, long-service, low-wage workers might be guaranteed a minimum benefit equal to 125 percent of the poverty line. An even simpler and more target-efficient way to achieve the same goal is to liberalize the SSI program, which is squarely aimed at reducing old-age poverty. However, long experience suggests the goal is politically easier to accomplish in the popular Social Security program rather than in a less visible program targeted at the poor.

A policy that combines a gradual increase in the FRA with an improvement in basic benefits for long-service, low-wage workers offers the best prospect of reducing future benefit growth while still protecting the interests of the most vulnerable workers. As recognized by most actuaries and economists, but few voters, keeping pension formulas unchanged in the face of rising life expectancy is equivalent to offering younger workers a more generous pension plan than the one provided to older workers. Gradually increasing the FRA can keep pension generosity relatively constant over time while clearly communicating to workers the desirability of later exit from the workforce.

A number of recent reform proposals, even some aimed at slowing future benefit growth, include benefit hikes for specific populations thought to face special hardships. Besides long-service, low-wage workers, these populations include aged widows, retired women who took time out of their paid careers to rear children, and the very old, regardless of gender. One idea for helping widows is to guarantee that surviving spouses receive a benefit equal to at least 75 percent of the combined benefit received by the family when both spouses were alive. To make the guarantee less costly, it could be restricted to surviving spouses whose OASI benefits would otherwise be less than 125 percent of the poverty line. To help child caretakers, advocates have offered two approaches. One is to allow caretakers to reduce the number of years used to calculate their lifetime average earnings. The current formula uses the worker's 35 years of highest indexed earnings. The number of averaged years could be reduced by two for a mother's first child and by four if she has two or more children. Another approach is to credit new mothers with fictitious covered earnings for a specified number of years per child. Finally, Congress might help long-lived retirees and survivors by boosting their benefits after they reach 85. The case for this one-time benefit hike would be compelling if we adopted a cost-of-living-adjustment formula that increases benefits more slowly than the current formula. I see no good reason for increasing benefits more slowly than the CPI-W, so the case for a special benefit hike at 85 seems weak to me. It would be even weaker if we link benefit increases to a price index that increases faster than the CPI-W.

Conclusion

In the next 15 years voters and lawmakers must decide how Social Security's funding shortfall will be resolved. If past experience is any guide, lawmakers are likely to adopt a combination of tax hikes and benefit cuts, despite voters' apparent preference for tax increases over benefit cuts. A pension reform package that emphasizes benefit cuts would be more defensible if Congress required private employers to offer automatic payroll withholding for private retirement saving or, even better, obliged them to make at least modest contributions into workplace retirement plans. In the absence of such a mandate, a growing fraction of private sector workers will find themselves underprepared for retirement if Social Security benefits are cut substantially. This is likely to be the case even if benefit cuts are phased in gradually.

The simplest, most politically acceptable, and easiest to justify tax increase is a hike in the maximum earnings amount subject to the payroll tax. Raising the cap so that 90 percent of total earnings in covered employment is subject to the tax eliminates more than a quarter of the 75-year funding imbalance. A tougher political challenge is to impose a new payroll tax on earnings above the new cap. The justification for such a tax is that it would help to fill the missing reserve that should have been accumulated when early participants in Social Security were given benefits in excess of the pensions their contributions could pay for. Both tax increases fall solely on workers whose earnings are above the current taxable wage cap. To broaden the population facing higher taxes, Congress could modestly increase the payroll tax on earnings below the taxable wage cap. Of the benefit cuts I have mentioned, the easiest to defend is a gradual increase in the FRA that is linked to improvements in average longevity. To protect low-wage workers in low-income families, the reform should be combined with liberalization of the SSI asset test and benefit levels and an increase in OASI pensions for long-service, low-wage workers.

Conservative critics of OASI think it should be scaled back and at least partially replaced with a system of compulsory individual retirement accounts owned and largely controlled by workers themselves. The advantages of such a plan depend on its exact design, but these could include less distortion of workers' savings and retirement incentives. For the next few decades, however, these advantages are unlikely to be large, because the government will still require huge tax revenues to pay for Social Security benefits promised to retired Americans and those near retirement. The taxes needed to pay for legacy benefits would themselves cause distortions, and it is unclear whether the distortions would be any smaller than those produced by the current system. Voters seem at best lukewarm about the wisdom of replacing Social Security with individual accounts. In 2005, President George W. Bush tried to persuade the nation to divert some OASI payroll taxes into a system of voluntary individual accounts. His reform plan attracted little support among voters and even less in the GOP-controlled Congress. Many voters seem to prefer the humdrum dependability of a government pension to the excitement of placing more of their retirement savings in the stock market.

History suggests lawmakers will phase in major Social Security reforms in a way that largely spares current beneficiaries and most workers who will soon become eligible for pensions. This seems not only politically expedient, but also practical and humane. Workers need time to understand the implications of major reform for their own saving behavior and retirement planning. Of course, it would be far preferable if policy-makers acted with due deliberation well in advance of any funding emergency. But if it requires the prospect of an immediate 20 percent benefit cut to capture lawmakers' attention, so be it.

Notes

1. A surviving spouse who is disabled may receive survivor benefits starting as early as age 50, and a nondisabled surviving spouse may collect benefits so long as she or he is caring for a child of the deceased worker. The child must be under age 16 or disabled.

2. If a surviving spouse is dually entitled as both a retired worker and as the survivor of a deceased worker, he or she receives the larger of the two benefits rather than the sum of the two benefits. See Li (2019).

3. Wage indexation is based on the growth of average economy-wide annual earnings in the United States. The annual wage-growth factors are applied to adjust the worker's reported earnings up through age 60.

4. The FRA for workers born before 1938 is 65. For workers born between 1943 and 1954, it is 66. For workers born after 1959, it is 67.

5. Since 1990, the combined payroll tax for OASDI has been 6.2 percent on both employees and employers for a combined tax rate of 12.4 percent. However, the division of this tax between OASI and DI has been modified from time to time to reflect the changing financial fortunes of the two programs.

6. The benefit formula is based on a worker's average indexed monthly earnings (AIME). For workers attaining 62 in 2019, the formula is the following: 90 percent of the first $926 of AIME plus 32 percent of the AIME over $926 but below $5,583 plus 15 percent of the AIME above $5,583.

7. The SSA analysis is based on the assumption that high and low earners have the life expectancy predicted for workers born in the indicated years (Clingman, Burkhalter, and Chaplain 2019). Under the more realistic assumption that high earners can expect to live longer than low earners, the expected returns to high earners would be somewhat higher and the returns to low earners would be somewhat lower. The basic pattern of results displayed in Figure 2 would nonetheless remain (Bosworth, Burtless, and Zhang 2016).

8. Workers can of course contribute to IRAs outside the workplace. However, most of the assets currently in IRAs were accumulated in workplace plans and then transferred into IRAs as tax-free rollovers when workers separated from employers that sponsored a workplace plan.

9. For a good recent survey, see Coile (2018). The antiwork incentives in the Social Security benefit formula are nowadays mild compared with those in the program's early history. Until 2000, the earnings test applied to all pensioners between 62 and 69, rather than just those younger than the FRA. Moreover, the actuarial adjustment in monthly benefits to reflect delayed benefit claiming after the FRA was formerly much less generous. Compared with today's formula, the old formula provided stronger financial incentives to claim benefits and reduce earnings below the exempt amount at the FRA.

10. In fact, the tax hikes and benefit cuts would eventually need to be bigger than the ones mentioned, because operating deficits after the 75th year of the projection period means that the OASDI reserve fund would be quickly exhausted after that year.

11. The Social Security chief actuary maintains a useful website showing estimates of the impact of a variety of reforms on OASDI program solvency (https://www.ssa.gov/OACT/solvency/provisions/index.html). The estimates reported above are described here: https://www.ssa.gov/OACT/solvency/provisions_tr2018/payrolltax.html.

References

Arnone, William, and Griffin Murphy. 2019. *Social Security finances: Findings of the 2019 trustees report*. Washington, DC: National Academy of Social Insurance.

Bee, Adam, and Joshua Mitchell. 2017. Do older Americans have more income than we think? SESHD Working Paper 2017-39, U.S. Census Bureau, Washington, DC.

Blau, David M., and Ryan M. Goodstein. 2010. Can Social Security explain trends in labor force participation of older men in the United States? *Journal of Human Resources* 45 (2): 328–63.

Board of Trustees OASDI. 2018. *The annual report of trustees of the federal OASI and federal DI trust funds*. Washington, DC: Social Security Administration.

Board of Trustees OASDI. 2019. *The annual report of trustees of the federal OASI and federal DI trust funds*. Washington, DC: Social Security Administration.

Bosworth, Barry P., Gary Burtless, and Kan Zhang. 2016. *Later retirement, inequality in old age, and the growing gap in longevity between rich and poor*. Washington, DC: Brookings Institution.

Burtless, Gary. 1986. Social Security, unanticipated benefit increases, and the timing of retirement. *Review of Economic Studies* 53 (5): 781–805.

Burtless, Gary, and Eric Koepcke. 2018. The U.S. tax preference for retirement savings. In *The taxation of pensions*, eds. Robert Holzmann and John Piggott, 257–96. Cambridge, MA: MIT Press.

Center on Budget and Policy Priorities. 2018. Top ten facts about Social Security. Washington, DC: Center on Budget and Policy Priorities. Available from https://www.cbpp.org/sites/default/files/atoms/files/8-8-16socsec.pdf.

Clingman, Michael, Kyle Burkhalter, and Chris Chaplain. 2018. Replacement rates of hypothetical retired workers. Actuarial Note 2018.9. Baltimore, MD: Office of the Chief Actuary, Social Security Administration.

Clingman, Michael, Kyle Burkhalter, and Chris Chaplain. 2019. Internal real rates of return under the OASDI program for hypothetical workers. Actuarial Note 2018.5. Baltimore, MD: Office of the Chief Actuary, Social Security Administration.

Coile, Courtney. 2018. The demography of retirement. In *Future directions of the demography of aging: Proceedings of a workshop*, eds. Mark D. Haywood and Malay K. Majmandar, 217–46. Washington, DC: National Academies Press.

Congressional Budget Office. 1998. *Social security and private saving: A review of the empirical evidence*. Washington, DC: Congressional Budget Office.

Congressional Budget Office. 2018. The distribution of household income,2015: Additional data for researchers. Washington, DC: Congressional Budget Office. Available from https://www.cbo.gov/system/files/2018-11/54646-additional-data-for-researchers.zip.

Diamond, Peter A., and Peter R. Orszag. 2005. *Saving Social Security: A balanced approach*. Washington, DC: Brookings Institution Press.

Engelhardt, Gary V., and Jonathan Gruber. 2006. Social Security and the evolution of elderly poverty. In *Public policy and the income distribution*, eds. Alan Auerbach, David Card, and John Quigley, 259–87. New York, NY: Russell Sage Foundation.

Dushi, Irena, Howard Iams, and Jules Lichtenstein. 2015. Retirement plan coverage by firm size: An update. *Social Security Bulletin* 75 (2): 41–55.

Gelber, Alexander M., Adam Isen, and Jae Song. 2017. The effect of pension income on elderly earnings: Evidence from Social Security. University of California, Berkeley, Working Paper. Available from https://siepr.stanford.edu/system/files/Gelber%20Paper %20021617.pdf.

Krueger, Alan, and Jörn-Steffen Pischke. 1992. The effect of Social Security on labor supply: A cohort analysis of the notch generation. *Journal of Labor Economics* 10 (4): 412–37.

Leimer, Dean R. 1999. Lifetime redistribution under the Social Security program: A literature synopsis. *Social Security Bulletin* 62 (2): 43–51.

Leimer, Dean R. 2007. Cohort-specific measures of lifetime social security taxes and benefits. ORES Working Paper Series No. 110, Office of Research, Evaluation, and Statistics, Office of Policy, Social Security Administration, Washington, DC.

Li, Zhe. 2019. Social Security: Revisiting benefits for spouses and survivors. Report R41479. Washington, DC: Congressional Research Service.

Meyer, Bruce D., Wallace K. C. Mok, and James X. Sullivan. 2015. Household surveys in crisis. *Journal of Economic Perspectives* 29 (4): 199–226.

Short, Kathleen. 2012. The Research Supplemental Poverty Measure: 2012. Current Population Reports P60-247. Washington, DC: U.S. Census Bureau.

Social Security Administration. 2018. *Annual Statistical Supplement, 2018*. Washington, DC: Office of Research, Evaluation and Statistics, Social Security Administration. Available from https://www.ssa.gov/policy/docs/statcomps/supplement/2018/index.html.

U.S. Census Bureau. 2019. Historical poverty tables: People and Families – 1959 to 2017: Table 3. Washington, DC: U.S. Census Bureau. Available from https://www2.census.gov/programs-surveys/cps/tables/time-series/historical-poverty-people/hstpov3.xls.

Waldron, Hillary. 2007. Trends in mortality differentials and life expectancy for male social security-covered workers, by socioeconomic status. *Social Security Bulletin* 67 (3): 1–28.

Walker, Elisa, Virginia Reno, and Thomas Bethell. 2014. *Americans make hard choices on Social Security: A survey with trade-off analysis*. Washington, DC: National Academy of Social Insurance.

Economic Principles for Medicare Reform

In this article, we develop an economic framework for Medicare reform that highlights trade-offs that reform proposals should grapple with, but often ignore. Central to our argument is a tension in administratively set prices, which may improve short-term efficiency but do so at the expense of dynamic efficiency (slowing innovations in new treatments). The smaller the Medicare program is relative to the commercial market, the less important this is; but in a world where there are no market prices or the private sector is very small, the task of setting prices that are dynamically correct becomes more complex. Reforming Medicare should focus on greater incentives to increase competition between Medicare Advantage plans, which necessitates a role for government in ensuring competition; premium support; less use of regulated prices; and less appetite for countless "pay for performance" schemes. We apply this framework to evaluate Medicare for All proposals.

Keywords: Medicare; value-based care; health care reform; markets in health care

By
AMITABH CHANDRA
and
CRAIG GARTHWAITE

Whle the U.S. health care sector is often described as a private, market-based system, the government now controls more than 60 percent of spending (Martin et al. 2018). Public insurers provide insurance to several groups, including the elderly, the indigent, and

Amitabh Chandra is a professor at Harvard Business School and a professor at the Harvard Kennedy School of Government. He is a member of the Congressional Budget Office's (CBO) Panel of Health Advisors and is a research associate at the National Bureau of Economic Research (NBER).

Craig Garthwaite is a professor at the Kellogg School of Management at Northwestern University, the director of the Program on Healthcare at Kellogg (HCAK), and a research associate at NBER.

NOTE: We are grateful to Jim Ziliak, Robert Moffit, and conference participants for very helpful comments.

Correspondence: Amitabh_Chandra@Harvard.EDU

DOI: 10.1177/0002716219885582

the disabled. Of all insurers in the United States, Medicare—which provides health insurance for the elderly and a subset of the disabled population—is the largest in terms of spending and is expected to grow even more in coming years as a result of changing demographics. Given this breadth of coverage, Medicare's current coverage decisions and operations, as well as reforms to the program's structure, will likely have meaningful market-wide effects.

Medicare reform is important for a number of reasons. First, the demographics of the baby-boomers means Medicare enrollment is growing rapidly. This enrollment growth is important as we consider reform, because it creates a political constituency that will both demand improvements to the existing program and push back against any reforms that are seen to decrease the generosity of existing benefits—even if those reforms increase net social benefits (the net benefit to patients and producers of health care, including the net benefit to taxpayers).[1]

Second, even after the implementation of the Affordable Care Act (ACA), a meaningful fraction of the U.S. population remains without health insurance coverage (at the time of this writing, the percentage of uninsured hovers at 13 percent of the population, up from 10.9 percent in November 2016 [Witters 2019]). In addition, health care costs for even those who are insured are quite high, and many individuals are in plans with high cost sharing relative to their income, which leaves them underinsured to the financial risk of a health shock. Many see the relative success of the existing Medicare program in providing broad coverage to the elderly and want to expand it to others. Often described as "Medicare for All," these various policy proposals range from allowing progressively younger individuals to purchase Medicare coverage to the expansion of the existing Medicare program to serve as a single-payer system for the entirety of the U.S. population.[2] These proposals are popular, but popularity does not mean that the hard work of grappling with the underlying trade-offs has been started, let alone achieved.

Third, despite the ostensible "dual mandate" of the ACA to both increase coverage and control costs, health care costs in the United States continue to grow, albeit at a slower rate than in the past (Chandra, Holmes, and Skinner 2013). Concerns about rising costs and a lack of universal coverage has pushed policy-makers to call for an expanded role for the Medicare system because of the belief that a government-run program can be more administratively efficient than a complex web of private firms offering coverage. In addition, some supporters of such reforms believe a system of administratively set prices will be less expensive, because these prices will be below those determined by a market transaction. Other constituents, who are interested in the debt and tax ramifications of such a large health care program financed by the federal government, want to reform the program accordingly. Still other reformers do not want to shrink Medicare per se but believe it can be made more efficient—which increases its sustainability and reduces the extent to which this program may be crowding out other public spending priorities.

Finally, the last major changes to Medicare occurred in 2003 with the Medicare Modernization Act (which introduced Medicare Advantage [MA]) and in 2006 with the introduction of the prescription drug benefit (Medicare Part D). Medicare Part D, now nearly 15 years old, was effectively created from scratch and has allowed us to learn many things about the structure of the program over time. In addition, neither of the most recent reforms addressed fundamental challenges to the design and financing of the Medicare medical benefit, so even in the absence of the political and economic imperatives noted above, some amount of Medicare reform is long overdue.

Given the importance of Medicare today and its potential for serving as a centerpiece for even further health care reforms, our aim is to provide an economic framework for considering reforms to the existing Medicare program. Such a framework highlights the trade-offs with which all proposals—including those originating from purely normative or polling perspectives—must grapple. Our approach is distinct from the several excellent proposals by the Medicare Payment Advisory Commission (MedPAC) and many think tanks. Many of those proposals provide specific modifications to the existing program but are piecemeal—such as reforming the way physicians are paid for prescribing infusion therapies. In a desire for specificity, those proposals often ignore larger dynamic forces such as innovation and spillovers, whose long-term policy effects are often not empirically certain. But the lack of existing empirical evidence or the difficulty of persuading voters to understand these long-run forces does not mean that they are quantitatively small. There are potentially massive implications of changes to the Medicare program, and therefore it is incumbent on reform proposals to grapple with their long-run implications for societal well-being.

With the fundamentals of this framework in mind, we then propose a series of broad and specific reforms intended to provide structure for more competition in the existing program. One objective of this mutually reinforcing package of reforms is to provide the existing Medicare program with incentives for improving innovation in cost containment beyond the use of administrative rate setting. We view administrative rate setting as having two limitations: the process is routinely captured by provider groups, as demonstrated by how physicians determine their relative fees and how hospitals have lobbied Congress for ad hoc additional payments (Chan and Dickstein 2019). The process also requires the government to determine prices—this is not only hard without an external benchmark, but such prices are unlikely to reflect socially optimal compensation as government's size in health care approaches that of a monopsonist (i.e., a single buyer). Our second objective is to emphasize that the goal of Medicare reform must extend beyond simply reducing spending growth. Such a goal runs the danger of creating a fiscally sustainable program that does not offer sufficient insurance value. In our view, a more laudable goal is building a program that increases (or at a minimum maintains) the value of health insurance over time, which means designing a program where growing per capita Medicare spending is justifiable if it increases societal benefits more than its spending.

We believe that the innovations necessary to achieve these goals over the long term come through a greater reliance on market forces and market competition, which also necessitates a role for government in ensuring such competition, but a different role than government setting prices or expanding "pay for performance" schemes. This tension between administratively set prices, which may improve efficiency in a static (short-run) sense, but at the expense of dynamic efficiency (slowing innovations in the set of treatments available to patients), has been largely ignored in most previous Medicare reform proposals and by all Medicare for All proposals. The smaller the Medicare program is relative to the commercial market, the less important this omission is; but in a world where there are no market prices or the private sector is very small, the task of setting prices that are dynamically correct becomes vastly more complex. The reality that markets are beneficial even in health care is supported by the increasing reliance on competition even in one of the most notable government-run health care systems, Britain's National Health Service, which has undertaken several recent experiments with private markets and providers (Gaynor, Moreno-Serra, and Propper 2013; Propper and Van Reenen 2010). The British experience with introducing competition and incentives means market forces can be combined with government-run and -financed health care systems. In addition, to the extent that Medicare becomes a vehicle for a universal health insurance program, this second goal would moderate some of the potential negative consequences of an expanded use of buyer power.

A Primer on Medicare's Structure and Problems

Structure of Medicare

Medicare is the largest social-insurance program in the world, with spending continuing to increase over time. Medicare payments were $702 billion in 2017, up from $502 billion in 2007 (in 2017 dollars). This funding comes from several parts of Medicare. Part A provides insurance for hospital services and is available to everyone over age 65. Part B provides coverage for physician services and has a premium that is moderately adjusted by income. Part D provides coverage for prescription drugs. Unlike Parts A and B, which are entirely run by the government, Part D is subsidized by the government, but the plans are administered by private insurers, and individual enrollees are responsible for some portion of the premium. Within this time period, the share of total payments for Part A, Part B, and Part D has shifted, with spending on the latter two components increasing (from 41 to 44 percent and 11 percent to 14 percent, respectively), and the former decreasing (from 47 to 42 percent).

A final component of Medicare is Part C, often described as MA. This was introduced in the 1970s as a voluntary managed care version of Medicare, where private firms receive a risk-adjusted, capitated payment from the government and are financially responsible for medical expenses of all enrollees. Spending on the MA program also increased from 2007 to 2017, rising from 18 percent of total Medicare benefit spending to 30 percent ($210 billion).[3] About a third of Medicare beneficiaries are in MA plans, but there is geographic variation in its penetration. About 9.2 million Medicare beneficiaries are also eligible for Medicaid, which covers premiums for Part A; Part B; and a variety of copayments, coinsurance, and deductibles. Eligibility depends on income and the state of residence.

In dollar terms over the past decade, Medicare Part A spending has grown by just less than $100 billion to $300 billion, Part B spending increased by $150 billion to just over $300 billion, and Part D spending grew by $50 billion. In the same time, payments to MA grew by approximately $150 billion to a total of just over $200 billion. The entire program grew by over $407 billion in the past decade, and the size of the current program is now $700 billion, which is about 15 percent of the federal budget (Cubanski and Neuman 2018). In recent years, Medicare spending has grown more slowly than it had in previous years. Between 2010 and 2017, average annual growth in Medicare spending per beneficiary was 1.5 percent, compared to 7.3 percent between 2000 and 2010. Despite the slowing growth rate of per beneficiary spending in the recent past, changing population demographics in part point to the idea that overall spending will start to increase again in the coming years. In addition to the aging of the population, increased use of services, increased intensity of care, and new technologies have led actuaries to project that future spending growth will increase at a faster rate than in the recent past; projected net outlays are expected to increase from $583 billion in 2018 to $1.26 trillion in 2028. Average annual growth is expected to be higher between 2017 to 2027 (7.5 percent) than it was between 2010 and 2017 (4.5 percent). Per beneficiary spending is also expected to grow at a fast rate between 2017 and 2027 (4.6 percent) compared to 2010 to 2017 (1.5 percent). Over the long term, the Congressional Budget Office (CBO) predicts that net Medicare spending will grow from 2.9 percent of gross domestic product (GDP) in 2018 to 6.1 percent of GDP in 2047 (Cubanski and Neuman 2018). The CBO predicts that "excess" health care cost growth—defined as the extent to which the growth of health care costs per beneficiary, adjusted for demographic changes, exceeds the per person growth of potential (the maximum sustainable output of the economy)—will account for 60 percent of spending for Medicare, Medicaid, and subsidies for ACA Marketplace coverage, while the aging of the population will account for 40 percent of this spending.

The unique financing structure of Medicare also leads the program to use more resources than other government-funded programs. Other public payers such as Medicaid are constrained by the inability of state governments to run budget deficits. In contrast, Medicare is primarily funded from general revenues, payroll taxes, and beneficiary premiums (41 percent, 37 percent, and 14 percent, respectively), though it is also funded in small part by transfers from states, taxation of Social Security benefits, and interest. There is no hard budget constraint on many of these components. Part A, Part B, and Part D are funded by different levels of each of these sources of funding. One way of better understanding the current state of Medicare funding is to look at the solvency projections of the Medicare Hospital Insurance trust fund, from which Part A benefits are paid. Part A funding largely comes from payroll taxes. Actuarial analysis of the state of the trust fund posits that the Part A trust fund will be depleted by 2026 (leaving Medicare to be able to cover only 91 percent of Part A costs from payroll tax revenue). While Part B and Part D spending comes from beneficiary premiums and general revenues, which are set annually based on spending, increased future spending will require higher general revenue funding and higher beneficiary premiums (Cubanski and Neuman 2018). These demands mean higher taxes and higher beneficiary premiums for the elderly, most of whom are entirely dependent on Social Security income.

Problems confronting Medicare

Medicare's peculiar financing structure, whereby spending can be perpetually deficit financed, creates a number of problems. The first is that Medicare does not rely on cost-effectiveness in its coverage decisions (Chandra, Jena, and Skinner 2011). This means that a number of dubious medical therapies are routinely covered, including therapies that may work for some patients in some settings but may be overused in others. For example, proton beam therapy is an expensive new technology that has demonstrated valuable benefits for pediatric cancers, but it is routinely used for other cancers where the value is far less clear yet where the technology is no less expensive. These policies also induce innovation in wasteful therapies (Weisbrod 1991). Relatedly, Medicare does not use narrow networks to restrict access to lower-quality providers, which reduces the economic penalty associated with being a lower-quality provider and decreases the incentives to improve. Given Medicare's size, these effects spill onto other payers, while continuing to increase the debt-to-GDP ratio (CBO 2019).

Second, Medicare operates on a chassis of fee-for-service (FFS) payments, which means that care can be fragmented (for some conditions, hospitals are paid prospectively but the physicians in these hospitals are still paid FFS) because payments are also not coordinated across different types of care—hospitals, physicians, and pharmaceutical companies are paid separately, even though there may be complex spillovers from their treatment decisions. Beneficiaries in traditional Medicare (so about two-thirds of beneficiaries) have wraparound supplemental coverage (Medigap, employer-sponsored retiree benefits, or Medicaid) and a separate Part D prescription drug plan. There is no reason to believe that fragmented insurers, each responsible for a portion of a beneficiary's health in a particular setting, will result in an optimal insurance design from a patient perspective or taxpayer perspective (Chandra, Gruber, and McKnight 2010).

Third, Medicare's FFS rates are also determined by an administrative process, not a market process. This process pays hospitals based on average cost, not marginal cost and is tied to average industry cost, not marginal costs for a specific provider (meaning that payments are likely too generous). Physicians are paid on the basis of the resource-based relative value scale (RBRVS) that ties payment to (average) economy-wide time effort and practice expenses, not outcomes or marginal cost.

Because these prices are set by Congress, there are large incentives for associations to lobby Congress for ad hoc supplements to their payments. For example, Cooper et al. (2019) document how a series of hospitals were able to use political leverage to increase their Medicare reimbursement as a result of their local representative voting in favor of the creation of Medicare Part D. Pushing in the other direction is that Medicare can always reduce payments if hospitals and physicians reduce their costs—reducing their incentive to reduce cost in the first place. Another example of payment regulation that would not arise from a market process is the constant desire to tie spending to a set function of growth in GDP. The now-defunct Sustainable Growth Rate (SGR), which was repealed by Congress in 2015, highlights this desire. No economic principle would generate this goal—for these principles would tie health care spending to the value of that spending, which depends on the opportunity cost of that spending. This tying is likely to vary across services and specialties, none of which were accounted for in the SGR (Alhassani, Chandra, and Chernew 2012).

Confronted with the challenge of not being able to use cost-effectiveness for its FFS patients, Medicare has experimented with a variety of lackluster "pay for performance" schemes, the most recent one being the accountable care organization (ACO) program, almost all of which have shown anemic results on outcomes and spending. There are three reasons for this: first, performance in the form of concrete health outcomes is hard to measure, so these programs have collapsed into "pay for process." Nor is it clear that Medicare is able to figure out market demand for performance (the "pay" in pay for performance), so the payment for performance improvement may be substantially less than what it actually takes to induce improvement. Many of these proposals are also focused on improving quality and not lowering costs, and they increase costs, as providers are doing more, not less (McWilliams 2016).

Finally, Medicare has low administrative costs, but this is not automatically an asset—fraud detection, quality measurement, and utilization review increase administrative costs; and Medicare does less of these activities, piggybacking on the efforts of private payers.

To be clear, many of these problems do not affect the MA program, which is free to exclude hospitals from its network and pay providers in novel and more integrated ways. We discuss the challenges to MA later in this article.

Other reform proposals

Confronted with these challenges, a number of reform proposals exist for Medicare. We do not review each of them here, but we note that many are focused on specific ideas, like raising the age of eligibility of Medicare. Fifteen proposals, ranging from premium support in Medicare, raising Medicare premiums, and increasing cost sharing, are thoughtfully discussed in a report by the American Association of Retired Persons (AARP; n.d.). MedPAC also provides an excellent, and up-do-date list of proposals to improve Medicare (MedPAC 2019).

These various proposals highlight three features of Medicare reform. First, many reform proposals seek to improve some arbitrary aspect of price regulation, which has undesirable consequences, with another regulation. For example, regulators have figured out that paying physicians 6 percent over the cost of high-priced drugs induces physicians to prescribe high-cost drugs. They respond by lowering this percentage, but the lower percentage is not based on market forces, or research about the optimal percentage, or understanding that some of these drugs have different levels of spillover effects on hospital spending and so should not be treated like other drugs. This results in a perpetual cycle of regulation, updates, and opportunities for lobbying and rent-seeking. Second, many proposals seek to improve the way Medicare pays off services under the rubric of "payment reform." But payment reforms in Medicare are often still tied to FFS payments. Third, these proposals do not grapple with two key features of Medicare reform: the ability of a monopsonistic buyer to pay subcompetitive prices that will affect the incentives to innovate and the spillovers from Medicare policy onto payers.

Guiding Principles for Medicare Reform

We have discussed a number of challenges facing Medicare—principally cost growth that results from its peculiar financing and payment models. We begin by discussing economic principles for Medicare policy reform. Enumerating these principles is key to understanding our policy proposals. Our principles are grounded in economics, and so reflect knowledge of incentives and trade-offs. Consequently, they are unlikely to deliver political expediency or achieve ad hoc budget targets. The guiding principles are as follows:

One: The goal of any reform to Medicare is not simply to reduce spending but to increase the societal benefits of the program (i.e., its holistic value to society). It is true that policy solutions that supplant the market in favor of administrative prices decrease budgetary costs. However, the economic efficiency costs of such a decision are far less clear and could decrease the value of the insurance product over the long term.

Two: FFS Medicare has no residual claimant ("the insurer") and therefore lacks strong incentives to discourage overuse, decrease fragmentation, or encourage true preventative health care. In such situations, where there is no residual claimant and we lack perfect contracts to motivate public employees, the privatization of government services can enhance social benefits (Shliefer 1998; Hart, Shliefer, and Vishny 1997). Fundamentally, Medicare savings to date have been achieved using regulated prices rather than efficient quantities. The implications of these regulated prices increase as the size of the Medicare program grows. Using market forces in place of administrative rate setting can correct for this disincentive; but in the realm of social insurance, it can create additional problems if quality cannot be easily monitored and contracted. Effectively, Medicare must look for areas where the benefits of the cost incentives of privatization outweigh the potential adverse consequences of lower quality. This may require operation of both public and private versions of the system for different types of patients.

Three: Defining the "correct" price for innovation in a political environment is difficult, and those suffering from lack of treatments often lack a seat at the proverbial table. Fundamentally, this is a question of the salience of the lack of treatment access. Individuals who cannot purchase an existing drug are clearly observable and identifiable, while those who lack access because a treatment does not exist are more theoretical. After all, we cannot identify exactly which treatments are not emerging because of inefficiently lower prices. This lack of salience means that if prices are subject to the political process, they would undervalue the benefits for individuals who represent smaller constituencies or future constituencies, relative to current constituencies. This is important because medical innovations, preventive and therapeutic, have profound implications for future patients but may not be as beneficial for those who are currently sick.

Four: Medicare is fundamentally engaged with the private market, and Medicare reforms can have very large impacts on the behavior of private firms. Engagement with the private market varies across proposals. FFS Medicare pays private hospitals and providers—this is an example of the most limited engagement. However, Medicare recipients also enroll in plans operated by private insurance firms, including both the prescription drug insurance plans of Medicare Part D and the managed care plans of MA. Spillovers from Medicare can increase or decrease the efficiency of the entire system. For example, the creation of the prospective payment system likely helped to control the growth of hospital spending compared to a counterfactual world where Medicare paid cost-plus to hospitals. In contrast, Medicare's willingness to provide coverage for any treatment regardless of its relative efficacy makes it hard for private insurers to implement stricter utilization management programs to address moral hazard concerns in insurance. These spillover effects magnify the impact of both positive and negative aspects of Medicare's reforms.

Five: Medicare is potentially the best platform for enacting reforms to the health care system, which can have far-reaching implications that affect multiple parties. For example, changes to an insurance product that give providers incentives to provide more efficient care will likely affect all patients and not simply the innovative insurer. Given these investments could be costly for the innovative insurer, there may be concern about the competitive implications of the spillovers benefits to competitors. This could decrease the rate of innovation. Medicare can solve the potential "common agency" problem that exists in U.S. health care, where no single payer in the system is willing to make investments that will change provider behavior in a way that could have spillover benefits for competitors (Frandsen, Powell, and Rebitzer 2019).

Six: As Medicare increases its use of private firms for the provision of insurance, it must focus on creating the structures for these firms to create, rather than simply capture, value. This requires that firms bear risk while ensuring that they do not face incentives to avoid providing services to particular individuals. This means that the economic principal of risk adjustment is central to Medicare reform. Even if Medicare creates a single risk pool and eliminates private insurers completely (which would eliminate plan incentives to select healthier patients), individual hospitals and physicians still need to be compensated more when they see sicker patients.

Seven: While Medicare would like to ensure that private firms do not capture an inappropriate amount of value, it is important that reforms balance this desire with creating the appropriate incentives for these firms to make value-creating investments in the first place. Firms must remain convinced that the returns from their fixed and sunk investments are not subject to renegotiation in future periods. For example, if firms must make investments to improve efficiency, they must believe that they will be able to reliably benefit from the value created by such investments. Consider the case of bundled payments, ACOs, or MA plans—all involve private firms making investments to reduce unnecessary spending. If firms believe that regulators will observe the reduced spending and subsequently decrease the payments to these private firms, they will underinvest in these value-creating activities in the first place. This is the economic concept of "hold-up," and it is critical as Medicare considers its ongoing interactions with private firms.

Similarly, creating bundled pricing for services creates strong incentives for innovation that reduces costs for a given level of quality across a variety of related services, and, arguably, those incentives have generally been lacking in health care. However, bundles have difficulty providing incentives to develop products and processes that increase quality and charge a commensurately higher price. Unless firms are confident bundles will be updated to include the new technology or process, bundled payment initiatives will discourage investments in value-creating goods and services. Therefore, bundles may be more appropriate in areas of health care where existing treatment options are quite good, and efficiency is more likely to be created by cost savings.

In addition, reforms must consider the alignment of incentives within and across firms. For example, certain types of hospital global budgets cap total hospital spending to reduce the incentives for wasteful practices like duplicative tests and unnecessary treatments. But such budgets also create scope for zero-sum competition within various units of a hospital by eliminating the incentives to attract more patients—for example, a superior cardiology department would attract more cardiology patients, but the budget for their operations will come from the budget of other departments, reducing the incentives for the cardiology department to improve. Aspirational statements about professionalism and diligence in medicine do not substitute for these economic realities.

Eight: As we consider the scope of activities undertaken by the Medicare program, it is important to keep focus on the goal of the program. Medicare is intended to be a social health insurance system and not an income support program. The "social insurance" of Medicare occurs when observably healthy enrollees subsidize observably sicker ones (i.e., both enrollees enter the risk pool when they are already healthy and sick). Such a feature is not likely to be accomplished by private insurance markets alone, where products are intended to pool together people with similar health risk or to adjust premiums to account for differential risk. The goals of social insurance are to increase access to health care services, smooth consumption from negative health care shocks, and redistribute resources from the healthy to the sick.[4]

That is not to say that Medicare cannot serve as a means of income support or offer programs like housing or long-term care. However, this must be a conscious decision because the implications of income support programs are quite different from those of health insurance—and muddling that definition can lead to an inefficient expenditure of resources. Moreover, to the extent that insurance requires a residual claimant, and competition between insurers is desirable, the more services that are covered by insurance, the more difficult it becomes to measure plan outcomes or induce plan switching by enrollees.

Opportunities to Improve Medicare

While Medicare recipients have broad access to medical providers, the financial protection provided is more limited than many people likely understand. For example, a 2012 Kaiser Family Foundation study found that the actuarial value of Medicare is less than the average plan offered by large employers.[5] This lower actuarial value should not be surprising. Table 1 shows the various cost-sharing provisions for Medicare Part D, within FFS Medicare.

Concerns about this lack of financial protection can be seen by the emergence of both the Medigap and the MA program—both of which fill in some of the gaps in the traditional FFS program. Under the Medigap program, patients pick between a variety of standardized plans offered by private firms. These supplemental Medigap policies have a benefit design structure that does not take into account spillover effects on the rest of the Medicare program. For example, small increases in copayments for diabetes drugs would reduce their use, saving Medigap plans money, but some beneficiaries are hospitalized as a result, increasing Medicare spending elsewhere (Chandra, Gruber, and McKnight 2010). Conversely, to the extent that the cost sharing for Medicare is efficient, supplemental insurance plans can further increase Medicare spending. Cabral and Mahoney (2019) find that Medigap increase an enrollees Medicare spending by more than 22 percent.

Depending on the generosity of coverage, Medigap enrollees could construct a combination of plans that provide an actuarial value that exceeds the average private market plan. Of course, constructing plans in this way hinders perhaps the only utilization management tool for FFS Medicare. As a result, spending for enrollees in Medigap exceeds that of otherwise similar Medicare enrollees.

Another attempt to improve Medicare coverage is MA. Under MA, plans are administered by private firms that are reimbursed based on a benchmark. If firms submit a bid below the benchmark, they can receive a rebate that they must spend on additional medical services for their enrollees. This often involves services such

TABLE 1
Medicare Part D Standard Benefit Design (2019)

Benefit Phase	Limit	Payer Responsible (percent responsible)
Deductible	Below $415	Enrollee (100%)
Initial coverage period	Below $3,820 and above $415	Enrollee (25%) Plans (75%)
Coverage gap	Below $8,140 and above $3,820	Brand-name drugs: • Manufacturer discount (70%) • Enrollee (25%) • Plans (5%) Generic drugs: • Enrollee (37%) • Plans (63%)
Catastrophic coverage	Above $8,140	Enrollee (5%) Plans (15%) Medicare (80%)

SOURCE: An overview of the Medicare Part D prescription drug benefit. See https://www.kff .org/medicare/fact-sheet/an-overview-of-the-medicare-part-d-prescription-drug-benefit.

as paying enrollees' premiums for Medicare Part B, Part D, or providing additional coverage for services excluded from the traditional Medicare benefit, such as vision. These additional services are attractive to enrollees and, therefore, plans, which can successfully bid below the benchmark (i.e., those that can maintain a sufficiently low-cost structure) should expect to gain market share. That said, like any privatization system, there are concerns that the cost incentives for the private firms may be too large, resulting in adverse consequences for enrollees. MA attempts to address this through multiple channels. First, there is competition among the privatized firms, which should provide incentives for increased quality to retain enrollees. In addition, the amount of the rebate that firms receive is based on their quality star rating; that is, firms that receive a higher star rating receive a large share of the difference between their bid and the benchmark.

The policy goal of MA is for private firms to respond to competitive pressures to manage the care of Medicare enrollees. After all, firms are the residual claimant on the amount of their bid that is not consumed by enrollee health spending. However, at the time of its creation, policy-makers were cognizant of the fact that this payment structure would dissuade firms from enrolling individuals with conditions that require large amounts of medical spending. At the extreme, policy-makers were worried that firms would design plans to be so sufficiently unattractive to sick individuals that these enrollees would not sign up for coverage in the first place. Therefore, policy-makers created a system of risk adjustment where MA firms receive greater payments from Medicare for individuals with documented medical conditions. Ideally, under such a system, firms are rewarded for managing the spending of sick individuals and not avoiding them entirely. In practice, there are concerns that firms may be able to game the system by augmenting the codes of individuals to make them appear sicker than they would appear in the FFS data.[6]

MA plans broadly increase the financial protection of Medicare while providing incentives for firms to innovate on plan design. Various features of MA result in these plans effectively adopting the administrative price schedule for Medicare.[7] Multiple studies find that the provider prices paid by MA insurers are quite close to the Medicare price schedule (Curto et al. 2019; Baker et al. 2016). This is quite different from the commercial market, where prices for insurers are meaningfully higher than Medicare (White and Whaley 2019). Given an inability to secure prices below the Medicare schedule, the only means of increasing profits is to find ways to manage the quantity of care—an incentive that is largely absent from FFS Medicare but one that MA plans do extremely well.

A Package of Market-Based Reforms

We propose a series of reforms to Medicare to increase competition and the insurance value of the program. These proposals will increase the economic efficiency of the existing program. In addition, if Medicare serves as the vehicle for either a large expansion of social insurance or, at the extreme, universal health coverage, these reforms will create a program that is more amenable to having a larger (or even dominant) presence in the health care market.

At a high level, these market-based reforms are an attempt to translate our guiding principles into a series of tractable policies that would increase the economic efficiency of the Medicare program. Certainly, for any of these reforms, there are a number of legal and regulatory issues that would need to be addressed before a final policy could be implemented—a task that is beyond the skill set of economists but one that is readily taken on by administrative lawyers. Our goal is primarily to highlight the economic rationales for these various concepts to serve as a starting point for policy development and to emphasize that the Medicare Advantage program could serve as a vehicle for reform efforts.

One: Introduce pricing pressure on Part B (or physician-administered) drugs

Currently, physician-administered drugs under Part B are reimbursed based on a "buy-and-bill" system. Physicians purchase the drugs and, once they are administered, the physicians are paid the average sales price (ASP) of the drug plus a percentage markup (i.e., ASP + 4.3 percent). There are multiple channels through which this system provides incentives for higher spending on drugs. First, physicians have an incentive to prescribe more expensive drugs.

Second, profit-maximizing pharmaceutical manufacturers have the incentive to charge inefficiently high prices in the private market (i.e., profits that are above the profit-maximizing level) because the lost commercial sales can be made up for by higher payments from the public payer. Third, public spending is higher because they are a multiple of the inefficiently high private prices. As a result, the buy-and-bill system results in higher spending for both the public and the private market.

There is widespread agreement among economists that the buy-and-bill system is an inefficient method of procuring these physician-administered products. However, the best replacement program is unclear. Moving to a simple flat fee for administering the drugs would eliminate the incentives for manufacturers to raise prices and for physicians to prescribe higher priced drugs. However, because physicians take ownership of the product (i.e., they must actually purchase the drug), their inventory and capital costs increase as a function of the drug's price. Therefore, simply moving to a flat fee would create a disincentive for physicians to provide more expensive but clinically appropriate drugs. In addition, a flat fee system does not (without other changes to the system) create negotiating pressure on manufacturers.

A second proposal is to move all prescription drugs to the Part D program regardless of where they are administered. This would allow pharmacy benefit managers (PBMs) to negotiate lower prices. However, the cost-sharing provisions of Part D mean that this would expose patients to potentially meaningfully higher costs (the equilibrium impacts for patients could be lower if all our proposed policies are implemented as a package).

Perhaps the best solution for injecting more competition into the pricing of Part B drugs would be to establish a series of vendors that maintain a financial title to the drug and manage the inventory of physician offices. This would be like the goal of the Competitive Acquisition Program (CAP), which was created with the intent of establishing a series of vendors for Part B drugs. Unfortunately, CAP never attracted enough vendors to establish a competitive market, which is a concern for any attempt to reform the Part B market. There are several potential reasons why the CAP program failed to gain traction, and it is important to learn from these concerns as we reform payment for Part B drugs. At a minimum, any vendor program must provide firms with the tools and ability to use utilization management to secure discounts. This must include the ability to exclude products when manufacturers are unwilling to give sufficiently large discounts.

In addition to the direct benefits to Medicare, given the role of Medicare in many of these drug markets, the purchasing decisions of the public payer increases private prices. This is both a direct impact of the fact that manufacturers may find higher private prices optimal to increase public payments and of indirect spillovers, as many private firms pay prices that are effectively just a function of the Medicare price (Duggan and Morton 2006). Thus, to the extent that the Medicare price is too high, these private prices are also inefficient.

Two: Fix incentives for high-priced drugs in Part D

When the Part D program was created, the underlying concept was to use the expertise and incentives of the private market to secure discounts on pharmaceutical products.

However, to entice a sufficiently large number of competitors to this newly emerging market, the program provided a reinsurance program that shielded firms from the costs of very expensive drugs. Specifically, once a patient's annual drug spending exceeds a preset limit ($8,140 in 2019), the government is responsible for 80 percent of additional spending. While this generous reinsurance did attract several firms to the market, it also markedly decreased the incentives for these firms to strongly negotiate with manufacturers for drugs whose annual spending falls into the catastrophic range.

In addition, the existence of catastrophic coverage increases the incentives for Part D firms to prefer drugs that have high list prices because patient cost sharing is tied to list prices. As list prices increase, patient cost sharing increases, which increases total drug spending and the likelihood of a patient reaching the level of catastrophic coverage (where patient cost sharing decreases). These incentives have little to do with improved health care or lowering costs and should be reformed.

The combination of these incentives has made the reinsurance payments under Part D one of the largest budget components of the plan. For example, Figure 1 from MedPAC shows that expected payments from reinsurance are now the largest component of a plans' expected bids (MedPAC 2018).

To restore the appropriate incentives to Part D, we propose that a greater share of the responsibility for exceptionally high-cost patients be shouldered by the private firms that are responsible for negotiating prices. These proposals will raise premiums because of lowered cost sharing but will also increase competition between Part D plans, primarily by increasing the incentives to negotiate lower prices for drugs that are currently over the catastrophic threshold.

Three: Eliminate coinsurance for prescription drugs—replace with flat copayments

Enrollees in Medicare Part D are exposed to high levels of cost sharing on the execution of their purchases. This includes both high deductibles and coinsurance (i.e., patients paying a percentage of the price of the medication). This cost sharing is intended to accomplish two goals: decreasing the use of low-value drugs and moving patients toward products that offer a large price discount. However, after patients are exposed to a certain level of cost sharing, the payments are unlikely to affect their choice of products. Therefore, if patients are exposed to high cost-sharing payments without another option in the therapeutic class, these payments unwind the benefits of the insurance product.

Therefore, we propose that the only acceptable form of cost sharing for prescription drugs under the Part D program is flat copayments. Given that firms use high cost sharing to move patients across products, an alternative rule would

FIGURE 1
National Average Plan Bid for Basic Part D Benefits

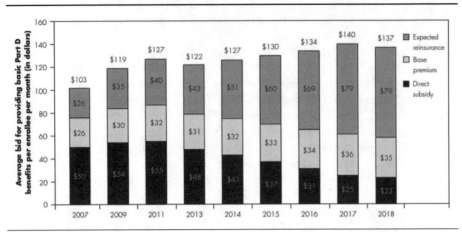

SOURCE: MedPAC based on data from the Centers for Medicare and Medicaid Services (CMS), available at http://www.medpac.gov/docs/default-source/reports/mar18_medpac_ch14_sec.pdf.
NOTE: The averages shown are weighted by the previous year's plan enrollment. Amounts do not net out subsequent reconciliation amounts with CMS. Components may not sum to stored totals due to rounding.

be that firms must provide at least one product in each therapeutic class that has a flat copayment.

An added benefit of this policy change is that it would blunt the distortions created by rebates in the market. Under the current system, rebates are confidential discounts negotiated between manufacturers and PBMs. Economic research shows that confidentiality results in larger discounts. As a result, PBMs require that coinsurance (i.e., percentage-based cost sharing) be based on the list price of the drug. Therefore, patients who pay coinsurance increasingly do not benefit from negotiations in this sector. However, in a world of copayments, this is no longer a problem.

Four: Limit protected classes in Part D

When Medicare Part D was created, there was a concern that firms would create incomplete formularies (i.e., lists of drugs that the insurance plan covers) that did not provide sufficient therapeutic options for patients. As a result, Congress created several restrictions on what must be included in the formulary. These six protected classes include drugs that are anticonvulsants, antidepressants, antineoplastics, antipsychotics, antiretrovirals, and immunosuppressants. The antineoplastics category includes many oral chemotherapy drugs. Within these classes, Part D plans have to cover "all or substantially all drugs" within each of the classes, but these restrictions also mean that plans cannot build closed formularies to secure discounts. According to the Centers for Medicare and Medicaid Services (CMS), "typical private market discounts for these drugs are in the 20 to 30 percent range, but the average discount across all protected classes in Part D is just 6 percent" (Azar and Verma 2019). At their core, these classes reflect a preference by society to provide complete access to all products in these categories. However, the trade-off for this access is very high prices in these categories. In addition, these high prices can distort manufacturers' investment decisions away from more competitive categories if capital markets are constrained in some manner, even if those competitive markets need additional treatment options.

CMS has recently proposed a rule allowing plans to exclude protected class drugs with price increases that are greater than inflation from their formularies, as well as certain new drug formulations that are not a significant innovation over the original product. Plans would also be allowed to use prior authorization and step therapy (approving coverage for a more expensive treatment after a cheaper one has failed) for protected class drugs.

We propose that we either eliminate or greatly reduce the restrictions within these protected classes, along the lines that CMS has suggested. If eliminated, these categories would revert to the existing formulary restrictions for other classes. Moreover, the central concern that plans would withhold valuable drugs would be addressed by competition and marketing: at the time of this writing, there are 901 stand-alone Part D plans, and it is difficult to imagine that skimping on valuable drugs would persist in an environment where there is high plan competition and where prescription drug manufacturers can advertise their products. These concerns are probably more likely to be true for therapeutics that target extremely small or rare diseases that are not part of the protected classes to begin with.

Five: Reference pricing for drugs

Reference pricing for drugs is an alternative to using deductibles and copayments and can be deployed well when there are drug classes with therapeutic alternatives that are generally equivalent. The idea is for the plan to label a set of therapies as the reference therapy for a condition or a patient. These would have no cost sharing, but patients who want something other than the reference treatment will pay more for such treatments. The extra payment need not be the full additional cost of the new drug but could be a copayment or coinsurance amount.

The key challenge is determining the reference product: if drugs in a class are genuinely equivalent, then the reference product should be the cheapest product (for example, a generic should clearly be the reference product in a class that includes a brand-name product and its generic competitor). When there is heterogeneity within a class in the form of multiple branded drugs, the reference product could be the most cost-effective one—which creates strong incentives for manufacturers to lower their prices and obtain this designation, as it will beget a large volume of patients. A novel drug that is substantially better than older alternatives could still qualify as the reference product if its outcomes are substantially superior even in comparison to its higher price. One area for improvement is to rethink the use of "drug classes" as the grouping for reference pricing (these classes are mostly a statement about a drugs mechanism of action) and redefining the grouping as a medical condition (so drugs for congestive heart failure and drugs for heart attacks would be different classes, even though the classes may have overlapping drugs).

In situations where a medical condition can be treated by a generic drug and a branded drug with a different composition, it may be tempting to make the generic drug the reference product because of its substantially lower price. This would not be right if incremental improvements cost proportionately more (e.g., a 10 percent improvement means that prices are higher than 10 percent). In these settings, to ensure that there is a viable market for better drugs, one may want to use the pregeneric entry price for the now generic drug to determine its cost-effectiveness. Such a price more closely reflects willingness to pay for the product.

In principle, the reference product could be defined differently for different patients—a patient with a particular mutation may have a reference product that works on that mutation; patients without this mutation may have another reference product. In this manner, there is no tension between reference pricing and indication-based pricing, where the same drug is sold at different prices based on the drug's efficacy in different conditions (Chandra and Garthwaite 2017). As such, reference pricing does not by itself lower drug spending but provides stronger incentives to demonstrate effectiveness and tie patient cost sharing to the likelihood of moral hazard. We note that reference pricing is not applicable for drugs in classes where there is no competition (e.g., orphan drugs).

Reference pricing for health care is not a new idea. It has been successfully implemented in Germany, a nation in which the government does not determine prices or make coverage decisions (Robinson, Penteli, and Ex 2019). It has also been extensively discussed in policy reports for the United States and developed for the specific context of Medicare (Bagley, Chandra, and Frakt 2015; Pearson and Bach 2010). More recently, an employer alliance implemented a version of reference pricing where enrollees paid the full marginal cost of nonreference drugs (as opposed to a copayment or coinsurance to access these drugs). The program led to a 13.9 percent reduction in price per prescription (Robinson, Whaley, and Brown 2017). This number is a lower bound—to the extent that if all Medicare Part D plans moved to this model, there would be larger equilibrium responses.

Six: Reforms to risk adjustment and reimbursement in MA

As discussed above, a primary goal of the MA program is to provide incentives for firms to develop programs that control the use of medical services by their enrollees while disincentivizing firms to skimp on valuable care for patients. MA plans have an advantage over traditional FFS Medicare in doing this for two reasons. First, they are owned by companies that are residual claimants, as opposed to the federal government, which has no immediate incentive to manage costs given its ability to debt-finance spending (the threat of long-term tax increases or debtors demanding higher yields is not a proven recipe for cost containment). Second, because MA plans are responsible for all health care spending (as opposed to just pharmaceutical or just medical spending), they face strong incentives to coordinate benefits—for example, by spending more on drugs or physician care now, MA plans reduce a costly hospitalization later.

Successfully operating the MA program requires determining the appropriate compensation for plan sponsors. The appropriate payment provides firms with sufficient returns for investing in efforts to reduce costs without overcompensating them or creating inefficient distortions. In addition, given the goal of MA is for firms to manage the care of enrollees, the system must provide the appropriate incentives for firms to accept and manage risk. At some level, this involves providing larger payments to firms that accept patients who are expected to have higher spending. This is currently done through a risk adjusted benchmark that is intended to reflect FFS spending in that county. However, this system faces two primary challenges: (1) accurately determining the appropriate benchmark for payments and (2) the dynamic incentives created by risk adjustment. We consider each in turn.

Under an MA plan, if a plan's bid to provide services in a county is above the FFS benchmark, it receives a rate from the government that is equal to the benchmark, and enrollees pay a premium that equals the difference. If a plan bid falls below the FFS benchmark, the plan receives a base rate equal to its bid. Therefore, the benchmark is a key determinant in the number of participants in the market and the generosity of benefits that enrollees receive. The key here is that the benchmark is calculated using all FFS enrollees in a county, even those who only enroll in either Medicare Part A or Part B. This is puzzling given that MA plans are required to cover both Part A and Part B services. MedPAC estimates that enrollees who enroll in only Part A have lower spending on average; thus, including them in the benchmark determination likely means that, in general, MA benchmarks are too stingy (MedPAC 2017). This is particularly a problem in counties where a relatively large fraction of FFS enrollees chooses to enroll only in Part A. Given that the MA plan must cover both Part A and Part B services, it attracts part of the population with a preference for both services. Therefore, as MA penetration in a county grows, the share of the population with only Part A *or* Part B increases, and their distortion to determining the benchmark grows.

Medicare acknowledges this concern—for example, the benchmark in Puerto Rico (where half the population does not sign up for both Parts A and B) is determined only using FFS enrollees who are in both plans. Hawaii is currently petitioning for similar treatment. That said, MedPAC identifies that there are a large number of counties with high MA penetration where the resulting FFS benchmark involves a large fraction of enrollees who are only in Part A. At the very least, all MA benchmarks should be set using only FFS patients who are enrolled in both Parts A and B of Medicare FFS. Some may argue that MA firms currently are overpaid or capture too much value from the existing benchmark; we believe that this problem (to the extent it exists) should be dealt with directly. It is hard to imagine that deliberately mismeasuring the benchmark to decrease payments to MA plans based on how much of their FFS population elects Part B coverage increases efficiency.

This brings us to the second concern with MA: that firms will be able to cream-skim the risk pool such that enrollee expenditures are lower than payments from the government without any effort required of the firm. In addition to concerns about overpaying firms, such cream-skimming may make it difficult for individuals with potentially high spending to secure coverage through MA. We know that MA enrollees are healthier than FFS enrollees, as MA enrollees have about a third fewer chronic conditions than those who enrolled in FFS (Geruso and Layton 2019).

Currently, these goals are accomplished through a system of risk adjustment. MA firms gather information on the acuity of patients based on their various diagnoses. Payments to MA plans are then adjusted by these risk codes based on the use of medical services by individuals in the FFS system with similar risk codes. Unsurprisingly, when profit-maximizing firms are provided strong incentives to document the sickness of individuals, they expend resources to do so. These expenditures can be quite significant, and it is unclear whether they create economic value or are simply inefficient expenditures by firms attempting to capture value.

A further concern is that an individual with a particular risk code gathered based on the incentives of MA may not result in the same expected costs as a patient with a similar risk code that emerged as part of the FFS system. This would result in overpaying MA plans. The potential for this problem is recognized in the current system by the existence of a "coding intensity factor"—a blunt tool whereby payments to MA plans are reduced across the board.

Rather than attempting to reduce the impact of more intensive coding (an activity that represents economic waste in the system), another option would be to base coding on immutable characteristics such as race, gender, and geographic location. However, to the degree that spending is not based on specific illnesses, firms would avoid sick individuals conditional on the immutable characteristics that are used.

Fundamentally, there is no perfect answer to the question of risk adjustment, which ultimately represents a tension of balancing the incentive for gaming with the opportunity for cream-skimming. Ideally, we would want to settle on a metric for risk adjustment that is not gameable but that rewards firms for attracting and managing a sick patient population. We know from economics literature that MA plans engage in particular forms of coding: they are more likely to code at the intensive margin than at the extensive margin, as evidenced by a greater number of patients who are coded with the least severe form of a disease.

To circumvent these incentives, we might consider a risk-adjustment system based on plan-wide characteristics such as Consumer Assessment of Healthcare Providers and Systems (CAHPS) survey scores or other measures that assess the sickness of the population, such as the incidence of conditions (e.g., metastatic cancer, pulmonary embolisms, and heart attacks) for which it is harder to code diagnosis at the intensive. In principle, with the increase in genome sequencing and the growing literature on the high predictiveness of risk scores for many illnesses, a polygenic risk score could be used for risk adjustment. Our interest in using CAHPS scores, which are patient surveys rating health care experiences, is that CAHPS scores are obtained from patients and not from physicians. The challenge with using them in their current form is that they measure patient experiences, which are an ex-post measure of outcomes. However, they could be modified to include a section on self-reported outcomes, such as the SF-36 survey, which captures information on vitality, physical functioning, bodily pain, mental health, and social functioning. The SF-36 has a median completion time of 8 minutes, with 85 percent of respondents completing it in under 10 minutes.

The key point for patient measures is that we do not need these data for all members to operate plan-level risk adjustment. Data from a random panel of a plan's patients would be enough to fully perform this adjustment. For adequate risk adjustment, however, we should be cognizant that medical spending depends on much more than illness. It also depends on patients' preferences, including their preferences for expensive care and the propensity to engage in moral hazard. These are notoriously hard to measure in claims data, but it is possible that more of these features can be observed in patient surveys.

The two problems with determining optimal MA compensation demonstrate the difficulty of determining efficient administrative prices in health care. Even something as simple as determining the appropriate measure of FFS services is complicated, and implementing simple fixes to the benchmark involves a cumbersome legislative and regulatory process. Note that in 2017, all seventeen MedPAC commissions voted in favor of adjusting the FFS benchmark, and the change has still not been implemented. In addition, the problem of risk adjustment illustrates the dynamic effects of incentives created by regulatory systems. We note that as MA evolves, there will be additional dynamic concerns that grow from basing payments in MA on the administratively determined FFS rates. If those rates are set too low, firms' dynamic incentives to invest in quality and innovation will be hampered.

Seven: Premium support in Medicare

MA has been an extremely popular program for which enrollment has exceeded most expectations. Enrollment in MA has rapidly increased, with more than 20 million Medicare beneficiaries enrolled in the program in 2019. High levels of enrollment generate benefits to enrollees in the form of improved plan design and coordination and to the federal government in the form of large reductions in the quantity of services (but not price reductions for a given service). In a pure FFS system, neither of these benefits is possible, as a lack of competition also means a lack of incentives to improves one's offerings.

These features of MA also allow for cost control on a different dimension, by allowing the federal government to subsidize the premium for one health insurance plan (which could be traditional Medicare or an MA plan) and letting enrollees pick another plan by supplementing this "premium support" with their own dollars. In principle, the premium support for a plan could be tied to an enrollee's income (or Social Security income), which would be a way to reduce the generosity of the Medicare program for higher-income individuals. The exchanges constructed by the ACA have this design feature, and premiums offer a way to consolidate the "dual-eligibles" (those covered by both Medicare and Medicaid) into one program.

There are three concerns with premium support. The first is how to determine which plan to subsidize. The subsidy could be tied to the lowest plan bid or the average plan bid. The CBO has noted that if the payments to plans were tied to the average plan bid, then beneficiaries' total out-of-pocket costs (including premiums) would decrease while federal payments would increase. If the payments were tied to the second-lowest plan bid, then beneficiaries' total out-of-pocket costs would increase while federal payments would decrease. This reveals the central trade-off between subsidy generosity and benefits to the private purse versus the public purse. This trade-off is unlikely to be solved with economics alone, although it should be noted that economic theory would argue that the political process has a bias toward today's enrollees because of their ability to vote, suggesting that the subsidy levels will be more generous than what a social planner, balancing the needs of today's beneficiaries against tomorrow's taxpayers, would choose.

The second issue for premium support is what to require plans to cover and how. Allowing plans to cover whatever they want could induce innovation in skinny plans that offer low benefits and low premiums, competing for beneficiaries with this model. The same is true for discretion over patient cost sharing— plans could, in principle, compete for enrollees with low premiums and high patient cost sharing. At a minimum, it seems reasonable to require plans to be actuarially equivalent but to allow them latitude in how they determine cost sharing, formularies, and network generosity. This approach would provide high-powered incentives to MA plans to find ways to cut waste and compete on services that enrollees want.

The third concern is how to grow the subsidy over time. If the growth is tied to GDP growth, then a growing number of beneficiaries will not be able to afford health care, because the growth rate of health care exceeds that of GDP growth. Ultimately, the right subsidy depends on the value of the insurance that is being provided, which in turn depends on the quality of underlying health care and its improvement. But these are hard to measure and know in advance. As such, tying the growth rate to something similar to GDP growth+1 may provide an attractive compromise between fiscal prudence and economic sense.

The fourth concern with premium support is the role of Medicare FFS. In theory, Medicare FFS is not needed for premium support to flourish, but it may be necessary in some rural areas where MA plans do not want to compete. Alternatively, one could increase the payment to MA plans in those areas (it does not seem essential to create an entire FFS service). Medicare FFS could also create competition, as its presence increases the incentives for MA plans to compete. This is possible, but it has fairly dubious logic, as it is hard for private firms to compete with an entity that cannot go out of business. The Medicare FFS program does not have a residual claimant, making it harder for MA plans to compete. Therefore, if one of the policy goals is to grow MA, then the appropriate response is not to have a "public option" where Medicare FFS competes (unfairly) with MA. But this approach raises the question about how to devise a payment for MA plans. Here, our intuition is to rely on the architecture of the exchanges in the ACA, where there is no public option. With enough competition, MA plans will bid at cost, and no FFS benchmark will be necessary.

There is empirical support for our conjecture. Duggan, Starc, and Vabson (2016) find that more generous MA reimbursement increases the number of firms offering MA and also an increase in the number of Medicare recipients in these plans.

Eight: Payment reforms to increase incentives for managing costs

The capitated payment structure of MA does an effective job of providing firms with the appropriate incentives to consider the externalities of spending across various categories. This can be seen in the coverage of prescription drugs, where MA programs offer more generous coverage for medications that offset future medical spending.

The existing FFS program, however, has few such natural incentives built into the program. For example, Medicare Part D plans have no exposure to future health expenditures, resulting in little coordination of benefit design across the programs.

In addition, under the existing FFS system, medical providers have little incentive under the traditional program to control costs. Medicare operates under a prospective payment system based on diagnosis related groups (DRGs) where, broadly speaking, hospitals are compensated based on the condition they treat. Therefore, firms want to minimize the costs of treating a specific DRG, but they have little incentive to reduce the number of DRGs in the population. At the extreme, this lack of incentive is exemplified by the fact that many hospitals find it profitable when patients are readmitted, that is, the hospital is paid both for the initial visit and for the readmission.

Recognizing this concern about cost containment in FFS Medicare, CMS has created several ACOs, which attempt to provide incentives for providers to reduce the spending of enrollees, provided they meet certain quality criteria. Our reading of ACOs' performance is that they have resulted in small cost savings, and perhaps not nearly enough to justify payment reform as a general approach that should be directly pursued by the government. Rather, our view is that MA plans are free to create whatever payment reform they need to manage costs— including creating ACOs.

One commonly stated (incorrect) reason that the performance of ACOs has been relatively jaundiced is that the program is new; however, the program has been in existence since 2012, resulting in seven years of data for analysis. A second reason is that through the end of 2015, 99.2 percent of ACOs were in so-called one-sided contracts that rewarded ACOs with bonuses if spending was sufficiently below benchmarks but did not impose a risk of financial losses for spending above benchmarks. This is not a sufficient explanation for the general lack of savings. A third reason may be that ACO savings depend on Medicare

FFS rates, and as these rates are cut (as they have been), it becomes harder for an ACO to save money. This challenge represents the general "hold-up" problem that we mentioned in our design principles. It highlights that the key to allowing private firms to lower costs (assuming ACOs are like private firms) is not to remove the incentives for cost reduction.

One new result from the recent performance of ACOs is intriguing: a recent report finds that ACOs' savings may be partly explained by the strength of incentives facing different ACOs. ACOs that are large health systems containing a hospital, offering many specialties and services, will find it harder to lower spending than smaller organizations that offer a narrower suite of services. There are two reasons for this: the first is that the larger the team (organization), the lower the incentives for any given physician in that organization to reduce costs. The second is that the larger the organization, the more likely it is to serve FFS patients who are not in the ACO program. Reducing waste and unnecessary procedures for these patients would lower total revenues for the ACO, muting the incentives to reduce waste in ACO patients. In contrast, physician groups that formed smaller ACOs face stronger incentives to save. Moreover, they do not lose revenue when they reduce unnecessary procedures for a patient, regardless of whether that patient is covered by an ACO contract.

The evidence for this theory is striking. Hospital-integrated ACOs have not saved any money once one accounts for their bonus payments. In contrast, physician-group ACOs have saved somewhere between 1.5 and 3.6 percent relative to FFS (McWilliams et al. 2018). The first-order point is that the savings are meager relative to the size of the fiscal challenge. But the heterogeneity in performance suggests that smaller ACOs, unaffiliated with hospitals, may hold the most promise.

These results on ACO performance are consistent with our emphasis on using MA as the vehicle for lowering Medicare costs. MA plans have reduced use far more than ACOs do, despite being much larger than ACO plans. They have also saved money by doing exactly the sorts of things that ACOs were supposed to do, like shifting patients into less expensive settings, such as primary over specialist care, and outpatient care over inpatient care; and by employing various types of use management to discourage the use of grey-area services. Therefore, the key to savings may not be an organization's size as much as the incentives to save. Economists have found that after adjusting for enrollee mix, spending per enrollee in MA is 9 to 30 percent lower than in FFS Medicare (Curto et al. 2019), and there is evidence that MA plans achieve these savings by substituting less expensive care and engaging in use management (Curto et al. 2019). Even at the lower-bound 9 percent number, the savings are about three times larger than the most successful ACOs.

Conclusion: An Economic Analysis of Medicare for All Proposals

To illustrate the use of economic principles to evaluate Medicare reform proposals, we analyze the underlying principle of Medicare for All proposals that were being proposed at the time of this writing (Kliff 2018).[8] We avoid discussing specific proposals, mostly because they are incomplete, but emphasize the broader principles and trade-offs that all reform proposals should grapple with but often ignore. Regardless of their exact slogans and specifics, these policies have two goals: to achieve universal health insurance coverage and to decrease the growth rate of this spending (some proposals claim to reduce the level of health care spending, but we view them as unserious because they privilege political expediency over the hard work of grappling with the underlying trade-offs).

With respect to the first goal, either allowing individuals to buy into Medicare or establishing Medicare as the single-payer insurance system for the United States would likely close the coverage gap and establish universal coverage for the country's population. The reduction in uninsurance would be accompanied by an increase in spending for at least four reasons—and would immediately conflict with the second goal of reducing spending growth. Spending would increase because people would receive access to valuable medical care (which costs money) and would be insured (making them substantially less price sensitive); providers would also be incentivized to do more (because their patients are insured); and over the long term, the increase in insurance will induce new medical innovations (because there is greater willingness to pay for innovation) (Chandra and Skinner 2012).

In terms of reducing spending growth, there are a variety of channels by which the proposed policies could potentially accomplish this goal. For example, collapsing the existing market of multiple insurers (Medicaid, Medicare, many employers, the VA, and military systems) into a single entity would likely decrease administrative costs from redundant and conflicting billing practices. In addition, a single firm would not need to market products that would decrease these expenditures. The exact magnitude of the reduced economic cost of lower administrative spending is less clear, but it has been estimated to be substantial (almost 40 percent) in the context of U.S.-Canada comparisons (Cutler and Ly 2011). While administrative costs like prior authorization are viewed as waste in most media reports, private insurers rely on these methods to reduce use of dubious technologies that reduce premiums growth. To the extent that their marketing costs better match consumers to efficient plan designs, there could be negative effects from the reduced spending. Put differently, reducing the reliance on private insurance does not automatically reduce health care spending or its growth; and even when it does, it does not automatically imply that the enrollees' well-being has improved, for some would have preferred more generous plans.

The greatest source of savings from a single-payer system would be the adoption of Medicare's regulated price schedule, which currently reimburses providers (doctors and hospitals) at rates far lower than the commercial market. Commercial insurers are generally viewed as being unable to achieve Medicare's prices because they lack Medicare's market power with providers. However, the economic benefits of a greater use of monopsony (single purchaser) power are unclear because of the countervailing effects of lower payments on the incentives to pursue certain types of medical innovation. As we note, price setting by a monopsonist introduces scope for the related ability to engage in the classic "hold-up" problem, in which a new innovation introduced by a private firm is paid a subcompetitive price by the monopsonist, which discourages the innovation in the first place. Both forces mean that lower prices achieved through regulation should not be judged solely by the reduced budgetary costs in the short term, but also by their effect on subsequent innovation.

Proposing Medicare as the correct vehicle for accomplishing the twin goals of growing coverage and lowering spending rests on the implicit belief that the existing social insurance program for the elderly is the most cost-effective means of providing health insurance coverage in the United States. However, there are many concerns about the existing system that challenge this belief. These concerns are perhaps more important when considering Medicare for All because some of the negative consequences of existing features of Medicare will be magnified as the program increases in size and scope.

At a minimum, there are many ways in which the existing Medicare program provides incomplete insurance coverage compared to many private products. FFS Medicare for those who lack supplemental coverage provides exceptionally incomplete financial coverage. For example, enrollees lack meaningful insurance for outpatient coverage and have no limits on the financial costs they can incur. About 20 percent of Medicare beneficiaries in FFS Medicare lack supplemental coverage, and, despite reducing use, this is not a feature that ought to be extended to others (Cubanski et al. 2018).

In addition, FFS Medicare places few limits on the coverage of medical services or the use of step-therapy and prior authorization to reduce access. All services are covered, and there is far less use management than is typically seen in commercial insurance products (as noted above, Medicare relies on a blunt set of cost-sharing measures to reduce use). Furthermore, lacking pressure from a competitive market, there is little incentive for the FFS Medicare program to develop innovative methods of controlling the use of medical services. Medicare has experimented with a variety of pay-for-performance programs, with lackluster results (Frakt and Jha 2018).

Medicare's primary tool for reducing spending growth is lower regulated prices (as opposed to cost-effectiveness analysis)—these prices could have insidious effects when there is no private market and the program exerts monopsony pricing. The reliance on lower prices rather than the more efficient consumption of medical services is not an accident and represents the benefits of a greater use of monopsony power in the procurement of health care services. Fundamentally, the relative costs and benefits of the use of this market power are partly a function of the size of the Medicare program. This is effectively a statement of the elasticity of supply of medical services and devices, which is a function of the size of the insurer in the overall market.

While Medicare is a large public insurer, it is not the only large payer in the market. In 2017, there were approximately 55 million enrollees (17 percent of the population). To put that in perspective, United Healthcare currently provides health care coverage for 38 million individuals and represents only one of many private insurers in the United States.[9] The fact that Medicare is not the only large payer in the market limits some of the negative consequences of its exercising its market power as a large purchaser. However, if Medicare expands to be a dominant (or, depending upon the plan, the only) health insurance plan, then the impact of the use of buyer power could be quite large. To illustrate this point briefly, Medicare introduced a prescription drug benefit (Medicare Part D) several decades after private insurers had. Had there been no private insurers, the missing innovation from Medicare's reliance on monopsony power (as opposed to competition) would be harder to spot. The trade-off between the benefits of lower prices that provide greater access but at the cost of less innovation in plan design is central to all Medicare reform proposals.

In summary, current Medicare for All proposals do not grapple with the central economic trade-offs that require more attention for these proposals to be successful (which is not an impossibility). The inattention to central economic issues has been a theme that runs through other proposals to reform Medicare—perhaps because of a combination of political expediency and uncertainty about the magnitude of these effects. Many effects are hard to know—such as the magnitude of incentives necessary to create and capture value, the link between payment and future innovation, and the point at which Medicare starts to resemble a monopsony payer. But the current approach of believing that regulation is immune to these forces, or can circumvent them through more regulation, is not different from believing them to be small or zero. This is an unfortunate state of affairs for Medicare, as it is a large program with great economic, medical, and insurance significance for the disabled and elderly and, through spillover effects, for all Americans.

In contrast to this approach, we believe that Medicare's long-term significance can be increased with a greater appreciation for the economic forces that underlie the program. Our approach relies on reforming and expanding the MA program, as we believe that it represents the best vehicle for creating a social insurance program that balances access and coverage with long-term innovation in new therapeutics, prevention, and care-delivery models. But we also note that simply expanding the current MA is insufficient, for current reimbursement and risk adjustment in the MA program should be improved before the program is expanded. An expansion of the MA program also serves as a substitute for Medicare running its own pay-for-performance schemes, which are prone to tinkering and moving the goalposts. These proposals can also be paired with premium support, mirroring the approach that was set up by the ACA. These reforms can also be augmented by a number of proposals to make sense of high prescription drug prices—an area that will likely require more attention in coming years. Reforming how Part B drugs are paid for by delegating the task of price negotiation to vendors, reforming plan design in Medicare Part D to make payers more price-conscious about expensive drugs, and removing the requirement that drugs in "protected classes" must be covered are fruitful areas for Medicare reform efforts.

Notes

1. Throughout this article, we use the term *social benefits* in lieu of the conventional *social welfare* term from economics and public finance. We do this to avoid confusing the reader who is interested in welfare reform.

2. For a broad summary of these various plans, please see https://www.vox.com/2018/12/13/18103087/medicare-for-all-explained-single-payer-health-care-sanders-jayapal.

3. Medicare payments equal the amount that Medicare has paid out to different sources, excluding any income from premiums and other offsetting repayments. Net Medicare outlays equal Medicare payments minus income from premiums and other offsetting payments. Medicare payments will therefore always be higher than net Medicare outlays.

4. We acknowledge that health insurance provides more than the traditional economic definition of insurance (i.e., smoothing consumption across negative and positive states of the world).

5. "How Does the Benefit Value of Medicare Compare to the Benefit Value of Typical Large Employer Plans? A 2012 Update," The Henry J. Kaiser Family Foundation (blog) (April 5, 2012), https://www.kff.org/health-reform/issue-brief/how-does-the-benefit-value-of-medicare/.

6. For more information on how risk-adjustment is conducted by CMS, see https://www.cms.gov/Regulations-and-Guidance/Guidance/Manuals/downloads/mc86c07.pdf.

7. These features include both explicit and implicit regulations. Explicitly, providers that choose not to enroll in an MA network can only charge a provider the out-of-network rate. This reduces the bargaining power of providers. Implicitly, providers realize that if prices raise the premiums of MA plans too high, enrollees will default to the FFS system, and the provider will only earn the FFS rate.

8. "Compare Medicare-for-All and Public Plan Proposals," The Henry J. Kaiser Family Foundation (blog) (April 11, 2019), https://www.kff.org/interactive/compare-medicare-for-all-public-plan-proposals/.

9. This includes 27 million commercial lives, 5 million Medicare advantage enrollees, and 6.4 million Medicaid managed care enrollees. In addition, United Healthcare provides supplemental Medicare coverage for 4.5 million customers.

References

Alhassani, Ali, Amitabh Chandra, and Michael E. Chernew. 2012. The sources of the SGR "hole." *New England Journal of Medicine* 366 (4): 289–91.

American Association of Retired Persons (AARP). n.d. The future of Medicare: 15 proposals you should know about. Available from https://www.aarp.org/content/dam/aarp/health/medicare-and-medicaid/2012-05/The-Future-Of-Medicare.pdf.

Azar, Alex, and Seema Verma. 2019. Proposed changes to lower drug prices in Medicare Advantage and Part D. Available from https://www.cms.gov/blog/proposed-changes-lower-drug-prices-medicare-advantage-and-part-d.

Bagley, Nicholas, Amitabh Chandra, and Austin Frakt. 7 October 2015. Correcting signals for innovation in health care. Brookings (blog). Available from https://www.brookings.edu/research/correcting-signals-for-innovation-in-health-care/.

Baker, Laurence C., M. Kate Bundorf, Aileen M. Devlin, and Daniel P. Kessler. 2016. Medicare Advantage plans pay hospitals less than traditional Medicare pays. *Health Affairs* 35 (8). Available from https://doi.org/10.1377/hlthaff.2015.1553.

Cabral, Marika, and Neale Mahoney. 2019. Externalities and taxation of supplemental insurance: A study of Medicare and Medigap. *American Economic Journal: Applied Economics* 11 (2): 37–73.

Chan, David C., and Michael J. Dickstein. 2019. Industry input in policy making: Evidence from Medicare. *Quarterly Journal of Economics.* Available from https://doi.org/10.1093/qje/qjz005.

Chandra, Amitabh, and Craig Garthwaite. 2017. The economics of indication-based drug pricing. *New England Journal of Medicine* 377 (2): 103–6.

Chandra, Amitabh, Jonathan Gruber, and Robin McKnight. 2010. Patient cost-sharing and hospitalization offsets in the elderly. *American Economic Review* 100 (1): 193–213.

Chandra, Amitabh, Jonathan Holmes, and Jonathan Skinner. 19 September 2013. Is this time different? The slowdown in health care spending. Brookings (blog). Available from https://www.brookings.edu/bpea-articles/is-this-time-different-the-slowdown-in-health-care-spending.

Chandra, Amitabh, Anupam B. Jena, and Jonathan S. Skinner. 2011. The pragmatist's guide to comparative effectiveness research. *Journal of Economic Perspectives* 25 (2): 27–46.

Chandra, Amitabh, and Jonathan Skinner. 2012. Technology growth and expenditure growth in health care. *Journal of Economic Literature* 50 (3): 645–80.

Congressional Budget Office. 2019. *The 2019 long-term budget outlook*. Washington, DC: CBO. Available from https://www.cbo.gov/publication/55331.

Cooper, Zack, Amanda E. Kowalski, Eleanor N. Powell, and Jennifer Wu. 2019. Politics and health care spending in the United States. NBER Working Papers 23748, National Bureau of Economic Research Cambridge, MA.

Cubanski, Juliette, Anthony Damico, Tricia Neuman, and Gretchen Jacobson. 28 November 2018. Sources of supplemental coverage among Medicare beneficiaries in 2016. The Henry J. Kaiser Family Foundation (blog). Available from https://www.kff.org/medicare/issue-brief/sources-of-supplemental-coverage-among-medicare-beneficiaries-in-2016/.

Cubanski, Juliette, and Tricia Neuman. 22 June 2018. The facts on Medicare spending and financing. The Henry J. Kaiser Family Foundation (blog). Available from https://www.kff.org/medicare/issue-brief/the-facts-on-medicare-spending-and-financing/.

Curto, Vilsa, Liran Einav, Amy Finkelstein, Jonathan Levin, and Jay Bhattacharya. 2019. Health care spending and utilization in public and private Medicare. *American Economic Journal: Applied Economics* 11 (2): 302–32.

Cutler, David M., and Dan P. Ly. 2011. The (paper)work of medicine: Understanding international medical costs. *Journal of Economic Perspectives* 25 (2): 3–25.

Duggan, Mark, and Fiona M. Scott Morton. 2006. The distortionary effects of government procurement: Evidence from Medicaid prescription drug purchasing. *Quarterly Journal of Economics* 121 (1): 1–30.

Duggan, Mark, Amanda Starc, and Boris Vabson. 2016. Who benefits when the government pays more? Pass-through in the Medicare Advantage program. *Journal of Public Economics* 141:50–67.

Frakt, Austin B., and Ashish K. Jha. 2018. Face the facts: We need to change the way we do pay for performance. *Annals of Internal Medicine* 168 (4). Available from https://doi.org/10.7326/M17-3005.

Frandsen, Brigham, Michael Powell, and James B. Rebitzer. 2019. Sticking points: Common-agency problems and contracting in the US healthcare system. *RAND Journal of Economics* 50 (2): 251–85.

Gaynor, Martin, Rodrigo Moreno-Serra, and Carol Propper. 2013. Death by market power: Reform, competition, and patient outcomes in the national health service. *American Economic Journal: Economic Policy* 5 (4): 134–66.

Geruso, Michael, and Timothy Layton. 2019. Upcoding: Evidence from Medicare on squishy risk adjustment. *Journal of Political Economy*. https://doi.org/10.1086/704756.

Hart, Oliver, Andrei Shliefer, and Robert W. Vishny. 1997. The proper scope of government: Theory and an application to prisons. *Quarterly Journal of Economics* 112 (4): 1127–61.

Kliff, Sarah. 13 December 2018. We read Democrats' 9 plans for expanding health care. Here's how they work. *Vox*. Available from https://www.vox.com.

Martin, Anne B., Micah Hartman, Benjamin Washington, and Aaron Catlin, and The National Health Expenditure Accounts Team. 2018. National health care spending in 2017: Growth slows to post–Great Recession rates; share of GDP stabilizes. *Health Affairs* 38 (1). Available from https://doi.org/10.1377/hlthaff.2018.05085.

McWilliams, J. Michael. 2016. Cost containment and the tale of care coordination. *New England Journal of Medicine* 375 (23): 2218–20.

McWilliams, J. Michael, Laura A. Hatfield, Bruce E. Landon, Pasha Hamed, and Michael E. Chernew. 2018. Medicare spending after 3 years of the Medicare Shared Savings Program. *New England Journal of Medicine*. Available from https://doi.org/10.1056/NEJMsa1803388.

Medicare Payment Advisory Commission (MedPAC). 2017. Status report on the Medicare Advantage program. Washington, DC: MedPAC. Available from http://medpac.gov/docs/default-source/reports/mar17_medpac_ch13.pdf?sfvrsn=0.

Medicare Payment Advisory Commission (MedPAC). 2018. The Medicare Prescription Drug Program (Part D): Status report. Washington, DC: MedPAC. Available from http://www.medpac.gov/docs/default-source/reports/mar18_medpac_ch14_sec.pdf.

Medicare Payment Advisory Commission (MedPAC). 2019. *Medicare and the health care delivery system*. Washington, DC: MedPAC.

Pearson, Steven D., and Peter B. Bach. 2010. How Medicare could use comparative effectiveness research in deciding on new coverage and reimbursement. *Health Affairs* 29 (10): 1796–1804.

Propper, Carol, and John Van Reenen. 2010. Can pay regulation kill? Panel data evidence on the effect of labor markets on hospital performance. *Journal of Political Economy* 118 (2): 222–73.

Robinson, James C., Dimitra Penteli, and Patricia Ex. 2019. *Reference pricing in Germany: Implications for U.S. drug purchasing.* Washington, DC: Commonwealth Fund. Available from https://doi .org/10.26099/5xrf-wb19.

Robinson, James C., Christopher M. Whaley, and Timothy T. Brown. 2017. Association of reference pricing with drug selection and spending. *New England Journal of Medicine.* Available from https://doi .org/10.1056/NEJMsa1700087.

Shliefer, Andrei. 1998. State versus private ownership. NBER Working Paper 6665, National Bureau of Economic Research, Cambridge, MA.

Weisbrod, Burton A. 1991. The health care quadrilemma: An essay on technological change, insurance, quality of care, and cost containment. *Journal of Economic Literature* 29 (2): 523–52.

White, Chapin, and Christopher Whaley. 2019. *Prices paid to hospitals by private health plans are high relative to Medicare and vary widely: Findings from an employer-led transparency initiative.* Santa Monica, CA: RAND Corporation.

Witters, Dan. 2019. U.S. uninsured rate rises to four-year high. *Gallup.* Available from https://news.gallup .com.

Identifying Work Capacity and Promoting Work: A Strategy for Modernizing the SSDI Program

By
NICOLE MAESTAS

The Social Security Disability Insurance (SSDI) program, which provides income support to individuals who become unable to work because of a disability, has not been substantially reformed since the 1980s, despite sweeping changes in health, medical technology, and the functional requirements of jobs. I review how the SSDI program works, its history in terms of caseloads and reforms, and findings from the research evidence that offer lessons for the future. I then propose two interlocking reforms that would modernize the core functions of the program. The first is to improve SSDI's process for determining whether an applicant has remaining capacity to work by replacing the outdated medical-vocational "grid" with a new system of individual work capacity measurement. Second, I propose the introduction of partial disability benefits, which would make use of the new system for measuring work capacity and allow beneficiaries to combine benefit receipt with work. Partial benefits could be paired with a generalized benefit offset to further encourage work by beneficiaries, and the Social Security Administration's complex array of work-related rules could be eliminated.

Keywords: Social Security Disability Insurance (SSDI); disability; work capacity; partial benefits

The U.S. Social Security Disability Insurance (SSDI) program provides income support to individuals who become unable to work because of a disability. SSDI is one of the largest social insurance programs in the United

Nicole Maestas is an associate professor of health care policy at Harvard Medical School and a research associate of the National Bureau of Economic Research (NBER), where she directs the NBER's Retirement and Disability Research Center. She studies the economics of aging, health care, and disability insurance. Her current work investigates work capacity among older individuals and people with disabilities, working conditions in the American labor force, the effects of the Medicaid and Medicare programs on health care utilization and health, and the causes and consequences of the opioid epidemic.

Correspondence: maestas@hcp.med.harvard.edu

DOI: 10.1177/0002716219882354

States. In 2017, it paid \$144.3 billion in benefits to 8.7 million disabled workers and 3.0 million of their dependent family members (Social Security Administration [SSA] 2018d). SSDI disabled workers as a group equate to 5.4 percent of the U.S. labor force (SSA 2018d; U.S. Bureau of Labor Statistics [BLS] 2019b).

The central policy trade-off for the SSDI program is to provide protection against disability-related earnings losses, but in a way that does not induce labor force nonparticipation among people who could otherwise work. Balancing "insurance" against "incentives" is exceptionally difficult, and the political discourse surrounding SSDI throughout its history of expansion and retrenchment has reflected this deep tension. By 2014, the program had expanded in nearly every year since its birth in 1956 and was inching dangerously close to insolvency. Some of the caseload growth was predictable, resulting from deliberate expansions of eligibility, rising labor force participation by women (increasing the number of SSDI-insured workers), or population aging (Reno 2011; Liebman 2015). But much of the growth was due to the eroding labor market prospects of lower-skilled workers, who, despite significant health problems, might have otherwise worked (Autor and Duggan 2003; Liebman 2015). In 2014, the SSDI program began transitioning to a smaller steady-state size (Munnell et al. 2015), due to the natural fading of earlier demographic pressures and administrative changes at the appellate level. The program now appears solvent until 2052 (Board of Trustees 2019).

With the caseload contracting, the case for SSDI reform is no longer primarily a fiscal one.[1] As emphasized by Liebman (2015), the case for SSDI reform rests on the need to reoptimize the program to account for change in the composition of applicants. Originally a program for older men with clear-cut, permanent impairments (e.g., circulatory diseases), SSDI now serves men and women of all ages who more often than not have a musculoskeletal or mental impairment and diminished employment opportunities. Many of these individuals have some degree of residual work capacity. The case for reform is bolstered by the fact that the last major reform of the SSDI program was in the 1980s. The core structures that define who does and does not have work capacity have not been updated to keep pace with advancements in medicine, technology, or the functional requirements of jobs. SSA's listings of automatically qualifying impairments have been updated infrequently, despite decades of medical progress (SSA Office of the Inspector General 2015). Similarly, there have been no updates to the "medical-vocational grid" used by disability adjudicators to determine whether an applicant can do any other job in the national economy, despite broad structural change in the nature and skill demands of jobs.

Decades of research highlight five high-level takeaways that should guide reform. First, SSDI participation is not just a reflection of individuals' underlying

NOTE: I thank Jason Fichtner, Jason Seligman, and the editors and attendees of *The ANNALS of the American Academy of Political and Social Science* authors' conference for helpful feedback. Michael Jetsupphasuk provided outstanding research assistance. The reform ideas proposed here were made possible in part by research support from the National Institute on Aging (R01AG056238, R01AG056239).

health. It also reflects their labor market outcomes and prospects for future employment. Second, a significant portion of SSDI entrants have substantial work capacity. Third, they lose further work capacity during the SSDI application process because program rules require them to sit out of the labor market while they wait for a disability determination, a process that takes several years for some. Fourth, once people finally enter the SSDI program, they are unlikely to return to work, even when offered work incentives. Repeated policy efforts to incentivize work among beneficiaries have largely failed to increase work activity. Finally, SSDI provides immensely valuable social insurance benefits for American workers who experience a disabling health problem; it is essential to maintain this protection.

In light of these findings, the goals of reform should be to allow SSDI applicants to stay in the labor force for as long as possible, improve identification of what work capacity SSDI applicants have, and help them to use and augment their available work capacity before it is too late. I propose two major, interrelated reforms to the SSDI program that address these goals. The first is to improve measurement of work capacity and eliminate the outdated medical-vocational grid. The second is to award partial disability benefits for partial disabilities. Under a system that included partial benefits as well as full benefits, applicants could apply while still working, and the new system of work capacity measurement would more precisely identify their amount of remaining work capacity.

The article proceeds as follows. I first explain how the SSDI program works and how it has been changed over time. I then describe historical and recent trends, showing that the caseload has begun to decline after decades of unrelenting growth, while concurrently, employment among people with disabilities has risen. I next review the evidence from the literature that provides the basis for reform. I then present my reform proposals. I close by commenting on some of the other reforms that have been proposed in recent years.

Overview of SSDI

How SSDI works

SSDI is a federal social insurance program established in 1956 to protect individuals against loss of earnings due to a disability. Individuals and their employers pay SSDI insurance "premiums" in the form of payroll taxes, in the same way they contribute to the Social Security retirement program and to Medicare.[2] Once individuals begin making payroll tax contributions, they become insured only after accruing sufficient "work credits." The required number of credits increases with age, and at least half must have been earned recently.[3]

Although it is necessary to be insured for SSDI to obtain SSDI benefits, insured status is not enough to guarantee benefits. The SSA must also determine that an applicant has a "medically-determinable mental or physical impairment" that *prevents* them from engaging in "substantial gainful activity" (SGA). SGA is defined as earnings of $1,220 per month[4] or higher (in 2019), an amount roughly equivalent to a full-time job at the federal minimum wage. Individuals are not permitted to even apply for SSDI benefits if they are working at or above SGA. In addition, an applicant's impairment must be severe and long-lasting—expected to result in death or last for at least 12 months. Importantly, partial disabilities resulting in partial loss of earnings capacity do not meet SSA's definition of disability (unless the remaining work capacity is below SGA).[5]

SSA's medical review process is designed to identify and award benefits to two types of applicants: (1) those who have one or more especially severe medical impairments on the "listing of impairments"; and (2) those whose functional limitations in *combination with* vocational background—their education, skills, and age—prevent them from performing any job in the national economy at or above the SGA level.[6] The initial disability review is performed by disability examiners in state agencies. If an applicant is initially denied SSDI benefits, he or she may appeal the decision.

Similar to Social Security retirement benefits, an individual's SSDI benefit is based on her or his average lifetime earnings, except there is no actuarial reduction in benefits for claiming before full retirement age. The average monthly benefit for a disabled worker was $1,197 in 2018 (SSA 2018e). In addition to cash benefits, SSDI beneficiaries automatically qualify for Medicare following a 29-month waiting period.

Once benefits begin, SSDI beneficiaries are allowed to try working again, and a small number of beneficiaries are referred for SSA-financed vocational rehabilitation services. Beneficiaries may reengage in work *above SGA* for up to nine months during what is called the trial work period.[7] But after that, any amount of earnings above SGA results in suspension of monthly cash benefits.[8] This abrupt loss of the entire benefit amount for as little as $1 in additional earnings is often called the "cash cliff." Once cash benefits are stopped because of work activity, the beneficiary enters a 36-month "extended period of eligibility," during which time benefits can be restarted whenever earnings fall below SGA. After that, benefits are terminated but can be reinstated on an expedited basis during the next five years.

The early years of the SSDI program were marked by intentional program expansions. Benefits that were originally only for disabled workers aged 50 to 64 were quickly extended to disabled workers of all ages, as well as their dependent spouses, children, and disabled widow(er)s, and disabilities no longer had to be permanent, just "long-lasting," which was defined as lasting at least 12 months (SSA, n.d.). SSDI's first work incentive initiative, the trial work period, was established in 1960.

The caseload growth that followed this period of expansion was met with concerns about fiscal solvency. To curb program costs, in the late 1970s SSA tightened the medical eligibility criteria and pressured states to reduce initial allowance rates. As a result, the award rate fell from 45 percent in 1976 to 32 percent in 1980 (Autor and Duggan 2003). Adding to this effort, Congress passed the 1980 Social Security Amendments, which placed a cap on family benefits, revised the benefit computation formula, and established several work incentive initiatives (Kearney 2005/2006).[9] To encourage work, the SGA earnings test would now be applied to beneficiary earnings *net of* impairment-related work expenses, and if benefits were suspended for work activity, individuals could keep their Medicare coverage for an extended period. Furthermore, cash benefits could be restarted if a former beneficiary became unable to continue working during the new extended period of eligibility (originally just 15 months but extended to 36 months in 1987).

More controversially, the 1980 amendments added a requirement that beneficiaries be reassessed regularly to ensure continued qualification for benefits (called continuing disability reviews [CDRs]) (SSA, n.d.). The reassessment requirement, which resulted in a large number of terminations (especially among people with mental disorders), was met with intense resistance by states, administrative law judges, the courts, and the public. This backlash led to further amendments in 1984 that limited benefit terminations to cases of demonstrated medical improvement, or error in the initial determination. In addition, the functional capacity of applicants with multiple impairments was to be assessed taking into account the *combined effect* of all impairments (even if no one impairment was sufficiently severe on its own), the list of automatically qualifying mental impairments was to be revised, and it was clarified that pain could be a contributing (though not sole determining) factor in a disability award (SSA, n.d.).

Since the 1980s, Congress has enacted no major reforms of the SSDI program. Incremental changes include the elimination of substance abuse disorder as a qualifying disability in 1996 and the creation of the Ticket to Work and Self-Sufficiency Program in 1999, which provides employment services and supports to SSDI beneficiaries interested in returning to work. The most impactful program change has come not from Congress, but from SSA itself. Beginning in 2010, SSA's Appeals Council launched a management initiative to improve policy compliance and decisional consistency among administrative law judges, who hear appeals of denied claims (Ray and Lubbers 2014).[10] The initiative, which included case reviews, direct feedback to individual judges, and a redesigned judge training curriculum, was associated with a large decline in the hearing-level allowance rate (Maestas, Mullen, and Strand 2018)—from 52 percent in 2010 to 38 percent in 2016 (SSA 2018d). Although the causes of the decline are not known with certainty, it appears the SSDI program may have recently undergone a major tightening.

SSDI trends

SSDI has long been characterized as a program undergoing unsustainable growth (see, e.g., Autor and Duggan 2006). Indeed, the DI trust fund was on course for depletion in 2016, when Congress averted benefit cuts of 19 percent by temporarily shifting a larger share of payroll tax revenues to the DI trust fund.[11] Since then, however, two surprising trends have shifted the narrative about the SSDI program. The first is that the SSDI caseload is unexpectedly and persistently declining. The second is that employment among people with

FIGURE 1
Number of SSDI Disabled Worker Beneficiaries, 1960–2017

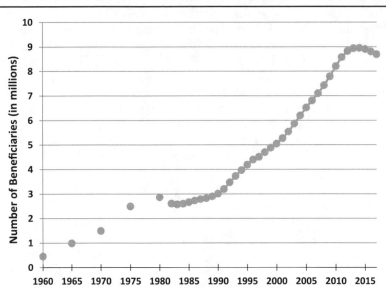

SOURCE: Social Security Administration (SSA; 2018d, Table 19).

disabilities is steadily rising, a surprising reversal of a decades-long downward trend. This section discusses these new facts in greater detail.

Figure 1 shows the SSDI disabled worker caseload from 1960 to 2017. The caseload increases during the 1960s and 1970s reflect the early expansions in eligibility, and the sharp decline in the early 1980s reflects the controversial terminations. The subsequent backlash restored the caseload to its upward trajectory. Between 1982 and 2013, the caseload more than tripled—from 2.6 million to 8.9 million, the latter number equivalent to 5.8 percent of the U.S. civilian labor force (BLS 2019b). Correspondingly, annual expenditures on cash benefits for disabled workers grew from $13.8 billion to $123.0 billion during this period (SSA 2018d). In 2014, the SSDI caseload plateaued, and in 2015 it began declining—for only the second time ever.

Initially, the growth in new SSDI awards was concentrated among people with circulatory system impairments (e.g., cardiovascular disease), as shown in Figure 2. The policy changes that followed the terminations in the 1980s made it easier for people with mental impairments and with pain to qualify, which shifted growth to mental impairments, followed by musculoskeletal impairments (e.g., back pain). The figure also shows a recent, sharp reduction in the number of new awards—primarily awards due to mental and musculoskeletal impairments—reflecting the sharp reduction in the hearing allowance rate (discussed above) and suggesting that sharply reduced inflows are at least part of the reason for the recent caseload decline.

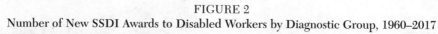

FIGURE 2
Number of New SSDI Awards to Disabled Workers by Diagnostic Group, 1960–2017

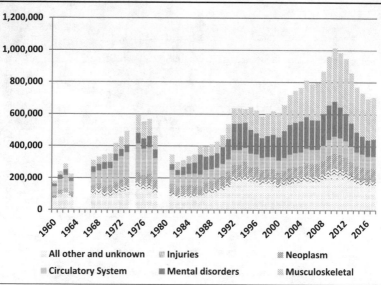

SOURCE: SSA (2018d, Table 40).

But the recent caseload decline is also in part due to an increase in exits. Figure 3 plots the annual number of awards and exits (right axis), against the caseload stock (left axis), focusing on the period since 2001. The annual number of exits has nearly doubled (from 459,073 in 2001 to 859,020 in 2017) and beginning in 2014 has exceeded the annual number of new awards. Figure 4 shows that the vast majority of SSDI exits are accounted for by ever-larger numbers of Baby Boomers aging out of the program (and into the Social Security retirement program) at full retirement age, in demographically predictable fashion. Not predicted, however, was the surprising rise in program exits due to successful return to work, as shown in Figure 5. Although work exits are rare (just 0.5 percent of beneficiaries exit in this manner), it is nonetheless striking that work exits have nearly doubled since 2013.

It is possible that the strong labor market is driving the trend in work exits. During this period, there has been an unexpected and remarkable increase in employment among people with disabilities. Figure 6 shows the employment rate for people with and without work-limiting disabilities from 1988 to 2018. In approximately 2014, the employment rate among people with disabilities began to rise, after several decades of decline. The shaded areas denote the timing of recessions. While the employment rate has risen during the long recovery since the Great Recession, there was no such rise during the recovery from the 2001–2002 recession (shown) or prior recessions (not shown). Although speculative, this may point to structural changes in employers' willingness to hire individuals with disabilities, perhaps in response to growing labor demand pressures associated with population aging (Maestas, Mullen, and Powell 2016).

FIGURE 3
SSDI Inflows and Outflows

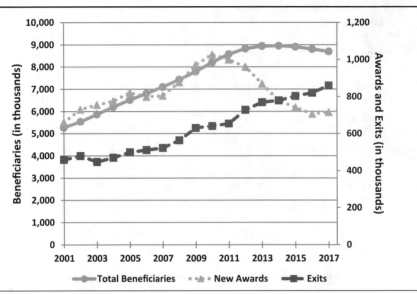

SOURCE: SSA (2018d, Tables 19, 40, and 49).
NOTE: Exits include exits due to death, attainment of retirement age, return to work, election of a lower retirement benefit, entitlement to an equal or larger benefit, medical improvement, failure to cooperate, miscellaneous medical reasons, and other.

FIGURE 4
Exits due to Age, Death, and Return to Work among SSDI Disabled Workers, 2001–2017

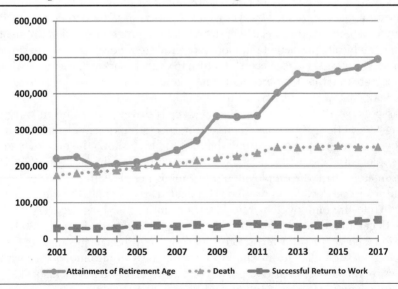

SOURCE: SSA (2018d): 2001, Table 39; 2002, Table 45; 2003–2004, Table 46; 2005–2017, Table 50.

FIGURE 5
Number of SSDI Beneficiaries Who Exited due to Successful Return-to-Work

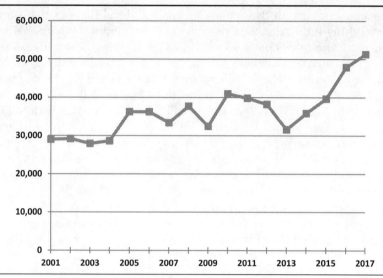

SOURCE: SSA (2018d): 2001, Table 39; 2002, Table 45; 2003–2004, Table 46; 2005–2017, Table 50.

FIGURE 6
Employment Rate of People with and without Disabilities (ages 16–64)

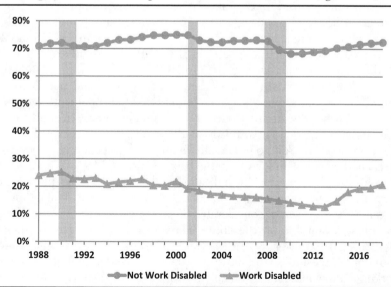

SOURCE: Flood et al. (2018).
NOTE: "Work disability" is defined as a disability or health problem that limits or prevents work. Beginning in 2016, the wording of this question in the Annual Social and Economic Supplement of the Current Population Survey changed by covering the entire previous year and including issues that affected work even for short periods of time.

What the Research Evidence Tells Us

The research evidence to date points to five high-level findings that provide a basis for crafting future disability reforms. The first finding is that SSDI participation is not just a reflection of an individual's underlying health. It also reflects his or her labor market outcomes and prospects for future employment, both of which are affected by cyclical and structural labor demand conditions (see, e.g., Black, Daniel, and Sanders 2002; Autor and Duggan 2003; Charles, Li, and Stephens 2018; Maestas, Mullen, and Strand 2018) and interact with SSDI program features. That economic factors should play an important role in SSDI participation is not surprising: nonparticipation in the labor market (technically, earnings below SGA) is a precondition for application, and some of SSA's decision rules are based on assumptions about the number of jobs for unskilled workers in the national economy (this is described in detail in the next section). Nonetheless, experts have disagreed about how much of the program's growth has been due to nonhealth factors, such as economic incentives. On one hand, as the program expanded after the mid-1980s, there was no evidence of a decline in population health (Autor and Duggan 2010; Burkhauser and Daly 2011), but strong evidence of weakening demand for low-skilled workers that occurred just as the 1984 amendments made the program more lenient and rising earnings inequality made the SSDI benefit more generous relative to the earnings of low-skilled workers (Autor and Duggan 2003). In contrast, others argued that even though the percentage of the population in poor health had not increased, the *number* of people insured for disability benefits had risen dramatically—primarily women (who were acquiring work credits in greater number) and Baby Boomers (who were reaching middle age in ever-larger numbers) (Reno 2011). Liebman (2015) resolved the debate by showing that the sources of program growth differed over time. During 1985 to 1993 (the period immediately following the 1984 amendments),[12] women becoming insured, and population aging accounted for very little program growth, implying that nonhealth factors were the primary drivers. But from 1993 to 2007, women becoming insured and population aging accounted for two-thirds of the growth, thus ascribing a smaller, though still important, role to nonhealth factors such as economic incentives.[13]

The second takeaway follows from the first: many SSDI beneficiaries retain (or recover) "residual" work capacity, indicating that for many, SSDI participation is an alternative to employment. But how much work capacity is retained or recovered has been the subject of considerable debate. Parsons (1980) found the SSDI program was responsible for the entire increase in labor force *non*participation among men aged 45 to 54 between 1948 and 1976.[14] In other words, had the SSDI program not been established (and subsequently expanded), all of the additional nonworking men would have been able to work to some degree. This finding was critiqued for its reliance on nonrandom variation in the SSDI benefit amount, which, as a function of lifetime earnings, was potentially confounded with underlying health and labor force attachment (Haveman and Wolfe 1984a, 1984b; Bound 1989; Gruber 2000). Bound (1989) countered that the SSDI program was responsible for, at most, one-quarter of the rise in male nonparticipation. To obtain this estimate, he used denied applicants as a control group for SSDI beneficiaries, arguing that since denied applicants were healthier than beneficiaries (by virtue of having failed to meet SSDI's medical criteria), their postdenial labor supply was an *upper bound* on the work capacity of SSDI beneficiaries. Specifically, he found that the employment rate among SSDI beneficiaries would have been at most 35 percentage points higher, had they not been awarded SSDI benefits.[15] In response, Parsons (1991) argued that Bound's (1989) estimate was not an upper bound on the total effect of the SSDI program if denied SSDI applicants had *lower* labor force attachment than allowed applicants, or if the long SSDI application process eroded human capital. Evidence of both effects has since emerged.

Recent advances have made use of quasi-experimental variation and administrative data to pin down the residual work capacity of SSDI beneficiaries. Maestas, Mullen, and Strand (2013) found that approximately 23 percent of applicants were "on the margin" of an SSDI award, meaning that their chances of SSDI receipt depended entirely on the allowance propensity of the disability examiner to which they were randomly assigned.[16] Using the examiner's allowance propensity as an "instrumental variable" for an applicant's chances of receiving an SSDI award, Maestas, Mullen, and Strand (2013) found that the employment rate among this subset of SSDI beneficiaries would have been 28 percentage points higher in the absence of SSDI receipt. Furthermore, the employment rate would have been as much as 50 percentage points higher in the absence of SSDI receipt among the least impaired applicants in the group. Overall, their estimates imply that 43 percent of SSDI applicants have residual work capacity, of which about 18 percent ultimately qualify for benefits (calculations based on Maestas, Mullen, and Strand 2013), sometimes under the listings but more often under the outdated medical-vocational criteria. That said, the residual work capacity of these beneficiaries is a *partial* capacity, in the sense that their potential earnings in the absence of SSDI are substantially less than their predisability earnings; that is, even though many could work, they have nonetheless experienced a significant, disability-induced loss in potential earnings (see, e.g., Maestas, Mullen, and Strand 2013).[17]

The third high-level finding relates to the second: residual work capacity declines even further the longer people spend out of the labor force (Autor et al. 2015). Although initial SSDI decisions are rendered in a matter of months, applicants who are initially denied and file an appeal often wait several years, during which time most do not risk disqualification by working, even though, strictly speaking, they could work as long as their earnings were below the SGA level. During this time out of the labor force waiting for a disability determination, their work capacity declines, likely due to skill depreciation or loss of attachment to employers or employment networks. If they are ultimately denied, they are less likely to work *because they applied for SSDI benefits*. If they are ultimately awarded benefits, they are less likely to work because they applied and also because (as discussed above) receiving benefits deters employment for some.[18] This means the SSDI program reduces the subsequent employment of applicants—both allowed *and* denied—by far more than the prior literature suggests. Furthermore, Autor et al. (2015) find that accounting for the effect of processing delays *increases* the magnitude of the deterrent effect of SSDI receipt on labor supply: indeed, the employment rate of SSDI beneficiaries on the margin of award would be *48 percentage points higher* had they not received SSDI benefits (compared to 28 percentage points in Maestas, Mullen, and Strand 2013). In other words, their residual work capacity was also far greater than previously estimated.

The decay in work capacity that occurs with time out of the labor force may offer an important clue as to why policy efforts to incentivize work among SSDI beneficiaries have repeatedly failed. Indeed, the fourth high-level finding is that we still do not understand how to increase work effort among SSDI beneficiaries, despite decades of research. Early studies noted low levels of work activity; limited awareness of work incentives like the trial work period; and extended period of eligibility, low rates of benefit termination, and a high likelihood of reenrollment among those who did terminate (Muller 1992; Hennessey and Muller 1994). Similarly, the Ticket to Work Program has suffered from low participation and has had little impact on beneficiary employment and earnings (Livermore et al. 2013). More recently, the Benefit Offset National Demonstration (BOND) Project to test the effect of replacing the SSDI "cash cliff" with a less abrupt "benefit offset" or partial reduction in benefits ($1 for every $2 in earnings) found no impact of the weakened work disincentive on employment and earnings (Gubits et al. 2018). What these policies have in common is that they target individuals only after they have enrolled in SSDI, having already spent significant time out of the labor force.[19]

Last, despite long-standing concerns about moral hazard among some beneficiaries (who choose not to work even though they have work capacity) and perhaps also among some employers (who choose not to provide reasonable accommodations to disabled workers), an emerging body of economic research finds that the *benefits* associated with the SSDI program are substantial (Low and Pistaferri 2015; Deshpande, Gross, and Su 2019) and may offset the distortionary costs (Low and Pistaferri 2015). It is important to note that this in turn suggests that the optimal SSDI program is *not* no SSDI but, rather, an SSDI program that retains its protective aspects while at the same time reducing its labor-market efficiency costs.

Reforms to Identify and Promote Work

The implication of the major research findings I have reviewed here is that an effective reform strategy must achieve three goals. First, we should encourage individuals to stay engaged in the labor force when reasonably possible, while increasing access to vocational rehabilitation and other supports while they still have an employer or still have skills that employers value. Second, we should identify who has work capacity and specifically what jobs they could do. Currently, we know work capacity exists in the SSDI population, but the available evidence does not offer any specificity about who has what capacities and what alternative jobs use those capacities. Third, we should help individuals to use and even augment their available work capacity before it is too late.

In this section, I propose two interrelated reforms to the SSDI program that address these goals: (1) improve measurement of work capacity and eliminate the medical-vocational grid and (2) award partial disability benefits for partial disabilities. The reforms are interrelated in the sense that payment of partial benefits would be greatly facilitated by replacing SSA's current method of determining work capacity with a modernized approach with greater discriminatory power. In addition, I discuss several reform proposals put forth by others, highlighting those that are complementary with those that I have proposed.

Proposed reform #1: Improve measurement of work capacity and eliminate the "grid"

The medical-vocational guidelines, also known as the "grid," are used by SSA to determine whether an applicant can perform any other job in the national economy. In their recent proposal to eliminate the grid, Warshawsky and Marchand (2015) argue that the grid is "no longer fair, necessary, or reflective of current conditions" (p. 33). Instead, disability determinations should be focused solely on remaining earnings capacity combined with an evaluation of potential jobs suitable for the claimant (and without relaxed standards for older, less educated, and non-English-speaking workers). In this spirit, my first proposal is to eliminate the medical-vocational grid and replace it with a robust system for measuring earnings capacity.

Estimating applicants' remaining earnings capacity is the core objective of the SSDI determination process. The current process is sequential. SSA first checks whether the applicant has a listed impairment.[20] Applicants with listed impairments are presumed to have *no* earnings capacity (as opposed to the less stringent standard of less-than-SGA capacity), and therefore they qualify on medical grounds alone. If the applicant's impairment is not listed but it nonetheless prevents them from performing any of their "vocationally relevant" past jobs, then SSA assesses whether the applicant's skills are *transferable* to *other* occupations that fall within the applicant's functional capacity range. SSA makes these skill transferability assessments by first determining the applicant's level of residual functional capacity based on medical evidence, and then determining whether the applicant is disabled by applying the medical-vocational guidelines (SSA 2018c). The guidelines are a "grid" of rules specifying whether an applicant is disabled based on combinations of residual functional capacity, age, education, and skills gained from work experience. Table 1 shows how SSA defines these factors. Residual functional capacity has just four categories that describe the applicant's maximum exertional capability (i.e., strength): sedentary work, light work, medium work, and heavy work. Age is divided into "closely approaching retirement age" (60+), "advanced age" (55–59), "closely approaching advanced age" (50–54), and "younger individual" (18–49). Education has three categories:

TABLE 1
Grid Categories Used to Determine Skill Transferability

Dimension	Categories (ordered from least to most transferable)
Residual functional capacity	Sedentary work Light work Medium work Heavy work
Age	Closely approaching retirement age (60+) Advanced age (55–59) Closely approaching advanced age (50–54) Younger individual (18–49)
Education	Illiterate or unable to communicate in English Limited (high school nongraduate) High school graduate or more
Work experience	Unskilled or none Skilled or semiskilled—skills not transferable Skilled or semiskilled—skills transferable

SOURCE: SSA (2018c).

"illiterate or unable to communicate in English," "limited" (high school nongraduate), and "high school graduate or more." Work experience also has three categories: "unskilled or none," "skilled or semiskilled—skills not transferable," and "skilled or semiskilled—skills transferable."[21]

To illustrate how the grid rules work, Table 2 shows several segments of it. For someone with sedentary functional capacity, limited education, and skills that are not transferable, the disability decision hinges on age: if the applicant is 45 to 49, she or he is not disabled; but if 50 to 54, the applicant is disabled. If the applicant with sedentary capacity is illiterate and unskilled—the disability-age cutoff is 45 instead of 50. If the individual has capacity for light work (i.e., more work capacity than sedentary), but limited education and nontransferable skills, he or she is not disabled if 50 to 54 but disabled if 55 to 59. For someone who can handle "light" work but is illiterate and unskilled, the disability-age cutoff is 50 instead of 55.

While the grid is a convenient heuristic that enables adjudicators without medical or vocational training to render disability decisions, it has major limitations.[22] The first is that the grid has not been updated to reflect changes in the functional demands of jobs. The regulations indicate that if a particular grid rule directs a decision of *not* disabled, it is to be assumed that a reasonable number of "unskilled" jobs[23] are available to an applicant with that medical-vocational profile across the national economy. But this assessment of job availability is based on the Dictionary of Occupational Titles (DOT), which saw its final publication in the 1990s. The ensuing decades have seen a dramatic shift in the nature of work; most relevantly, the rise in industrial automation has eliminated many

TABLE 2
Example Grid Rules

Rule	Residual Functional Capacity	Education	Previous Work Experience	Age	Decision
201.19	Sedentary work	Limited or less	Skilled or semiskilled—skills not transferable	45–49	Not disabled
201.10				50–54	Disabled
201.23	Sedentary work	Illiterate/no English	Unskilled or none	18–44	Not disabled
201.17				45–49	Disabled
202.11	Light work	Limited or less	Skilled or semiskilled—skills not transferable	50–54	Not disabled
202.02				55–59	Disabled
202.16	Light work	Illiterate/no English	Unskilled or none	18–49	Not disabled
202.09				50–54	Disabled

SOURCE: SSA (2018c).

physically demanding tasks and made others less demanding. Furthermore, advances in medical care and assistive technologies have likely altered the set of tasks that can be performed in a given range of functional capacity. Although SSA has a decade-long initiative to create an updated occupational information system, disability decisions today continue to use grid rules based on the obsolete DOT.[24]

The second limitation of the grid is that the medical-vocational combinations it delineates are coarsely defined and lack consideration of individual variability. The grid's reliance on fixed age thresholds to distinguish the disabled from the nondisabled is particularly problematic given the individual variation in health at any given chronological age (see, e.g., Mitnitski 2018; Sudharsanan and Bloom 2018), dramatic gains in life expectancy (Oeppen and Vaupel 2002), and secular improvements in many dimensions of health (Crimmins 2015).

A third limitation of the grid is that residual functional capacity is conceptualized in terms of a single ability domain: the ability to exert physical strength.[25] In determining an applicant's maximum exertional level, adjudicators are instructed to consider whether the applicant can also perform the *nonexertional* requirements of unskilled occupations at that level,[26] but this is a secondary consideration, and the grid otherwise provides little direct guidance for disability cases that are primarily nonexertional—cases involving mental impairments, sensory disorders, skin disorders, or pain symptoms. Perhaps not surprisingly, mental impairments and those associated with pain have been a major driver of program growth (see Figure 2).

I propose SSA modernize its method of assessing skill transferability. Several principles should guide this effort. First, the assessment should be individualized. Second, it should measure the full range of remaining work abilities possessed by the individual. Third, the assessment should use validated data collection methods and evidence-based guidelines for assessing function. The more systematic and comprehensive the measurement system, the greater will be the potential gains in efficiency and equity as standardization enhances consistency across adjudicators and provides decision support to enhance application processing speed.

In practice, the system would measure the applicant's functional capacity across a full range of ability domains, use that information to query a database of job requirements, identify the set of jobs the applicant has the functional capacity to perform, and then assess whether the applicant's education and skills are transferable to any of those jobs with only a limited amount of on-the-job retraining.[27]

The key to the approach is to measure individual function in the same terms as the functional demands of occupations. The disability assessment system in the Netherlands offers an informative model. First, an applicant's functional capacity across a range of domains is assessed by a social security physician using a specially designed survey instrument. The applicant's information is then compared to a database of occupations that exist in all regions of the country and that have been rated along the same functional dimensions as the survey instrument. An algorithm combines the applicant information and the occupational information to identify a list of feasible occupations for the applicant. A social security labor expert reviews the list of feasible occupations, pruning the list to take into account any extenuating information not captured by the algorithm. The feasible occupations are then ranked by average earnings, and the average earnings of the second-ranked occupation become the applicant's estimated residual earnings capacity. The percent difference between the applicant's prior earnings and her or his estimated earnings capacity is the applicant's estimated percent earnings loss, which then determines the benefit amount.

There are at least two promising efforts underway in the United States that could be integrated to create a modern system of work capacity measurement based on the principles above. First, SSA has already invested in development and testing of an instrument for measuring individual work capacity. The instrument, known as the Work Disability Functional Assessment Battery (WD-FAB), was developed over a 10-year period by experts at the National Institutes of Health and Boston University under an interagency agreement with SSA (Marfeo et al. 2013). The WD-FAB has many advantages. It is broad, measuring function across eight physical and behavioral domains.[28] It provides coverage across the continuum of function within each domain by using computerized adaptive testing to iteratively select relevant items from a bank of more than three hundred hierarchical items (Marfeo et al. 2015). Precisely because it is adaptive, it can be administered in just 15 to 20 minutes in different modes (e.g., in-person, phone, or online). In extensive testing in samples of SSDI applicants and the general adult population, WD-FAB displayed good test-retest reliability, measurement accuracy, and convergent validity with legacy instruments (Marfeo et al. 2015; Chan 2018). Last, the WD-FAB was designed to evolve over time with ongoing research and development; items can be added and removed, measurement precision can be adjusted, and scoring algorithms can be modified.

The drawback of the WD-FAB is that its items reference functional tasks performed in the home domain, rather than in work settings. This was intentional because people who apply for disability benefits are not working and might not be able to reference their functioning against work-related tasks. But this feature makes it difficult to identify which specific work tasks—and thus which occupations—an applicant can perform. Nonetheless, the WD-FAB could be adapted to this purpose if a team of occupational analysts created a crosswalk between WD-FAB items and specific job demands.

A second promising effort is the Occupational Requirements Survey (ORS) being developed by SSA and the BLS. ORS is an establishment survey designed to elicit detailed information about job requirements from the employer perspective. ORS is part of the occupational information system SSA is building to replace the DOT. The DOT was maintained by a team of analysts who visited workplaces around the country to observe and record the requirements of jobs. In contrast, ORS collects data by interviewing employers and establishment representatives, an approach that yields similar measurements as direct observation while being less costly and time-consuming (Smyth 2018). Further, by randomly sampling establishments, ORS is nationally representative; as of 2018, ORS represents about 90 percent of civilian employed workers (BLS 2019a, 2019c) (although a substantially smaller percent of occupations). To fulfill its potential, the ORS should be synchronized with a functional measurement system like the WD-FAB so that it can be used to produce realistic, individualized, and multidimensional assessments of work capacity and a complete list of feasible jobs.

In addition to enhancing equity and efficiency across the SSDI system, the use of a modern, integrated work capacity measurement system would open the door to new types of interventions to improve outcomes for people with disabilities. For example, such data would facilitate targeting of return-to-work interventions to precisely those individuals with residual work capacity. The data generated by the system could be used to identify retraining opportunities for individuals who have the functional capacities for other occupations but who lack the necessary vocational skills or certifications. It would also make possible other types of SSDI reforms, such as my second proposal, to allow for partial disability benefits.

Proposed reform #2: Allow partial disability benefits

The SSDI program uses an all-or-nothing definition of disability, when in reality medical conditions reduce some abilities but not others, and the reductions may be full or partial. Although there is no definitive estimate, it is possible that 20 percent of SSDI beneficiaries are only partially disabled (see e.g., Benitez-Silva, Buchinsky, and Rust 2004). For those who have experienced partial loss of work capacity, the optimal arrangement would be to combine partial earnings with partial disability benefits. Without a partial option, these individuals must either forgo disability benefits or attempt to qualify as fully disabled. Typically, such applicants stop working altogether, further weakening their labor force prospects should they be denied or subsequently attempt to return to work.

I propose the SSDI program add partial disability benefits for individuals with partial disabilities. There are many ways to structure partial benefits, with examples from the U.S. Workers Compensation system, the Veterans Affairs Disability Compensation system, and the disability systems in several other countries.[29] The core component is estimation of applicants' residual earnings capacity—that is, the amount they could be expected to earn given their remaining functional abilities. Anyone with residual earnings capacity below the SGA floor would receive a disability rating of 100 percent, as under the current system. Those with residual earnings capacity above the SGA floor would receive a disability rating equal to ([1 − residual earnings capacity ÷ pre-disability earnings] × 100) percent. A ceiling could be placed on predisability earnings to restrict insurable earnings to a desired multiple of the SGA level.[30] Under this structure, an applicant with residual earnings capacity of $30,000 and predisability earnings of $50,000 would receive a disability rating of 40 percent. If instead her residual earnings capacity were $10,000, the disability rating would be 100 percent because $10,000 is below SGA. If her predisability earnings were $100,000 (and residual earnings capacity $30,000), then her disability rating would be 70 percent if there were no ceiling on predisability earnings, but 60 percent if a ceiling on predisability earnings were set at, for instance, 5 × SGA (approximately $75,000). The estimation of residual earnings capacity would be greatly facilitated by a modernized system for measuring work capacity (see Proposal #1).

Disability ratings could correspond to exact percentage reductions in an individual's full SSDI benefit amount, or they could be grouped into ranges defining discrete benefit levels, say 25 percent, 50 percent, 75 percent, and 100 percent. The choice of benefit schedule should depend on the precision with which work capacity can be measured. The more precise the measurement instrument, the more articulated the benefit schedule can be.

Such a system would have several advantages. Most importantly, people could apply while still working and receive a partial disability rating. This would preserve unique employer accommodations and attachment to the labor force while providing replacement of lost earnings. Beneficiaries would maintain their SSDI entitlement until their full retirement age, as long as they continued to be medically eligible. Regular continuing disability reviews (CDRs) would be used to ensure ongoing *medical* eligibility at the initially determined level or to revise the initial disability rating up or down as needed.[31] "Work" CDRs would be eliminated.[32] Eligibility for Medicare benefits would be extended indefinitely, even for those whose employers offer health insurance coverage.[33] Allowing employers to be the secondary insurer would create an incentive for employers to retain and hire people with disabilities.[34]

Partial benefits could be usefully paired with a "generalized benefit offset" to provide beneficiaries with a strong incentive to increase work effort beyond their partial rating, if they can. Unlike a standard benefit offset that imposes a tax on earnings (albeit lower than the sky-high tax rate implied by the cash cliff), the generalized benefit offset taxes earnings only when earnings are low and *subsidizes* earnings when earnings are higher. The earnings subsidies act as a strong work incentive (see Gokhale [2015] for a detailed proposal). With the possibility of entitlement to partial benefits and postentitlement incentives to increase work levels above the initial rating level—and without risk of entitlement termination—there would be no need for a Trial Work Period, the Extended Period of Eligibility, or provisions for Expedited Reinstatement.[35]

The biggest drawback of partial benefits is the possibility that they would *increase* SSDI expenditures by inducing program entry by people who currently choose work instead of SSDI participation. To see the issue, consider the hypothetical individual above who had predisability earnings of $50,000 and residual earnings capacity of $30,000. Under current rules, if she works and earns $30,000, she does not qualify for SSDI benefits. If she does not work, she may qualify, depending on her impairments, age, and vocational background. If successful, she would receive *full* SSDI benefits, or approximately $15,000 on average. But if she were awarded partial benefits of 40 percent, she would receive $6,000 in SSDI benefits in addition to $30,000 from employment. The individual is financially better off under partial benefits, which allow her to combine employment with SSDI receipt for a total income of $36,000. But the SSDI system saves money only if she would have received full benefits under current rules. It loses money if she would have worked.[36]

Nonetheless, this risk could be managed with careful analysis to determine optimal program parameters (e.g., the ceiling on insurable earnings). Indeed, recent research finds that a system of partial benefits would *reduce* disability expenditures on net (Yin 2015). On one hand, more people would apply for benefit support when partial benefits are available than when only full benefits are available. But these increases in caseload and costs are more than offset by two factors. First, some new beneficiaries who would receive full benefits under the current system would receive partial benefits instead.[37] Second, even though the SSDI caseload would increase, the expected program duration at full benefits would shorten since transitions to full benefits are postponed to later in life, and the total years spent receiving full benefits decrease on average (Yin 2015). Other important concerns are administrative complexity and the need to process more applicants than under the current system. While these are real concerns, partial benefits implemented along with several of the administrative simplifications noted above would help to offset the added complexity.[38]

Because partial benefits allow beneficiaries to work, they complement and even enhance other proposed SSDI reforms. For example, partial benefits and the generalized benefit offset both provide for reduced benefits with employment, but partial benefits are established at entitlement while the generalized benefit offset allows further flexibility during the postentitlement period. Together they deliver incentive-compatible programmatic flexibility; they combine formal disability assessment with an incentive for individuals to reveal their true work capacity at a given point in time by allowing them to self-select into higher work activity. But because SSDI eligibility is maintained at the last established level, beneficiaries are not penalized if they are no longer able to sustain employment at higher levels or if they are laid off. Individuals whose conditions worsen would have a right to be reassessed for a higher disability rating through a medical CDR. Another example would be a pairing of partial benefits with an early intervention system of integrated employment and eligibility services (see, e.g., Stapleton, Ben-Shalom, and Mann 2016), which would emphasize rehabilitation and supported work attempts with the goal of increasing employment to the degree possible while maintaining access to the SSDI safety net.

Other possible reforms

Making employers put skin in the game. SSDI's work incentives are misaligned not only for disabled workers (many of whom work less than they are able), but also for employers. Although employers are required by law to provide reasonable accommodation to employees with disabilities, accommodation can be costly, and firms pay no penalty should their employees enter the SSDI program instead. Several reforms have been proposed to make employers internalize the costs of not accommodating their employees. These include requiring employers to cover the cost of SSDI benefit payments during the first two years, as is currently done in the Netherlands (Fichtner and Seligman 2019); requiring employers to provide temporary disability insurance to their workers (Autor and Duggan 2010); and introducing experience rating through the payroll tax system (Burkhauser and Daly 2011).

All these proposals would make employers internalize costs they do not currently bear. But there are at least three reasons for caution. First, by making employers cover costs associated with a worker becoming disabled, firms may avoid hiring workers with disabilities or those who might plausibly become disabled.[39] Detrimental effects on hiring have been attributed to the employer-responsibility policy in the Netherlands (Hullegie and Koning 2015; Koning and Lindeboom 2015), although not to antidiscrimination laws in the United States that have required employers to provide reasonable accommodations to employees with disabilities (Neumark, Song, and Button 2017).

Second, the idea of experience rating is rooted in an economic theory that implies employers whose former employees enter SSDI at a relatively high rate should pay higher SSDI payroll taxes (or "premiums") than those who send employees at relatively low rates. Experience rating is used in insurance settings and in state workers' compensation systems. For experience rating to work, there needs to be enough pooling of individuals with high and low disability risks within firms to promote a stable system. The system breaks down if the high-risk types cluster in the same firms, while the low-risk types cluster in different firms. As firms have evolved in recent years, workplaces have become more fissured, with support occupations clustered in subcontractor firms (Weil 2014). Further research is needed to assess whether the structure of occupations within firms would support adequate risk-pooling. Last, SSDI is not the same as workers' compensation, where employers can control injury rates to some degree by improving workplace safety. It seems unlikely that employers could prevent disability onsets that arise from genetic predisposition or environmental factors beyond the workplace, and accommodation may be unreasonably costly for some kinds of disabilities in some work settings.

Early interventions to promote return-to-work. Currently, people with disabilities do not have access to federally financed vocational rehabilitation services until after they are awarded SSDI benefits. People who are denied benefits never receive such federal support. Intervention after the long SSDI application process comes too late for many and misses earlier opportunities to restore work capacity, develop transferable skills, or identify potential accommodations while the individual may still be attached to an employer.

Several have proposed reforms designed to take advantage of opportunities for early intervention, in the hopes of avoiding (or at least delaying) SSDI entry. In general, early intervention would complement partial benefits, since efforts would be made to restore as much work capacity as possible while the individual was still partially employed. In addition, the new work capacity assessment system could be used to identify specific areas where work capacity could be generated or restored. Stapleton, Ben-Shalom, and Mann (2016) propose an integrated employment/eligibility services (EES) system where once a worker experiences a serious medical condition, she would undergo triage and be fast-tracked to either SSDI benefits, employment supports, or neither benefits nor supports. The triage decision would be based on the severity of the condition and the individual's work history. If the individual is assigned supports, she would only be awarded SSDI benefits if she attempted to return to work but was unable to do so, even with the work supports. The EES system differs from the current system by providing individuals with work supports quickly after the onset of their medical condition, *before* an SSDI determination is made.

Similarly, Christian, Wickizer, and Burton (2019) propose a Health and Work Service (HWS) that would coordinate various resources and supports—such as referrals for specialized services and creation of a stay-at-work and return-to-work (SAW/RTW) plan—for individuals who experience a serious medical condition. The goal is to provide these supports as soon as a week after the onset of the work disability. Additionally, there is empirical evidence for the effectiveness of the HWS. The HWS is partly modeled on the Centers of Occupational Health and Education (COHE) in Washington State, which reduced long-term work disability for workers with musculoskeletal injuries by 30 percent (Wickizer, Franklin, and Fulton-Kehoe 2018). Moreover, early intervention efforts might also be particularly effective for mental health disorders, in part compensating for the wide variation in mental health service availability across states (Manchester 2019).

Yet another way to keep individuals connected to the labor force after onset of a work disability is to offer transitional jobs, as Kerksick, Riemer, and Williams (2016) propose. Under this system, both SSDI applicants and current beneficiaries would have an opportunity to work in subsidized, wage-paying jobs tailored to their work capacity. These jobs would pay an amount greater than the benefit amount (e.g., the authors propose $10 per hour) to encourage uptake. The authors further propose modifying the Earned Income Tax Credit to increase the credit for workers without children and who are unmarried—a subpopulation that makes up a large portion of individuals with disabilities. Both proposals would increase the incentive to work and keep applicants more connected to the labor force to prevent deterioration of skills.

Temporary benefits. Making SSDI benefits temporary for all new beneficiaries has been proposed as a way to limit long-term dependence by those who might benefit from return-to-work interventions (Fichtner and Seligman 2016, 2019). Under a temporary benefits scheme, all new beneficiaries would receive SSDI benefits for a time-limited period (e.g., two years), during which time they would receive rehabilitation and other return-to-work interventions, such as the early interventions described above. At the end of the temporary benefit period, all beneficiaries would be reassessed to determine their eligibility for long-term benefits. Long-term benefits would not be time limited. Temporary benefits would complement a system of partial long-term benefits, so that those who recover partial work capacity can transition to partial benefit support and partial work (Fichtner and Seligman 2016, 2019). Temporary benefits can also be paired with employer responsibility requirements, such as a requirement that employers finance the temporary benefit period. However, in this case, the same cautions apply about the risks of creating hiring disincentives or destabilizing employers with many high-risk workers.

$1-for-$2 benefit offset. The "benefit offset" proposal is less creation of a work incentive than it is weakening of an existing work disincentive. Instead of losing their entire benefit when their earnings exceed the SGA level, beneficiaries would lose $1 in benefits for every $2 in earnings above an earnings disregard amount.[40] Although, this implicit 50 percent marginal tax rate on earnings is much less than the astronomically high implicit tax rate associated with the current cash cliff, it nonetheless represents a substantial tax on earnings.

Of all the disability reforms that have been proposed, the $1-for-$2 benefit offset has been studied the most (per congressional mandate), first during the decade-long BOND Project and currently through the Promoting Opportunity Demonstration. As noted above, a weakness of the standard benefit offset policy is that applicants still have to demonstrate that they are fully disabled by not working during their application period; the inducement to reengage in work comes after benefits are awarded, which is too late for many. Perhaps not surprisingly, the BOND showed no positive employment effects (Gubits et al. 2018). A generalized benefit offset (Gokhale 2015) is an appealing alternative, but it should be paired with a partial benefit scheme that would allow applicants to continue working during the application process (see Proposal #2). Otherwise, it too is likely to target individuals too long after they have left the labor market.

Conclusion

The reforms proposed here are not about requiring SSDI beneficiaries to work. Rather, their intention is to encourage people who retain work capacity to work while they maintain complementary SSDI support in the amount needed, for as long as it is needed, and with the flexibility to adjust to changes in beneficiary health and employment prospects over time.

In this article, I have proposed two interrelated reforms. First, I propose SSDI eliminate the outdated and incomplete "grid" framework for assessing disability. In its place would be a new system that would measure residual functional capacity across an array of multidimensional abilities and would make use of this information to identify potential new jobs and estimate potential earnings.

Second, I propose that partial benefits be offered to applicants who have partial disabilities. Residual earnings capacity would be assessed during the application process, using my proposed work capacity measurement system. Those with partial earnings capacity would receive a partial benefit proportional to their lost earnings capacity. Applicants who have lost their entire earnings capacity would continue to receive full benefits, as they would currently. Importantly, any applicant could apply for SSDI benefits while still working to whatever degree they are able. Beneficiaries would be reassessed regularly to ensure continuing medical eligibility for SSDI and to adjust their disability rating up or down as needed. SSDI entitlement would continue until beneficiaries age out of the program or are found to no longer be medically eligible. A generalized benefit offset—which features a true work incentive unlike the standard benefit offset—would further enhance the proposed partial benefits scheme by providing all beneficiaries (both full and partial) with *postentitlement* flexibility to further increase work effort when employment opportunities arise.

Notes

1. Liebman (2015) argues the case was never primarily a fiscal one because SSDI's share of GDP grew by only 0.13 percent in the 30 years preceding the Great Recession—far slower than the SSDI caseload.

2. SSDI payroll taxes are collected under FICA, the Federal Insurance Contributions Act. Self-employed individuals are responsible for the entire tax amount (12.4 percent of taxable earnings up to an annual limit), while wage-and-salary workers split the payments evenly with their employers.

3. One work credit is earned for every $1,360 in earnings (in 2019), and a maximum of four credits may be earned each year. Those who become disabled at ages 31 to 42 are insured for SSDI if they have accrued 5 years' worth of work credits and at least half the credits were earned in the most recent 10-year period. Those who become disabled before age 31 need fewer credits to be insured, while those disabled after 42 need more. The maximum number of credits required is forty, for individuals age 62 or older. The minimum number is six, for individuals younger than 24. The requirement that credits be earned recently does not apply to individuals with statutory blindness.

4. The SGA threshold is higher for statutorily blind individuals ($2,040 in 2019).

5. This stands in contrast with state workers' compensation systems and disability insurance systems in many other countries that provide partial benefits for partial disabilities.

6. These medical criteria are the same as those used by the Supplemental Security Income (SSI) Program, the means-tested disability insurance program for individuals with low incomes and minimal work history.

7. The nine months of the trial work period may be nonconsecutive and are followed by a three-month grace period, before benefits are suspended.

8. Although cash benefits are suspended, Medicare benefits are maintained for 93 months. After this period ends, Medicare benefits may be continued under buy-in provisions. Some states offer premium assistance through Medicaid.

9. The 1980 amendments also included performance standards to improve decisional consistency among adjudicators at the initial and appellate levels.

10. Other notable changes by SSA included a ruling in 2015 that all evidence relating to a disability claim must be submitted—including unfavorable evidence, and, in 2017, elimination of the long-standing rule that the treating physician's opinion should carry the most weight.

11. See Fichtner and Seligman (2019, 4) for further information about the payroll tax reallocation legislated in the Bipartisan Budget Act of 2015 (Pub. L. No. 114-74, 129 Stat. 584).

12. This is largely the time period examined by Autor and Duggan (2003).

13. It is difficult to precisely identify the relative contribution of economic factors from Leibman's (2015) analysis for two reasons. First, the effects of the business cycle on the SSDI program are held constant by the inclusion of the annual unemployment rate as a control variable. Other research demonstrates the importance of cyclical effects (see, e.g., Black, Daniel, and Sanders 2002; Charles, Li, and Stephens 2018; Maestas, Mullen, and Strand 2018). Second, the effects of (noncyclical) economic conditions are not estimated separately but are captured by the portion of the disability incidence rate that is not explained by the demographic factors. The "disability incidence rate" is not the incidence of disability in the working-age population but, following SSA convention, the incidence of *SSDI award* in the working-age population.

14. Labor force nonparticipation by males 45 to 54 rose from 4.2 percent to 8.4 percent between 1948 and 1976 (Parsons 1980).

15. Von Wachter, Song, and Manchester (2011) corroborated Bound's (1989) estimate in more recent data.

16. French and Song (2014) obtain a similar estimate using the award propensities of disability judges who hear appeals of initial denials. Specifically, employment among SSDI beneficiaries would be 26 to 48 percentage points higher in the absence of SSDI receipt (Maestas, Mullen and Strand 2013; French and Song 2014; Autor et al. 2015).

17. Unfortunately, the available evidence does not reveal what specific types of work these individuals could perform, only what they could potentially earn in the absence of SSDI.

18. These program-induced losses in employability occur in addition to losses arising from the disability itself.

19. The same is true for federally financed vocational rehabilitation services; individuals become eligible for these services only *after* they are awarded SSDI benefits.

20. SSA's Listing of Impairments includes over one hundred impairments, such as serious and persistent depressive disorders, major dysfunction of a joint, inflammatory bowel disease with obstructions, epilepsy, chronic kidney disease with impairment of kidney function, and metastatic cancers. For the complete list, see https://www.ssa.gov/disability/professionals/bluebook/AdultListings.htm.

21. According to SSA, transferable skills are "skilled or semi-skilled work activities done in past work that can be used to meet the requirements of skilled or semi-skilled work activities of other jobs or kinds of work. This depends largely on the similarity of occupationally significant work activities among different jobs. Transferability is most probable and meaningful among jobs in which (i) the same or a lesser degree of skill is required; (ii) the same or similar tools and machines are used; and (iii) the same or similar raw materials, products, processes or services are involved" (SSA 2018a).

22. See also Warshawsky and Marchand (2015) for a detailed review of the grid's many limitations.

23. The grid is calibrated to the number of unskilled jobs in the national economy because it is used when the applicant can no longer perform "vocationally relevant" occupations. Unskilled jobs require no particular skills, training, or education.

24. The DOT was replaced by the Occupational Information network (O°NET). O°NET collects occupational information through national surveys of workers who self-report about their job requirements. O°NET has less occupational coverage than the DOT.

25. Specifically, the grid takes account of strength available for sitting, standing, walking, lifting, carrying, pushing, and pulling (SSA 2018b).

26. The nonexertional capacities consist of postural and manipulative abilities, vision, hearing or speaking abilities, tolerance for environmental exposures, and the mental requirements of unskilled work (defined as ability to understand, carry out, and remember simple instructions, make simple decisions, respond appropriately to supervision, coworkers and work situations, and deal with routine changes).

27. SSA's disability criteria ("unable to do any job in the national economy") does not take account of local job availability. That said, the grid rules are based on the notion that a given alternative job should be reasonably prevalent across the national economy.

28. The WD-FAB domains are Basic Mobility, Upper Body Function, Fine Motor Function, Community Mobility, Communication and Cognition, Mood and Emotions, Resilience and Sociability, and Self-Regulation.

29. Countries with partial benefit provisions include Sweden, the Netherlands, Finland, Norway, Germany, Switzerland, Czech Republic, Greece, Hungary, Korea, France, Poland, Portugal, Spain (Yin 2015), Japan (Mitra 2008), and Slovenia (OECD 2016).

30. With a ceiling on insurable earnings set at 5 × SGA, the disability rating would be ([1 − residual earnings capacity ÷ min{predisability earnings, 5 × SGA}] × 100) percent.

31. As Fichtner and Seligman (2016) put it, beneficiaries would have a right to due process that guarantees a timely CDR.

32. Elimination of work CDRs will be tested under SSA's planned Work Incentive Simplification Pilot (WISP).

33. Indefinite continuation of Medicare coverage will be tested by WISP. Current law already provides for extended Medicare eligibility for at least 93 months (7.75 years) after SSDI benefits are suspended for work activity.

34. Requiring employers to be the primary insurer would tend to disincentivize hiring because individuals with disabilities have relatively high medical expenditures.

35. Research is currently under way that may shed light on the value of such simplifications. The Promoting Opportunity Demonstration, which is testing a $1 for $2 benefit offset without a Trial Work Period or Extended Period of Eligibility, includes one treatment arm in which beneficiaries maintain entitlement indefinitely no matter how long their benefits are suspended due to work. The other treatment arm terminates entitlement after 12 consecutive months of fully suspended benefits.

36. Although she would earn more from employment than SSDI participation under current rules, other factors influence claiming decisions, such as whether her employer would allow her to work part time, whether she would qualify for employer-sponsored health insurance, the probability of future layoff, and her disutility of work (often a function of pain).

37. For humanitarian reasons, partial benefits should be considered for new beneficiaries, with current beneficiaries grandfathered in. This would extend the period of transition to the program's new steady-state size.

38. WISP will test similar simplifications of work incentive rules. Like this partial benefits proposal, the Promoting Opportunity Demonstration is testing elimination of the Trial Work Period and Extended Period of Eligibility.

39. One way to offset a negative hiring effect of payroll tax penalties would be to include payroll tax *discounts* to employers who hire (or retain) disabled workers (Fichtner and Seligman 2019).

40. The disregard amount can be the SGA level (as was tested by the BOND) or another level. The Promoting Opportunity Demonstration is testing a disregard amount that is less than SGA (either an amount equal to the beneficiary's impairment-related work expenses or $810 in 2016).

References

Autor, David H., and Mark G. Duggan. 2003. The rise in the disability rolls and the decline in unemployment. *Quarterly Journal of Economics* 118 (1): 157–206.

Autor, David H., and Mark G. Duggan. 2006. The growth in the Social Security Disability rolls: A fiscal crisis unfolding. *Journal of Economic Perspectives* 20 (3): 71–96.

Autor, David H., and Mark G. Duggan. 2010. *Supporting work: A proposal for modernizing the U.S. disability insurance system.* Washington, DC: Center for American Progress and The Hamilton Project.

Autor, David H., Nicole Maestas, Kathleen J. Mullen, and Alexander Strand. 2015. Does delay cause decay? The effect of administrative decision time on the labor force participation and earnings of disability applicants. NBER Working Paper no. w20840, National Bureau of Economic Research, Cambridge, MA.

Benitez-Silva, Hugo, Moshe Buchinsky, and John Rust. 2004. How large are the classification errors in the Social Security Disability award process? NBER Working Paper no. w10219, National Bureau of Economic Research, Cambridge, MA.

Black, Dan, Kermit Daniel, and Seth Sanders. 2002. The impact of economic conditions on participation in disability programs: Evidence from the coal boom and bust. *American Economic Review* 92 (1): 27–50.

The Board of Trustees, Federal Old-Age and Survivors Insurance and Federal Disability Insurance Trust Funds (Board of Trustees). 2019. *The 2019 annual report of the Board of Trustees of the Federal Old-Age and Survivors Insurance and Federal Disability Insurance Trust Funds*. Washington, DC: Board of Trustees.

Bound, John. 1989. The health and earnings of rejected disability insurance applicants. *American Economic Review* 79 (3): 482–503.

Burkhauser, Richard V., and Mary Daly. 2011. *The declining work and welfare of people with disabilities: What went wrong and a strategy for change*. Washington, DC: AEI Press.

Chan, Leighton. 2018. The WD-FAB: Development and validation testing. Available from https://www.eumass.eu/wp-content/uploads/2018/03/Leighton-Porcino.pdf (accessed 24 May 2019).

Charles, Kerwin Kofi, Yiming Li, and Melvin Stephens Jr. 2018. Disability benefit take-up and local labor market conditions. *Review of Economics and Statistics* 100 (3): 416–23.

Christian, Jennifer, Thomas Wickizer, and Tim Burton. 2019. Implementing a community-focused Health and Work Service (HWS). Available from http://www.crfb.org/project/ssdi/developing-social-security-disability-ssdi-reform-demonstrations-improve-opportunities (accessed 13 May 2019).

Crimmins, Eileen M. 2015. Lifespan and healthspan: Past, present, and promise. *The Gerontologist* 55 (6): 901–11.

Deshpande, Manasi, Tal Gross, and Yalun Su. 2019. Disability and distress: The effect of disability programs on financial outcomes. NBER Working Paper no. w25642, National Bureau of Economic Research, Cambridge, MA.

Fichtner, Jason, and Jason Seligman. 2016. Beyond all or nothing: Reforming Social Security Disability Insurance to encourage work and wealth. In *SSDI solutions: Ideas to strengthen the Social Security Disability Insurance Program*, eds. Jim McCrery and Earl Pomeroy, 357–88. West Conshohocken, PA: Infinity Publishing.

Fichtner, Jason, and Jason Seligman. 2019. Developing Social Security Disability (SSDI) reform demonstrations to improve opportunities and outcomes based on lessons learned. Available from http://www.crfb.org/project/ssdi/developing-social-security-disability-ssdi-reform-demonstrations-improve-opportunities (accessed 13 May 2019).

Flood, Sarah, Miriam King, Renae Rodgers, Steven Ruggles, and J. Robert Warren. 2018. Integrated public use microdata series, Current Population Survey: Annual Social and Economic Supplement (1988–2018), version 6.0. Available from https://doi.org/10.18128/D030.V6.0 (accessed 8 May 2019).

French, Eric, and Jae Song. 2014. The effect of disability insurance receipt on labor supply. *American Economic Journal: Economic Policy* 6 (2): 291–337.

Gokhale, Jagadeesh. 2015. SSDI reform: Promoting return to work without compromising economic security. Wharton Public Policy Initiative Issue Brief 3.7, Wharton School, Philadelphia, PA.

Gruber, Jonathan. 2000. Disability insurance benefits and labor supply. *Journal of Political Economy* 108 (6): 1162–83.

Gubits, Daniel, David Stapleton, Stephen Bell, Michelle Wood, Denise Hoffman, Sarah Croake, David R. Mann, Judy Geyer, David Greenberg, Austin Nichols, Andrew McGuirk, Meg Carroll, Utsav Kattel, and David Judkins. 2018. *BOND implementation and evaluation: Final evaluation report*, vol. 1. Cambridge, MA: Mathematica Policy Research, for Social Security Administration.

Haveman, Robert H., and Barbara L. Wolfe. 1984a. The decline in male labor force participation: Comment. *Journal of Political Economy* 92 (3): 532–41.

Haveman, Robert H., and Barbara L. Wolfe. 1984b. Disability transfers and early retirement: A causal relationship? *Journal of Public Economics* 24 (1): 47–66.

Hennessey, John C., and L. Scott Muller. 1994. Work efforts of disabled-worker beneficiaries: Preliminary findings from the new beneficiary followup survey. *Social Security Bulletin* 57 (3): 42–51.

Hullegie, Patrick, and Pierre Koning. 2015. Employee health and employer incentives. IZA DP No. 9310, Institute of Labor Economics. Available from https://www.iza.org/publications/dp/9310/employee-health-and-employer-incentives.

Kearney, John R. 2005/2006. Social Security and the "D" in OASDI: The history of a federal program insuring earners against disability. *Social Security Bulletin* 66 (3). Available from https://www.ssa.gov/policy/docs/ssb/v66n3/v66n3p1.html.

Kerksick, Julie, David Riemer, and Conor Williams. 2016. Using transitional jobs to increase employment of SSDI applicants and beneficiaries. In *SSDI solutions: Ideas to strengthen the Social Security Disability Insurance Program*, eds. Jim McCrery and Earl Pomeroy. West Conshohocken, PA: Infinity Publishing.

Koning, Pierre, and Jan-Maarten Lindeboom. 2015. The rise and fall of disability insurance enrollment in the Netherlands. *Journal of Economic Perspectives* 29 (2): 151–72.

Liebman, Jeffrey B. 2015. Understanding the increase in disability insurance benefit receipt in the United States. *Journal of Economic Perspectives* 29 (2): 123–50.

Livermore, Gina, Arif Mamun, Jody Schimmel, and Sarah Prenovitz. 2013. *Executive summary of the Seventh Ticket to Work evaluation report*. Cambridge, MA: Mathematica Policy Research.

Low, Hamish, and Luigi Pistaferri. 2015. Disability insurance and the dynamics of the incentive insurance trade-off. *American Economic Review* 105 (10): 2986–3029.

Maestas, Nicole, Kathleen Mullen, and David Powell. 2016. The effect of population aging on economic growth, the labor force and productivity. NBER Working Paper no. w22452, National Bureau of Economic Research, Cambridge, MA.

Maestas, Nicole, Kathleen J. Mullen, and Alexander Strand. 2013. Does disability insurance receipt discourage work? Using examiner assignment to estimate causal effects of SSDI receipt. *American Economic Review* 103 (5): 1797–1829.

Maestas, Nicole, Kathleen Mullen, and Alexander Strand. 2018. The effect of economic conditions on the disability insurance program: Evidence from the Great Recession. NBER Working Paper no. w25338, National Bureau of Economic Research, Cambridge, MA.

Manchester, Joyce. 2019. Targeting early intervention based on health care utilization of SSDI beneficiaries by state, with emphasis on mental disorders and substance abuse. Available from http://www.crfb.org/project/ssdi/developing-social-security-disability-ssdi-reform-demonstrations-improve-opportunities (accessed 13 May 2019).

Marfeo, Elizabeth E., Stephen M. Haley, Alan M. Jette, Susan V. Eisen, Pengsheng Ni, Kara Bogusz, Mark Meterko, Christine M. McDonough, Leighton Chan, Diane E. Brandt, and Elizabeth K. Rasch. 2013. Conceptual foundation for measures of physical function and behavioral health function for Social Security work disability evaluation. *Archives of Physical Medicine and Rehabilitation* 94 (9): 1645–52.

Marfeo, Elizabeth E., Pengsheng Ni, Leighton Chan, Elizabeth K. Rasch, Christine M. McDonough, Diane E. Brandt, Kara Bogusz, and Alan M. Jette. 2015. Interpreting physical and behavioral health scores from new work disability instruments. *Journal of Rehabilitation Medicine* 47 (5): 394–402.

Mitnitski, Arnold B. 2018. Epigenetic biomarkers for biological age. In *Epigenetics of aging and longevity*, eds. Alexey Moskalev and Alexander M. Vaiserman, 153–70. London: Academic Press.

Mitra, Sophie. 2008. Temporary and partial disability programs in nine countries: What can the United States learn from other countries? *Journal of Disability Policy Studies* 20 (1): 14–27.

Muller, L. Scott. 1992. Disability beneficiaries who work and their experience under program work incentives. *Social Security Bulletin* 55.2.

Munnell, Alicia H., Katharine G. Abraham, David Autor, Jeffrey R. Brown, Peter Diamond, Claudia Goldin, Sam Gutterman, Michael S. Teitelbaum, Ronald R. Rindfuss, and Joseph J. Silvestri. 2015. *2015 technical panel on assumptions and methods: Report to the Social Security Advisory Board*. Washington, DC: Social Security Advisory Board.

Neumark, David, Joanne Song, and Patrick Button. 2017. Does protecting older workers from discrimination make it harder to get hired? Evidence from disability discrimination laws. *Research on Aging* 39 (1): 29–63.

OECD. 2016. Assuring work motivation and work incentives in the Slovenian benefit system. In *Connecting people with jobs: The labour market, activation policies and disadvantaged workers in Slovenia*. Paris: OECD Publishing.

Oeppen, Jim, and James Vaupel. 2002. Broken limits to life expectancy. *Science* 296 (5570): 1029–31.

Parsons, Donald O. 1980. The decline in male labor force participation. *Journal of Political Economy* 88 (1): 117–34.

Parsons, Donald O. 1991. The health and earnings of rejected disability insurance applicants: Comment. *American Economic Review* 81 (5): 1419–26.

Ray, Gerald K., and Jeffrey S. Lubbers. 2014. A government success story: How data analysis by the Social Security Appeals Council (with a push from the Administrative Conference of the United States) is transforming social security disability adjudication. *George Washington Law Review* 83:1575–1608.

Reno, Virginia P. 2011. Securing the future of Social Security Disability Insurance program. Available from https://www.nasi.org/research/2011/testimony-virginia-p-reno-securing-future-social-security-di (accessed 10 July 2019).

Smyth, Kristin. 2018. Observational collection compared to critical task threshold interview collection in the Occupational Requirements Survey. Available from https://www.bls.gov/ors/research/collection/pdf/observational-collection-compared-interview-2018.pdf (accessed 15 May 2019).

Social Security Administration (SSA). 2018a. 20 C.F.R. 404.1568: Skill requirements. Available from https://www.ssa.gov/OP_Home/cfr20/404/404-1568.htm (accessed 21 June 2019).

Social Security Administration (SSA). 2018b. 20 C.F.R. 404.1569a, 416.969a: Exertional and nonexertional limitations. Available from https://www.ssa.gov/OP_Home/cfr20/404/404-1569a.htm (accessed 21 June 2019).

Social Security Administration (SSA). 2018c. 20 C.F.R., Part 404, Subpart P, Appendix 2: Medical-vocational guidelines. Available from https://www.ssa.gov/OP_Home/cfr20/404/404-app-p02.htm (accessed 21 June 2019).

Social Security Administration (SSA). 2018d. Annual statistical report on the Social Security Disability Insurance Program, 2001–2017. Available from https://www.ssa.gov/policy/docs/statcomps/di_asr/ (accessed 26 April 2019).

Social Security Administration (SSA). 2018e. The facts about Social Security's Disability Program. Available from https://www.ssa.gov/disabilityfacts/materials/pdf/factsheet.pdf (accessed 27 February 2019).

Social Security Administration (SSA). n.d. Legislative history of the Social Security Disability Insurance Program. Available from https://www.ssa.gov/legislation/DI%20legislative%20history.pdf. (accessed 25 February 2019).

Social Security Administration, Office of the Inspector General. 2015. The Social Security Administration's listing of impairments, A-01-15-50022. Available from https://oig.ssa.gov/sites/default/files/audit/summary/pdf/Summary%2050022.pdf (accessed 5 March 2019).

Stapleton, David, Yonatan Ben-Shalom, and David Mann. 2016. The employment/eligibility service system: A new gateway for employment supports and social security disability benefits. In *SSDI solutions: Ideas to strengthen the Social Security Disability Insurance program*, eds. Jim McCrery and Earl Pomeroy, 51–82. West Conshohocken, PA: Infinity Publishing.

Sudharsanan, Nikkil, and David E. Bloom. 2018. The demography of aging in low-and middle-income countries: Chronological versus functional perspectives. In *Future directions for the demography of aging: Proceedings of a workshop*, eds. Mark D. Hayward and Malay K. Majmundar, 309–38. Washington, DC: National Academies Press.

U.S. Bureau of Labor Statistics (BLS). 2019a. Civilian employment level [CE16OV]. Available from https://fred.stlouisfed.org/series/CE16OV#0 (accessed 5 June 2019).

U.S. Bureau of Labor Statistics (BLS). 2019b. Civilian labor force [CLF16OV]. Available from https://fred.stlouisfed.org/series/CLF16OV (accessed 14 May 2019).

U.S. Bureau of Labor Statistics (BLS). 2019c. Occupational requirements survey: Handbook of methods. Available from https://www.bls.gov/opub/hom/ors/pdf/ors.pdf (accessed 5 June 2019).

von Wachter, Till, Jae Song, and Joyce Manchester. 2011. Trends in employment and earnings of allowed and rejected applicants to the Social Security Disability Insurance program. *American Economic Review* 101 (7): 3308–29.

Warshawsky, Mark J., and Ross A. Marchand. 2015. Modernizing the SSDI eligibility criteria: A reform proposal that eliminates the outdated medical-vocational grid. Mercatus Working Paper, George Mason University, Fairfax, VA.

Weil, David. 2014. *The fissured workplace: Why work became so bad for so many and what can be done to improve it*. Cambridge, MA: Harvard University Press.

Wickizer, Thomas M., Gary M. Franklin, and Deborah Fulton-Kehoe. 2018. Innovations in occupational health care delivery can prevent entry into permanent disability. *Medical Care* 56 (12): 1018–1123.

Yin, Na. 2015. Partial benefits in the Social Security Disability Insurance program. *Journal of Risk and Insurance* 82 (2): 463–504.

Unemployment Insurance Reform

The Unemployment Insurance (UI) system is the largest general social insurance program for working-age individuals in the United States and currently insures more than 140 million workers against temporary income losses related to unemployment. UI has been the bedrock of U.S. social policy in recessions, but the system has remained largely unchanged since the mid-1970s despite substantial changes in the labor market that include deindustrialization, higher female participation, increases in wage inequality, and technological changes. This article summarizes existing empirical evidence on the state of the UI system and its effectiveness in achieving its stated goals. A range of reform proposals are discussed that aim to address both the well-known, long-term issues with UI, as well as UI's readiness to support the workforce of the twenty-first century.

Keywords: unemployment insurance; experience rating; worker behavior; firm behavior

By
TILL VON WACHTER

The unemployment insurance (UI) program has been the bedrock of U.S. social policy in response to job loss and swings in unemployment during recessions. The UI program provides temporary benefits to employees who lost their job through no fault of their own. Individuals with a minimal degree of prior labor market attachment are insured but benefits are only a fraction of a worker's prior earnings.

Since its inception in the mid-1930s, the primary goals of the UI program have been to

Till von Wachter is a professor of economics at the University of California–Los Angeles, faculty director of the California Policy Lab, and associate dean for research of the Social Science Division. His research examines how labor market conditions affect the well-being of workers and the role of social insurance programs in buffering economic shocks.

NOTE: I thank Brenda Garcia Lemus for excellent and indispensable research assistance and the two editors of the special issue for helpful guidance. All remaining errors or omissions are my own.

Correspondence: tvwachter@econ.ucla.edu

DOI: 10.1177/0002716219885339

prevent declines in consumption of individuals who lose their jobs and their families without their having to spend down or liquidate their assets. In addition, the
program is meant to enable unemployed workers to find productive employment
rather than quickly take available lower-wage jobs. One important function of the
UI system is to also help unemployed workers continue to spend as a means of
automatically stabilizing the economy in hard-hit local labor markets.

The UI program is the largest social insurance program available to the general working-age population in the United States. As of the fourth quarter of
2018, the program provided monthly benefit payments to around 1.6 million
unemployed individuals. During the Great Recession in 2007 to 2008 and its
aftermath, the UI system saw a massive expansion of its program from a duration
of six months to as long as two years, and it provided benefits to more than 10
million individuals (see Vroman 2011).

Despite important secular changes in the labor market over the last decades,
the core UI program has remained relatively unchanged since the mid-twentieth
century, with little reforms since the 1980s, with the exception of a brief reform
push in the course of the American Recovery and Reinvestment Act (ARRA). In
the face of an evolving labor market and difficulties of the UI system during the
Great Recession, including delays in approving benefit extensions and funding
shortfalls, an increasing number of observers have called for a systemic approach
to reforming UI. Absent such a system-wide approach, in the aftermath of the
Great Recession, several states have begun to cut UI benefits and UI durations
to address recent financing shortfalls of their UI state programs.

Some of the potential issues in the UI system have been well known to policy-
makers and researchers alike. On one hand, as with any program involving both
conditional benefits and taxation, the UI system has been shown to affect employment decisions of both workers and employers. While the value of the insurance
provided is usually found to outweigh such costs, these considerations are relevant
for setting the right parameters of the system. On the other hand, problems of
solvency of the UI state trust funds have plagued the UI system, especially in the
aftermath of larger recessions, highlighting the need to address the financing of
the system and the state-federal partnership embedded in the UI program.

This article provides an overview of the UI program as it stands today and
summarizes some of the main reform proposals put forward to address the various issues that the system is facing. These deal with, among others, whether the
current UI program adequately supports a workforce that has undergone substantial changes in recent decades, including a higher female labor force participation rate, increased inequality, deindustrialization and the rise of service jobs,
ongoing technological changes, and the recent rise in contract work. Reform
proposals also address concerns over states' ad hoc benefit reductions to address
financing needs, as well as the current way in which the UI program is extended
in recessions to account for rising unemployment. I also discuss extensions of the
UI system that have been proposed to address the large costs of layoffs through
temporary wage subsidies, sometimes called job sharing, and options to keep
some of the benefits as workers resettle into initially lower-paying jobs. I do not
provide a thorough analysis of proposals to replace the UI program as a whole,

such as Universal Basic Income or Unemployment Savings Accounts, but I do discuss them in the conclusion.

An Overview of the UI Program and Its Effect on Behavior

UI in the United States is a federal-state unemployment compensation system that was established in 1935 by the Social Security Act.[1] The system was designed to provide partial temporary compensation to workers who become unemployed through no fault of their own and to serve as an economic stabilizer during economic recessions.[2] Workers quitting a job on their own are not eligible, with some exceptions (see National Employment Law Project [NELP] 2012).[3] The program requires applicants to demonstrate a work history as measured in terms of past wages or prior weeks of work (NELP 2012). The prior work is typically measured by the amount of earnings received in a base period. While this differs by state, the typical state requires a minimal amount of earnings in four of five calendar quarters prior to job loss.[4] As a result, labor market entrants or workers with unstable earnings histories are not typically eligible for UI. To receive benefits, beneficiaries must be actively seeking work. Most states set a maximum benefit period of 26 weeks; however, the federal government provides ad hoc extended benefits through times of high unemployment. During periods of severe economic hardship such as throughout the Great Recession, Congress approved federally funded supplemental benefits to further extend the benefit period. As of the end of fiscal year 2018, around 142.7 million workers were covered by the unemployment compensation program and $29.3 billion of benefits were paid.[5] During the peak of the Great Recession, the regular UI benefits more than doubled from $31 billion in 2007 to $72 billion in 2009.[6] However, as further discussed below, typically less than half of the unemployed receive UI benefits.

These state-level unemployment compensation systems are administered by the states within a general framework set by federal law.[7] As a result, the eligibility and benefit terms, along with the financing structure, greatly vary by state as each has the flexibility to design its own program within general federal requirements. For example, Hawaii's UI maximum weekly benefit amount is $619 compared to $454 in Texas.[8] In addition, the duration of the benefits varies by state. Many states have 26 weeks of maximum duration, but for instance, in Florida, the maximum duration of benefits ranges from 12 to 23 weeks depending on the state's unemployment rate; whereas in Missouri, the maximum duration is set at 13 weeks.[9] States can also set the earnings history and the type of job moves that determine eligibility. As a result, for example, low-income or younger workers with limited earnings histories may be eligible for UI in some states but not in others. Similarly, the so-called State Unemployment Tax Act (SUTA) tax rate and the tax base vary across states. The key functions of the federal government are to provide broad guidelines on administering the program, inspect state performance, offer technical assistance, determine funding requirements, ensure compliance with state law, and hold and invest the money provided by the states in the unemployment trust fund.[10]

In recessions, the duration of UI benefits is typically extended. This occurs either through a jointly financed Extended Benefit (EB) program, or a federally financed Emergency Unemployment Compensation (EUC) program. These programs are further discussed in detail in the next section.

Program financing: Experience rating and reserve ratios

While the state-federal UI system allows states to set their own financing structures, nearly all states fund their programs through employer payroll taxes. The U.S. Treasury manages the state-level trust fund accounts and ensures compliance with federal guidelines. Currently, the states determine UI tax rates based on each employer's history of layoffs, also known as an "experience rating." Under a full-cost experience rating, each firm would incur a tax rate accurately reflecting its past layoffs. Currently, states set a maximum rate on payroll tax schedules, leading to so-called imperfect experience rating.

Currently, states use one of the following four formulas that capture some form of experience rating to determine payroll taxes: the reserve ratio, benefit ratio, benefit-wage ratio, or payroll decline. The Employment Development Department (EDD) in California uses the reserve ratio formula, which is equal to the reserve account balance of a firm divided by the average base payroll.[11] The reserve account balance captures the prior reserve balance of a firm's insurance account plus the interest rate earned by the account minus the amount of UI benefits paid to former employees. The reserve ratio is then used to determine the UI tax rate based on the contribution schedule defined by the EDD.[12] I return to this point below.

In addition to taxes levied by the states, the UI system is also financed at the federal level based on the 6 percent Federal Unemployment Tax Act (FUTA) tax rate on wages up to $7,000, where some employers receive credits of up to 5.4 percent under an approved state unemployment compensation program.[13] The federal funds are used to fund administrative costs, the share of federal extended benefits, advances paid to states, and benefits under federal supplemental or emergency programs.[14]

During the Great Recession, the unemployment compensation system faced serious challenges, as states started to borrow from the federal government to pay benefits (Vroman et al. 2017). The unemployment compensation system continues to be out of balance, as payroll taxes are not indexed to provide sufficient benefits and revenues over time (Balducchi et al. 2018). Consequently, during economic downturns, states are faced with the choice of either borrowing funds from the federal government or reducing the generosity of the benefits (Balducchi et al. 2018). In addition, states continue to use imperfect experience rating formulas to collect payroll taxes from employers, even though this has been shown to lead to more layoffs and distorted incentives for unstable firms (Rejda and Rosenbaum 1990). While the unemployment compensation system is in need of reform to address the vitality of the system in future recessions, the federal government has failed to modernize the system since the 1970s via the passage of newer federal guidelines.

FIGURE 1
Overview of Individuals Claiming Unemployment Insurance Benefits,
by Year and Program Type

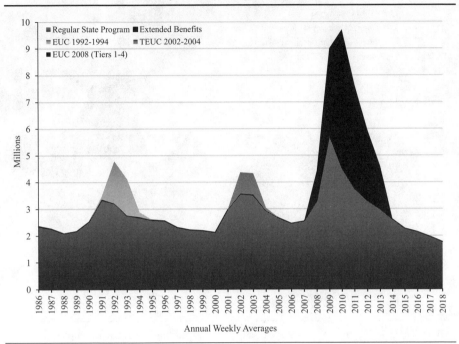

Annual Weekly Averages

SOURCE: U.S. Department of Labor data. See https://oui.doleta.gov/unemploy/Data
Dashboard.asp.
NOTE: EUC = Emergency Unemployment Compensation; TEUC = Temporary Extended
Unemployment Compensation.

Basic trends in the UI program

Figure 1 shows the number of individuals claiming UI benefits under different programs, as measured by the annual average over weekly claims. The regular state UI program provides the vast majority of benefits. In times of economic distress, Congress has approved a series of emergency UI programs to provide additional federally funded benefits to claimants across the country. This practice began during the large recessions in the mid-1970s and early 1980s and continued with the EUC program during the Great Recession.[15] The EUC program started in July 2008 and ended in December 2013. This was the longest emergency UI program approved by Congress, providing coverage for up to 99 weeks, compared to 56 weeks during the 1982 recession.[16]

The EUC program was rolled out in four tiers, where each tier provided additional benefit weeks. Under tier 1, the EUC program provided an additional 14 weeks of benefits in all states; whereas in tiers 2–4, the benefits were only provided to states with high unemployment rates.[17] The EUC program had to be approved by Congress under each tier, which led to much-discussed delays in approval and lapses in coverage, among other problems. The federal-state EB UI

FIGURE 2
Unemployed Workers Served by the Unemployment Insurance System, by Year

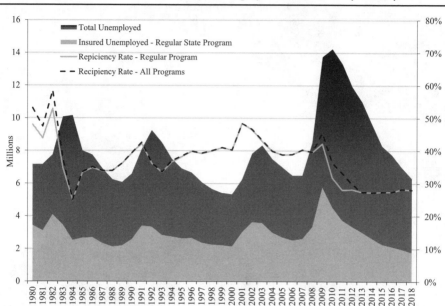

Annual Quarterly Averages

SOURCE: U.S. Department of Labor data. See https://oui.doleta.gov/unemploy/data_sum
mary/DataSum.asp.

program grants benefits to those who reside in a state experiencing high unemployment.[18] The EB program was approved under the Federal-State Extended
Unemployment Compensation Act of 1970.[19] Given that the payments in the EB
program are partially funded by the states, the program has been used sparingly
in recent recessions.

Figure 2 shows the number of total unemployed workers compared to those
who claim benefits from the UI system. The recipiency rate measures the number of unemployed individuals receiving UI benefits across all programs as a
percentage of the total number of unemployed, whether insured by the program
or not.[20] The graph shows that a vast portion of unemployed individuals do not
receive UI benefits (see also Vroman 2009). After falling in the early 1980s, the
recipiency rate has been trending down again since the end of the Great
Recession and is now below 30 percent.

Figure 3 shows how the recipiency rate varies substantially by state. For
instance, New Jersey has a much higher recipiency rate compared to North
Carolina. This is a result of different eligibility criteria set by each state, where
some states set much stricter criteria than others. In addition, the differences
may capture different application rates across states. Overall, it is clear that the
current unemployment insurance system highly varies by state, leading to differences in coverage of unemployed workers and benefits.

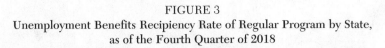

FIGURE 3
Unemployment Benefits Recipiency Rate of Regular Program by State,
as of the Fourth Quarter of 2018

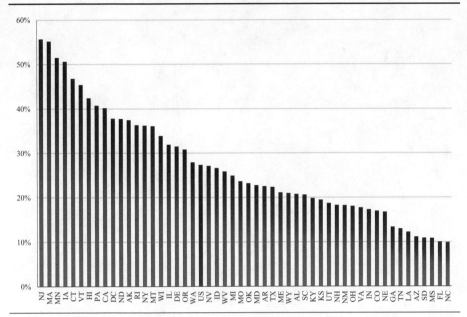

SOURCE: U.S. Department of Labor data. See https://oui.doleta.gov/unemploy/data_sum
mary/DataSum.asp.

Figure 4 displays the number of exhaustions of regular UI benefits over time. As depicted in the figure, a large number of unemployed workers exhausted their benefits during the peak of the Great Recession. Generally, exhaustions of regular benefits tend to peak during recessionary periods and then level down during economic expansions. Partly in response, the U.S. Congress has typically passed ad hoc emergency UI programs during recessions to provide additional benefits to those who have exhausted their regular benefits.

Figure 5 provides an example of a tax schedule set under a system of experience rating. For instance, in California, the reserve ratio is a function of the amount of benefits paid out to prior laid-off employees, which reflects the experience rating built into the system.[21] Then, depending on the overall schedule that is based on the solvency of the state fund, the employer's specific tax rate reflects its reserve ratio. Consequently, those employers with a stronger history of layoffs will face a higher tax rate compared to those with fewer layoffs. Most states use a system based on an imperfect experience rating to determine each employer's tax rate, as discussed in more detail in the section that follows.

Effects on the economy and worker and firm behavior

One of the key objectives of the UI system in the United States is to serve as an economic stabilizer during recessions. The UI benefits smooth consumption

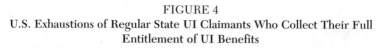

FIGURE 4
U.S. Exhaustions of Regular State UI Claimants Who Collect Their Full
Entitlement of UI Benefits

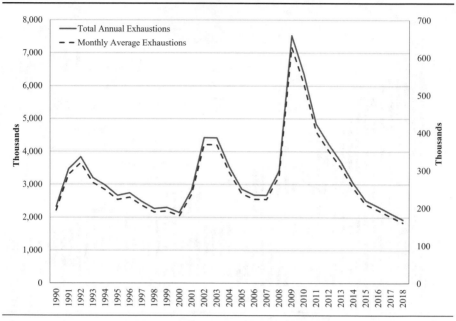

SOURCE: U.S. Department of Labor data. See https://oui.doleta.gov/unemploy/chartbook
.asp.

during the period of initial job loss and do not permanently impact consumption
levels. For instance, empirical research shows that food consumption decreases
by 7 percent when the main breadwinner becomes unemployed; however, in the
absence of UI benefits, that decrease would have been a substantial 22 percent
(Gruber 1994). As a result, the system serves as a consumption buffer during job
loss. The UI system also serves as an economic stimulus by partially replacing lost
income and mitigating reductions in consumption due to job loss (Orszag 2001).
At least one study has found that economic recessions, as measured by GDP in
real terms, would have been up to 15 percent worse in the absence of the UI
system (Chimerine et al. 1999).

At the same time, economists have long been concerned that UI benefits may
lead unemployed workers to stay out of work longer, as they reduce the relative
value of employment. A long and ongoing empirical literature has indeed shown
that both higher UI benefits and longer-benefit durations lead employees to stay
out of the workforce for a longer period of time (e.g., Solon 1979; Moffitt 1985;
Katz and Meyer 1990; Krueger and Meyer 2002, Schmieder and von Wachter
2016). Two important hurdles in studying whether UI benefits have this effect are
that measures of total duration of nonemployment are typically not available, and
identifying variation comes from recession-induced benefit expansions. Recent
studies suggest the effect of recent UI expansions during the Great Recession had

FIGURE 5

Example of California's Experience Rating Tax Schedule Tax Rate Determined by the Reserve Ratio and the Solvency of the System

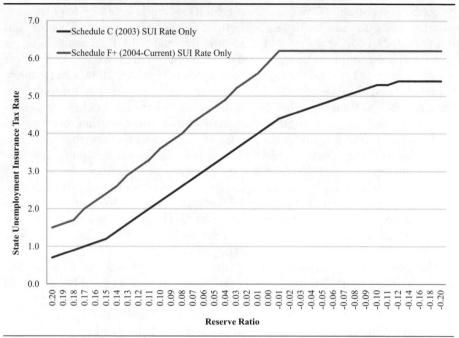

precisely estimated but moderate negative effects on unemployment duration (e.g., Rothstein 2011; Valletta 2014; Farber and Valletta 2015; Kroft and Notowidigdo 2016).[22]

A key question is whether these reductions are indeed a cost to society. Among others, this depends on whether access to UI benefits relaxes preexisting income constraints, rather than reduces the value of working, and whether they allow workers to find better jobs. The first question depends to an important extent on whether individuals are credit constrained, and this has been difficult to assess because of a lack of widely available data on assets. Chetty (2008) estimates that the effects of UI benefits on labor supply are to an important degree nondistortionary income effects in addition to being distortionary substitution effects due to a lower incentive to look for work. The second question has been hard to answer in the United States because of a lack of larger longitudinal datasets on the unemployed. In countries where such data are available, longer UI durations tend to lead to zero or small negative effects (e.g., Schmieder, von Wachter, and Bender 2016), though this may depend on the duration of unemployment (e.g., Nekoei and Weber 2017). While research on these questions of interpretation is still ongoing, it is likely that a program such as UI has some behavioral consequences that need to be considered when addressing potential reforms of the system.

Based on these fundamental trade-offs, researchers have developed a conceptual framework for assessing the optimal amount and duration of UI benefits. Current estimates of this framework suggest that average replacement rates at or below 50 percent and 26 weeks' benefit durations are likely to be *too low* compared to the optimum levels (e.g., Chetty 2008; Schmieder, von Wachter, and Bender 2012). In the conceptual framework, the value of UI payments in terms of reduced consumption losses as workers become unemployed are traded off against any costs from providing the insurance (e.g., Bailey 1984; Chetty 2008; Schmieder and von Wachter 2016). Since workers effectively pay for their own benefits through their contributions to the system, these costs consist of behavioral distortions deriving from reductions in labor supply, either because UI benefits lead workers to take longer to search for jobs or because they work less once employed in response to higher UI tax rates.[23] The empirical implementation of this framework typically relies on estimates of the effects of UI benefit payments on labor supply and on consumption. For benefit levels, two separate studies have confirmed that current UI benefit levels are likely to be too low (Chetty 2008; Kroft and Notowidigdo 2016). For UI benefit durations, Schmieder and von Wachter (2016) review the literature and conclude that at current benefit durations, a further increase would improve worker well-being.

The conceptual framework for evaluating the optimal level of benefit amounts and benefit durations at any given point in time has also been used to assess the extent to which UI benefits should be more generous during recessions. Findings based on this framework suggest that during recessions, UI benefits should indeed be given for longer periods of time and be more generous. The key question is again the trade-off between the benefit of consumption smoothing, that is, avoiding large reductions in consumption at unemployment, and any potential negative effect from a reduction in employment. Thereby, a key question in recessions is whether employment reductions of UI are smaller, because more workers compete for fewer jobs, or larger, because businesses have a harder time filling jobs because workers spend more time looking for better jobs. Since UI exhaustion rates typically rise substantially in recessions, there is an unambiguous rise in the benefit of extending UI durations. At the same time, the so-called efficiency costs of UI benefits tend to be either unchanged or smaller in recessions (e.g., Schmieder, von Wachter, and Bender 2012; Johnston and Mas 2018).

It is also well understood that employers' behavior can also be affected by the UI system. Per se, payroll taxes can impose a cost on hiring that depends on whether the incidence of the tax falls on workers, consumers, or the firm. Furthermore, research has shown that the experience rating feature of the UI tax system can affect employment decisions by affecting the cost of a layoff (e.g., Anderson and Meyer 1994). These potential responses are again relevant when evaluating different reform proposals. Finally, the financial health of the UI system is determined in part by the political process at the state level that is responsible for choosing the key parameters of the system. Hence, policy-makers' behavior and incentives can play an important role in the overall health of the system, but they have not yet been systematically analyzed.

Recent Reforms to the UI System

Federal reforms before ARRA

The latest major federal reform of the UI program took place as part of the Unemployment Compensation Amendments of 1976. The most significant change as part of the amendments was the expansion of the program to cover nearly all wage and salary workers in the United States (U.S. Congress 1976). In addition, Congress permitted the creation of the National Commission on Unemployment Compensation (NCUC) to make additional recommendations to improve the UI system (Committee on Finance of U.S. Senate 1976). In 1981, the commission submitted a report making a series of recommendations to improve the UI system, such as establishing federal minimum benefit standards.[24] Subsequently, the Unemployment Compensation Amendments of 1981 made minor changes to the UI system to reduce costs to the program. Most notably, it eliminated the national trigger for the extended benefits program to lower federal costs.[25] And, in 1991, Congress passed the Emergency Unemployment Compensation Program to address the 1990 to 1991 recession, which also established the Advisory Council for Unemployment Compensation to conduct empirical studies of the U.S. system.[26] Since then, in recognition of the need to reform the UI system, the Obama administration submitted several proposals in the 2017 fiscal year budget to expand coverage, restore the 26-week minimum benefit duration, create a better extended benefits program, and restore the solvency of the state UI funds; however, none of the proposals passed.[27]

State-level reforms targeted by ARRA

The ARRA of 2009 provided $7 billion in federal funding as modernization incentive payments to states that implemented changes to expand eligibility and the level of benefit generosity in their unemployment compensation systems.[28] The incentive payments were provided until October 1, 2011, and the changes made by the states must have been permanent.[29] The states received one-third of their designated total share of incentive payments if they set an alternative base period to raise eligibility among workers with lower or unstable earnings that met federal guidelines.[30] Moreover, the states were eligible for the remaining two-thirds of their share if they first enacted an alternative base period and then implemented at least two of the following four requirements:[31]

(1)   Individuals should not be denied regular unemployment compensation if they are only part-time workers,

(2)   Permit those with voluntary separations from employment due to compelling family reasons to be eligible for regular unemployment compensation,

(3)   Provide extended unemployment compensation to exhaustees of regular unemployment benefits who were enrolled in a state-approved training program covered by the Workforce Investment Act of 1998, and

(4)   Grant dependent allowances to those receiving regular unemployment compensation who have dependents.

Last, the ARRA of 2009 provided $500 million in federal funding to the states for the administration of the modernization of their programs, to improve outreach to individuals who might be eligible for regular unemployment insurance benefits, and for reemployment services.[32]

State-based changes since the Great Recession

Since the Great Recession, several states have enacted laws to reduce the maximum duration of their unemployment compensation benefits or changed the weekly benefit amount, mainly to address funding shortfalls in the UI system. For instance, in 2011, Arkansas, Florida, Illinois, Michigan, Missouri, and South Carolina passed state laws to reduce their UI benefit duration. Later, in 2012, Georgia reduced its benefit duration, followed by Kansas and North Carolina in 2013. Afterwards, Arkansas and Missouri (later found unconstitutional) reduced their benefit durations in 2015, followed by Idaho in 2016, and Arkansas passed a third benefit duration reduction in 2016 (Isaacs 2018). Following the peak of the recession, in February 2011, around $42.4 billion of unemployment trust fund loans were outstanding, as states had to borrow money to meet their unemployment compensation obligations.[33] Consequently, many states faced severe financial pressures and decreased unemployment compensation spending by reducing the generosity or duration of their benefits.

Proposals for Basic Reforms to UI

Policy analysts and researchers have discussed the need to modernize the UI system for some time. This discussion gained momentum during the Great Recession. The result has been a series of well-articulated proposals and convergence on a list of basic fixes. Several of these reform proposals had made it into President Obama's Budget Proposal for Fiscal Year (FY) 2017, and some have been taken up by the Trump administration. The following is a list of the core proposals, including a brief summary of their justification.

Prevent erosion of benefit generosity by mandating minimum benefits

Partly to counter funding difficulties in the aftermath of the Great Recession, several states have cut benefit durations below the typical 26-week mark. Similarly, there is substantial heterogeneity in benefit levels across states. Yet there are no compelling reasons why similar workers in different states should be treated differently by the UI system. Research provides justification for the optimal generosity of UI benefits and when these should vary with characteristics of workers or local labor markets. Hence, the choice of benefit parameters and how they vary in the population or over time should not be a function of the local political process or short-term funding needs.

Federal law should mandate a minimum amount of potential duration of UI benefit of 26 weeks, an average effective replace rate of 50 percent of benefits (with gradual adjustments of the maximum benefit amount), and a dependent allowance to support families with children with higher consumption commitments. To ensure states update their laws, the federal government can limit the credit for the State Unemployment Tax employers receive against the Federal Unemployment Tax.

Institutionalize federal emergency UI benefits as a function of local unemployment rates

Research clearly indicates that UI benefits should be extended in recessions. This is because the benefits to workers at risk of exhausting their benefits are greater, the inefficiency costs are not larger and perhaps smaller, and the potential of stimulating effects is greater. The experience in the aftermath of the Great Recession has shown that leaving extensions of UI benefits to the political process can lead to gaps in coverage that are damaging to affected workers. For most recessions, there is no evidence indicating a need for wasteful and potentially harmful discretion.

The federal Emergency Unemployment Compensation program should be made a permanent program. A straightforward way to achieve this is to reform the current trigger-based extended benefit program and make it 100 percent federally financed. In the course of such a reform, the trigger structure should be modified to keep the fraction of workers covered by UI approximately constant over the business cycle.

Fix outdated data collection so evidence can guide policy

To maintain daily operations of their UI programs, states collect information on workers' wages, UI claimants' benefits, and their employers' UI taxes. This information is vital for an efficient administration of the UI system, including understanding which parts of the system are cost-effective. Yet the current law only requires states to share the data with federal agencies for extremely limited purposes. Moreover, many of the datasets lack basic information, such as worker age or gender. Researchers are now well equipped to manage and analyze sensitive administrative data stored by government agencies to uncover critical trends that could inform policy-makers.

The data collection should be modernized by adopting four complementary strategies: (1) enhance data collection by states, (2) establish a national data clearinghouse of UI data at either the Bureau of Labor Statistics or the Census Bureau, (3) support these changes by providing a common software and offering moderate grants to upgrade hardware, and (4) establish a protocol to allow access to the data for research purposes and to improve the UI system. It is important to include an enforcement mechanism to ensure states' compliance with this last requirement.

The UI system in the United States collects several sources of data that not only are vital to a better understanding of how UI benefits and related programs work but also provide crucial information on the labor market needed to address many other issues. These are quarterly earnings records collected to assess workers' eligibility for UI benefits; UI claims records recording when workers file and receive benefits; records on job search assistance received by unemployed workers (funded under the Wagner-Payser Act); and records on job training received, mostly but not exclusively, by lower-income unemployed workers (funded under the Workforce Innovation and Opportunity Act [WIOA]). At present, the administrative worker-level records from WIOA services are sent annually by each state to the U.S. Department of Labor, chiefly for reporting purposes. The earnings records are sent to the Department of Health and Human Services to become part of the National Directory of New Hires (NDNH), which can be used to only enforce child support orders. No similar national collection of UI claims data exists, and the NDNH or the WIOA data are currently not accessible to researchers. Efforts by the Census Bureau to collect earnings data directly from the states has been hampered by the need to enter into legal agreements with fifty states. Yet the automated electronic collection processes already in place for the NDNH and the WIOA data shows that in principle, national databases of vital labor market data could be easily created as soon as appropriate legal frameworks are in place to guard the confidentiality and access of these data for research purposes.

Expand coverage of UI to fit structure of modern workforce

The current UI system does not serve a large fraction of the unemployed. This is partly due to changes in the structure of the workforce, with an increasing number of low-wage workers in unstable jobs or rising part-time employment, especially among women. Through incentives provided by the ARRA, a substantial number of states have now made benefits more easily accessible by adopting a range of proposals. Yet the ARRA reforms were implemented very unevenly across the country, leading to a patchwork of eligibility for UI across the United States.[34]

A reform should provide pathways to harmonize eligibility for UI across states and increase take-up rates among eligible individuals. There is little justification for the current patchwork of eligibility, and meetings of state and federal UI officials should provide a system of best practices for eligibility requirements and outreach. Eligibility requirements should include those proposed in the ARRA, among them allowing for training of UI beneficiaries, enabling part-time workers to claim benefits, enhancing the mobility of working couples by making moves for family-related reasons a qualifying event for UI, and instituting the alternative base period. In addition, some of the gradual restrictions imposed over the last three decades to lower UI payments should be reviewed and possibly modified as well (Evangelist 2012).

Incentives provided by the ARRA led nineteen states to adopt an alternative base period and eleven states implemented a part-time inclusionary definition (Mastri et al. 2016, 8–9). One research study found that if all states implemented all the provisions, eligibility would have increased by 20 percent (Linder and Nichols 2012, 13). While the ARRA provisions improved coverage, not all states implemented all the provisions to fully improve eligibility. As part of broader UI reform efforts, the federal government should consider fully extending provisions, such as the alternative base period, to workers regardless of geographic location.

Resolve financing shortfalls in states' UI trust funds

As a consequence of growing wages and low taxable wage bases that are not indexed to covered wages, just 25 percent of earnings covered by UI laws nationally are currently subject to state UI payroll taxes. The minimum taxable wage base, set by the federal government, is currently $7,000 and has not changed since 1983. While most states have set a state wage base higher than the required federal minimum, most are relatively low, with taxable wage bases of $15,000 or less.[35] Some states, such as California and Florida, continue to use the bare minimum $7,000 base to charge their state unemployment insurance taxes.[36] Similarly, the net federal tax rate—as defined under the FUTA—has been 0.8 percent for more than 30 years, depressing revenues that pay, among others, for UI administration by federal and state agencies (Dixon 2013). Many states' UI tax rates—as defined by their SUTAs—have remained low as well, and states have increasingly resorted to borrowing to finance UI benefits during recessions. Hence, even without the large increase in UI payments during and after the Great Recession, the financial soundness of the UI system has been steadily eroding (NELP 2010).

Policy-makers and researchers have proposed several sensible reforms to improve the complex financing system and solvency of the state UI funds. One proposed solution is to raise the federal taxable wage base by indexing it to wage growth, while lowering the FUTA tax rate.[37] Another possible solution is to institute federal penalties for states that fail to carry sufficient forward balances in their trust funds during expansions (West et al. 2016). A third proposed reform is to prevent payroll taxes from rising in the midst of a protracted recovery by extending the two-year window until the FUTA tax credit expires, institutionalizing interest wavers, and encouraging states to also delay automatic tax triggers aimed at balancing their trust funds.

While the solvency of the state unemployment insurance funds has improved greatly over the last few years since the aftermath of the Great Recession, as of March 2019, twenty-four states and U.S. territories continue to face solvency levels below the recommended standard. The Department of Labor measures the forward-funding solvency of the states' funds via the Average High Cost Multiple (AHCM), which is equal to the average of the three highest benefit cost rates over the last 20 years compared to the reserve ratio. The states with an AHCM value of greater than one have reached the minimum level of solvency needed before entering the next recession to cover UI benefits.[38] As the economy approaches the next recession, many states across the country continue to be at risk of once again entering federal debt to meet their UI benefit obligations. As a result, it is critical to reform the current financing structure of the federal-state UI system to ensure its vitality over the next recession and course of future business cycles.

The Congressional Budget Office (CBO) found that administering the afore-mentioned first proposed change to the current financing system via increasing the federal taxable wage base by indexing it to wage growth while decreasing the FUTA tax rate would result in an additional $18 billion in revenue from 2019 to 2028.[39] Under the CBO analysis, the states would receive additional revenues if their state wage base met the wage base set by the federal government via FUTA. The proposed reform would significantly improve the financial state of the federal part of the UI system along with the individual state UI systems.

Moreover, the Trump administration proposed as part of its FY2019 budget that states should be required to have a balance in their state trust fund accounts reflecting an AHCM of at least 0.50 (see Congressional Research Service 2018). For those states with an AHCM of less than 0.50, a penalty would be reflected via a higher net FUTA tax rate on those states' employers. The change would help to incentivize states to maintain enough funding to cover UI benefits claimed during the next recession and help to ensure financial soundness of their state's trust fund.

Additional proposals worthy of consideration

There are interesting proposals meant to fix additional shortcomings of the current UI system. In addition, there are challenging open questions that have not yet been addressed. These proposals and open questions include, among others, the following:

- A modernization of the administration of UI, including information technology used to administer claims, which is found to be outdated and under-funded (see NELP 2010; West et al. 2016).

The states have encountered various challenges related to the administration of their UI programs, mostly due to insufficient funding for newer information technology (O'Leary and Wandner 2018). State analysts such as in California have reported as a challenge insufficient federal funding to properly administer the state UI program (Legislative Analyst's Office 2017). As a result of a lack of proper federal funding to administer the state UI programs, during the peak of the Great Recession in the first quarter of 2009, 40 percent of states failed to meet the federal guidelines on their benefit payment obligations due to the large volume of claims submitted.[40] Policy researchers have proposed updating the current administration and information technology of the UI system by improv-ing data collection, setting up a national database at a government entity like the Census, providing funding and technical support to implement the changes, and setting guidelines for researchers on how to access the data (von Wachter 2016).

- A reform of firms' UI tax rates to better internalize the costs of layoffs, reduce the cost to the UI system, and achieve similar cost of layoffs across states.

The academic literature shows that implementing a full-cost experience rating system to replace the current imperfect experience rating structure would incentivize employers to reduce the number of layoffs during recessions and lead to stable hiring during expansions (e.g., Rejda and Rosenbaum 1990). Further research finds that allowing volatile industries to use more UI benefit resources than more stable industries induces a 5 percent increase in layoff unemployment (Deere 1991). The most volatile industries receiving subsidies as a result of imperfect experience ratings are construction, manufacturing, and mining (Anderson and Meyer 1993). Increasing the degree of experience ratings can lead to lower seasonal variations in temporary layoffs in volatile industries, especially in construction and durable manufacturing (Card and Levine 1994).

More recent empirical research finds that an increase of 5 percent in experience rating on average leads to a 1.4 percent decrease in job flows and a decrease of 0.21 percentage points in the unemployment rate (Ratner 2013). The impact of the increase in experience rating on tax revenues is less clear (Ratner 2013). Policy advocates and researchers recommend improving the current UI payroll system by increasing the degree of experience rating such that a tax schedule must include at least ten different tax rates capturing a firm's layoff history (O'Leary and Wandner 2018).

- An optional private unemployment account to cover the self-employed or independent contractors

Currently, private UI is not widely available and can only be purchased from a handful of private insurance companies to partially cover lost wages during times of unemployment.[41] The rate of covered workers by the UI system has fallen over the last few decades, and as a result, a lower share of workers can access UI benefits (McKay 2017b). As a result, some have proposed that a private UI system should be created for independent workers and the self-employed by pooling resources among these workers through an intermediary (e.g., Kletzer and Rosen 2006; Harris and Krueger 2015). Further, policy-makers could consider developing policies to induce the growth of the private UI market as an alternative for those not covered by the public UI system.

- A "job seeker allowance" to aid workers with limited work history who do not qualify for UI because of a lack of earnings history (West et al. 2016).

Traditional UI benefits require applicants to meet certain past earnings or work history levels, such as in California, where a worker must have earned at least $1,300 during the highest-earning quarter.[42] Consequently, unemployed individuals with limited work history, such as young workers, those with health issues, and those who exited the labor market for caregiving purposes do not qualify for traditional UI benefits. Some policy reform advocates have proposed implementing a job seeker allowance to help low-income workers mitigate the financial hardship due to job loss or lower income volatility, and to help improve job outcomes (West et al. 2016).

Proposals for Innovation in UI

Even if sufficiently modernized according to the basic reforms reviewed above, UI as it is currently designed can neither prevent nor buffer much of the large and lasting earnings losses due to layoffs. This also affects the UI system's efforts to reemploy workers, who may wait too long to engage in the process of rebuilding their careers. Yet several innovations of the existing UI system have been proposed that could greatly expand the reach of UI without the need to establish a new program.

Institute a functioning system of work sharing to prevent costly layoffs

An increasing number of U.S. states have instituted programs of work sharing—also called short-term compensation, or STC—that allow workers to draw prorated UI benefits while on the job as an alternative to layoff. Evidence from other countries suggests work sharing can achieve substantial reductions in layoffs. Yet take-up of the programs by employers in the United States has been low, partly because of restrictive program rules and a lack of awareness about the program.

Several policy options are available to strengthen the use of STC across and within states, especially during recessions. One would be to continue to incentivize adoption of the program, with 100 percent of STC outlays funded federally for the first three years after adoption, or alternatively require states to establish STC programs. To raise attractiveness to employers, during this period states should be required to not charge employers for their uses (meaning there should be no experience rating). Another policy option would be to encourage states to share best practices, harmonize their efforts in outreach, and consider targeting employers using industry-level indicators of economic activity or those in the Worker Adjustment Retraining and Notification (WARN) system. A third policy option would be to encourage widespread use of short-term compensation during recessions when extended benefits are turned on by having STC benefits 100 percent federally financed, by suspending experience ratings, and by not having STC benefits deducted from worker's maximum UI eligibility. Finally, research should continue to assess what prevents the adoption of the STC program and how to develop best practices for eligibility requirements.

The current U.S. STC program provides regular unemployment benefits prorated by a partial work reduction. For example, employers can adapt the program by lowering the hours of all their workers by 25 percent instead of laying off 25 percent of their full-time workforce when business is slow, where the STC program would replace the lost wages. At the moment, the STC program is underutilized, and only the following twenty-six states have operational programs that meet the new federal definition: Arizona, Arkansas, California, Colorado, Connecticut, Florida, Iowa, Kansas, Maine, Maryland, Massachusetts, Michigan, Minnesota, Missouri, Nebraska, New Hampshire, New Jersey, New York, Ohio, Oregon, Pennsylvania, Rhode Island, Texas, Vermont, Washington, and Wisconsin.[43] One key benefit of the STC program is a reduction of those who become long-term unemployed during recessionary periods (Hassett and Strain 2014).

Policy advocates and researchers have identified three main potential advantages of the STC program compared to traditional layoffs. First, STC leads to more equitable outcomes, as the negative effects from a recession are distributed across workers rather than only a subgroup of workers. Second, STC serves as a macroeconomic stabilizer, as more workers continue to receive traditional work earnings. Third, STC mitigates economic hysteresis that occurs when a severe recession reduces the economy's production capacity for the future (Hassett and Strain 2014). Moreover, Hijzen and Martin (2013) found that STC programs increase the productivity of those working and help to preserve jobs during an economic recession. While the impact of the STC program on productivity in the short-term is of little or no concern, the long-term impact remains ambiguous, and some critics argue that it could deter the shift of workers from eroding to growing industries (D. Baker 2011).

The current STC system in the United States needs major reforming as it currently does not have nationwide coverage to better serve workers and employers regardless of location. Abraham and Houseman (2014) found that the STC program saved a significant number of jobs in the manufacturing sector during the Great Recession; however, it did not serve as an aggregate mitigation tool to reduce overall layoffs due to the program's small scale and patchy regional coverage. Due to the program's popularity as another tool to help the unemployed, policy-makers need to consider expanding the current STC program in terms of regional coverage and the number of employers it can serve.

Experiment with wage insurance to aid workers returning to employment

Since UI only insures a minor fraction of the total earnings risk of job losers, its role as an insurance mechanism and automatic stabilizer in recessions performs substantially below its potential. As a result, a growing number of researchers have suggested complementing the current UI system with a system of wage insurance. Wage insurance is likely to provide substantial additional insurance value. It may provide cost savings by lowering UI payments. And it is unlikely to further reduce wages and may raise them by shortening unemployment.[44] Yet currently little is known on potential effects of wage insurance.

A series of proposals have been made to extend existing wage-insurance plans for trade-related layoffs to all workers covered by UI (Wandner 2016). Given the evidence on job loss, introducing a version of wage insurance is a sound policy, but an experimental evaluation will be important to better understand its effects.

Policy parameters should be set with core facts in mind—for example, average wage losses of displaced workers with three years or more of tenure from good employers in a recession are about $15,000 per year in the first couple of years (von Wachter, Song, and Manchester 2011), so $10,000 over two years replaces only 30 percent of the loss.[45] Similarly, insurance benefits should be extended to workers earning more than $50,000 on their new job since this would exclude substantially affected middle-class employees and their families from insurance.[46] Since most evidence suggests that earnings losses last at least three years, and likely many more, a proposal with sharp limits has to educate workers about the long path to recovery.

At the moment, the United States only operates a small-scale wage insurance program, known as the Alternative Trade Adjustment Assistance Program, as part of the Trade Adjustment Assistance Act (TAAA) (McKay 2017a). The program offers a wage subsidy of 50 percent of the difference between wages at the time of separation and current wages from reemployment to dislocated workers who are at least 50 years old and had a multiyear tenure in a TAAA-certified industry. The benefits provided to dislocated workers are capped at a maximum amount of $10,000 over the course of two years, along with a credit for health insurance and relocation costs.[47]

In 2016, the Obama administration proposed a federally funded wage insurance program mimicking the current Alternative Trade Adjustment Assistance Program. The proposed program was released as part of the FY2017 Presidential Budget Request, which would offer 50 percent of a dislocated worker's lost wages with a maximum amount of $10,000 during a period of up to two years. The eligibility criteria were more generous as the program would have included all displaced workers making less than $50,000 per year in their new job who had been with their prior employer for at least three years (see Wandner 2016). Ultimately the program was not adopted, but it may provide a good point of departure for future policy considerations regarding wage insurance.

Currently, there is a lack of rigorous empirical research on any evaluation of the impact of a wage insurance program on worker's outcomes in the United States due to the program's narrow coverage (Wandner 2016, 8). However, the Canadian Government conducted an experiment to evaluate the causal impact of their wage insurance known as the Earnings Supplement Program (ESP) (Bloom et al. 1997). The randomized controlled trial consisted of a sample of 5,912 displaced workers from various provinces, with a control versus a treatment group (Bloom et al. 1997). Interestingly, among those in the treatment group, only 20 percent received the earnings supplement with an average weekly payment of $127 (Bloom et al. 2001). Researchers leading the Canadian experiment found that the supplemental wage had little impact on job-search efforts, employment outcomes, and use of UI (Bloom et al. 2001). As a result of the findings and the costs associated with the program, the Canadian government decided against implementing the ESP program on a larger scale (McKay 2017a).

Even while the Canadian ESP experiment did not yield the desired results, the findings from that study are not fully transferable to the U.S. context in any case, as the benefits and eligibility were different from those proposed by the

Obama administration and used for the Alternative Trade Adjustment Assistance program. Moreover, prior work has shown that similar programs can improve job-finding rates (e.g., Meyer 1995) and be cost effective if appropriately targeted (O'Leary, Decker, and Wandner 2005).[48] Hence, if the goal is to help reintegrate the long-term unemployed into the labor market and reduce income shocks among displaced workers, then a wage insurance program is a policy tool worth careful consideration and additional research.

Conclusion

This article provided an overview of the UI program and a range of reform proposals, along with research evidence to support those reforms. Some of the proposals are recent and responded to new challenges of the UI program, while some of them are older and aimed to address well-known issues with the current UI system. Throughout, I have focused on reforms that keep the central tenets of the current UI system in place but try to address some of the core issues with the program summarized at the outset of the article.

Overall, there are a range of sensible proposals to reform the UI system, several of which would find broad backing among academics and policy-makers alike. Yet in many cases there are important open questions, in particular for empirical research. Progress on several fronts is currently severely hampered by a lack of mostly administrative micro data that are, in principle, available but currently not accessible because of a missing legal framework. This in itself constitutes an important proposal for reform.

There are a few reforms discussed here that are soundly grounded in empirical academic research or longstanding regulatory experience, or both: mandating minimum UI benefits at the federal level to prevent states from arbitrarily cutting benefits to fix budget shortfalls; replacing the current ad hoc Emergency Unemployment Compensation by a federally financed, trigger-based system to ensure a smooth temporary expansion of the UI system in recessions; considering several proposals for stabilizing funding of the system, including expanding the tax base and requiring minimal reserves; and creating a national system of data collection and access for research purposes.

Other reforms are sensible, but additional research is important for making recommendations thoroughly grounded in empirical evidence. While many agree that the UI system could better serve a broader group of workers, not enough research is available on longer-run trends in the take up of UI benefits or effects of recent reforms; preventing dramatic long-term earnings losses associated with job displacements could be addressed by a system of job sharing, but little U.S.-based evidence is available; finally, once large wage losses are incurred, further evidence on effective ways of reintegrating displaced workers more quickly would be beneficial. Other reform ideas are promising but are relatively new and may need more discussion, such as UI for the self-employed or reform of experience ratings. Here, evidence from other countries, most notably Europe, may show the potential for this and other programs to help make the UI system more flexible and effective.

UI has been a successful program worthy of being strengthened through appropriate reforms. There have been proposals that would replace UI altogether that were not covered here. One more recent proposal has been Universal Basic Income (UBI). UBI proposals have been discussed elsewhere in detail (e.g., Hoynes and Rothstein 2019). Overall, while by design they sidestep the issue of reducing the relative benefit of working that affects a conditional program such as UI (e.g., moral hazard effects), they may simply be too expensive and have adverse distributional consequences despite promises to the contrary. Another alternative to UI that has been proposed in the past that again sidesteps the issue of moral hazard by design are personal savings accounts that would allow workers to self-insure for temporary employment shocks. While not without conceptual appeal, such a program would still need to rely on a final insurance pool for those who exhaust their savings account. Moreover, the difficulties in incentivizing participation in savings accounts, and the tight link to the stock market, bring additional implementation challenges worthy of a separate discussion.

Notes

1. See https://oui.doleta.gov/unemploy/pdf/partnership.pdf.

2. Ibid.

3. See https://oui.doleta.gov/unemploy/uifactsheet.asp. The ARRA provided incentive payments to states that would modernize their UI system such as by extending eligibility to those who quit their jobs for compelling reasons such as due to domestic violence, spousal relocation, or illness.

4. See https://oui.doleta.gov/unemploy/uifactsheet.asp.

5. Ibid.

6. See https://www.stlouisfed.org/publications/regional-economist/october-2012/unemployment-insurance-payments-overpayments-and-unclaimed-benefits.

7. See https://oui.doleta.gov/unemploy/pdf/partnership.pdf.

8. See https://www.nolo.com/legal-encyclopedia/collecting-unemployment-benefits-hawaii.html and https://www.nolo.com/legal-encyclopedia/collecting-unemployment-benefits-texas-32500.html.

9. See https://eligibility.com/unemployment/florida-fl-unemployment-benefits and https://www.cbpp.org/research/economy/policy-basics-how-many-weeks-of-unemployment-compensation-are-available.

10. Ibid.

11. See https://www.edd.ca.gov/pdf_pub_ctr/de2088c.pdf.

12. See https://www.edd.ca.gov/pdf_pub_ctr/de231z.pdf.

13. See https://oui.doleta.gov/unemploy/pdf/partnership.pdf.

14. Ibid.

15. See https://oui.doleta.gov/unemploy/euc.asp.

16. See https://oui.doleta.gov/unemploy/supp_act.asp.

17. See https://oui.doleta.gov/unemploy/pdf/euc08.pdf.

18. Ibid.

19. See https://fas.org/sgp/crs/misc/R45478.pdf.

20. See https://oui.doleta.gov/unemploy/data_summary/definitions.pdf.

21. See https://www.edd.ca.gov/pdf_pub_ctr/de231z.pdf.

22. Presence of UI benefits can have other effects on worker behavior. For example, given that eligibility for UI benefits typically depends on a minimum amount of employment, unemployed workers may face

an added incentive to search for jobs if they do not qualify or if their UI benefits come toward an end (Mortensen 1977). Empirical work has found evidence of such an "entitlement effect" (e.g., Christofides and McKenna 1996; M. Baker and Rea 1998), although the net effect on employment can either be positive or negative (Hamermesh 1979). There have also been studies of UI on spousal labor supply, as benefits may lower the need of a spouse to increase labor supply to make up for lost income (e.g., Cullen and Gruber 2000).

23. In principle, the ability to search longer may improve job quality. However, current evidence suggests these effects may be small or even negative (e.g., Schmieder and von Wachter 2016).

24. See https://pdfs.semanticscholar.org/b3a5/e169a456b105a2d23773086a560d70a20922.pdf.

25. See https://www.congress.gov/bill/97th-congress/house-bill/2880.

26. See https://www.congress.gov/bill/102nd-congress/house-bill/3575.

27. See https://obamawhitehouse.archives.gov/omb/budget.

28. See Section 2003, "Special Transfers for Unemployment Compensation Modernization," in https://www.congress.gov/bill/111th-congress/house-bill/1/text.

29. Ibid.

30. Ibid. The federal definition defined an *alternative base period* as a state that (A) uses a base period that includes the most recently completed calendar quarter before the start of the benefit year for purposes of determining eligibility for unemployment compensation; or (B) provides that, in the case of an individual who would not otherwise be eligible for unemployment compensation under the State law because of the use of a base period that does not include the most recently completed calendar quarter before the start of the benefit year, eligibility shall be determined using a base period that includes such calendar quarter.

31. See Section 2003(B)(2) in https://www.congress.gov/bill/111th-congress/house-bill/1/text.

32. See Section 2003(g)(1), "Special Transfer in Fiscal Year 2009 for Administration," in https://www.congress.gov/bill/111th-congress/house-bill/1/text.

33. See https://oui.doleta.gov/unemploy/solvency.asp.

34. See Table I.1 on page 8 of https://www.dol.gov/asp/evaluation/completed-studies/UCP_State_Decisions_to_Adopt.pdf. There have been no further federal reforms of UI since the ARRA.

35. See https://www.apspayroll.com/resources/payroll-taxes-rates-and-changes/suta-wage-bases/.

36. The other states or U.S. territories are Arizona, Puerto Rico, and Tennessee. See https://www.apspayroll.com/resources/payroll-taxes-rates-and-changes/suta-wage-bases/.

37. See White House (2017).

38. Per a change in 2013 to code CFR 606.32, the AHCM will be used as a solvency measure to determine whether a state qualifies for an interest-free loan for a federal advance after January 1 of a given year to cover unemployment insurance benefits if the loan is repaid by September 30 of the same year. See pages 1–3 in https://oui.doleta.gov/unemploy/docs/trustFundSolvReport2019.pdf and https://www.law.cornell.edu/cfr/text/20/606.32.

39. The CBO conducts the analysis by first raising the FUTA taxable wage base from $7,000 to $40,000 in 2019 where the wage base can be indexed to wage growth in future periods, while decreasing the FUTA tax rate from the current 0.6 percent to 0.167 percent. See https://www.cbo.gov/budget-options/2018/54809.

40. See https://www.nasi.org/sites/default/files/research/Unemployment_Insurance_Administration.pdf.

41. See https://www.thebalancecareers.com/is-private-unemployment-insurance-worth-it-4161288.

42. See https://www.nolo.com/legal-encyclopedia/collecting-unemployment-benefits-california-32504.html.

43. See https://oui.doleta.gov/unemploy/docs/stc_fact_sheet.pdf.

44. In Canada, workers taking up wage insurance saw substantial income increases (see Bloom et al. 1997); yet, consistent with evidence from reemployment bonuses in the United States (see Meyer 1995), the cost saving from lower UI spells from wage insurance in Canada was moderate. All estimates from the United States indicate that UI benefits do not affect wages, and UI benefits tend to lower wages for those with longer spells (see Schmieder and von Wachter 2016).

45. See the proposal in White House (2017).

46. Ibid.

47. See https://www.ctdol.state.ct.us/TradeAct/ataa%20presentation2a.pdf.

48. In the 1980s, the U.S. government experimentally evaluated reemployment bonuses that provided incentives to unemployed workers to find a job. While the bonus is not necessarily a function of past or future earnings levels, it also works through improving the attractiveness of finding a job.

References

Abraham, Katharine G., and Susan N. Houseman. 2014. Short-time compensation as a tool to mitigate job loss? Evidence on the US experience during the recent recession. *Industrial Relations: A Journal of Economy and Society* 53 (4): 543–67.

Anderson, Patricia M., and Bruce D. Meyer. 1993. Unemployment Insurance in the United States: Layoff incentives and cross subsidies. *Journal of Labor Economics* 11 (1, part 2): S70–S95.

Anderson, Patricia M., and Bruce D. Meyer. 1994. The effects of unemployment insurance taxes and benefits on layoffs using firm and individual data. NBER Working Paper w4960, National Bureau of Economic Research, Cambridge, MA.

Bailey, Kent R. 1984. Asymptotic equivalence between the Cox estimator and the general ML estimators of regression and survival parameters in the Cox model. *Annals of Statistics* 12 (2): 730–36.

Baker, Dean. 2011. *Work sharing: The quick route back to full employment*. No. 2011-15. Washington, DC: Center for Economic and Policy Research.

Baker, Michael, and Samuel Rea. 1998. Employment spells and unemployment insurance eligibility requirements. *Review of Economics and Statistics* 80 (1): 80–94.

Balducchi, David E., Christopher J. O'Leary, Suzanne Simonetta, and Wayne Vroman. 2018. *Unemployment insurance reform: Fixing a broken system*. Kalamazoo, MI: WE Upjohn Institute.

Bloom, Howard, Barbara Fink, Susanna Lui-Gurr, Wendy Bancroft, and Doug Tattrie. 1997. *Implementing the earnings supplement project: A test of a re-employment incentive*. No. r-98-1a. Ottawa: Social Research and Demonstration Corporation.

Bloom, Howard S., Saul Schwartz, Susanna Lui-Gurr, Suk-Won Lee, Jason Peng, and Wendy Bancroft. 2001. Testing a financial incentive to promote re-employment among displaced workers: The Canadian Earnings Supplement Project (ESP). *Journal of Policy Analysis and Management: The Journal of the Association for Public Policy Analysis and Management* 20 (3): 505–23.

Card, David, and Phillip B. Levine. 1994. Unemployment insurance taxes and the cyclical and seasonal properties of unemployment. *Journal of Public Economics* 53 (1): 1–29.

Chetty, Raj. 2008. Moral hazard versus liquidity and optimal unemployment insurance. *Journal of Political Economy* 116 (2): 173–234.

Chimerine, Lawrence, Theodore S. Black, Lester Coffey, and Martha K. Matzke. 1999. *Unemployment insurance as an economic stabilizer: Evidence of effectiveness over three decades*. Washington, DC: U.S. Department of Labor, Employment and Training Administration.

Christofides, L. N., and C. J. McKenna. 1996. Unemployment insurance and job duration in Canada. *Journal of Labor Economics* 14 (2): 286–312.

Congressional Research Service. 19 November 2018. *Unemployment insurance: Legislative issues in the 115th Congress*. Washington, DC: Congressional Research Service.

Cullen, Julie, and Jonathan Gruber. 2000. Does unemployment insurance crowd out spousal labor supply? *Journal of Labor Economics* 18:546–72.

Deere, Donald R. 1991. Unemployment insurance and employment. *Journal of Labor Economics* 9 (4): 307–24.

Dixon, Rebecca. November 2013. Federal neglect leaves state unemployment systems in a state of disrepair. New York, NY: NELP. Available from https://s27147.pcdn.co/wp-content/uploads/2015/03/NELP-Report-State-of-Disrepair-Federal-Neglect-Unemployment-Systems.pdf.

Evangelist, Mike. 31 July 2012. Lessons left unlearned: Unemployment insurance financing after the Great Recession. National Employment Law Project Policy Brief, New York, NY. Available from http://www.nelp.org/content/uploads/2015/03/Policy_Brief_UI_Lessons_Unlearned.pdf.

Farber, Henry S., and Robert G. Valletta. 2015. Do extended unemployment benefits lengthen unemployment spells? Evidence from recent cycles in the U.S. labor market. *Journal of Human Resources* 50 (4): 873–909.

Gruber, Jonathan. 1994. The consumption smoothing benefits of unemployment insurance. NBER Working Paper w4750, National Bureau of Economic Research, Cambridge, MA.

Hamermesh, Daniel S. 1979. Entitlement effects, unemployment insurance and employment decisions. *Economic Inquiry* 17 (3): 317–32.

Harris, Seth D., and Alan B. Krueger. 2015. *A proposal for modernizing labor laws for twenty-first-century work: The independent worker.* Washington, DC: Hamilton Project, Brookings Institution.

Hassett, Kevin A., and Michael R. Strain. 2 April 2014. Worksharing and long-term unemployment. Washington, DC: Center on Budget and Policy Priorities. Available from http://www.aei.org/wp-content/uploads/2014/04/-hassett-strain-workshairng-and-long-term-unemployment_173834868095 .pdf.

Hijzen, Alexander, and Sebastien Martin. 2013. The role of short-time work schemes during the global financial crisis and early recovery: A cross-country analysis. *IZA Journal of Labor Policy* 2 (1): 5.

Hoynes, H. W., and J. Rothstein. 2019. Universal basic income in the U.S. and advanced countries. NBER Working Paper 25538, National Bureau of Economic Research, Cambridge, MA.

Isaacs, Katelin P. 2018. *Unemployment insurance: Consequences of changes in state unemployment compensation laws.* Washington, DC: Congressional Research Service.

Johnston, Andrew C., and Alexandre Mas. 2018. Potential unemployment insurance duration and labor supply: The individual and market-level response to a benefit cut. *Journal of Political Economy* 126 (6): 2480–2522.

Katz, Lawrence F., and Bruce D. Meyer. 1990. The impact of the potential duration of unemployment benefits on the duration of unemployment. *Journal of Public Economics* 41 (1): 45–72.

Kletzer, Lori G., and Howard Rosen. 2006. *Reforming unemployment insurance for the twenty-first century workforce.* Washington, DC: Brookings Institution.

Kroft, Kory, and Matthew J. Notowidigdo. 2016. Should unemployment insurance vary with the unemployment rate? Theory and evidence. *Review of Economic Studies* 83 (3): 1092–1124.

Krueger, Alan B., and Bruce D. Meyer. 2002. Labor supply effects of social insurance. *Handbook of Public Economics* 4:2327–92.

Legislative Analyst's Office (LAO). 10 May 2017. Major issues facing the unemployment insurance program. Washington, DC: LAO. Available from https://lao.ca.gov/handouts/socservices/2017/UI-Program-Issues-051017.pdf.

Linder, Stephan, and Austin Nichols. 2012. How do unemployment insurance modernization laws affect the number and composition of eligible workers? Washington, DC: The Urban Institute. Available from http://www.urban.org/sites/default/files/publication/25471/412582-How-Do-Unemployment-Insurance-Modernization-Laws-Affect-the-Number-and-Composition-of-Eligible-.PDF.

Mastri, Annalisa, Wayne Vroman, Karen Needels, and Walter Nicholson. 2 March 2016. States' decision to adopt unemployment compensation provisions of the American Recovery and Reinvestment Act. Cambridge, MA: Mathematica Policy Research. Available from https://www.dol.gov/sites/dolgov/files/OASP/legacy/files/UCP_State_Decisions_to_Adopt.pdf.

McKay, Katherine Lucas. July 2017 (2017a). Bridging the gap: How wage insurance can address unemployment-related income volatility. Washington, DC: The Aspen Institute.

McKay, Katherine Lucas. August 2017 (2017b). Reforming unemployment insurance to support income stability and financial security. Washington, DC: The Aspen Institute.

Meyer, Bruce D. 1995. Lessons from the U.S. unemployment insurance experiments. *Journal of Economic Literature* 33 (1): 91–131.

Moffitt, Robert. 1985. Unemployment insurance and the distribution of unemployment spells. *Journal of Econometrics* 28:85–101.

Mortensen, D. 1977. Unemployment insurance and job search decisions. *Industrial and Labor Relations Review* 30 (4): 505–17.

National Employment Law Project (NELP). 9 April 2010. Understanding the unemployment trust fund crisis of 2010. NELP Data Brief. New York, NY: NELP.

National Employment Law Project (NELP). May 2012. Modernizing unemployment insurance: Federal incentives pave the way for state reforms. Briefing Paper. New York, NY: NELP. Available from https://www.nelp.org/wp-content/uploads/2015/03/ARRA_UI_Modernization_Report.pdf.

Nekoei, Arash, and Andrea Weber. 2017. Does extending unemployment benefits improve job quality? *American Economic Review* 7 (2): 527–61.

O'Leary, Christopher J., Paul T. Decker, and Stephen A. Wandner. 2005. Cost-effectiveness of targeted reemployment bonuses. *Journal of Human Resources* 40 (1): 270–79.

O'Leary, Christopher J., and Stephen A. Wandner. 2018. Unemployment insurance reform: Evidence-based policy recommendations. In *Unemployment insurance reform: Fixing a broken system*, 131–210. Kalamazoo, MI: W.E. Upjohn Institute for Employment Research.

Orszag, Peter. 2001. *Unemployment insurance as economic stimulus*. Washington, DC: Center on Budget and Policy Priorities.

Ratner, David. 2013. Unemployment insurance experience rating and labor market dynamics. The Federal Reserve Board Working Paper 2013-86, Washington, DC.

Rejda, George E., and David I. Rosenbaum. 1990. Unemployment insurance and full-cost experience rating: The impact on seasonal hiring. *Journal of Risk and Insurance* 57 (3): 519–29.

Rothstein, Jesse. 2011. Unemployment insurance and job search in the Great Recession. *Brookings Papers on Economic Activity* 2:143–213.

Solon, Gary. 1979. Labor supply effects of extended unemployment benefits. *Journal of Human Resources* 14:247–55.

Schmieder, Johannes F., and Till von Wachter. 2016. The effects of unemployment insurance benefits: New evidence and interpretation. *Annual Economic Review* 8:547–81.

Schmieder, Johannes F., Till von Wachter, and Stefan Bender. 2012. The effects of extended unemployment insurance over the business cycle: Evidence from regression discontinuity estimates over 20 years. *Quarterly Journal of Economics* 127 (2): 701–52.

Schmieder, Johannes F., Till von Wachter, and Stefan Bender. 2016. The effect of unemployment benefits and nonemployment durations on wages. *American Economic Review* 106 (3): 739–77.

U.S. Congress, Committee on Finance of the U.S. Senate and the Committee of Ways and Mean of the U.S. House of Representatives. 1976. *Unemployment compensation amendments of 1976*. 94th Cong., 2nd sess. Washington, DC: Government Printing Office.

Valletta, Robert. 2014. Recent extensions of U.S. unemployment benefits: Search responses in alternative labor market states. *IZA Journal of Labor Policy* 3 (1). Available from https://doi.org/10.1186/2193-9004-3-18.

von Wachter, Till. 31 October 2016. Unemployment insurance reform primer. Washington, DC: Washington Center for Equitable Growth. Available from https://equitablegrowth.org/unemployment-insurance-reform-primer.

von Wachter, Till, Jae Song, and Joyce Manchester. 2011. Trends in employment and earnings of allowed and rejected applicants to the social security disability insurance program. *American Economic Review* 101 (7): 3308–29.

Vroman, Wayne. 2009. Unemployment insurance recipients and non-recipients in the current population survey. *Monthly Labor Review*, October: 44–53.

Vroman, Wayne. 2011. *Unemployment insurance and the Great Recession*. Washington, DC: The Urban Institute. Available from https://www.urban.org/sites/default/files/publication/26766/412462-Unemployment-Insurance-and-the-Great-Recession.PDF.

Vroman, Wayne, Elaine Maag, Christopher J. O'Leary, and Stephen A. Woodbury. 2017. *A comparative analysis of unemployment insurance financing methods*. Washington, DC: Urban Institute.

Wandner, Stephen A. 2016. Wage insurance as a policy option in the United States. Upjohn Institute Working Papers, Kalamazoo, MI.

West, Rachel, Indivar Dutta-Gupta, Kali Grant, Melissa Boteach, Claire McKenna, and Judy Conti. 2016. *Strengthening unemployment protections in America*. Washington, DC: Center for American Progress.

The White House. 2017. The president's budget for fiscal year 2017. Available from https://www.whitehouse.gov/omb/budget (accessed 6 September 2016).

Means-Tested Transfer Programs

Medicaid: What Does It Do, and Can We Do It Better?

This article provides an overview of the Medicaid program and summarizes the evidence about its effectiveness in terms of providing insurance and promoting health. The evidence shows that Medicaid has improved the lives of low-income people since its creation in 1965. Expansions in Medicaid have led to increases in coverage and access to medical care, reductions in medical debt, and improvements in health outcomes with little evidence of significant reductions in beneficiaries' labor supply. Yet there are concerns around the program's high and increasing costs, the quality of care provided, and difficulty accessing Medicaid-funded care. We discuss some of the proposed Medicaid reforms meant to address these problems in light of previous evidence.

Keywords: Medicaid; health insurance; health care; medical care; health policy

By
JANET CURRIE
and
VALENTINA DUQUE

M edicaid—publicly funded health insurance for low-income people—is one of the largest U.S. social programs, currently providing health insurance coverage to 73 million Americans,[1] at a cost of $565.5 billion in 2016.[2] These costs accounted for 17 percent of total national health expenditures and for about 3 percent of the U.S. gross domestic product (GDP).[3]

The program serves four distinct populations: lower-income children and their mothers; the

Janet Currie is the Henry Putnam Professor of Economics and Public Affairs at Princeton University and codirects Princeton's Center for Health and Wellbeing and the NBER Children's program. She is a member of the National Academy of Sciences and of the National Academy of Medicine and a fellow of the AAPSS.

Valentina Duque is an assistant professor of economics at the University of Sydney, Australia.

NOTE: We would like to thank Robert Moffitt and James Ziliak for helpful comments, as well as Karen Dynan, Amitabh Chandra, Nicole Maestas, and participants at *The ANNALS* "Entitlement Reform" Conference. Owen Smith provided excellent research assistance.

Correspondence: valentina.duque@sydney.edu.au

DOI: 10.1177/0002716219874772

disabled; elderly people in nursing homes; and, since 2014, low-income nondisabled adults in states that have adopted Medicaid expansions that were allowed under the Affordable Care Act (ACA). This heterogeneity in the populations served, combined with the fact that each state runs its own Medicaid program subject to federal government regulations, makes it difficult to draw general conclusions about the functioning and impacts of the Medicaid program and the best options for reforming it.

In this article, we first provide a very brief overview of the program and its history and then summarize evidence about the effectiveness of Medicaid in terms of providing insurance and promoting health. There is considerable evidence that Medicaid has improved the lives of low-income people. Yet there is also dissatisfaction about the high cost of Medicaid, concerns about the availability of Medicaid-funded care and the quality of care provided, and lingering concerns about whether eligibility for Medicaid creates perverse incentives that discourage self-sufficiency in able bodied people who can work. Moreover, many Americans have incomes too high to qualify for Medicaid but too low to comfortably afford private health insurance, notwithstanding the health insurance exchanges created by the ACA (which we discuss further). The final part of this article discusses some proposed Medicaid reforms meant to address these problems.

Background

Medicaid was adopted in 1965, in an era when poor families had little access to private insurance or charity care and many people lacked health care. For instance, Goodman-Bacon (2018) shows that before Medicaid, only 40 to 50 percent of poor children had any doctor visits in a year. Medicaid greatly increased public spending on health care for the poor, mandating a defined set of services that were to be covered without requiring the patient to pay.

Figure 1 shows the number of Medicaid beneficiaries each year from 1975 to 2018, by eligibility category. Children are the largest single group of beneficiaries. While enrollment was initially flat, the growth in the coverage of children since the late 1980s was intentional. States were first allowed and then required to raise income eligibility limits for pregnant women and children. These expansions broke the link between welfare receipt and Medicaid coverage and allowed children in families with higher incomes to be covered. By 2010, 48 percent of all births in the United States were covered by Medicaid (Markus et al. 2013). The introduction of the state Child Health Insurance Program (CHIP or SCHIP) in 1998 further expanded coverage of low-income children.[4] Between 1986 and 2005, the share of children eligible for Medicaid/CHIP increased from between 15 and 20 percent of U.S. children, to between 40 and 50 percent of children, depending on the age group (Currie, Decker, and Lin 2008).

Coverage of low-income, nondisabled adults and the disabled also increased over time, especially beginning in the late 1990s, when some states raised income

FIGURE 1
Medicaid (and CHIP) Beneficiaries, By Eligibility Group, FY1975–2018 (thousands)

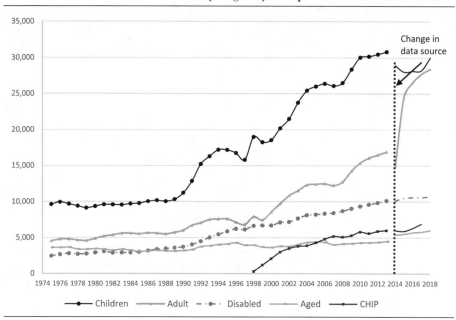

SOURCE: We used several sources of data to construct this figure: (1) the "MACStats: Medicaid and CHIP Data Book" provided information on Medicaid enrollment by group from 1975 to 2013 (https://www.macpac.gov/wp-content/uploads/2016/12/MACStats_DataBook_Dec2016.pdf), (2) the "CMS – Brief Summaries of Medicare & Medicaid" provided information from 2014 to 2016 (https://www.cms.gov/Research-Statistics-Data-and-Systems/Statistics-Trends-and-Reports/MedicareProgramRatesStats/SummaryMedicareMedicaid.html), and (3) the "CMS – Fast Facts" provided statistics in 2017 and 2018 (link: https://www.cms.gov/fastfacts/). We used the "CMS – Statistics Reference Booklet" that provided CHIP enrollment rates from 1998 to 2016 (https://www.cms.gov/Research-Statistics-Data-and-Systems/Statistics-Trends-and-Reports/CMS-Statistics-Reference-Booklet/2003.html) and the "CMS – Fast Facts" for CHIP enrollment in 2017 (https://www.cms.gov/fastfacts/). CHIP enrollment for 2018 was not available in the CMS Fast Facts.

NOTE: The numbers represent "person-year equivalents" or total individuals ever enrolled in Medicaid/CHIP in a fiscal year. CHIP is the Children's Health Insurance Program that was first implemented in 1998. For Medicaid and CHIP, data are reported by individual states and are representative of the unduplicated number of children ever enrolled in Medicaid and CHIP. The dotted line represents a change in the source of data.

cutoffs for these eligibility groups, and again after the passage of the ACA in 2014.

Coverage of the elderly has been remarkably constant, in part because most medical expenditures for the aged are covered under a separate federal program, Medicare. Medicaid primarily covers low-income elderly people in nursing homes, who have spent down their assets so that they are poor enough to qualify. Medicaid now covers six out of ten nursing home residents.[5]

FIGURE 2
Real Spending Per Beneficiary by Eligibility Group, FY1975–2016

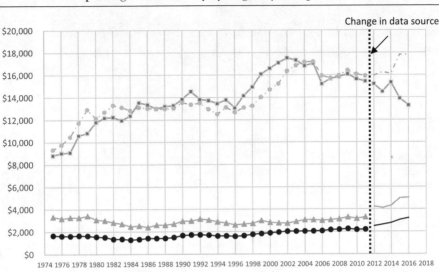

SOURCE: We used two data sources to construct this figure: (1) the CMS Tables (2012) from 1975 to 2011 (https://www.cms.gov/Research-Statistics-Data-and-Systems/Statistics-Trends-and-Reports/MedicareMedicaidStatSupp/Downloads/2013_Section13.pdf#table13.11) and (2) the "CMS – Brief Summaries of Medicare & Medicaid" from 2012 to 2016 (https://www.cms.gov/Research-Statistics-Data-and-Systems/Statistics-Trends-and-Reports/MedicareProgramRatesStats/SummaryMedicareMedicaid.html).
NOTE: Amounts are in 2010 dollars. The dotted line represents a change in the data source.

Figure 1, which shows the number of Medicaid-eligible individuals, should be contrasted with Figure 2, which shows spending per beneficiary by eligibility category. Although the majority of recipients are children, annual spending per child is low, at approximately $3,000 (2010 U.S. dollars). Low-income, nondisabled adults are also relatively inexpensive to cover. Figure 2 shows clearly that the disabled and the elderly are the high-cost groups, with costs more than four times the average per capita cost for a child or nondisabled adult. Thus, although the majority of recipients are children, the elderly and disabled account for about 60 percent of Medicaid's costs.

Since Medicaid is run at the state level under federal guidelines, these averages mask considerably the variability in the generosity of the programs and in the eligibility rules across states. Income cutoffs for the elderly and disabled range from 74 to 100 percent of the federal poverty rate, while cutoffs for pregnant women varied from 145 to 375 percent of poverty as of April 1, 2019.[6] These differences in generosity across states mean that similar families will be treated quite differently in terms of health care coverage, depending on where they live.

In constructing these figures, we were forced to rely on different sources of data before and after 2012.[7] The Center for Medicare and Medicaid Services

FIGURE 3
Real Federal and State Medicaid Expenditures (Millions), Fiscal Years 1966 to 2017

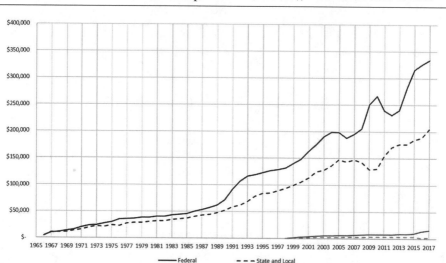

SOURCE: We used two sources of data to construct this figure: (1) the CMS, Office of the Actuary, National Health Statistics Group: "National Health Expenditures by Type of Service and Source of Funds: Calendar Years 1960 to 2016" from 1966 to 2016 (https://www.cms.gov/Research-Statistics-Data-and-Systems/Statistics-Trends-and-Reports/NationalHealthExpendData/NationalHealthAccountsHistorical.html) and (2) the "MACStats: Medicaid and CHIP Data Book" for 2017 (https://www.macpac.gov/publica-tion/macstats-medicaid-and-chip-data-book-2/).
NOTE: Amounts are in 2010 dollars.

(CMS) is working on a new database (Transformed Medicaid Statistical Information System, or TMSIS), which has caused delays in the public release of information on enrollments and per capita spending levels. These data series changes mean that it may not be possible to determine the effects of the ACA (whose main provisions came into effect in 2014) on Medicaid with absolute certainty.[8]

Figure 3 shows trends in state and federal expenditures on Medicaid and CHIP. State governments run Medicaid and receive a federal "match" of state expenditures. These matching funds now account for over half of the program's total costs. Figure 3 shows the relief that the federal government provided to states during the Great Recession (2007–2009), when economic hardship caused Medicaid coverage to increase at a time when state budgets were already under severe strain from a downturn in tax receipts.[9] Without this increase, states would have had to implement painful cuts in Medicaid or other important areas such as education.

Figure 4 shows that despite increases in federal aid, Medicaid has consumed a growing share of state budgets over time. Much of the increase is because infla-tion in health care costs has generally outstripped overall inflation. Despite the

FIGURE 4
Medicaid as a Share of State Budgets, Including and Excluding Federal Funds,
FY1990–2016

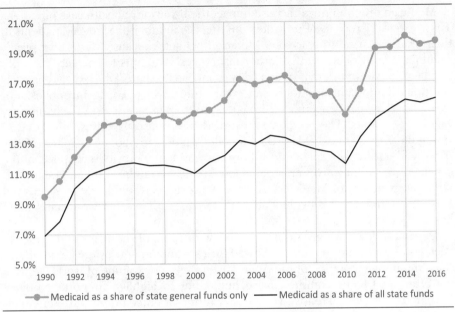

SOURCE: Medicaid and CHIP Payment and Access Commission. These data are taken from the following source: https://www.macpac.gov/publication/medicaid-as-a-share-of-state-budgets-including-and-excluding-federal-funds/.

growth in costs, however, total Medicaid spending in 2019 is expected to be 20 to 30 percent lower than the actuaries' initial estimates, suggesting that Medicaid provides health care in a relatively efficient way (Glied and Tavenner 2019).

The Effects of Medicaid on Health, Well-Being, and Behavior

Whether Medicaid affects people's health is a first-order question. But to affect health, Medicaid must impact other aspects of people's lives, such as health insurance coverage, quantity and/or quality of care received, or financial well-being. Medicaid may also affect people's economic behavior: most obviously, healthy people are more likely to be able to work and will likely be able to work to older ages than unhealthy people. To the extent that Medicaid makes people better off financially, they may also choose to consume some of this "wealth" by working fewer hours. In the United States, most privately insured people obtain health insurance through their employers. Consequently, Medicaid could allow some people with employer health insurance to drop out of the labor force or reduce their work hours. Medicaid's sharp income cutoffs might discourage people from earning more than these cutoffs if increasing their earnings means that they would lose their Medicaid coverage.

Medicaid program rules can also impact the behavior of health care providers. There are many reports of providers limiting the number of Medicaid patients in their practice (or refusing to treat Medicaid patients) because Medicaid typically reimburses providers less than other insurances. Attempts to correct this problem by giving hospitals that treat a "disproportionate share" of Medicaid patients additional lump sum payments can create their own perverse incentives. For example, they can encourage providers to "cream skim" relatively healthy Medicaid patients. The literature on provider responses is ably summarized in Bitler and Zavodny (2017) and Buchmueller, Ham, and Shore-Sheppard (2016), so we will not further delve into it here. By and large, providers respond in the expected way to incentives created by low Medicaid reimbursement. Hence, differential treatment of Medicaid patients by providers would likely be reduced if Medicaid reimbursed providers at market rates, an idea that we discuss more here.

In what follows, we give a brief overview of some of the main findings from decades of Medicaid research, followed by a section on new evidence on effects since the implementation of the ACA. Given the sheer volume of work, we have not attempted to be comprehensive but rather to highlight important points. Research on Medicaid tends to emphasize different outcomes for different eligibility groups, in part because there are differences in the types of services that are covered. Hence, we have opted to have separate discussions of low-income women and children; elderly people in nursing homes; low-income, nondisabled adults; and the disabled.

Low-income women and children

Pregnant women and children are the majority of Medicaid recipients. The staggered implementation of the Medicaid expansions of the late 1980s and 1990s provided an opportunity to examine the effect of eligibility for public health insurance in these groups. Some studies focus on pregnant women and infant health outcomes, while other studies examine the combined effects of coverage in the in utero period and early childhood on later child outcomes.

Effects of the expansions for pregnant women on infant health outcomes were significant and immediate. For example, Currie and Gruber (1996a) show that the 30 percent increase in the eligibility of pregnant women that took place was associated with an 8.5 percent decline in the infant mortality rate. The Medicaid expansions to pregnant women had little effect on fertility (Zavodny and Bitler 2010; DeLeire, Lopoo, and Simon 2011). However, expansions of Medicaid funding for family planning services increased contraceptive use and reduced births (Kearney and Levine 2009; Zavodny and Bitler 2010).

The roughly 15 percent increase in Medicaid eligibility for children that occurred over the same period reduced the probability that a child went without any doctor visits during the year by 9.6 percent and reduced preventable hospitalizations (Currie and Gruber 1996b; Kaestner, Joyce, and Racine 2001; Aizer, Currie, and Moretti 2007; Dafny and Gruber 2005; Howell and Kenney 2012). These results suggest that as many as 6 million children received increased access to basic preventive care. Being eligible for Medicaid conferred gains in access to care even without formal Medicaid coverage, as providers became aware that most low-income children were eligible and that they could be reimbursed for services rendered ex post.

These expansions in public health insurance for pregnant women and children dramatically reduced mortality among poor children and especially among poor African American children. The result is that inequality in mortality has been falling among children since 1990, even while it has increased for adults (Currie and Schwandt 2016). In fact, the child mortality rate in the United States converged toward the lower Canadian rate between 1990 and 2010 (M. Baker, Currie, and Schwandt 2017).

Goodman-Bacon (2018) uses historical data about the rollout of Medicaid across states in the late 1960s and finds that mortality fell more rapidly among infants and children in states with bigger Medicaid expansions. Among nonwhite children, who were poorer on average and therefore most likely to be affected, mortality fell by 20 percent. Thus, the historical results mesh well with those from the more recent Medicaid expansions.

Many recent studies look at the long-term effects of Medicaid coverage in early childhood on adult outcomes. Goodman-Bacon (2016) finds that the rollout of Medicaid in the 1960s reduced adult disability and increased labor supply measured up to 50 years later, while Boudreaux, Golberstein, and McAlpine (2016) find that access to Medicaid in early childhood reduces high blood pressure, diabetes, heart disease, and obesity.

Several recent papers look at the long-term effects of the expansions of maternal and child Medicaid eligibility in the late 1980s and early 1990s (D. Brown, Kowalski and Lurie 2015; Cohodes et al. 2016; Miller and Wherry 2019; Wherry and Meyer 2016; Wherry et al. 2018). These studies follow cohorts who received Medicaid coverage in utero or early childhood over time. Levine and Schanzenbach (2009) find long-run effects of Medicaid on child educational attainment and achievement test scores, while Currie, Decker, and Lin (2008) find that they are in better health in adolescence. As young adults, covered cohorts are more likely to work, have higher earnings, have more education, and are in better health (using self-reported health, mortality, and hospitalization rates as outcomes) than cohorts who were not covered by the Medicaid/CHIP expansions. East et al. (2017) find that the effects of the Medicaid expansion are being felt intergenerationally: women who were covered by Medicaid as infants because of the expansions in the late 1980s and early 1990s are giving birth to healthier children today.

Finally, Buchmueller, Ham, and Shore-Sheppard (2016) provide an in-depth overview of an earlier body of literature examining the effects of Medicaid expansions in the 1980s and 1990s on the work effort of mothers with young children and of the disabled. They conclude that there is little evidence of any effect.

In summary, there is overwhelming evidence that expansions of Medicaid coverage to low-income pregnant women and children have had dramatic positive effects on their health and well-being and have improved the quality of the labor force as the children enter adulthood. Recent cuts to Medicaid coverage of children threaten these gains. For example, recent changes to the rules governing when immigrants are deemed a "public charge" threaten health care coverage for children who are U.S. citizens but have undocumented family members.[10]

Elderly people in nursing homes

About a fifth of Medicaid expenditures are for the elderly—primarily through spending on long-term care services such as nursing homes.[11] Eligibility requirements require elderly people to "spend down" their assets and have low enough incomes to qualify for Medicaid coverage of their nursing home care.[12] In most states with an income cap, individuals may not have monthly incomes higher than $2,205. In states that use "medically needy" criterion for eligibility, an individual must spend all her or his income on medical expenses except for a small personal allowance of $50 to $100 per month to qualify. Single individuals applying for Medicaid's Long-Term Care coverage are allowed to have a maximum of $2,000 in "countable" assets. Income and asset cutoffs are slightly higher for married couples.

Research into the role of Medicaid in the nursing home market has focused on four main areas: (1) whether increases in Medicaid generosity affect nursing home utilization; (2) whether there are shortages of nursing home beds for Medicaid patients; (3) whether the quality of nursing home care for Medicaid recipients is worse than the care received by private-pay elderly; and (4) the relationship between Medicaid reimbursement levels, service quality, and patient health.

The demand for nursing home care seems to be unresponsive to Medicaid's generosity, which suggests that people who use nursing homes have few viable alternatives and an urgent need for care (Grabowski and Gruber 2007). In the past, Medicaid patients have faced shortages of nursing home beds perhaps because Medicaid's payment rate for nursing home care tends to be significantly below the private market rate or the Medicare rate (although Medicare does not pay for long-term care, it does pay for short-term rehabilitative stay) (Reschovsky 1996). However, nursing home occupancy rates have declined nationwide from 93 percent in 1977 to 82.3 percent in 2014 (Laes-Kushner 2018). States such as Oregon are struggling with occupancy rates of only 52 percent. As the cost of maintaining empty beds tends to be reflected in overall nursing home costs, states have experimented with policies such as "bed buybacks" to encourage providers to voluntarily retire licensed beds and increase occupancy rates. However, the oldest baby boomers are only in their 70s, and as this large cohort enters extreme old age, demand for nursing homes may rise.

Once Medicaid patients receive a bed, Medicaid-funded residents in nursing homes receive care that is of similar quality compared to private-pay patients (Grabowski 2001, 2004; Grabowski, Gruber, and Angelelli 2008). Moreover, reductions in Medicaid reimbursements to nursing homes affect service quality and patients' health for all patients. Mor et al. (2011) show that a cut in the Medicaid reimbursement rate of around 10 percent led to a functional decline of almost 10 percent in nursing home residents (that is, a decline in their ability to walk or use the restroom by themselves). Reductions in Medicaid reimbursement rates raise the odds that patients will be in persistent pain and that they will have bedsores (Grabowski, Gruber, and Mor 2017; Grabowski and Angelelli 2004).

Looking after nursing home patients is a labor-intensive job, and so having enough staff and having high-quality staff are critical to providing good care. Hence, lower Medicaid reimbursement rates can affect patient's health if nursing homes react by reducing staff. Stevens et al. (2015) suggest that one reason that recessions appear to improve the health of older people is that by lowering labor costs, recessions allow for improved levels of staffing in nursing homes.

Policy discussions about nursing homes have been dominated by the issue of escalating costs. Some estimate that the average cost of nursing home care is around $125,000 per year (The Association for Long Term Care Planning 2019).[13] State governments pay approximately half of Medicaid costs, and in many states, the rising cost of nursing home care threatens to crowd out other necessary spending, such as spending on education. At the same time, when there are shortages of nursing home beds, or when the quality of nursing home care is poor, it can result in people being hospitalized, which is even more expensive.

One-quarter of nursing home residents are hospitalized each year, and the daily cost of caring for them more than quadruples when they move to the hospital. Research shows that a reduction in nursing home reimbursements of around 10 percent leads to a 5 percent rise in the odds that residents will be hospitalized (Intrator et al. 2007). However, to the extent that care in hospitals is paid for by Medicare, which does not require state cost-sharing, it may be in the fiscal interest of state governments to allow people to be pushed into hospitals rather than to have them stay in nursing homes.

The main approaches that states have employed to lower nursing home costs are reducing Medicaid payment rates and directly limiting the number of nursing home beds via certificate-of-need laws and construction moratoria. These laws are effective in limiting nursing home construction and state Medicaid expenditures (Grabowski, Ohsfeldt, and Morrisey 2003) but reduce nursing home competition and lower both quality of care and access to services for Medicaid residents (Grabowski, Angelelli, and Mor 2004; Grabowski et al. 2004). Lowering costs by denying nursing home care to needy people does not seem like good public policy. Not surprisingly, the laws do little to control hospital costs (Lanning, Morrisey, and Ohsfeldt 1991; Conover and Sloan 1998; Salkever 2000).

Capitated payments are another policy measure that has been implemented to contain costs. In managed care plans, providers typically receive a fixed amount for each enrolled individual. In principle, this system should encourage lower utilization of nursing home services and increase the use of cheaper home- or community-based services. However, health care quality may also decline as providers are no longer compensated for providing additional services (Grabowski 2004).

Another type of policy aimed at reducing the public cost of nursing home care involves encouraging people to purchase private long-term care (LTC) insurance policies. Currently, only 10 to 12 percent of the U.S. population has LTC insurance (Johnson 2016),[14] a fraction that is declining as the cost of LTC insurance has risen. Goda (2011) evaluates a tax-incentive policy that aimed to encourage purchases of LTC plans and shows that it did increase private LTC insurance coverage (by 2.8 percentage points) but only among high-income or wealthy individuals who were already more likely to have the option to purchase LTC policies from their employers (and were less likely to be covered by Medicaid).

Low-income, nondisabled adults

Until quite recently, low-income adults who were not mothers of young children and who were not disabled were seldom eligible for Medicaid. Hence, it is not surprising that there has been less research on the impact of Medicaid on low-income, nondisabled adults than on other groups. Most research on this subject prior to the ACA focuses on one-off state-level expansions of Medicaid, especially the expansion in Oregon, which is discussed further below. Research on this group has focused on (1) insurance coverage; (2) financial security; (3) health care use; (4) health outcomes; and (5) measures of work effort including participation, employment, and job mobility.

Perhaps the least controversial finding from this literature is that Medicaid expansions increase health insurance coverage. There is a large body of literature examining crowd out of private health insurance by public health insurance, beginning with Cutler and Gruber (1996). See Buchmueller, Ham, and Shore-Sheppard (2016) and Bitler and Zavodny (2017) for excellent recent summaries of this work.

Medicaid coverage also improves financial security and reduces medical debt. The evidence from both experimental evaluations and natural experiments suggests that health insurance reduces out-of-pocket medical spending and, in particular, reduces catastrophic out-of-pocket expenditures that might impose huge consumption costs on individuals (Clemans-Cope et al. 2013; Hu et al. 2016; Mazumder and Miller 2016; Michalopolous et al. 2011). Gross and Notowidigdo (2011) examine the effect of the Medicaid expansions between 1992 and 2004 on bankruptcies and find that a 10 percent increase in eligibility for Medicaid reduces bankruptcy by 8 percent. Since catastrophic medical bills can push people into poverty, these results suggest that Medicaid provides a safety net that may reduce poverty.[15]

The evidence also suggests that Medicaid improves access to health services and increases the consumption of health care among low-income able-bodied adults. Sommers et al. (2017) find a 41-percentage-point increase in the probability of having a regular source of care among uninsured people gaining coverage. Measures such as having a usual source of care, receiving an annual checkup, and self-reported ability to pay for needed treatment also increased (Sommers et al. 2016, 2017; Miller and Wherry 2017; Courtemanche et al. 2018), while the probability of delaying care because of cost fell (Sommers, Baicker, and Epstein 2012).

The Oregon Health Insurance Experiment was a social experiment designed to examine the effects of providing Medicaid coverage to low-income, uninsured adults. The state received federal permission to expand Medicaid coverage of this group but did not have funds to cover all low-income adults. Therefore, adults were randomly chosen from those who applied. The results regarding effects on insurance coverage, utilization of care, and financial security are consistent with those from the nonexperimental studies discussed here. There was no crowd out of private health insurance coverage. Medicaid coverage increased health care use across all dimensions including outpatient care, preventive care, prescription drugs, hospital admissions, and emergency room visits. For instance, the average person in the control group visited an emergency room 1.02 times, but people in the treatment group increased ER use by 0.41 visits per person, or 40 percent (Finkelstein et al. 2012; Baicker et al. 2013; Taubman et al. 2014; Baicker et al. 2014; Finkelstein et al. 2016). Receiving Medicaid also reduced the risk of catastrophic out-of-pocket medical expenditures, defined as expenditures of 30 percent of household income or greater (Finkelstein, Mahoney, and Notowidigdo 2018).

Findings regarding the health effects of Medicaid coverage are more heterogeneous. Sommers, Baicker, and Epstein (2012) employ a difference-in-difference strategy comparing changes in county-level mortality rates in New York, Maine, and Arizona—three states that expanded their Medicaid programs in the early 2000s—to those in neighboring states that did not implement such expansions, before and after the policy change. They find that Medicaid expansions were associated with a significant 6.1 percent reduction in mortality, concentrated among adults 35 to 64, nonwhites, and residents of poorer counties. These expansions also improved self-reports of "excellent" or "very good" health (by 3.4 percent).

The Oregon Health Insurance Experiment finds improvements in self-reported health and especially in mental health but does not find any significant effects on physical health measures (such as blood pressure) or on mortality, although an important caveat to both the Oregon study and the earlier one is that one might not expect to see a large mortality effect within a few years of a change in health insurance status. It is possible that the differing findings across studies reflect heterogeneity across groups in addition to statistical uncertainty. Sommers et al. (2015) find that the largest improvements in coverage and in access to medical care occurred among racial and ethnic minorities, a finding that echoes the result that the earlier Medicaid expansions to children had their largest effects on minority children. Sommers, Baicker, and Epstein (2012) show that the declines in mortality were particularly concentrated among older adults, nonwhites, and residents of poorer counties. It may be that the health impacts are also concentrated in these groups.

The most controversial issue associated with extending Medicaid to low-income adults who are not disabled concerns possible effects on the incentive to work. Income cutoffs for the program may cause people to lower their incomes by reducing work hours to maintain their Medicaid coverage. In addition, if public health insurance is available, it may remove an incentive to try to find a job that offers private health insurance.

The Oregon Health Insurance Experiment finds no statistically significant effect of Medicaid coverage on employment or earnings (Baicker et al. 2013). Dague, DeLeire, and Leininger (2017) examine a policy change in Wisconsin, which had expanded Medicaid coverage of low-income adults but then placed a sudden cap on new enrollments in the Medicaid program in October 2009. Using state administrative data from 2005 to 2011, they compare people who enrolled before the cap to those who had applied but were waitlisted after the announcement of the cap. They find that Medicaid coverage reduced employment in the covered group by about 12 percent relative to the waitlisted group.

At the other end of the spectrum, Garthwaite, Gross, and Notowidigdo (2014) compare childless adults to other adults in Tennessee and in other southern states before and after a Medicaid policy change in Tennessee. Beginning in July 2005, Tennessee disenrolled around 170,000 people from Medicaid, and the authors find that this disenrollment led to a 60 percent increase in the labor supply of affected adults. These large estimates have been critiqued, largely on the basis that the dataset they use, the March Current Population Survey, yields a relatively small sample with an imprecise measure of Medicaid status. A study of the effect of this same policy change using administrative data does not find statistically significant effects (Gouskova 2015). Similarly, Ham and Ueda (forthcoming) find little effect of the policy change on labor supply using alternative data sources. In any case, the Tennessee estimates, published as they were on the eve of implementation of the ACA, have proven influential in part because they suggested that the new law might have a large effect on employment. But it is important to note that these results are an outlier relative to the other studies of this issue.

The disabled

Although research on Medicaid has mostly focused on low-income children and their mothers and on the institutionalized elderly, Medicaid spends more on disabled adults than on any other group. In 2011, although the disabled only represented 12 percent of the total Medicaid population, they accounted for 36 percent of the cost (Musumeci and Young 2017). Their cost per capita is substantially higher than for other groups, given their often complex health care needs, the persistence of their health conditions, and their often low employment rates.

Studies about Medicaid and the disabled focus on four key areas: (1) health care coverage, (2) the quality of care, (3) interactions with other programs, and (4) effects on labor-market outcomes. Surprisingly, there are few studies about the effects of Medicaid on the health of the disabled, which may be due to data limitations. The National Health Interview Survey has had questions about limitations on activities of daily living since the 1990s, but it has little information about health per se. Questions about activity limitations were added to the

American Community Survey and the Current Population Surveys in 2008, but again, these datasets have little information about underlying health status.

States are required to give Medicaid coverage to disabled people who qualify for federal Supplemental Security Income (SSI). SSI is available to those who have low income and assets and a disability that impairs their ability to work. The SSI federal benefit rate is generally less than the federal poverty level. Disabled nonelderly people who have a substantial work history may be eligible for Social Security Disability Insurance (SSDI), which is a completely different and separate program with benefit levels geared to a person's earnings history. Those who become eligible for SSDI can receive Medicare coverage after two years, reflecting a more generous package than Medicaid.

When the federal SSI program replaced state-only programs for the disabled in 1972, states were given the option to retain some of their pre-1972 rules for Medicaid eligibility in place of the federal rules. Currently, eleven states have retained such rules, which typically make their programs less generous than the federal program.[16]

Many disabled people are unable to access Medicaid via the SSI program, which is not surprising given relatively onerous requirements for proving eligibility. Benitez-Silva, Buchinsky, and Rust (2004) estimate that up to 60 percent of those whose claims are denied are actually disabled and that the adjudication of claims can take years. Hence, general increases in the generosity of public health insurance coverage can also increase coverage of the disabled. For example, the Massachusetts health care reform reduced the probability that working age people with disabilities lacked health insurance by about 50 percent and also reduced the probability of going without care due to cost (Gettens, Mitra, and Himmelstein 2011).

Research has also focused on how Medicaid coverage affects labor force participation and employment among the disabled. There is a large branch of literature suggesting that increasing the generosity of disability programs (which generally include public health insurance coverage) can discourage people from working (see, for example, Autor et al. 2016; Deshpande 2016). Here, we consider the narrower question of how changes in Medicaid eligibility of the disabled can affect labor market outcomes and participation in disability insurance programs.

It is difficult and time-consuming to qualify for SSI, and SSI recipients must maintain a low income to remain qualified. People on SSI may be discouraged from working because if their incomes exceed the cutoff, they lose SSI eligibility and, consequently, health insurance coverage. Baicker et al. (2014) show, however, that the Oregon Health Experiment had no effect on enrollees' take-up of disability insurance. Similarly, Maestas, Muellen, and Strand (2014) find no evidence that the Massachusetts health care reform led to a change in the number of SSI applications. Hence, there is little evidence so far that disabled adults are changing their work effort to qualify for health insurance.

In addition to the possible interactions between Medicaid generosity and SSI, there may be trade-offs between what the government spends on the disabled under Medicaid and what it spends under Medicare. Autor, Chandra, and Duggan (2011) show that there is substantial variation in spending under these two programs across geographic regions and that areas with high Medicaid spending tend to have lower Medicare spending on the disabled. The variation in Medicaid spending on the disabled tends to be driven by variation in the intensity of care. These findings suggest that some of the cost of increasing the level of Medicaid expenditures on the working-aged disabled today may be offset by lower Medicare costs on the disabled elderly tomorrow. Given the high cost of this part of the program, further investigation of the reasons for variations in spending on the disabled under Medicaid and possible trade-offs with expenditures on Medicare is warranted.

Medicaid and the ACA

The ACA is the most important health care reform legislation enacted in the United States since the creation of Medicare and Medicaid in 1965. The primary aim of the ACA was to reduce the number of Americans without health insurance and to improve the accessibility, affordability, and quality of health care for consumers (Obama 2016). For example, the ACA required most insurance plans to cover ten classes of benefits, including treatment of mental illness, which historically had been covered less generously than other health care services (Garfield, Lave, and Donohue 2010).

The ACA contained few provisions that were expected to directly address health care prices and, therefore, had little hope of reducing costs (Gruber 2008). For instance, the ACA tried to address the high cost of long-term care by creating a voluntary system of LTC insurance (i.e., the CLASS Act), but due to high cost, this system never actually got off the ground (James, Gellad, and Hughes 2017).

As enacted in March 2010, the ACA created subsidized marketplaces (exchanges) where uninsured individuals with incomes less than 400 percent of the federal poverty line could purchase private health insurance. The ACA initially required all states to extend eligibility for Medicaid to adults in families with incomes less than 138 percent of the federal poverty line, as these people were viewed as too poor to be able to purchase health insurance even in the subsidized exchanges. The ACA also changed the rules regarding the determination of gross income and required every state to increase income eligibility for Medicaid by 5 percentage points above the March 2010 level, effective January 1, 2014.

But in 2012, the Supreme Court ruled that requiring states to expand their Medicaid programs was unconstitutional. As of December 2018, thirty-six states and the District of Columbia had chosen to expand Medicaid, with the remainder of the states refusing to do so, even with the offer of large federal subsidies to help pay for newly eligible individuals. However, Frean, Gruber, and Sommers (2017) find that even in states that did not increase their income limits, more individuals who were eligible under existing criteria enrolled in Medicaid, a phenomenon they dub a "welcome mat effect." Still, states that have not expanded Medicaid have ended up with a large number of people with incomes too high to qualify for Medicaid but too low to benefit from the exchanges.

There is no doubt that the ACA was successful in increasing the fraction of Americans with health insurance (Gruber and Sommers 2019; Frean, Gruber, and Sommers 2017; Courtemanche et al. 2017; Kaestner et al. 2017; Wherry and Meyer 2016). For example, Courtemanche et al. (2017) show that the ACA increased the proportion of residents with insurance by 5.9 percentage points compared to 3.0 percentage points in states that did not expand Medicaid.

Effects of the ACA on health and health care

These increases have had positive effects on the use of health care and on some measures of health. Sommers et al. (2017) use survey data collected through the end of 2016 from Kentucky and Arkansas, which both expanded coverage, compared to Texas, which did not. They find a 23-percentage-point increase in "excellent" self-reported health in Kentucky and Arkansas relative to Texas. Other studies have shown positive effects of Medicaid expansions following from the ACA on health measures such as better self-assessed health, lower incidence of depression, and smoking cessation (Simon, Soni, and Cawley 2017; Winkelman and Chang 2018; Koma et al. 2017).

Ghosh, Simon, and Sommers (2017) show that within the first 15 months of the ACA expansion, Medicaid-paid prescriptions increased by 19 percent, which represented approximately seven additional prescriptions per year per newly enrolled beneficiary.[17] MacLean et al. (2017) show that Medicaid expansions between 2011 and 2017 increased the use of psychotropic prescriptions by 22.3 percent relative to nonexpansion states. These effects were experienced across most major mental illness categories and across states with different levels of patient need, system capacity, and scope for expansion. The study, however, finds no evidence that Medicaid expansions reduced suicide, a proxy for the most serious mental illnesses.

A recent study by Black et al. (2018) also finds no evidence that ACA expansions have changed mortality for nonelderly adults. They comment, however, that their estimated confidence intervals are large and that even the national natural experiment of the ACA is underpowered to find effects on mortality of the size that one might expect given past research on the relationship between medical care and shorter-term mortality changes in nondisabled adults.

One caveat to the generally improved outlook for the health and health care of patients receiving Medicaid because of the ACA is that the sudden influx of newly insured people into the system increased waiting times for appointments, reflecting a shortage of primary care physicians available to treat Medicaid patients (Miller and Wherry 2017).

Effects of the ACA on work

Because the ACA Medicaid expansions primarily cover able-bodied working age adults, much of the attention has been focused on changes in their work effort. It is worth considering that any work reductions experienced by childless adults who suddenly were covered, would imply that people were working only because they needed health insurance. It is questionable whether as a social policy, one wants to force people to work to get health care, if they have health problems and have difficulty working.

In any case, Gooptu et al. (2016) directly examine the effects of the ACA on labor market outcomes among adults with incomes below 138 percent of the federal poverty level. They compare states that expanded Medicaid and those that did not, looking at groups who were eligible and groups who were not eligible for Medicaid before and after the ACA (2005 to 2013 versus 2014 to 2015), and find no statistically significant effect of Medicaid coverage on employment. Similarly, Leung and Mas (2018) find no effect of the ACA on employment. Overall then, with the sole exception of the Garthwaite, Gross, and Notowidigdo's (2014) pre-ACA study where there may be some issues of data quality, the literature about the labor supply effects of Medicaid on nondisabled adults suggests that these effects are modest.

Turning to disabled adults, a small-scale survey using difference-in-difference methods finds that adults with disabilities living in states that expanded eligibility for Medicaid under the ACA were significantly more likely to be employed than those in nonexpansion states (38.0 percent versus 31.9 percent) (J. Hall et al. 2017).

Several studies have examined the impact of the ACA on young adults, a group with historically low rates of health insurance coverage, on education and employment. The ACA allowed parents to cover children up to age 26 under their parents' plans. However, Slusky (2017), using standard data sources such as the Current Population Surveys, shows that difference-in-differences estimates for this group are unreliable due to small sample sizes.

Possible Reforms to the Medicaid Program

In this section, we first explore some of the most persistent complaints about the Medicaid program and then consider reform options that have been suggested.

Cost and access to care: The main complaints about Medicaid

One common complaint is that even in states that expanded Medicaid after the ACA, there are still people who lack health insurance coverage because they cannot afford even the subsidized insurance available on the exchanges. In states that did not expand Medicaid, there are a large number of people whose incomes are too high for Medicaid but too low to qualify them to participate in the federal or state health insurance exchanges. This is not a complaint about Medicaid per se, but about the way that free or subsidized public insurance is means-tested.

One of the most persistent complaints about Medicaid itself is its high and rising cost to government. Rising health care costs are likely to put a strain on both state and federal budgets for the foreseeable future. When considering costs, it is important to consider that both the quantity of health care demanded and its price affect total cost. As a society, we have deliberately chosen to expand Medicaid coverage to millions of previously uninsured low-income pregnant women, children, disabled people, and now to nondisabled adults. We should not be surprised that people who previously had no health insurance consume more care when care becomes free for them. That is the intention of the policy.

Compared to most European countries, Americans pay more for specific health services as well as for prescription drugs (Kamal and Cox 2018). That is, high prices are the main aspect of health care costs that have not been implicitly chosen through public policy. Consistent with the higher prices, Americans typically consume *less* health care (e.g., fewer doctor visits and fewer hospital days) than residents of other wealthy countries, while paying twice as much per capita for our care. Rising drug prices are a particular problem for state Medicaid programs. For some diseases, like severe mental illnesses or cystic fibrosis, most patients are considered to be disabled and so are covered by Medicaid. Drugs for these conditions are expensive and getting more so over time. Cooper et al. (2019) show that there are vast and unexplained differences in the prices of similar services across U.S. hospitals, suggesting that there is little underlying market rationale for the high prices we pay. Instead, high prices may reflect a noncompetitive and highly concentrated market for health care (National Academy of Social Insurance 2015).

This discussion suggests that any policy that reduced the cost of Medicaid without greatly increasing the number of uninsured would have to tackle the systemic problem of high U.S. health care prices. So far, there has been little political will to do this. The leading options for controlling prices include measures to encourage price transparency, vigorously enforcing existing antitrust laws, and allowing government agencies to negotiate with providers over prices. To be clear, state governments do set the prices paid for services under Medicaid. But in the absence of any negotiation about prices in Medicare, this simply creates an incentive for providers to prefer Medicare to Medicaid patients.

A second common complaint about the Medicaid program involves difficulty in accessing care. For example, Alexander and Currie (2017) show that children with asthma (the most common reason for childhood hospitalization) were less likely to be hospitalized after presenting at the emergency room if they had public health insurance (though this had no measurable effect on their health outcomes). As discussed above, some providers do not participate in Medicaid because of low reimbursements. Just as eligibility varies a great deal across states, so does provider reimbursement, so access issues are more acute in some states than in others. Access is a particular problem for specialist care. In addition to low reimbursements, providers cite administrative difficulties with reimbursement as a reason for limiting their participation in the program.

Medicaid managed care: The dominant reform idea to date

One attempted solution to both the high cost of Medicaid and the access problem has been for state Medicaid agencies to contract with managed care organizations. Increasingly, the same third-party companies administer both private and public health insurance plans. From 1991 to 2009, the fraction of Medicaid recipients who shifted from the traditional fee-for-service model to Medicaid managed care (MMC) increased from 11 percent to 71 percent (Duggan and Hayford 2013).

MMC has not proven to be a panacea, however. Using data on state and local level MMC mandates and detailed data from CMS on state Medicaid expenditures, Duggan and Hayford (2013) show that the shift to MMC increased Medicaid spending, a finding that echoes Duggan (2004). However, the effects of the shift to MMC on Medicaid spending varied significantly across states as a function of the generosity of the state's baseline Medicaid provider reimbursement rates. MMC can increase costs to the state when insurance companies negotiate reimbursement formulas that turn out to be more advantageous to them than the state presumably foresaw. MMC can also increase costs by negotiating a reimbursement rate based on average Medicaid costs and then systematically encouraging only low-cost individuals to enroll in their plans (called "cream skimming").

Studies examining the estimated effects of MMC on access to care have shown mixed results. Bindman et al. (2005) study the welfare population and find reductions in hospitalization for ambulatory care sensitive conditions, which were larger for minority patients. They interpret this as evidence of improved access to preventive care, though it could also reflect decreased access to hospital care. L. Baker and Afendulis (2005) find that MMC did shift care away from emergency rooms and toward outpatient visits, but it also led to increases in the reporting of unmet medical needs and decreases in having a usual source of care. Herring and Adams (2011) also find reductions in access to care.

Studies of MMC implementation in Tennessee and North Carolina (Conover, Rankin, and Sloan 2001) and California (Aizer, Currie, and Moretti 2007) find that compulsory managed care had a negative impact on the use of prenatal care and on birth outcomes. In California, this may be because Medicaid managed care contracts "carved out" care for sick newborns—that is, high-cost newborns were covered by a state fund rather than by the managed care companies, so that companies had little incentive to act to prevent poor birth outcomes. The example suggests that the contracts governing these plans have important effects on the quality of care provided.

The switch to managed care may also affect who receives services if MMC organizations are actively trying to select low-risk patients. Kuziemko, Meckel, and Rossin-Slater (2018) find that managed care companies in Texas were less likely to enroll African American women than other women, leading to lower use of prenatal care and poorer birth outcomes among this population. Currie and Fahr (2005) report similar findings for California. Kaestner, Dubay, and Kenney (2005) also find that compulsory MMC for pregnant women was associated with increases in the incidence of low birth weight and prematurity.

On the other hand, Chorniy, Currie, and Sonchak (2018) find that in South Carolina, a move to managed care increased screening and treatment of chronic conditions in children, in part because providers received higher reimbursements for children with such conditions. Layton et al. (2019) also find that switching the disabled Medicaid caseload to managed care increased spending and improved health outcomes. One mechanism for these effects was that the Texas Medicaid program released the prescription drug cap when privatization was introduced, leading to an increase in drug spending across a range of medications used for management of acute and chronic conditions (e.g., asthma, antidepressants, etc.), and a reduction in mental health–related hospitalizations.

There is also mixed evidence on how the transition to managed care affected the disabled. On one hand, using the National Health Interview Survey, Coughlin, Long, and Graves (2008) find some evidence of improved access to care under MMC relative to fee-for-service (FFS) Medicaid, with most of the gains limited to beneficiaries in urban areas. Their findings suggest that under MMC, the disabled experienced increases in having a usual source of care for preventative care, having received some type of health care in the past 12 months, and having had contact with both general practitioners and specialists. On the other hand, LoSasso and Freund (2000) look at two California counties and find that increases in MMC enrollments among the disabled were associated with increases in the use of ambulatory services and prescription drug expenditures but also with increases in emergency department and hospital admissions. Burns (2009a) shows that disabled adults in MMCs still face large out-of-pocket expenses: 82 percent of enrollees reported incurring an out-of-pocket health care expense during the year, mostly for prescription medicines. Burns (2009b) shows that compared to disabled FFS enrollees, MMC enrollees are 24.9 percent more likely to wait more than 30 minutes to see a provider, 32 percent more likely to report a problem accessing a specialist, and 10 percent less likely to receive a flu shot within the past year.

The trend toward managed care for Medicaid patients seems unlikely to be reversed, so it is not an active policy debate. However, we have discussed the research on it in some detail because it offers a cautionary example of how a "private-public" partnership can turn out for state governments. Private health insurance companies have proven adept at outmaneuvering the state when it comes to negotiating contracts, so Medicaid costs have often gone up rather than down under MMC. Additionally, state governments have often proven relatively ineffectual in requiring that MMC provide improved access to care.

The examples suggest that the main issue with MMC has to do with the structure of provider reimbursements and the incentives that they provide to serve (or not serve) particular types of clients. That is, the specific details of the contracts matter. At the state level, greater cooperation among states in terms of sharing contract language and experiences might be helpful. At the federal level, CMS might consider offering technical assistance and "best practices" for managing these contracts.

Additional possible reforms

In this subsection, we first discuss some proposed changes to the Medicaid program itself and then briefly consider some proposals that would subsume Medicaid in a reform of the United States' larger health insurance system.

Block grants. One perennial proposal for Medicaid reform would involve making it an entirely state-run program that receives a "block grant" from the federal government. The idea is similar to the 1996 welfare reform that transformed the old Aid for Families with Dependent Children (AFDC) program, which was jointly funded by the federal government and the state, into the state-only Temporary Assistance for Needy Families Program (TANF). Under AFDC, states were entitled to unlimited matching funds to support needy families but set their own benefit levels and administrative rules under federal guidelines. Under TANF, states received block grants that initially were well above the matching grants that they had been receiving for AFDC and were given much more freedom to change program rules. Critics of this change argue that states yielded to a powerful temptation to use block grants for other purposes and that harsh new program rules (e.g., imposing mandatory job search at application, cutting time limits from five years to two, etc.) have resulted in shrunken programs that were of little use during the economic downturn that began in 2008 (Dilger and Boyd 2014).

In some ways, the argument for block-granting Medicaid is at least as strong as that for block-granting welfare, given that regulating health insurance is constitutionally a function of state governments. However, states have been wary about embracing this idea, largely because the rate of growth of health care costs has outstripped the overall inflation rate for decades. Therefore, even a generous block grant indexed to the rate of overall inflation would likely prove insufficient to cover future health care costs. Currently, Tennessee is considering petitioning the federal government to replace its Medicaid program with a block grant. The state is attempting to build in indexing to inflation in health care costs to protect against future erosion of state health care financing.

Even if this newer approach to block-granting Medicaid goes forward, it does not address a fundamental critique of state-level control over Medicaid programs. Many people believe that all Americans should have access to at least a core set of covered services, regardless of which state they live in, which implies a more limited role, rather than a broader role, for states in rule-making about what Medicaid covers and who should be eligible. Block-granting Medicaid would likely reduce Medicaid costs mainly by limiting the amount that some states could or would spend, which would lead to cuts in coverage and in covered services and greater inequities in health care access across states.

Work requirements. A second proposal that has gained currency recently is to impose work requirements on "able-bodied," working-age, adult Medicaid recipients. The best-case scenario is that work requirements would encourage Medicaid recipients to find jobs that included private health insurance and that these jobs would provide a steppingstone to a better life. However, even if such jobs are out of reach for many Medicaid recipients, some observers want to impose work requirements because they find it objectionable to offer benefits to people who are able to work if they are not working.

In January 2018, CMS invited states to solicit proposals for imposing work requirements. As of December 2018, six state proposals had been approved by

CMS and another nine states had submitted applications. Work requirements exempt children, pregnant women, and the disabled, and may or may not exempt primary caregivers for young children or the disabled. Typically, they require nonexempt individuals to work, volunteer, or go to school for 80 hours a month. Some proposals also count hours of job search toward the 80-hour total. Unlike work requirement programs for TANF and SNAP (the Supplemental Nutrition Assistance Program, or Food Stamps), the Medicaid work requirement programs do not build in any funds for job training, job search assistance, child care assistance, or other types of assistance that support employment.

Medicaid work requirements have been controversial and subject to legal challenge. They aim to fix a problem that does not exist: the research literature reviewed above suggests that only one study has ever found large effects of Medicaid on employment. The Oregon Health Insurance Experiment, which has arguably the best research design, found no effect on employment. Most able-bodied welfare recipients work already but have low-wage jobs that do not offer private health insurance coverage. Thus, work requirements in Medicaid have more to do with making a political point than with addressing a real social problem.

While they are highly unlikely to lead to large employment gains, the evidence indicates that Medicaid work requirements lead to large losses in health insurance coverage. This should not be surprising given a great deal of evidence that imposing administrative hurdles (such as proving that one has work or is exempt from work requirements) generally reduces coverage in any public program (Currie and Gahvari 2008).

However, there is also a specific example available to policy-makers. Arkansas' work-requirement program began in June 2018 and is continuing in the face of a legal challenge. In the first six months of Arkansas' program, seventeen thousand people lost coverage out of about sixty-five thousand people who needed to fulfill the work requirements (Scott 2018). Under the Arkansas rules, once people lose coverage, they are ineligible to reapply for Medicaid until the next calendar year. Many of the people who lost coverage in Arkansas may actually have been in compliance with the new requirements but simply failed to report. They may have been unaware of the new requirement, been unable to navigate the state's complicated web interface for reporting (use of the web interface is compulsory), or simply lacked Internet access. Arkansas' experience suggests that work requirements will reduce Medicaid costs, primarily by disenrolling previously eligible low-income recipients. However, keeping in mind that the elderly and the disabled account for 60 percent of Medicaid costs, the cost savings obtained by disenrolling nondisabled adults may prove less than what legislators expected when imposing these measures.

Long-term care. There are few reforms under discussion that would address the large fraction of Medicaid costs consumed by elderly and disabled people in nursing homes. In principle, Medicaid funding could be used to encourage aging in place by providing home health care.[18] One demonstration, the "Community Aging in Place—Advancing Better Living for Elders" (CAPABLE), provides home visits by teams of clinicians (i.e., occupational therapists, nurses, and "handy workers") combined with adaptation of the home (i.e., home repairs, adaptive modifications, or installation of assistive devices valued up to $1,300 in 2013 USD). The intervention led to significant reductions in expenditures and other medical service use in this population compared to a matched control over the first 17 months (Szanton et al. 2018). The problem with expanding these types of programs is that they would likely draw many more people into Medicaid by making long-term care arrangement more appealing. Lieber and Lockwood (2019) suggest that the increase in demand for Medicaid services could be very large, placing additional financial pressure on the program. That is, for every dollar saved by allowing an existing nursing home resident to stay in his or her home, more than a dollar would likely be spent on new entrants to the Medicaid program who would be attracted by more generous home health benefits.

Attempts to encourage people to purchase private long-term care insurance have shown little success, as we discussed. Another potential option would be to use the Social Security system to provide a form of long-term health insurance, allowing new Social Security recipients to choose lower income payments in exchange for using insurance for LTC (see J. Brown and Dynan 2017). This proposal would in effect allow people to use their Social Security benefits to purchase LTC insurance, but it is unclear at this point how many people would take up such an option, especially if publicly funded nursing home care continues to be provided to those who have not "purchased" such coverage.

Another proposal for long-term care involves ending Medicaid coverage of nursing home care and instead creating a new, universal Medicare benefit similar to the way the government created a new Medicare prescription drug benefit (Medicare Part D). At present, elderly people must spend down their assets to qualify for Medicaid coverage of long-term nursing home care and Medicare currently pays for only 100 days of rehabilitative nursing home care. Presumably, states would embrace a proposal to transfer the responsibility for covering nursing home care from Medicaid to Medicare as it would make funding nursing home care a solely federal responsibility. Moreover, elderly people would no longer have to become destitute to receive assistance with nursing home costs. However, such a proposal would greatly increase rather than decrease overall costs. The Trump administration has been moving in the opposite direction, with proposals for large cuts in Medicaid, which would necessitate reductions in state expenditures on nursing home care, and proposals to shift more of the financial burden of LTC to family members (Rau 2017).

Reimbursement rates. Leaving aside the issue of long-term care, another proposal to reform Medicaid involves raising Medicaid reimbursement rates to match Medicare rates but leaving the structure of the program otherwise unchanged. Such a change would increase provider participation in Medicaid and overall quality but would greatly increase costs given that Medicaid reimburses about 70 percent of what Medicare pays on average.[19] To make such a proposal viable might require a fundamental rethinking of the way Medicare sets fees. Unlike in other rich countries, CMS is forbidden by law from negotiating Medicare fees with private providers, resulting in the government being unable to use its market power to lower provider prices.

Single-payer schemes. A more radical proposal that has been gaining traction would be to eliminate Medicaid and offer "Medicare for All." This proposal is not equivalent to a "single-payer" system because Medicare currently offers the option to select "Medicare Advantage" plans offered by private insurers. Medicare's drug benefit (Medicare Part D) is also offered through private health insurers. Medicare for All would be an expensive proposal, especially given that many employers would likely stop offering full-service private insurance if high-quality public insurance were freely available to people younger than 65. (Private insurers might continue to offer "Medi-gap"-like policies to pay for services that Medicare did not cover.) Once again, making this proposal feasible would likely require a commitment to negotiate Medicare fees with providers and private insurers, as well as higher taxes to pay for the program. Also, given that Medicare currently only pays for 100 days of nursing home care, Medicare for All would need to include a new benefit covering longer-term care currently paid for by Medicaid.

Another alternative would be a single-payer health insurance system like Canada's. This proposal is often regarded as politically unfeasible in the United States, where private insurers are large and powerful companies, and many consumers are suspicious of attempts to standardize care and restrict consumer choice. Canada's single-payer system is an outlier among rich countries. Most developed countries have systems that mix privately and publicly funded care (Stabile and Thompson 2014). Even the United Kingdom's National Health Service has moved in this direction in recent years. Hence, it seems likely that the United States will continue to operate some type of hybrid public/private system of health insurance rather than moving to a truly single-payer system.

In fact, one could argue that the ACA moved the United States much closer to many European models of health insurance coverage by patching together a mix of public and private health insurance sources that has come close to achieving full coverage even in the face of considerable political resistance. While far from perfect, the most pragmatic and feasible policy option is likely to be to work within the ACA framework to strengthen regulation of health care providers (including some consideration of some form of price controls), continue to expand and reform Medicaid, and strengthen health care exchanges. The increasing prevalence of Medicaid-managed care plans operated by private companies may offer one mechanism for eventually allowing people who are not low income the option of purchasing Medicaid coverage.

Conclusion

Medicaid directly affects not only poor women and children but many middle-class people who become disabled, spend down their assets, and require nursing home care. In fact, although the majority of Medicaid recipients are women and children, the majority of the spending is on the elderly and disabled. Because of its size and impact on state and federal budgets, Medicaid also has indirect effects on the health care system and on other public spending. Medicaid has improved the health of low-income pregnant women and children, and the elderly and disabled increasingly depend upon it. There is less evidence about the longer-term effects of Medicaid for nondisabled adults, given that wide-spread Medicaid coverage of this group is quite new. However, the available evidence suggests that the program increases well-being and reduces financial uncertainty without having much effect on labor-force outcomes in any group. At the same time, the program is extremely expensive, and costs continue to grow along with overall U.S. health care costs.

Some of the proposals for reforming Medicaid include transforming Medicaid into a "block grant" to states rather than a federal program or allowing states to impose work requirements on recipients. Given our discussion of this reform option, we do not feel that these proposals would achieve the goal of providing minimally acceptable health care coverage for all Americans. Other proposals focus on replacing Medicaid with a universal program such as Medicare for All. This may prove a heavy lift, given that policy-makers have tried and failed to implement such a program before. Still other proposals would keep Medicaid's basic framework but make major changes, such as finding an alternative mecha-nism for funding universal LTC (perhaps through Medicare) or making Medicaid payments to health care providers more comparable to those of Medicare and private payers. While such changes would not be easy, we feel they are worth pursuing. Finally, basic reforms that would affect Medicaid and all other health insurers include strengthening antitrust regulation of health care providers, adopting some form of price regulation, encouraging price transparency, and strengthening health insurance exchanges. These smaller changes likely have the best chance of success and should be pursued vigorously.

As the political tug-of-war over expanding or contracting Medicaid continues, it is worthwhile to ask how much spending on medical care is too much from a social perspective? R. Hall and Jones (2007) argue that as a society becomes wealthier and people have more things, the marginal value of consumption falls relative to the marginal value of having additional healthy life years to enjoy them. Cutler, Rosen, and Vijan (2006) argue that the increased spending on medical care in the United States since 1960 has been "worth it" given any rea-sonable valuation of the improvements in health and life expectancy. From this perspective, the most important question is how we can improve both the equity and the efficiency of health care provision in the United States, rather than how we can reduce spending. Although expansions of the Medicaid program have improved the equity of health care provision, targeting both equity and efficiency may require more fundamental reforms of the U.S. health care system.

Notes

1. https://www.medicaid.gov/medicaid/program-information/medicaid-and-chip-enrollment-data/report-highlights/index.html.

2. https://www.cms.gov/research-statistics-data-and-systems/statistics-trends-and-reports/national-healthexpenddata/nhe-fact-sheet.html.

3. Medicaid is often confused with *Medicare*, a public health insurance program that covers all elderly people and is run by the federal government. In 2016, Medicare accounted for 20 percent of national health expenditures.

4. Medicaid targets children in the poorest households, those living in families with incomes up to 133 percent of the federal poverty level (FPL) (for children 0–6 years of age) or up to 100 percent of the FPL (for children ages 6–18). CHIP covers children starting at the point at which a state's Medicaid eligibility threshold ends, providing coverage to children in families with income up to 200 percent of the FPL or higher.

5. https://www.kff.org/infographic/medicaids-role-in-nursing-home-care/.

6. https://www.medicaid.gov/medicaid/program-information/medicaid-and-chip-eligibility-levels/index.html.

7. For instance, MACStats: Medicaid and CHIP Data Book (2017, 141) says, "One consequence of the transition from the MSIS to the T-MSIS is that there is now a gap in available data from many states. Several states began the transition to the T-MSIS in 2014 and do not have complete information for fiscal year (FY) 2014 available in the MSIS. Although many of these states have submitted data for these missing months through the T-MSIS, the data are still being validated by CMS and are not available for publication at this time. As a result, MACPAC was not able to fully update several exhibits that provide enrollment and spending data by eligibility group."

8. While Figure 1 shows a gentle increase in participation among the aged after 2012, Figure 2 shows a marked decline in spending per beneficiary on this group. Since there is no major reason for this decline in real spending among the elderly, we attribute this pattern to the change in data source.

9. Bitler, Hoynes, and Kuka (2016) examine the role of the safety net (including Medicaid) in mitigating the adverse effects of the Great Recession on child poverty.

10. According to the American Immigration Council (2018), roughly 8 million U.S.-citizen children have a family member who is undocumented.

11. Long-term care spending includes spending on nursing home and continuing care retirement communities, home health care, and residential and personal care. The major form of insurance for nursing home utilization is Medicaid, which provides some support to approximately 65 percent of nursing home residents and pays for 45 percent of the total nursing home bill. Medicare does not pay for long-term care, but the program covers up to 100 days of skilled nursing home care per benefit period, and Medicare pays for 17 percent of nursing home care (Georgetown University, Long-Term Care Financing Project, "National Spending for Long-Term Care," fact sheet, 2007).

12. See https://www.familyassets.com/nursing-homes/resources/medicaid for a useful summary of the rules pertaining to income and asset limits.

13. http://www.altcp.org/long-term-care/long-term-care-cost/.

14. https://www.urban.org/research/publication/who-covered-private-long-term-care-insurance.

15. The flip side of increasing financial security is that Medicaid eligibility may reduce savings. Gruber and Yelowitz (1999) find that the Medicaid expansions of the late 1980s and early 1990s reduced asset holdings, although the sensitivity of their results has been critiqued (Gittleman 2011). Maynard and Qiu (2009) find effects on savings for households in the middle of the income distribution, which makes sense given that poor families have little savings in any case.

16. For example, states may have lower income cut offs or tougher criteria for determining eligibility. For more details about these programs see Watts, Cornachione, and Musumeci (2016) and https://aspe.hhs.gov/report/understanding-medicaid-home-and-community-services-primer-2010-edition/state-209b-option. The law requires states to continue to offer Medicaid coverage to "medically needy" recipients whose SSI benefits place their income above the income cut off.

17. Medication classes that experienced relatively large increases included contraceptives (a 22 percent increase) and cardiovascular drugs (a 21 percent increase). Several drug classes more consistent with acute conditions such as allergies and infections experienced significantly smaller increases.

18. Like nursing home care, home health care can be paid for either by Medicaid, if it is long-term or by Medicare if it is up to 100 days. Even though the statutory eligibility criteria have varied little, changes in the interpretations of the criteria and in the licensing of home health care agencies have led to large swings in the availability and cost of home health care over time (Davitt and Choi 2008).

19. The Kaiser Family Foundation creates a Medicaid-to-Medicare fee index, which is available at: https://www.kff.org/medicaid/state-indicator/medicaid-to-medicare-fee-index/?currentTimeframe=0&sort

Model=%7B%22colId%22:%22Location%22,%22sort%22:%22asc%22%7D. The index shows a great deal of variation across states and is generally lower for primary care than for specialist care.

References

Aizer, Anna, Janet Currie, and Enrico Moretti. 2007. Does managed care hurt health? Evidence from Medicaid mothers. *Review of Economics and Statistics* 89 (3): 385–99.

Alexander, Diane, and Janet Currie. 2017. Are publicly insured children less likely to be admitted to hospital than the privately insured (and does it matter)? *Economics and Human Biology* 25:33–51.

American Immigration Council (AIC). 23 May 2018. US citizen children impacted by immigration enforcement. Fact Sheet. Washington, DC: AIC.

Association for Long Term Care Planning. 2019. *Costs of long term care across states*. Fort Myers, FL: Association for Long Term Care Planning. Available from http://www.altcp.org/long-term-care/long-term-care-cost.

Autor, David, Amitabh Chandra, and Mark Duggan. 2011. Public health expenditures on the working age disabled: Assessing Medicare and Medicaid utilization of SSDI and SSI recipients. MIT Working Paper, Massachusetts Institute of Technology, Cambridge, MA.

Autor, David, Mark Duggan, Kyle Greenberg, and David S. Lyle. 2016. The impact of disability benefits on labor supply: Evidence from the VA's disability compensation program. *American Economic Journal: Applied Economics* 8 (3): 31–68.

Baicker, Katherine, Amy Finkelstein, Jae Song, and Sarah Taubman. 2014. The impact of health insurance expansions on other social safety net programs. *American Economic Review: Papers and Proceedings* 104 (5): 322–28.

Baicker, Katherine, Sarah L. Taubman, Heidi L. Allen, Mira Bernstein, Jonathan H. Gruber, Joseph P. Newhouse, Eric C. Schneider, Bill J. Wright, Alan Zaslavsky, and Amy N. Finkelstein. 2013. The Oregon experiment — Effects of Medicaid on clinical outcomes. *New England Journal of Medicine* 368:1713–22.

Baker, Lawrence, and Christopher Afendulis. 2005. Medicaid managed care and health care for children. *Health Services Research* 40 (5): 1466–88.

Baker, Michael, Janet Currie, and Hannes Schwandt. 2017. Mortality inequality in Canada and the US: Convergent or divergent trends. NBER Working Paper 23514, National Bureau of Economic Research, Cambridge, MA.

Benitez-Silva, Hugo, Moshe Buchinsky, and John Rust. 2004. How large are the classification errors in the Social Security Disability award process? NBER Working Paper 10219, National Bureau of Economic Research, Cambridge, MA.

Bindman, Andrew, Arpita Chattopadhyay, Denis Osmond, William Huen, and Peter Bacchetti. 2005. The impact of Medicaid care on hospitalizations for ambulatory care sensitive conditions. *Health Services Research* 40 (1): 19–38.

Bitler, Marianne, Hillary Hoynes, and Emily Kuka. 2016. Child poverty, the Great Recession and the social safety net in the United States. *Journal of Policy Analysis and Management* 36 (2): 358–89.

Bitler, Marianne, and Madelyn Zavodny. 2017. Medicaid: A review of the literature. In *Handbook in law and economics federalism*, ed. Jonathan Klick, 183–213. Cheltenham: Edward Elgar.

Black, Bernard, Alex Hollingsworth, Leticia Nunes, and Kosali Simon. 2018. The effect of health insurance on mortality: What can we learn from the Affordable Care Act coverage expansions? Institute for Policy Research Working Paper, Washington, DC. Available from https://aysps.gsu.edu/files/2018/08/insurance_mortality_2018-08-16-forcomments-1.pdf.

Boudreaux, Michel H., Ezra Golberstein, and Donna D. McAlpine. 2016. The long-term impacts of Medicaid exposure in early childhood: Evidence from the program's origin. *Journal of Health Economics* 45:161–75.

Brown, David W., Amanda Kowalski, and Ithai Z. Lurie. 2015. Medicaid as an investment in children: What is the long-term impact on tax receipts? NBER Working Paper 20835, National Bureau of Economic Research, Cambridge, MA.

Brown, Jason, and Karen Dynan. 2017. Increasing the economic security of older women. The Hamilton Project, Policy Proposal 2017-11. Available from http://www.hamiltonproject.org/assets/files/increasing_economic_security_older_women _BrownDynan.pdf.

Buchmueller, Thomas, John Ham, and Lara Shore-Sheppard. 2016. The Medicaid program. In *Economics of means-tested transfer programs in the United States*, ed. Robert Moffitt, 21–136. Chicago, IL: National Bureau of Economic Research.

Burns, Marguerite E. 2009a. Medicaid managed care and cost containment for adult beneficiaries with disabilities. *Medical Care* 47 (10): 1076–96.

Burns, Marguerite E. 2009b. Medicaid managed care and health care access for adult beneficiaries with disabilities. *Health Services Research* 45 (5): 1521–41.

Chorniy, Anna, Janet Currie, and Lydmila Sonchak. 2018. Exploding asthma and ADHD caseloads: The role of Medicaid managed care. *Journal of Health Economics* 60:1–15.

Clemans-Cope, Lisa, Sharon K. Long, Teresa Coughlin, Alshadye Yemane, and Dean Resnick. 2013. The expansion of Medicaid coverage under the ACA: Implications for health care access use and spending for vulnerable low-income adults. *Inquiry* 50 (2): 135–49.

Cohodes, Sarah, Daniel Grossman, Samuel Kleiner, and Michale Lovenheim. 2016. The effect of child health insurance access on schooling: Evidence from public insurance expansions. *Journal of Human Resources* 51 (3): 727–59.

Conover, Chistopher J., Peter J. Rankin, and Frank Sloan. 2001. Effects of Tennessee Medicaid managed care on obstetrical care and birth outcomes. *Journal of Health Politics Policy and Law* 26 (6): 1291–1324.

Conover, Chris J., and Frank A. Sloan. 1998. Does removing certificate-of-need regulations lead to a surge in health care spending? *Journal of Health Politics, Policy and Law* 23 (3): 455–81.

Cooper, Zachary, Stuart V. Craig, Martin Gaynor, and John Van Reenen. 2019. The price ain't right? Hospital prices and health spending on the privately insured. *Quarterly Journal of Economics* 134 (1): 51–107.

Coughlin, Teresa, Sharon Long, and John Graves. 2008. Does managed care improve access to care for Medicaid beneficiaries with disabilities? A national study. *Inquiry* 45:395–407.

Courtemanche, Charles, James Marton, Benjamin Ukert, Aaron Yelowitz, and Daniela Zapata. 2018. Early effects of the Affordable Care Act on health care access risky health behaviors and self-Assessed health. *Southern Economic Journal* 84 (3): 660–91.

Courtemanche, Charles, Benjamin Ukert, Daniela Zapata, James Marton, and Aaron Yelowitz. 2017. Impacts of the Affordable Care Act on health insurance coverage in Medicaid expansion and non-expansion states. *Journal of Policy Analysis and Management* 36 (1): 178–210.

Currie, Janet, Sandra Decker, and Wanchuan Lin. 2008. Has public health insurance for older children reduced disparities in access to care and health outcomes? *Journal of Health Economics* 27 (6): 1407–1652.

Currie, Janet, and John Fahr. 2005. Medicaid managed care: Effects on children's Medicaid coverage and utilization of care. *Journal of Public Economics* 89 (1): 85–108.

Currie, Janet, and Fahrooz Gahvari. 2008. Transfers in cash and in-kind: Theory meets the data. *Journal of Economic Literature* 46 (2): 333–83.

Currie, Janet, and Jonathan Gruber. 1996a. Health insurance eligibility utilization of medical care and child health. *Quarterly Journal of Economics* 111 (2): 431–66.

Currie, Janet, and Jonathan Gruber. 1996b. Saving babies: The efficacy and cost of recent changes in the Medicaid eligibility of pregnant women. *Journal of Political Economy* 104 (6): 1263–96.

Currie, Janet, and Hannes Schwandt. 2016. Mortality inequality: The good news from a county-level approach. *Journal of Economic Perspectives* 30 (2): 29–52.

Cutler, David, and Jonathan Gruber. 1996. Does public insurance crowd out private insurance? *Quarterly Journal of Economics* 111 (2): 391–430.

Cutler, David, Allison Rosen, and Sandeep Vijan. 2006. The value of medical spending in the United States 1960–2000. *New England Journal of Medicine* 355:920–27.

Dafny, Leemore, and Jonathan Gruber. 2005. Public insurance and child hospitalizations: Access and efficiency effects. *Journal of Public Economics* 89 (1): 109–29.

Dague, Laura, Thomas DeLeire, and Lindsey Leininger. 2017. The effect of public insurance coverage for childless adults on labor supply. *American Economic Journal: Economic Policy* 9 (2): 124–54.

Davitt, Joan K., and Sunha Choi. 2008. Tracing the history of Medicare home health care: The impact of policy on benefit use. *Journal of Sociology & Social Welfare*: 35 (1): Article 12.

DeLeire, Thomas, Leonard M. Lopoo, and Kosali Simon. 2011. Medicaid expansions and fertility in the United States. *Demography* 48 (2): 725–47.

Deshpande, Manasi. 2016. Does welfare inhibit success? The long-term effects of removing low- income youth from the disability rolls. *American Economic Review* 106 (11): 3300–3330.

Dilger, Robert, and Eugene Boyd. 15 July 2014. *Block grants: Perspectives and controversies*. Washington, DC: Congressional Research Service. Available from http://fas.org/sgp/crs/misc/R40486.pdf.

Duggan, Mark. 2004. Does contracting out increase the efficiency of government programs? Evidence from Medicaid HMOs. *Journal of Public Economics* 88:2549–72.

Duggan, Mark, and Tamara Hayford. 2013. Has the shift to managed care reduced Medicaid spending? Evidence from state and local-level mandates. *Journal of Policy Analysis and Management* 32 (3): 505–35.

East, Chloe, Sarah Miller, Marianne Page, and Laura Wherry. 2017. Multi-generational impacts of childhood access to the safety net: Early life exposure to Medicaid and the next generation's health. NBER Working Paper 23810, National Bureau of Economic Research, Cambridge, MA.

Finkelstein, Amy, Neale Mahoney, and Matthew J. Notowidigdo. 2018. What does (formal) health insurance do, and for whom? *Annual Review of Economics* 10 (1): 261–86.

Finkelstein, Amy N., Sarah L. Taubman, Heidi L. Allen, Bill J. Wright, and Katherine Baicker. 2016. Effect of Medicaid coverage on ED use — Further evidence from Oregon's experiment. *New England Journal of Medicine* 375:1505–7.

Finkelstein, Amy, Sarah Taubman, Bill Wright, Mira Bernstein, Jonathan Gruber, Joseph Newhouse, Heidi Allen, and Katherine Baicker, and The Oregon Health Study Group. 2012. The Oregon health insurance experiment: Evidence from the first year. *Quarterly Journal of Economics* 127 (3): 1057–1106.

Frean, Michael, Jonathan Gruber, and Benjamin Sommers. 2017. Premium subsidies, the mandate and Medicaid expansion: Coverage effects of the Affordable Care Act. *Journal of Health Economics* 53:72–86.

Garfield, Rachel I., Judith R. Lave, and Julie M. Donohue. 2010. Health reform and the scope of benefits for mental health and substance use disorder services. *Psychiatric Services* 61 (11): 1081–86.

Garthwaite, Craig, Tal Gross, and Matthew Notowidigdo. 2014. Public health insurance labor supply and employment lock. *Quarterly Journal of Economics* 129 (2): 653–96.

Gettens, J. M., Henry A. D. Mitra, and J. Himmelstein. 2011. Have working-age people with disabilities shared in the gains of Massachusetts health reform? *Inquiry: The Journal of Health Care Organization Provision and Financing* 48 (3): 183–96.

Ghosh, Ausmita, Kosali Simon, and Benjamin D. Sommers. 2017. The effect of state Medicaid expansions on prescription drug use: Evidence from the Affordable Care Act. NBER Working Paper No. 23044, National Bureau of Economic Research, Cambridge, MA.

Gittleman, Maury. 2011. Medicaid and wealth: A re-examination. *B.E. Journal of Economic Analysis* 11 (1). Available from doi.org/10.2202/1935-1682.3029.

Glied, Sherry, and Marilyn Tavenner. 2019. Medicaid through the crystal ball of historical CMS projections. *Health Affairs*. doi 10.1377/hblog20190226.922368.

Goda, Gopi S. 2011. The impact of state tax subsidies for private long-term care insurance on coverage on Medicaid expenditures. *Journal of Public Economics* 95 (7): 744–57.

Goodman-Bacon, Andrew. 2016. The long-run effects of childhood insurance coverage: Medicaid implementation adult health and labor market outcomes. NBER Working Paper 22899, National Bureau of Economic Research, Cambridge, MA.

Goodman-Bacon, Andrew. 2018. Public insurance and mortality: Evidence from Medicaid implementation. *Journal of Political Economy* 126 (1): 216–62.

Gooptu, Angshuman, Asako Moriya, Kosali Simon, and Benjamin Sommers. 2016. Medicaid expansion did not result in significant employment changes or job reductions in 2014. *Health Affairs* 35 (1): 111–18.

Gouskova, Elena. 2015. Public health insurance labor supply and employment lock: Effects or data artifacts? Available from https://ssrn.com/abstract=2688582.

Grabowski, David. 2001. Medicaid reimbursement and the quality of nursing home care. *Journal of Health Economics* 20 (4): 549–69.

Grabowski, David. 2004. A longitudinal study of Medicaid payment private-pay price and nursing home quality. *International Journal of Health Care Finance and Economics* 4 (1): 5–26.

Grabowski, David, and Joseph J. Angelelli. 2004. The relationship of Medicaid payment rates bed constraint policies and risk-adjusted pressure ulcers. *Health Service Research* 39 (4): 793–812.

Grabowski, David, Joseph J. Angelelli, and Vincent Mor. 2004. Medicaid payment and risk-adjusted nursing home quality measures. *Health Affairs* 23 (5): 243–52.

Grabowski, David, Zhanlian Fend, Orna Intrator, and Vincent Mor. 2004. Recent trends in state nursing home payment and the role of provider taxes. *Medical Care Research and Review* 61 (1): 89–115.

Grabowski, David, and Jonathan Gruber. 2007. Moral hazard in nursing home use. *Journal of Health Economics* 26 (3): 560–77.

Grabowski, David, Jonathan Gruber, and Joseph J. Angelelli. 2008. Nursing home quality as a public good. *Review of Economics and Statistics* 90 (4): 754–64.

Grabowski, David, Jonathan Gruber, and Vincent Mor. 13 June 2017. You're probably going to need Medicaid. *New York Times*.

Grabowski, David, Robert Ohsfeldt, and Michael Morrisey. 2003. The effects of CON repeal on Medicaid nursing and long term care expenditures. *Inquiry* 40 (2): 146–57.

Gross, Tal, and Matthew Notowidigdo. 2011. Health insurance and the consumer bankruptcy decision: Evidence from expansions of Medicaid. *Journal of Public Economics* 95 (7): 767–78.

Gruber, Jonathan. 2008. Covering the uninsured in the United States. *Journal of Economic Literature* 46 (3): 571–606.

Gruber, Jonathan, and Benjamin Sommers. 2019. The Affordable Care Act's effects on patients, providers, and the economy: What we know so far? NBER Working Paper 25932, National Bureau of Economic Research, Cambridge, MA.

Gruber, Jonathan, and Aaron Yelowitz. 1999. Public insurance and private savings. *Journal of Political Economy* 107 (6): 1249–74.

Hall, Jean P., Adele Shartzer, Noelle K. Kurth, and Kathleen C. Thomas. 2017. Effect of Medicaid expansion on workforce participation for people with disabilities. *American Journal of Public Health* 107 (2): 262–64.

Hall, Robert, and Charles Jones. 2007. The value of life and the rise in health spending. *Quarterly Journal of Economics* 122 (1): 39–72.

Ham, John, and Kenneth Ueda. Forthcoming. Comparing the Conley-Taber and the standard approaches to inference in difference-in-difference models based on small policy variation: The case of TennCare. *Journal of Labor Economics*.

Herring, Bradley, and Esther K. Adams. 2011. Using HMOs to serve the Medicaid population: What are the effects on utilization and does the type of HMO matter? *Health Economics* 20 (4): 446–60.

Howell, Embry, and Genevieve Kenney. 2012. The impact of the Medicaid/CHIP expansions on children: A synthesis of the evidence. *Medical Care Research and Review* 69 (4): 372–96.

Hu, Luojia, Robert Kaestner, Bashkar Mazumder, Sarah Miller, and Ashley Wong. 2016. The effects of the Patient Protection and Affordable Care Act Medicaid expansions on financial well-being. NBER Working paper 22170, National Bureau of Economic Research, Cambridge, MA.

Intrator, Orna, David C. Grabowski, Jacqueline Zinn, Mark Schleinitz, Zhanlian Feng, Susan Miller, and Vince Mor. 2007. Hospitalization of nursing home residents: The effects of states' Medicaid payment and bed-hold policies. *Health Service Research* 42 (4): 1651–71.

James, Everette, Walid Gellad, and Meredith Hughes. 2017. In this next phase of health reform we cannot overlook long term care. Health Affairs Blog. Available from 10.1377/hblog20170316.059218.

Johnson, Richard W. 2 August 2016. *Who is covered by private long-term care insurance?* Washington, DC: The Urban Institute.

Kaestner, Robert, Lisa Dubay, and Genevieve Kenney. 2005. Managed care and infant health: An evaluation of Medicaid in the US. *Social Science & Medicine* 60:1815–33.

Kaestner, Robert, Bowen Garrett, Jiajia Chen, Anuj Gangopadhyaya, and Caitlyn Fleming. 2017. Effects of ACA Medicaid expansions on health insurance coverage and labor supply. *Journal of Policy Analysis and Management* 36 (3): 608–42.

Kaestner, Robert, Theodore Joyce, and Andrew Racine. 2001. Medicaid eligibility and the incidence of ambulatory care sensitive hospitalizations for children. *Social Science & Medicine* 52 (2): 305–13.

Kamal, Rabah, and Cynthia Cox. 8 May 2018. *How do healthcare prices and use in the US compare to other countries?* San Francisco, CA: The Kaiser Family Foundation.

Kearney, Melissa, and Phillip Levine. 2009. Subsidized contraception fertility and sexual behavior. *Review of Economics and Statistics* 91:137–51.

Koma, Jonathan W., Julie M. Donohue, Colleen L. Barry, Haiden A. Huskamp, and Marian Jarlenski. 2017. Medicaid coverage expansions and cigarette smoking cessation among low-income adults. *Medical Care* 55 (12): 1023–29.

Kuziemko, Ilyana, Katherine Meckel, and Maya Rossin-Slater. 2018. Does managed care widen infant health disparities? Evidence from Texas Medicaid. *American Economic Journal: Economic Policy* 10 (3): 255–83.

Laes-Kushner, Rebecca. 27 March 2018. Skilled nursing facilities: Too many beds. Commonwealth Medicine. Available from https://commed.umassmed.edu/blog.

Lanning, Joyce A., Michael Morrisey, and Robert Ohsfeldt. 1991. Endogenous hospital regulation and its effects on hospital and non-hospital expenditures. *Journal of Regulatory Economics* 3 (2): 137–54.

Layton, Timothy J., Nicole Maestas, Daniel Prinz, and Boris Vabson. 2019. Private vs. public provision of social insurance: Evidence from Medicaid. NBER Working Paper, National Bureau of Economic Statistics, Cambridge, MA.

Leung, Pauline, and Alexandre Mas. 2018. Employment effects of the Affordable Care Act Medicaid expansions. *Industrial Relations* 57 (2): 206–34.

Levine, Phillip, and Diane Schanzenbach. 2009. The impact of children's public health insurance expansions on educational outcomes. NBER Working Paper, National Bureau of Economic Statistics, Cambridge, MA.

Lieber, Ethan, and Lee M. Lockwood. 2019. Targeting with in-kind transfers: Evidence from Medicaid home care. *American Economic Review* 109 (4): 1461–85.

LoSasso, Anthony, and Deborah Freund. 2000. A longitudinal evaluation of the effect of Medi-Cal managed care on Supplemental Security Income and Aid to Families with Dependent Children enrollees in two California counties. *Medical Care* 38 (9): 937–47.

MacLean, Johanna C., Benjamin Cook, Nicholas Carson, and Michael Pesko. 2017. Public insurance and psychotropic prescription medications for mental illness. NBER Working Paper 23760, National Bureau of Economic Statistics, Cambridge, MA.

Maestas, Nicole, Kathleen J. Muellen, and Alexander Strand. 2014. Disability insurance and health insurance reform: Evidence from Massachusetts. *American Economic Review* 104 (5): 329–35.

Markus, Anna R., Ellie Andres, Kristina D. West, Nicole Garro, and Cynthia Pellegrini. 2013. Medicaid covered births 2008 through 2010 in the context of the implementation of health reform. *Women's Health Issues* 23 (5): e273–80.

Maynard, Alex, and Jiaping Qiu. 2009. Public insurance and private savings: Who is affected and by how much? *Journal of Applied Econometrics* 24 (2): 282–308.

Mazumder, Bhashkar, and Sarah Miller. 2016. The effects of the Massachusetts health reform on household financial distress. *American Economic Journal: Economic Policy* 8 (3): 284–313.

Medicaid and CHIP Payment and Access Commission. 2017. MACStats: Medicaid and CHIP data book 2017. Available from https://www.macpac.gov/wp-content/uploads/2015/12/MACStats-Medicaid-CHIP-Data-Book-December-2017.pdf.

Michalopolous, Charles, David Wittenburg, Dina Israel, Jennifer Schore, Anne Warren, Aparajita Zutshi, Stephen Freedman, and Lisa Schwartz. 2011. *The accelerated benefits demonstration and evaluation project: Impacts on health and employment at 12 months.* New York, NT: MDRC.

Miller, Sarah, and Laura Wherry. 2017. Health and access to care during the first 2 years of the ACA Medicaid expansions. *New England Journal of Medicine* 376 (10): 947–56.

Miller, Sarah, and Laura Wherry. 2019. The long-term effects of early life Medicaid coverage. *Journal of Human Resources* 54 (3): 785–824.

Mor, Vincent, Andrea Grunerir, Zhanlian Feng, David Grabowski, Orna Intrator, and Jacqueline Zinn. 2011. The effect of state policies on nursing home resident outcomes. *Journal of American Geriatric Association* 59 (1): 3–9.

Musumeci, MaryBeth, and Katherine Young. 1 May 2017. *State variation in Medicaid per enrollee spending for seniors and people with disabilities.* San Francisco, CA: Kaiser Family Foundation.

National Academy of Social Insurance (NASI). April 2015. *Addressing pricing power in health care markets*. Washington DC: NASI.

Obama, Barack. 2016. United States health care reform progress to date and next steps. *JAMA* 316 (5): 525–32.

Rau, J. 24 June 2017. Medicaid cuts may force retirees out of nursing homes. *New York Times*.

Reschovsky, James. 1996. Demand for and access to institutional long-term care: The role of Medicaid in nursing home markets. *Inquiry* 33 (1): 15–29.

Salkever, David. 2000. Regulation of prices and investment in hospitals in the United States. *Handbook of Health Economics* 1 (Part B): 1489–1535.

Scott, Dylan. 18 December 2018. 16932 people have lost Medicaid coverage under Arkansas's work requirements. *Vox*.

Simon, Kosali, Aparna Soni, and John Cawley. 2017. The impact of health insurance on preventive care and health behaviors: Evidence from the first two years of the ACA Medicaid Expansions. *Journal of Policy Analysis and Management* 36 (2): 390–417.

Slusky, David. 2017. Significant placebo results in difference-in-differences analysis: The case of the ACA's parental mandate. *Eastern Economic Journal* 43 (4): 580–603.

Sommers, Benjamin, Katherine Baicker, and Andrew Epstein. 2012. Mortality and access to care among adults after state Medicaid expansions. *New England Journal of Medicine* 367:1025–34.

Sommers, Benjamin, Robert J. Blendon, John Orav, and Andrew Epstein. 2016. Changes in utilization and health among low-income adults after Medicaid expansion or expanded private insurance. *JAMA Internal Medicine* 176 (10): 1501–9.

Sommers, Benjamin, Munira Z. Gunja, Kenneth Finegold, and Thomas Musco. 2015. Changes in self-reported insurance coverage access to care and health under the Affordable Care Act. *JAMA* 314 (4): 366–74.

Sommers, Benjamin, Bethany Maylone, Robert J. Blendon, E. John Orav, and Arnold M. Epstein. 2017. Three-year impacts of the Affordable Care Act: Improved medical care and health among low-income adults. *Health Affairs* 36 (6). Available from https://doi.org/10.1377/hlthaff.2017.0293.

Stabile, Mark, and Sarah Thompson. 2014. The changing role of government in financing health care: An international perspective. *Journal of Economic Literature* 52 (2): 480–518.

Stevens, Ann H., Douglas L. Miller, Marianne E. Page, and Mateusz Filipski. 2015. The best of times, the worst of times: Understanding pro-cyclical mortality. *American Economic Journal: Economic Policy* 7 (4): 279–311.

Szanton, Sarah L., Y. Natalia Alfonso, Bruce Leff, Jack Guralnik, Jennifer L. Wolff, Laura N. Gitlin, and David Bishai. 2018. Medicaid cost savings of a preventive home visit program for disabled older adults. *Journal of the American Geriatrics Society* 66 (3): 614–20.

Taubman, Sarah L., Heidi L. Allen, Bill J. Wright, Katherine Baicker, and Amy N. Finkelstein. 2014. Medicaid increases emergency-department use: Evidence from Oregon's health insurance experiment. *Science* 343 (6168): 263–68.

Watts, Molly O., Elizabeth Cornachione, and MaryBeth Musumeci. 2016. Medicaid financial eligibility for seniors and people with disabilities in 2015. Available from https://www.kff.org/report-section/medicaid-financial-eligibility-for-seniors-and-people- with-disabilities-in-2015-report/.

Wherry, Laura, and Bruce Meyer. 2016. Saving teens: Using a policy discontinuity to estimate the effects of Medicaid eligibility. *Journal of Human Resources* 51 (3): 556–88.

Wherry, Laura, Sarah Miller, Robert Kaestner, and Bruce Meyer. 2018. Childhood Medicaid coverage and later life health care utilization. *Review of Economics and Statistics* 100 (2): 287–302.

Winkelman, Tyler N. A., and Virginia W. Chang. 2018. Medicaid expansion mental health and access to care among childless adults with and without chronic conditions. *Journal of General Internal Medicine* 33 (3): 376–83.

Zavodny, Madelyn, and Marianne Bitler. 2010. The effect of Medicaid eligibility expansions on fertility. *Social Science & Medicine* 71 (5): 918–24.

The Earned Income Tax Credit

In this article, I review the most prominent provision of the federal income tax code that targets low-income tax filers, the Earned Income Tax Credit (EITC), as well as the structurally similar Child Tax Credit and Additional Child Tax Credit. I discuss the programs' goals: distributional, promoting work, and limiting administrative and compliance costs. The article reviews the history of the programs, the predicted economic effects, and what is known about program impacts and distributional consequences. I conclude that the EITC effectively targets low-income households and is efficient in reducing poverty while encouraging work and that increases in after-tax household incomes lead to improved outcomes over the life course for children of those households. I propose reforms to the program, including policies that expand the generosity of the credit and increase take-up, as well as structural reforms that include spreading benefits throughout the year and reducing reliance on paid tax preparers.

Keywords: safety net; poverty; labor supply; tax credits

By
HILARY HOYNES

Entitlements operate not only through the transfer system, such as food stamps, social security, and disability benefits, but also through the tax system. The most prominent provisions

Hilary Hoynes is a professor of economics and public policy and the Haas Distinguished Chair in Economic Disparities at the University of California, Berkeley, where she also codirects the Berkeley Opportunity Lab. She is a member of the American Academy of Arts and Sciences, the National Academy of Social Insurance, and is a fellow of the Society of Labor Economists.

NOTE: I thank Janet Holtzblatt, Elaine Maag, and the Center for Budget and Policy Priorities EITC team for discussions about policy reform and Krista Ruffini for excellent research assistance. The article draws heavily from my prior reviews including Eissa and Hoynes (2006a, 2006b); Hoynes and Rothstein (2017); and Hoynes, Rothstein, and Ruffini (2018). I thank these coauthors for the many useful discussions on these issues.

Correspondence: hoynes@berkeley.edu

DOI: 10.1177/0002716219881621

of the federal income tax code that target low-income tax filers are the Earned Income Tax Credit (EITC), the less prominent Child Tax Credit (CTC), and the Additional Child Tax Credit (ACTC). These programs are explicitly redistributive, designed to transfer money to families and individuals rather than tax it away from them.

The EITC is a tax credit available to lower-income families and individuals with positive earned income. The credit operates as an earnings subsidy at low levels of income (in the phase-in region), reaches a maximum credit amount, and then is phased out at higher income levels. For example, a family with two children earning less than $14,290 will receive 40 cents for every dollar earned up to a maximum of $5,716 (in 2018). For a single parent with two children, the credit is phased out at incomes between $18,660 and $45,802. The credit is refundable; therefore, if recipients' tax obligations are below the credit amount, they receive refund checks from the Internal Revenue Service (IRS). In 2016, 86 percent of the total tax expenditure of the EITC took the form of tax refunds (IRS 2018b, Table 2.5).

The EITC was introduced in 1975 as a modest tax credit to offset payroll taxes for those with low earnings. Expansions beginning in 1986 and continuing in the 1990s and 2000s have transformed the EITC into a central element of the U.S. social safety net for families with children (Bitler and Hoynes 2010; Hoynes and Schanzenbach 2018). While the EITC is available to all low-income wage earners, the tax credit is much more generous for families with children, reflecting the potential for intergenerational benefits (Hoynes and Schanzenbach 2018; Hendren and Sprung-Keyser 2019). In 2016, the EITC reached 27 million tax filers at a total cost of $67 billion. Almost 20 percent of all tax filers and 44 percent of filers with children receive the credit. The maximum credit in 2018 was $6,431 for families with three children, $5,716 for those with two children, $3,461 for those with one child, and $519 for those without children—this can be as much as 45 percent of a family's pretax income. Overall, the average credit amount for families with children is a substantial $3,200 (IRS 2018a). The program dwarfs traditional cash welfare (Temporary Assistance for Needy Families, or TANF), which reached only 1.2 million families in fiscal year 2018, a more than 75 percent decline since 1994.

The CTC is more recent; it has been available in the United States since 1997. The CTC is similar to the EITC (e.g., a phase-in, maximum credit, and phase-out regions), with a maximum credit of $2,000 per child under current law (up from $1,000 from 2003 to 2017). However, the CTC is much less targeted compared to the EITC, as eligibility extends very high into the income distribution (phase-out of the credit begins at $200,000 for single parents and $400,000 for married couples). Additionally, unlike the EITC, it is not fully refundable, and thus the lowest-income families do not gain fully from the credit. The refundable component of the CTC—the ACTC—requires $2,500 in earnings, is phased in slowly, and is capped at $1,400. In 2016, the cost of the CTC was $52 billion, on par with the EITC. After the 2018 expansion, the CTC's cost will likely far exceed that of the EITC.

What are the goals of these two tax credits? First, all means-tested programs are designed in part to achieve distributional objectives. In the case of the EITC (and the ACTC), these are to transfer funds to low- and moderate-income families, and particularly to those with children. The nonrefundable CTC distributes to families with children, but is not income targeted, given the eligibility up to the highest income percentiles. The CTC then may be better thought of as a near-universal (excluding the lowest earning and highest earning families) child benefit for working families. Second, the EITC is explicitly designed to encourage work. Third, by administering this benefit through the tax system, administrative costs associated with transfer programs are reduced.

In this article, I review the role of the EITC, what is known about its impacts and distributional consequences, and the possibilities for reform. I give less attention to the CTC given its less important role for lower-income families with children and the limited evidence on the behavioral effects of the credit.

I begin in the next section by reviewing the structure and history of in-work tax credits. Then, I discuss the economics of the EITC and briefly review the evidence from the research on the effectiveness of the EITC. The next section discusses possible reforms to the EITC, and I end with a concluding section that illustrates how the EITC has met its stated goals to date and possible reforms to improve on the program.

Current Policies and Recent Reforms

To be eligible for the EITC, a taxpayer—or tax filing unit—must have earned income during the tax year. The value of the credit is determined by a benefit schedule with three regions, known as the phase-in, flat, and phase-out. In the phase-in region, the credit increases by a share of each additional dollar earned. Once the credit reaches its maximum value, the taxpayer is in the second, flat region, where additional earnings do not affect the credit value. In the final region, the credit declines with each additional dollar of earnings (or, adjusted gross income [AGI], if that is higher) until it is zero.

The exact parameters of the schedule vary by filing status and by the number of qualifying children. The qualifying children definition for the EITC is complicated, occupying seven dense pages in IRS Form 596.[1] Figure 1 displays the EITC schedule in 2018 as a function of earned income for single taxpayers with zero, one, two, and three or more children. For families with children, the phase-in or subsidy rate is substantial at 34/40/45 percent for those with one/two/three or more children. The phase-out rate is modest, at 15.98 (21.06) percent for those with one (two or more) children. Maximum benefits range from $3,461 for families with one child to $6,431 for those with three or more. Eligibility for single taxpayers extends to incomes of $40,320 (with one child), $45,802 (with two children), or $49,194 (with three or more children). The credit for families without children is much less generous, with a phase-in rate of 7.65, a maximum credit of $519, and a maximum allowable income of $15,270. The dashed lines in Figure 1 denote the extended flat and phase-out regions for married couples ($5,680 in 2018) receiving the EITC.[2]

FIGURE 1
Earned Income Tax Credit Schedule, 2018

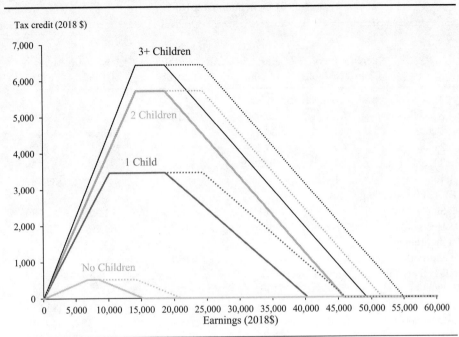

SOURCE: Internal Revenue Service, Revenue Procedure 2018-18, available from https://www.irs.gov/irb/2018-18_IRB.

The EITC is a refundable tax credit, meaning that if the credit exceeds a taxpayer's tax liability, he or she receives the difference as a refund. Typically, families with earnings below $20,000 to $25,000 will owe very little income tax, so the bulk of the EITC will arrive as a refund even when withholding is zero (86 percent of EITC costs in 2016 occured through refunds). EITC recipients receive the payment as an annual lump sum with most payments—about 80 percent— arriving in February and March (Lalumia 2013). The Advance EITC program allowed recipients to receive their credits throughout the year, but take-up was extremely low (under 1 percent), and this option was eliminated in 2011.

Table 1 shows the number of claimants and the cost of all claims for the EITC. In 2016, more than 27 million tax filers claimed the credit for a total of $67 billion. Almost 20 percent of all tax filers and 44 percent of filers with children receive the credit. About 75 percent of the EITC recipients and 97 percent of the total EITC benefits are for families with children. Married couples make up 22 percent of EITC filers and about a quarter of the total EITC spending. The average EITC payment is $3,200 for families with children.

Receiving the EITC requires filing a tax return and completing the necessary forms. The EITC take-up rate (defined as the share of eligible families/individuals that receive the credit) is approximately 80 percent for families with children and

TABLE 1
Number and Claim Amount of EITC Claims by Filing Status and Number
of Dependents (2016)

	Number of Claims (millions)	Claims, Share of Total	Total Claim Amount (billions of 2016$)	Claims, Share of Total	Average EITC
EITC filers by number of qualifying children					
No children	7.1	25.8%	$2.1	3.1%	$291
1 child	9.9	36.3%	$23.9	35.8%	$2,400
2 children	7.0	25.4%	$26.6	39.9%	$3,819
3+ children	3.4	12.5%	$14.2	21.3%	$4,152
Total	27.4		$66.7		$2,437
EITC filers by filing status					
Single	8.0	29.1%	$8.6	12.9%	$1,080
Head of household	13.2	48.4%	$41.7	62.5%	$3,148
Married	6.1	22.4%	$16.7	25.1%	$2,731
EITC filers with children by filing status					
Single	2.0	10%	$6.9	11%	$3,387
Head of household	13.1	65%	$41.7	64%	$3,179
Married	5.2	25%	$16.4	25%	$3,180
Total	20.3		$65.0		$3,200

SOURCE: Calculations based on unpublished tax year 2016 IRS data provided by the Center for Budget and Policy Priorities.

56 percent for taxpayers without children (Scholz 1994; Plueger 2009)—fairly high compared to other programs serving low-income families (Currie 2006).[3]

The CTC has the same basic structure as the EITC (requires income,[4] has phase-in, flat and phase-out regions) with a maximum credit of $2,000 per child under current law. However, the two programs are otherwise different. The CTC is not fully refundable, and thus the lowest-income families do not receive the full benefits of the credit. The refundable portion of the CTC (ACTC) is limited to those with earnings above $2,500 per year, is phased in at a 15 percent rate, and is capped at a maximum credit of $1,400. The CTC phase-in (15 percent) and phase-out (5 percent) rates are much smaller than the EITC and the ACTC. Additionally, the flat range for the credit is very large: the credit begins to phase out for single parents at incomes of $200,000 and for married couples at incomes of $400,000. The result is the CTC/ACTC is much less targeted than the EITC, and most of the spending on the program goes to families far above the poverty line (Hoynes and Rothstein 2017).[5]

Figure 2 presents the budget constraint for the combination of the EITC and the CTC for 2018. For illustration, I calculate the credits assuming a single

FIGURE 2
Budget Constraint for Combined EITC, CTC and ACTC, 2018

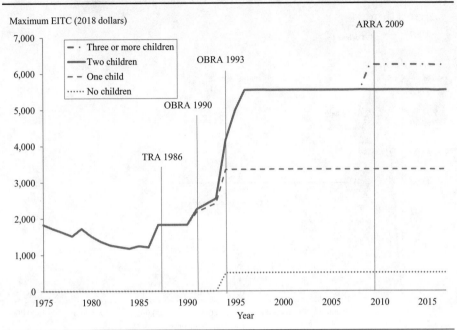

SOURCE: Author's tabulations based on Internal Revenue Service Revenue Procedure 2018-18 (EITC) and Publication 972 (CTC).

parent with two children. The figure separately identifies the portion of the CTC that is refunded and the portion that offsets other taxes. The figure also shows (labeled as "CTC forfeited") the portion of the credit that is forgone by very-low-income families for whom the refundability limit is binding. The figure shows the significantly greater targeting of the EITC compared to the CTC. Further, the refundable portion of the CTC effectively expands the EITC, serving approximately the same income range but increasing the benefit. By contrast, the portion of the CTC that offsets other tax liabilities rises much higher in the income distribution, not even beginning to phase out until income is four times the end of the phase-out region under the EITC.

The EITC and CTC/ACTC have expanded several times over their history. To illustrate these changes, Figure 3 plots the EITC maximum credit over time for families of different sizes, and Figure 4 shows the total tax cost of the EITC and CTC/ACTC over time (in real 2018 dollars).

The EITC was introduced in 1975, and in the early years inflation gradually eroded the real maximum benefit (Figure 3). The 1987 expansion of the EITC, passed as part of the Tax Reform Act of 1986, increased the generosity of the credit and indexed the credit schedule to inflation. The largest change was the 1993 expansion, which introduced a credit for families without children and

FIGURE 3
Maximum EITC, by Year and Number of Children

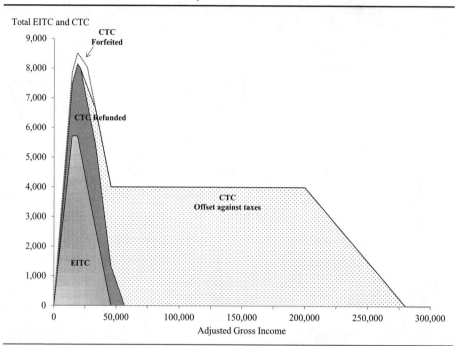

SOURCE: Author's tabulations based on Government Publishing Office (2004), Table 13–32 (1975–2003); Internal Revenue Service Publication 596 (2004–2018).
NOTE: TRA = Tax Reform Act; OBRA = Omnibus Budget Reconciliation Act; ARRA = American Recovery and Reinvestment Act.

greatly increased the credit for families with two or more children (and less so for one-child families). Elsewhere in the figure, one can see smaller expansions in the early 1990s, as well as the introduction of a separate three-child schedule in 2009 (as part of the stimulus package, which was later made permanent).

Overall, the EITC expanded from about $5 billion per year in the 1980s to nearly $50 billion in the mid-1990s (in real 2018 dollars), and it has grown gradually since then (Figure 4). The increases in the EITC tax cost follow the tax expansions in 1987, 1990, and 1993; the married couple expansions in 2002; and the three-child expansion in 2009. Another factor affecting the cost of the EITC is wage and earnings stagnation; as the earnings of lower-skill workers decline (Autor 2014), the cost of "toping up earnings" for these families increases.

Figure 4 also shows the cost of the CTC, the ACTC, and their combined cost over time. The CTC was introduced in 1997 with a nonrefundable credit of $500 per child, increased to $600 in 2001, $1,000 in 2003, and $2,000 per child in 2018. Unlike the EITC, the CTC maximum credit is set nominally, and the figure shows the real decline in periods between policy expansions. The ACTC began in 2001, allowing 10 percent of earnings over $10,000 to be refundable. It

FIGURE 4
Total Spending over Time (2018 dollars)

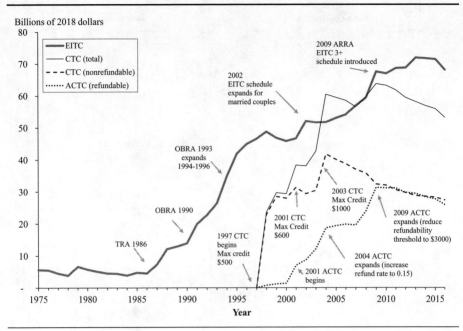

SOURCE: Author's tabulations based on Internal Revenue Service Statistics of Income Table 2.5 (EITC); Table 3.3 (CTC, ACTC).
NOTE: All amounts adjusted for inflation using the Consumer Price Index for All Urban Consumers (CPI-U).

expanded in 2004 (raising the refund rate to 15 percent), and the earnings threshold was lowered in 2008 (to $8,500), in 2009 (to $3,000), and in 2018 (to $2,500). As of 2016, the combined CTC/ACTC cost $52 billion, almost as large as the EITC ($67 billion), with about half on the nonrefundable CTC and half on the refundable ACTC.

As already discussed, and reported in Table 1, EITC spending disproportionately goes to single parents with children. Figure 5 explores this further by presenting histograms for tax-return-reported earned income in tax year 2012 from the Statistics of Income (SOI) 2012 data (shown in 2018 dollars). I present the histograms for six demographic groups (single vs. married, for each with no, one, or two or more children). For each, the dashed line shows the 2018 EITC schedule, and I limit the sample in each case to those returns with earned income between $1 and $200,000. I do not condition on receipt of the EITC but tabulate the total number of returns within each $1,000 bin of earned income to see how these counts stack up across various points in the EITC schedule. On each graph, I also indicate the share of total filers for that demographic group that is excluded from the histogram (those filers with earned income that is ≤$0 or greater than $200,000).

FIGURE 5
Distribution of Earnings and EITC Schedule, by Filing Status and Number of Children

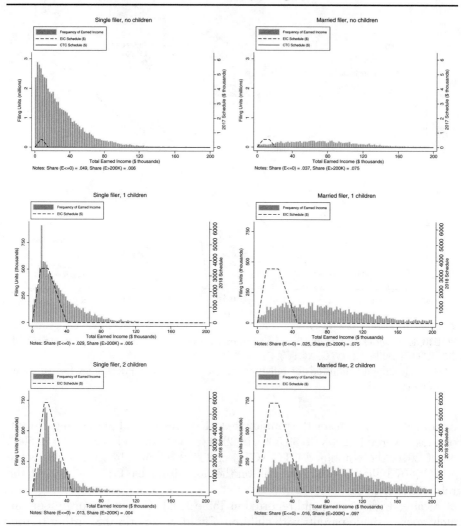

SOURCE: Earnings distribution calculated from Internal Revenue Service Statistics of Income Public Use Files (2012 tax year, earnings and EITC amounts in 2018 dollars using CPI-U). EITC schedule from Internal Revenue Service Procedure 2018–18, available from https://www.irs.gov/irb/2018-18_IRB.
NOTE: Notes to each figure provide the share of tax filers with earnings ≤$0 and above $200,000.

Several observations can be drawn from these figures. First, they illustrate well the variation in the generosity of the schedule across these six groups. The credit is substantially larger for families with children than for those without children, and the credit is larger for families with two or more children than for one-child families. Second, the distribution of earned income for single families

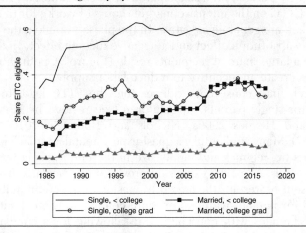

FIGURE 6
EITC Eligibility by Marital Status and Education

SOURCE: Author's calculation from the Annual Social and Economic Supplement to the Current Population Survey.
NOTE: Population includes women with children ages 24–48.

with children is shifted considerably to the left of the distribution for married families with children. Only 29 percent of singles with one child and 18 percent of singles with two children have earnings higher than the top of the EITC phase-out range (compared to 76 percent and 75 percent for married families with one and two children, respectively). Third, consistent with Saez (2010), there is evidence of clustering at the first kink of the EITC schedule for single families with children. On net, the higher income levels of married couples leads to lower rates of EITC eligibility (compared to single families). Figure 6, calculated using the March Current Population Survey, plots the EITC eligibility rates by marital status and maternal education level from 1984 to 2017. It shows the higher eligibility rates for single-parent families compared to married (about 60 percent of single parents with less than a college degree are eligible compared to 35 percent of married couples with mothers having less than a college degree) as well as the increases over time as the program has expanded.

Economic Effects and Evidence from the Research

Labor supply

The EITC generates incentives for employment as well as how much to work, but the effects differ based on the beneficiaries' marital status. Among single parents, who represent three-quarters of total EITC tax expenditures, the EITC increases the return to entering employment for those outside of the labor force and therefore results in a predicted increase in the extensive margin of labor supply. The incentives are quantitatively large due to the high phase-in rates in the credit (e.g., 40 percent for a single parent with two children). In contrast, the effects of the EITC on the intensive margin (hours of work), for those already in the labor market, are generally negative. In the phase-in region, the EITC generates a positive substitution effect and a negative income effect. In the phase-out region, where a large share of recipients reside (Figure 5), both substitution and income effects create an incentive to reduce labor supply.

The research finds consistent evidence that the EITC leads to increases in employment for single parents with children (see reviews by Hotz and Scholz 2003; Eissa and Hoynes 2006a; Nichols and Rothstein 2016; Hoynes and Rothstein 2017). Many studies take a quasi-experimental approach leveraging the variation across tax regimes and family size in the credit, using women without children as controls. The 1993 expansion provides a particularly attractive policy reform because it represents the largest expansion of the credit in its history, and the expansion for families with two or more children was much larger than the expansion for families with one child (thus allowing for a comparison among single women with children, comparing those with two or more children to those with one child). On the other hand, the 1993 expansion occurred during a period of broader changes including welfare reform and a very strong labor market (Blank 2001; Hoynes and Patel 2018).

Across the different studies and approaches, the evidence nearly universally points to a significant positive effect of the EITC on the employment of single women with children (Eissa and Liebman 1996; Meyer and Rosenbaum 2000, 2001). For example, Meyer and Rosenbaum (2001) find that the EITC raised labor force participation by 7.2 percentage points for single women with children relative to those without children between 1984 and 1996. The changes in employment are evident in the basic trends; Figure 7 uses the March Current Population Survey and plots the trend in annual employment for single women with no children, one child, and two or more children.

Quasi-experimental approaches (such as that described here) do not confirm the predictions on the intensive margin of labor supply. However, such quasi-experimental approaches are not well-suited to this question, because of the confounding effects of changes in the composition of workers due to the extensive margin labor supply effect. Bunching methods, starting with Saez (2010), take a different approach and find evidence that workers in the phase-in region adjust to increase their credits (Saez 2010; see also Chetty, Friedman, and Saez 2013; Chetty and Saez 2013; Mortenson and Whitten 2015). Most of this effect derives from self-employed workers who, and in contrast to wage and salary workers, self-report earnings on their tax return and have limited third-party verification. It is thus difficult to determine whether it is a real behavioral effect or a change in reporting. The bunching approach yields much weaker evidence for the predicted reduction in labor supply in the phase-out region.

Because the EITC is based on family income, the credit leads to a somewhat different set of incentives for married taxpayers. Overall, as with singles, we would expect higher rates of "family" employment (participation by at least one family member) for married couples, as a result of the credit being tied to work.

FIGURE 7
Employment Rates of Single Women, by Presence and Number of Children

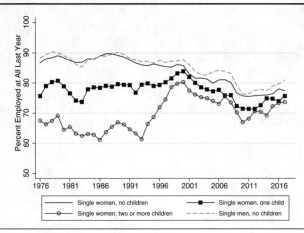

SOURCE: Author's calculation from the Annual Social and Economic Supplement to the Current Population Survey.
NOTE: Population includes unmarried women ages 19–44. Employment defined as any work in the previous year.

However, for most secondary earners, the EITC reduces the returns to work both on the extensive and intensive margin. Unless the primary earner has very low earnings (in the phase-in), the EITC reduces the after-tax wage for secondary earnings. There are fewer studies of married couples, but the available evidence shows that the EITC leads to small reductions in the employment of married women, consistent with the predictions above, and there is little evidence of any effects on men (Eissa and Hoynes 2004, 2006b).

Poverty and the distribution of income

Given the distributional goal of the EITC, it is useful to consider their expected effects on the distribution of income. In 2017, the poverty rate based on the supplemental poverty measure (SPM) was 13.9 percent, but the Census Bureau calculates that it would have been 16.5 percent without the EITC and CTC/ACTC (Fox 2018). The effect on child poverty is even larger: The SPM poverty rate for those under 18 years of age was 15.6 percent, but it would have been 21.7 percent without the refundable tax credits (Fox 2018). Based on these numbers, the EITC and CTC/ACTC are estimated to lift 8.3 million people, including 4.5 million children, out of poverty. These effects on child poverty are larger than any other government program. This measured antipoverty effect, however, captures only the *direct* effects of the tax credits. Additionally, there are *indirect* effects of the credit on after-tax and transfer income. Indirect effects come from earnings (with a positive effect if the extensive margin labor supply effect dominates) as well as a possible reduction in public assistance, Supplemental Nutrition Assistance

Program (SNAP), or other income that results from the increase in earnings. Several studies estimate the effect of the EITC on income or poverty (Bollinger, Gonzalez, and Ziliak 2009; Grogger 2003; Gunderson and Ziliak 2004; Hoynes and Patel 2018), all showing that the direct and indirect effects combine to lead to large effects of the EITC on income. Hoynes and Patel (2018) find that the 1993 expansion of the EITC led to a 7-percentage-point reduction in poverty rates among single-mother families with less than a college education; and fully half of this reduction is due to the behavioral response of labor supply. Thus, the static or direct effects of the EITC account for only half of the antipoverty effects for this group. More generally, Hoynes and Patel find that the income-increasing effects of the EITC are concentrated between 75 percent and 150 percent of income-to-poverty, with little effect at the lowest income levels (50 percent poverty and below where earnings and hence in-work credits play less of a role) and at levels of 250 percent of poverty and higher (beyond the phase-out range of the credit).

The EITC may affect *pretax* wages. Since the phase-in rate encourages increased employment, standard tax incidence models suggest that the credit will be shared between the buyers and sellers of labor (Rothstein 2008, 2010; Leigh 2010). Specifically, the credit may reduce pretax wages, allowing employers to capture a portion of the money spent on the tax credit. Additionally, workers who do not receive the tax credit, but compete in the same labor market as those receiving the tax credits, will also experience a reduction in pretax wages. The reductions in pretax wages will be smaller in settings with higher minimum wages. While these predictions have a strong theoretical basis, there is little knowledge of its size given fairly limited empirical evidence (Leigh 2010; Rothstein 2008, 2010). This remains an understudied topic and one that may be important for the consideration of expansions of the tax credits.[6]

These estimates of the effects of the EITC on after-tax income and poverty do not, however, take into account the recipients' out-of-pocket costs of tax filing. In 2017, 54 percent of EITC filers used paid tax preparers for a total cost (among all filers) of at least $0.5 billion (Government Accountability Office [GAO] 2019). These costs significantly reduce the net transfers of the EITC: Weinstein and Patten (2016) estimate the average cost (in 2016) of $400 or 13 to 22 percent of the refund. The total fees paid include tax preparation fees as well as additional financial products. Refund anticipation loans (RALs), widely used through 2008, provided short-term loans for refunds allowing filers to obtain a refund more quickly, as early as the day of filing. These highly profitable loans peaked in 2002, but by 2012 most banks were out of that market, partially due to the 2010 IRS elimination of a debt indicator, which alerted tax preparers to liens against filers (M. Jones 2017). With the decline in RALs, refund anticipation checks (RACs) increased. RACs are a short-term loan for tax preparation fees and do not allow the filer to receive the refund any sooner.[7] The RAC might charge a fee of $30 for a $200 filing fee for three weeks, implying an annual percentage rate (APR) of 260 percent (M. Jones 2017). It is widely reported that in addition to the RAC fees, tax preparers add on other fees—document processing fees, e-filing, and transmission fees. In 2014, 40 percent of EITC filers used an RAC, for a total of $424 million in RAC and add-on fees (Wu 2015).

Marriage and fertility

Children in two-parent families have substantially lower poverty rates than those in single-parent families, reflecting the potential for two earners in the household. In part, due to these disparities, there is interest in knowing how and whether elements of the social safety net incentivize or disincentivize marriage. The EITC creates a somewhat complicated set of incentives surrounding marriage. In particular, the EITC creates incentives for low-income, one-earner couples to legally marry; while for low-income, two-earner couples, the incentive is to avoid marriage or separate. These incentives are consequences of a progressive tax system based on family income, such as the marriage penalties/subsidies in the broader tax code (Eissa and Hoynes 2000). Additionally, because the credits increase with the number of children, they may incentivize additional births. There are a handful of studies that examine the effect of the EITC on marriage (e.g., Ellwood 2000; Rosenbaum 2000; Herbst 2011; Michelmore 2016); the results are largely inconclusive, and any effects are quite small. There is even less evidence on the effects of the EITC on fertility (Baughman and Dickert-Conlin 2009) and, again, the results suggest small effects.

Child and family well-being

To begin, it is useful to review the evidence about how the EITC is spent. Survey-based self-reports among EITC recipients at the time of tax filing indicate that 70 percent plan to spend their refunds on durable goods (Smeeding, Phillips, and O'Connor 2000). Several empirical studies reinforce this finding, in particular showing that expenditures on durables are higher in the beginning of the year (when EITC refunds are typically received) relative to the remainder of the year (Barrow and McGranahan 2000; Goodman-Bacon and McGranahan 2008; Gao, Kaushal, and Waldfogel 2009). Patel (2012), using tax reforms over the 1980s and 1990s, also finds an increase in durables at the beginning of the year but, overall, finds a larger effect of the EITC on work-related and housing expenditures uniformly increasing over the year.

A large and growing literature uses the established first stage finding that the EITC increases after tax and transfer income, to examine the credit effects on downstream outcomes of child and family well-being.[8] The research finds that the EITC leads to increases in infant health, including a reduction in low birth weight (Baker 2008; Hoynes, Miller, and Simon 2015; Strully, Rehkopf, and Xuan 2010); an increase in maternal health, including reducing the incidence of risky biomarkers such as measures of inflammation, high blood pressure, and elevated cholesterol; and improving mental health (Evans and Garthwaite 2014). There are several studies documenting a link between the EITC and human capital, including a positive effect of the EITC on child test scores (Dahl and Lochner 2012; Chetty, Friedman, and Rockoff 2011) and educational attainment (Bastian and Michelmore 2018; Manoli and Turner 2018).[9]

Possible Reforms

The evidence provided here indicates that the EITC is doing a good job of meeting its main objectives: it successfully targets low-income working families, bringing many of them out of poverty; and it has meaningful positive effects on labor force participation, with small or zero negative effects on the intensive margin and for secondary earners. In this section, I consider possible reforms to the EITC. One simple starting point is that the EITC has remained fixed in real terms for all but the largest families since the last expansion was fully phased in in 1996—more than 20 years ago. Yet since that time, wage stagnation and decline has been significant (Autor 2014), justifying an increase in the credit (Hoynes, Rothstein, and Ruffini 2018). More generally, the success of the EITC, and the consistent findings across the expansions to the credit over the past two decades (Nichols and Rothstein 2016) suggest that we should expand the EITC further. Several congressional proposals do just that (e.g., Senator Brown and Rep. Khanna's Gain Act, Senator Harris's Lift the Middle Class Act). One approach to increasing the EITC is to increase the credit along its current schedule. Given the evidence that the EITC increases the extensive margin of labor supply without much distortion due to the phase-out rate as well as the 2018 increase in the CTC (primarily benefiting those in the EITC phase-out and beyond), a more targeted expansion focused on the flat and phase in regions may be another choice.

Reforms aimed at equity across family types

One most commonly raised limitation of the EITC is the omission of a sizable credit for taxpayers without children. Figure 8 illustrates the variation in generosity of the credit by plotting the equivalence-scale-adjusted maximum EITC by filing status (married, single) and number of children (zero, one, two, three).[10] (The equivalence scale accounts for differences in family size.) For each family type, the equivalized maximum credit is expressed relative to the maximum benefit (equivalence scale adjusted) of a single adult with no children. If maximum benefits varied in a way that was consistent with equivalence scales, then all of the measures would equal 1. Clearly that is not the case. The largest deviation from equity across groups is the very low credit for childless tax filers; for example, the credit for single parents with one (two) children is more than five (seven) times as generous, taking into account differences in family size. The figure also shows that the EITC is less generous for married couples compared to singles (based on the maximum credit) and also exhibits variation in generosity across the number of children. Hoynes (2014) proposes reforming the credit such that it delivers an equitable benefit across different family sizes (thus the credit is equal in equivalence scale terms across groups).

This argument could be extended to argue for covering for a more significant credit for childless workers. Given the EITC's historical focus on targeting children (families with children), it is unclear whether support is sufficient for a sizable EITC to childless taxpayers. But given concerns about employment rates and

FIGURE 8

Equivalence Scale Adjusted Maximum EITC Credit by Filing Type and Family Size
(Relative to Maximum Credit for Single/No children)

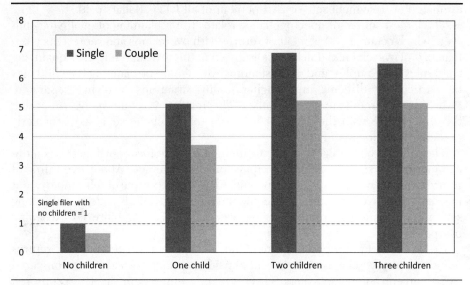

SOURCE: U.S. Internal Revenue Service, Revenue Procedure 2018-18, available from https://
www.irs.gov/irb/2018-18_IRB. Equivalence scale defined as OECD modified equivalence
scale; see OECD (2015).

poverty in this group (Joyce and Ziliak 2019) and the success of the EITC, there is
a strong argument to be made in favor of an expansion for childless workers.[11]

Reforms aimed at paid tax preparers

The discussion here described the large costs imposed on EITC filers through
the paid tax preparation industry. Clearly there are benefits to tax preparers—tax
filers may have limited knowledge of tax law, and the rules concerning refundable
credits are particularly complex. However, this is a largely unregulated industry
with predatory fees and little oversight. An often-proposed reform is to require
preparers to meet criteria, including education, training, continuing education, and
competency exams, as well as the requirement to register with the IRS.[12] A second
reform is requiring a standardized disclosure of fees. A third approach is to expand
IRS free filing and experimentation to improve use of these services. Currently the
IRS provides free filing for taxpayers with AGI below $66,000; GAO (2019) esti-
mates that 70 percent of taxpayers are eligible, yet only 3 percent use it.

Reforms aimed at reducing noncompliance

Noncompliance—errors in the claimed EITC—is an often-cited concern with
the program. This represents a potential cost of engaging in redistribution

through a complex tax system (where an often-cited benefit is the low administrative costs). The most recent IRS study (U.S. Department of the Treasury 2018), based on IRS audits of a sample of tax returns for tax year 2014, produces an estimated overpayment rate of 23.4 percent of all EITC dollars paid.[13]

The largest source of noncompliance relates to misclaiming of qualifying children, which occurs in 30 percent of returns with overclaims and represents more than half of overclaimed dollars. As discussed in this article, the EITC's qualifying child rules are complex, and understanding who should be claiming the child may be particularly difficult in changing family situations involving separated, divorced, or three-generation families. The residency requirement—requiring the child to live with the claimant for more than half the year—is particularly challenging to document.

The other major category of overclaiming is income misreporting; this is more common but results in smaller overpayments, on average. About two-thirds of returns with overclaims misreport income. Incorrect reporting of self-employment income is the primary source of income misreporting. This is widespread among self-employed and sole proprietors regardless of EITC eligibility, far exceeding overpayment costs in the EITC.

Commercial tax preparers account for a disproportionate share of returns found to have overclaims—60 percent of paid tax preparers had errors compared to 50 percent among self-filers (GAO 2014). Volunteers in the IRS-sponsored Volunteer Income Tax Assistance (VITA) and Tax Counseling for the Elderly (TCE) free assistance programs have the lowest error rates. One approach to reduce noncompliance could operate through the regulation of paid tax preparers. Additionally, we could adopt approaches to increase transparency, for example, in reporting tax preparer specific (or office specific) error rates. As with the development of compliance trainings for judges in the Social Security Disability Insurance (SSDI) program, high-noncompliance tax preparers could be required to engage in compliance training. In fact, the VITA volunteers are required to undergo rigorous certification training and pass a competency examination before they are allowed to prepare and file returns.

Additionally, expanding the EITC for taxpayers without children (and more generally equalizing EITC generosity across family types and family sizes as discussed) may have the added benefit of reducing noncompliance around qualifying children. Part of the EITC noncompliance around qualifying children may arise from the incentive to claim a child even if the rules are not satisfied—to move from a very small childless credit to the much larger credit for filers with children. The larger the childless credit, the smaller the incentives to misclaim.

One reform that would address this issue is to expand third-party reporting of self-employment income. By contrast, with third-party reporting of wage and salary income, there is very little noncompliance for wage and salary workers. Another approach would be to limit self-employment income for qualifying for the EITC, such as what California did in 2015 when it introduced the CalEITC. This limitation was ultimately eliminated, because of concerns for low-income self-employed workers being shut out of the state credit.

Structural reforms

As reviewed above, the EITC is highly effective at transferring income while encouraging work. But that leaves behind those that, for one reason or another, are not able to maintain stable work (in the short or longer run). In fact, after welfare reform and the reduction in the out-of-work cash safety net (Bitler and Hoynes 2010), there are concerns that our social safety net is inadequately protecting those not working. There are many ideas for how to address this, some that intersect with the tax credits that are the focus of this article. Shaefer et al. (2018) and Bitler, Hines, and Page (2018) proposed expansions of the CTC to extend to nonworking families. Senators Bennet and Brown have proposed the American Family Act, which extends the CTC to nonworking families and increases the maximum credit to $3,000 per child ($3,600 for younger children). This approach, also referred to as a child allowance, is present in many countries and was recently promoted in a National Academies of Sciences, Engineering, and Medicine (2019) report aimed at identifying policies to reduce child poverty. Dube (2018) proposed a reform to the EITC (called the Earned and Basic Income Tax Credit) where those with no earnings receive a benefit equal to some proportion (he suggests 50 percent) of the maximum benefits. Another approach gaining attention in the United States and around the world is to provide a Universal Basic Income (Hoynes and Rothstein 2019). All of these approaches would provide more assistance out of work but reduce the returns to entering work (illustrating the protection versus distortion trade-off present in all redistribution programs).[14]

Another way to improve the performance of the EITC is to increase the take-up rate. We know that take-up is lower among those eligible for smaller credits, notably those with low earning levels and childless filers (Plueger 2009). A challenge with increasing take-up for this group is that it disproportionately includes those not filing a tax return (and not legally required to). Recent evidence based on experimental designs and IRS partnerships shows that informational mailers can lead to significant increases in take-up (Bhargava and Manoli 2015; Guyton et al. 2016). Ongoing work in California, using various information treatments, is aimed at bringing in nonfilers for the new CalEITC (targeted at workers with earnings in the phase-in region). This work should be continued to establish best practices for increasing program take-up. Another approach that needs testing is the use of prepopulated tax returns, at least for earnings obtained by third-party reporting.

A final type of change to consider would be one aimed at distributing EITC payments periodically over the year rather than as annual lump sums, as this is commonly raised as an impediment to assisting families throughout the year. If EITC recipients are liquidity constrained, then an annual lump-sum payment has a smaller effect on the household's welfare than would one that is evenly distributed. Whether EITC recipients prefer periodic versus lump-sum payments is not well understood. Beginning in 1978, the Advance EITC provided a mechanism for recipients to receive their credits in their paychecks throughout the year, but take-up was extremely low (under 1 percent), and the option was canceled in 2010. This could indicate that recipients prefer their EITC payments as lump sums, seeing the program as a form of forced saving (Halpern-Meekin et al. 2015). On the other hand, the lack of use of the Advance EITC may stem in part because of lack of information or behavioral impediments to completing administrative processes and the power of changing defaults (Madrian and Shea 2001). Though prior experiments that informed recipients about the Advance EITC to overcome default behavior had only minor impacts on take-up (IRS and U.S. Department of the Treasury 1999; D. Jones 2010), recent evidence from the Chicago EITC Periodic Pilot suggests that there may be interest in a change to the delivery system (Bellisle and Marzahl 2015). In the pilot, the treatment group received half of their (projected) EITC payment in four quarterly payments (with the other half as the usual annual refund), while the control group had the status quo delivery system. At the end of the pilot, 90 percent of the treatment group stated a preference for this approach, and only 1.3 percent received overpayments (and often cited concern about period payments).

Conclusion

In this article, I examined the state of tax policy for low-income families with children. I focused primarily on the EITC but also discussed the much less targeted CTC. I discussed the goals of the programs (distributional, encouragement of work, and limiting of administrative costs) and summarized the existing research to assess how the programs meet the goals.

The EITC meets well all three of these goals. The policy provides substantial increases to income for low- to moderate-income families; it is the largest anti-poverty policy for families with children in the United States. A large body of research shows that the first-order behavioral effect of the policy is to increase employment among single mothers with children. Married couples also benefit from the program, although the policy does induce modest reductions in secondary earner employment. Administrative costs are low, particularly compared to the income-support-based alternatives to the EITC. However, fees for paid tax preparers lead to a reduction in the net benefits to the credit. Compliance remains an issue, with complicated rules for claiming children and lack of third-party reporting for all self-employment income. The CTC is much less favorable: it is not targeted (particularly with the 2018 expansion), with a credit of $2,000 per child extending high up the income distribution and with a lack of full refundability for the lowest-income workers.

I also discussed possible reforms to the EITC and to a lesser extent the CTC. I organized possible reforms into four categories including those aimed at improving equity across groups, regulating paid tax preparers, reducing noncompliance, and other design and delivery reforms.

An often-cited reform possibility is to extend the EITC more equitably to adults without children, who are largely left out of the benefits for the EITC. This should reduce poverty and increase employment for this group, their non-custodial children (if they have any), as well as having some potential to reduce noncompliance. More generally, I discussed using equivalence scales to create horizontal equity across tax filing units, those without children and those with a varying number of children.

Another high-value set of reforms would be focused on the paid tax preparation industry, with goals of improving quality, reducing noncompliance, and generating price transparency. The industry is largely unregulated, with a history of charging predatory fees. The fees lead to a substantial reduction in the net benefits of the credit and potentially higher noncompliance. I also call out the need for more research and experimentation to learn more about how to increase take-up of the EITC particularly for those with the lowest earnings levels. Additionally, many have argued for delivering the EITC more smoothly throughout the year rather than in a lump sum; I argued here for more research to gain insights into the possible benefits for this structural reform. Finally, I discussed the merits of a structural reform to the CTC, which extends the benefits more fully to the lowest-income families.

Notes

1. A qualifying child for the EITC is younger than 19 (or younger than 24 and a full-time student or any age if permanently and totally disabled), lives with the taxpayer for more than half the year, has a valid social security number, and is not claimed as a dependent by another taxpayer (IRS 2018).

2. Beginning in 2002, the flat and phase-out portions of the EITC were expanded for married couples. This expansion has increased over the years starting with a $1,000 expansion in 2002, $2,000 in 2005, and is $5,680 higher in 2018. Otherwise, the EITC does not vary with family structure.

3. Increases in the take-up rate of the food stamp program (SNAP) have reduced this distinction. Cunnyngham (2019) estimates an 85 percent SNAP take-up rate for 2016.

4. The nonrefundable CTC does not require earnings but is instead based on adjusted gross income.

5. A qualifying child for the CTC is under age 17. New in 2018, families with children ages 17–18, or those 19–24 and in school full time, and older dependents are eligible for a $500 per child credit.

6. These impacts on pretax wages represent general equilibrium effects and are difficult to estimate using credible research designs, especially given the widespread use of the variation by tax year and number of children, as wage effects would be common to all family types in the same year.

7. An RAC sets up a temporary bank account used to deposit the tax refund. The tax preparation fees are taken out of the refund, a bank card is issued for the balance, and the account is closed.

8. The above discussion makes clear that the EITC creates a "dual treatment"—it increases family resources and also increases maternal work. So while the EITC is generally viewed through the lens of increased resources (thus unambiguously good for family and child well-being), the effect of maternal employment could be positive or negative. In particular, the negative effect could result from low-quality childcare or a reduction in time investments from the child's parents.

9. On a more macro level, another question relates to how the EITC varies across boom and bust periods and the extent to which it serves as an automatic stabilizer. Bitler, Hoynes, and Kuka (2017) show that unlike most other elements of the social safety net, the EITC is fairly neutral to business cycle fluctuations. However, they show that this aggregate effect masks a procyclical effect for single filers (more jobs mean more EITC filers) and a countercyclical effect for married couples (for whom a negative earnings shock could lead to dropping into EITC eligibility).

10. This calculation is based on the OECD equivalence scale, which equals 1 for the head plus 0.5 for each additional adult (age 14 and over) plus 0.3 for each child (age <14).

11. Until recently, there was very little evidence on the likely labor supply impacts of a larger EITC on childless filers. The MDRC Paycheck Plus experiment implemented a randomized experimental design to estimate the impacts of a larger EITC (up to $2,000 compared to $519 under current law) for childless

workers. The final report for the experiment in New York City shows modest increases in employment rates, with effects concentrated among women and the more disadvantaged men (Miller et al. 2018).

12. These changes were proposed but ultimately turned down by a DC appeals court in 2014. Wu (2015) reports that five states have these types of regulations in place (including Connecticut, California, New York, Maryland, and Oregon). Wu (2018) has introduced a Model Individual Tax Preparer Regulation Act that includes obtaining a registration, passing a basic competency exam, requiring 60 hours of initial education and 15 hours per year of continuing education, and providing a standardized disclosure of their fees.

13. This is a *gross* overclaiming rate and does not take into account that an overpayment for one filer may be an underpayment for another.

14. A more modest but nonetheless important proposal would be to expand the CTC to allow for full refundability (Greenstein et al. 2018).

References

Autor, David. 2014. Skills, education, and the rise of earnings inequality among the "other 99 percent." *Science* 344 (6186): 843–51.

Baker, Kevin. 2008. Do cash transfer programs improve infant health: Evidence from the 1993 expansion of the Earned Income Tax Credit. Available from https://economics.nd.edu/assets/24011/baker_paper.pdf.

Barrow, Lisa, and Leslie McGranahan. 2000. The effects of the earned income credit on the seasonality of household expenditures. *National Tax Journal* 53 (4): 1211–44.

Bastian, Jacob, and Katherine Michelmore. 2018. The long-term impact of the Earned Income Tax Credit on children's education and employment outcomes. *Journal of Labor Economics* 36 (4): 1127–63.

Baughman, Reagan A., and Stacy Dickert-Conlin. 2009. The Earned Income Tax Credit and fertility. *Journal of Population Economics* 22 (3): 537–63.

Bellisle, Dylan, and David Marzahl. 2015. *Restructuring the EITC: A credit for the modern worker*. Washington, DC: Center for Economic Progress.

Bhargava, Saurabh, and Dayanand Manoli. 2015. Psychological frictions and the incomplete take-up of social benefits: Evidence from an IRS field experiment. *American Economic Review* 105 (11): 3489–3529.

Bitler, M., A. Hines, and M. Page. 2018. Cash for kids. *RSF: The Russell Sage Foundation Journal of the Social Sciences* 4 (2): 43–73.

Bitler, Marianne, and Hilary Hoynes. 2010. The state of the safety net in the post-welfare reform era. *Brookings Papers on Economic Activity*, Fall: 71–127.

Bitler, Marianne, Hilary Hoynes, and Elira Kuka. 2017. Do in-work tax credits serve as a safety net? *Journal of Human Resources* 36 (2): 358–89.

Blank, Rebecca. 2001. Declining caseloads increased work: What can we conclude about the effects of welfare reform? *Economic Policy Review* 7 (2): 25–36.

Bollinger, Christopher, Luis Gonzalez, and James P. Ziliak. 2009. Welfare reform and the level and composition of income. In *Welfare reform and its long-term consequences for America's poor*, ed. James P. Ziliak, 59–103. Cambridge: Cambridge University Press.

Chetty, Raj, John Friedman, and John Rockoff. 2011. *New evidence on the long-term impacts of tax credits*. Washington, DC: U.S. Internal Revenue Service.

Chetty, Raj, John N. Friedman, and Emmanuel Saez. 2013. Using differences in knowledge across neighborhoods to uncover the impacts of the EITC on earnings. *American Economic Review* 103 (7): 2683–2721.

Chetty, Raj, and Emmanuel Saez. 2013. Teaching the tax code: Earnings responses to an experiment with EITC recipients. *American Economic Journal: Applied Economics* 5 (1): 1–31.

Cunnyngham, Karen. 2019. *Reaching those in need: Estimates of State Supplemental Nutrition Assistance Program participation rates in 2016*. Cambridge, MA: Mathematica.

Currie, Janet. 2006. The take-up of social benefits. In *Poverty, the distribution of income, and public policy*, eds. Alan Auerbach, David Card, and John Quigley, 80–148. New York, NY: Russell Sage Foundation.

Dahl, Gordon B., and Lance Lochner. 2012. The impact of family income on child achievement: Evidence from the Earned Income Tax Credit. *American Economic Review* 102 (5): 1927–56.

Dube, Arindrajit. 24 October 2018. An anti-poverty tool with bipartisan support can be made even better. *The Hill*.

Eissa, Nada, and Hilary Hoynes. 2000. Explaining the fall and rise in the tax cost of marriage: The effect of tax laws and demographic trends, 1984–1997. *National Tax Journal* 53 (3): 683–711.

Eissa, Nada, and Hilary W. Hoynes. 2004. Taxes and the labor market participation of married couples: The Earned Income Tax Credit. *Journal of Public Economics* 88 (9): 1931–58.

Eissa, Nada, and Hilary W. Hoynes. 2006a. Behavioral responses to taxes: Lessons from the EITC and labor supply. In *Tax policy and the economy*, vol. 20, ed. J. M. Poterba, 74–110. Cambridge, MA: MIT Press.

Eissa, Nada, and Hilary W. Hoynes. 2006b. The hours of work response of married couples: Taxes and the Earned Income Tax Credit. In *Tax policy and labor market performance*, eds. Jonas Agell and Peter Birch Sorensen. Cambridge, MA: MIT Press.

Eissa, Nada, and Jeffrey B. Liebman. 1996. Labor supply response to the Earned Income Tax Credit. *Quarterly Journal of Economics* 11 (2): 605–37.

Ellwood, David T. 2000. The impact of the Earned Income Tax Credit and social policy reforms on work, marriage, and living arrangements. *National Tax Journal* 53 (4, part 2): 1063–1105.

Evans, William N., and Craig L. Garthwaite. 2014. Giving mom a break: The impact of higher EITC payments on maternal health. *American Economic Journal: Economic Policy* 6 (2): 258–90.

Fox, Liana. 2018. The Research Supplemental Poverty Measure: 2017. U.S. Census Bureau Current Population Report P60-265. Washington, DC: U.S. Census Bureau.

Gao, Q., N. Kaushal, and Jane Waldfogel. 2009. How have expansions in the Earned Income Tax Credit affected family expenditures? In *Welfare reform and its long-term consequences for America's poor*, ed. James Ziliak, 104–39. New York, NY: Cambridge University Press.

Goodman-Bacon, Andrew, and Leslie McGranahan. 2008. How do EITC recipients spend their refunds? *Economic Perspectives* 32 (2): 17–32.

Government Accountability Office (GAO). 2014. Paid tax return preparers: In a limited study, preparers made significant errors. GAO-14-467T. Washington, DC: GAO.

Government Accountability Office (GAO). 2019. Tax refund products: Product mix has evolved and IRS should improve data quality. GAO-19-269. Washington, DC: GAO.

Greenstein, Robert, Elaine Maag, Chye-Ching Huang, Emily Horton, and Choe Cho. 2018. *Improving the Child Tax Credit for very low-income families*. Washington, DC: US Partnership on Mobility from Poverty.

Grogger, Jeffrey. 2003. The effects of time limits, the EITC, and other policy changes on welfare use, work and income among female-headed families. *Review of Economics and Statistics* 85 (2): 394–408.

Gunderson, Craig, and James Ziliak. 2004. Poverty and macroeconomic performance across space, race, and family structure. *Demography* 41 (1): 61–86.

Guyton, John, Dayanand Manoli, Brenda Schafer, and Michael Sebastiani. 2016. Reminders and recidivism: Evidence from tax filing and EITC participation among low-income nonfilers. Working Paper, University of Texas.

Halpern-Meekin, Sarah, Kathryn Edin, Laura Tach, and Jennifer Sykes. 2015. *It's not like I'm poor: How working families make ends meet in a post-welfare world*. Berkeley, CA: University of California Press.

Hendren, Nathaniel, and Ben Sprung-Keyser. 2019. A unified welfare analysis of government policies. NBER Working Paper 26144, National Bureau of Economic Research, Cambridge, MA.

Herbst, Chris M. 2011. The impact of the Earned Income Tax Credit on marriage and divorce: Evidence from flow data. *Population Research Policy Review* 30:101–28.

Hotz, V. Joseph, and John Karl Scholz. 2003. The Earned Income Tax Credit. In *Means-tested transfer programs in the United States*, ed. Robert A. Moffitt, 141–197. Chicago, IL: University of Chicago Press.

Hoynes, Hilary. 2014. *Building on the success of the Earned Income Tax Credit, policies to address poverty in America*. Washington, DC: The Hamilton Project.

Hoynes, Hilary W., Doug L. Miller, and David Simon. 2015. Income, the Earned Income Tax Credit and infant health. *American Economic Journal: Economic Policy* 7 (1): 172–211.

Hoynes, Hilary W., and Ankur Patel. 2018. Effective policy for reducing inequality? The Earned Income Tax Credit and the distribution of income. *Journal of Human Resources* 53:859–90.

Hoynes, H., and J. Rothstein. 2017. Tax policy toward low-income families. In *Economics of tax policy*, eds. Alan Auerbach and Kent Smetters. Oxford: Oxford University Press.

Hoynes, H., and J. Rothstein. 2019. Universal basic income in the U.S. and advanced countries. *Annual Review of Economics* 11:929–58.

Hoynes, Hilary, Jesse Rothstein, and Krista Ruffini. 2018. Making work pay better through an expanded Earned Income Tax Credit. In *The 51% driving growth through women's economic participation*, eds. Diane Whitmore Schanzenbach and Ryan Nunn. Washington, DC: The Hamilton Project.

Hoynes, Hilary, and Diane Whitmore Schanzenbach. 2018. Safety net investments in children. Brookings Papers on Economic Activity. Available from https://www.brookings.edu/wp-content/uploads/2018/03/HoynesSchanzenbach_Text.pdf.

Internal Revenue Service (IRS) and U.S. Department of the Treasury. 1999. *Advanced Earned Income Tax Credit: 1994 and 1997 notice study: A report to Congress*. Washington, DC: IRS.

Internal Review Service (IRS). 2018a. Earned Income Credit (EIC). Publication 596. Washington, DC: IRS.

Internal Revenue Service (IRS). 2018b. Statistics of income—2016 individual income tax returns. Publication 1304. Washington, DC: IRS.

Jones, Damon. 2010. Information, preferences and public benefit participation: Experimental evidence from the Advance EITC and 401(k) savings. *American Economic Journal: Applied Economics* 2 (2): 147–63.

Jones, Maggie. 2017. *Tax preparers, refund anticipation products, and EITC noncompliance*. Washington, DC: Center for Administrative Records Research and Applications, U.S. Census Bureau.

Joyce, Rob, and James Ziliak. 2019. Poverty in the US and UK. Working Paper.

Lalumia, Sara. 2013. The EITC, tax refunds, and unemployment spells. *American Economic Journal: Economic Policy* 5 (2): 188–221.

Leigh, Andrew. 2010. Who benefits from the Earned Income Tax Credit? Incidence among recipients, coworkers and firms. *B.E. Journal of Economic Analysis & Policy* 10 (1).

Madrian, Brigitte, and Dennis F. Shea. 2001. The power of suggestion: Inertia In 401(k) participation and savings behavior. *Quarterly Journal of Economics* 116:1149–87.

Manoli, Dayanand, and Nick Turner. 2018. Cash-on-hand and college enrollment: Evidence from population tax data and policy nonlinearities. *American Economic Journal: Economic Policy* 10 (2): 242–71.

Meyer, B., and D. Rosenbaum. 2000. Making single mothers work: Recent tax and welfare policy and its effects. *National Tax Journal* 534 (part 2): 1027–62.

Meyer, Bruce D., and Dan T. Rosenbaum. 2001. Welfare, the Earned Income Tax Credit, and the labor supply of single mothers. *Quarterly Journal of Economics* 116 (3): 1063–1114.

Michelmore, K. 2016. The Earned Income Tax Credit and union formation: The impact of expected spouse earnings. *Review of Economics of the Household* 16 (2): 377–406.

Miller, C., L. Katz, G. Azurdia, A. Isen, C. Schultz, and K. Aloisi. 2018. *Boosting the Earned Income Tax Credit for singles final impact: Findings from the Paycheck Plus Demonstration in New York City*. New York, NY: MDRC.

Mortenson, Jacob A., and Andrew Whitten. 2015. How sensitive are taxpayers to marginal tax rates? Evidence from income bunching in the United States. Available from http://papers.ssrn.com/sol3/Papers.cfm?abstract_id=2719859.

National Academies of Sciences, Engineering, and Medicine. 2019. *A roadmap to reducing child poverty*. Washington, DC: The National Academies Press.

Nichols, Austin, and Jesse Rothstein. 2016. The Earned Income Tax Credit. In *Economics of means-tested programs in the United States*, vol. I, ed. Robert Moffitt. National Bureau of Economic Research Conference Report. Chicago, IL: University of Chicago Press.

Organisation for Economic Co-operation and Development. 2015. *In it together: Why less inequality benefits all*. Paris: OECD Publishing.

Patel, Ankur. 2012. The Earned Income Tax Credit and expenditures. Available from https://gspp.berkeley.edu/assets/uploads/research/pdf/Hoynes-Patel-EITC-Income-11-30-16.pdf.

Plueger, Dean. 2009. *Earned Income Tax Credit participation rate for tax year 2005*, 151–95. Washington, DC: Internal Revenue Service.

Rosenbaum, Dan T. 2000. Taxes, the Earned Income Tax Credit, and marital status, 1999–2000. Presented at ASPE Census Bureau Small Grants Sponsored Research Conference, May, Washington, DC.

Rothstein, Jesse. 2008. The unintended consequences of encouraging work: Tax Incidence and the EITC. Princeton University Working Paper, Princeton, NJ.

Rothstein, Jesse. 2010. Is the EITC as good as an NIT? Conditional cash transfers and tax incidence. *American Economic Journal: Economic Policy* 2 (1): 177–208.

Saez, Emmanuel. 2010. Do taxpayers bunch at kink points? *American Economic Journal: Economic Policy* 2 (3): 180–212.

Scholz, John Karl. 1994. The Earned Income Tax Credit: Participation, compliance, and antipoverty effectiveness. *National Tax Journal* 47 (1): 64–87.

Shaefer, H. Luke, Sophie Collyer, Greg Duncan, Kathryn Edin, Irwin Garfinkel, David Harris, Timothy M. Smeeding, Jane Waldfogel, Christopher Wimer, and Hirokazu Yoshikawa. 2018. A universal child allowance: A plan to reduce poverty and income instability among children in the United States. *RSF: The Russell Sage Foundation Journal of the Social Sciences* 4 (2): 22–42.

Smeeding, Timothy, K. Phillips, and M. O'Connor. 2000. The EITC: Expectation, knowledge, use, and economic and social mobility. *National Tax Journal* 53 (4): 1187–1210.

Strully, Kate W., David H. Rehkopf, and Ziming Xuan. 2010. Aspects of prenatal poverty on infant health: State Earned Income Tax Credits and birth weight. *American Sociological Review* 75 (4): 534–62.

U.S. Department of the Treasury. 2018. *Agency financial report, fiscal year 2018*. Washington, DC: U.S. Department of the Treasury.

Weinstein, Paul, Jr., and Bethany Patten. 2016. *The price of paying taxes II: How paid tax preparer fees are diminishing the EITC*. Washington, DC: Progressive Policy Institute.

Wu, Chi Chi. 2015. *Taxpayer beware: Unregulated tax preparers and tax-time financial products put taxpayers at risk*. Boston, MA: National Consumer Law Center.

Wu, Chi Chi. 2018. *Tax time products 2018: New generation of tax time loans surges in popularity*. Boston, MA: National Consumer Law Center.

Exploring Options to Improve the Supplemental Nutrition Assistance Program (SNAP)

By
DIANE WHITMORE
SCHANZENBACH

The Supplemental Nutrition Assistance Program (SNAP), previously known as the Food Stamp Program, is a cornerstone of the U.S. safety net. SNAP provides means-tested electronic vouchers that can be used to purchase most foods at participating retail outlets and helps low-income families afford the food that they need. It also helps to stabilize the economy in fiscal downturns, because more benefits are paid when jobs and income are scarce. SNAP households range widely in their demographic characteristics, from those with elderly or disabled members, to prime-age families (typically with children) who combine work and benefit receipt, to those with no or very low levels of income. Potential reforms, such as policies to encourage work or improve dietary outcomes, may have different impacts on various subgroups and should be designed with the heterogeneity of the caseload in mind. I review the theoretical and empirical research literature on SNAP's impacts and consider potential reforms by analyzing them in terms of the program's stated goals.

Keywords: SNAP; supplemental nutrition assistance program; food stamp program; safety net; nutrition assistance; means tested programs

The Supplemental Nutrition Assistance Program (SNAP), previously known as the Food Stamp Program, is a cornerstone of the U.S. safety net. SNAP is the only social benefits program universally available to low-income Americans, and in 2018 it assisted 40 million people in a typical month—about one out of every eight Americans. In 2018, $60.6 billion was spent on benefits and $65.0 billion was spent overall, including administrative costs. SNAP benefits typically are paid once per

Diane Whitmore Schanzenbach is the Margaret Walker Alexander Professor of Human Development and Social Policy at Northwestern University, where she also directs the Institute for Policy Research. She is an economist who studies policies aimed at improving the lives of children in poverty, including education, health, and income support policies.

Correspondence: dws@northwestern.edu

DOI: 10.1177/0002716219882677

ANNALS, *AAPSS*, 686, November 2019

FIGURE 1
SNAP Participation and Expenditures and Unemployment Rate over Time

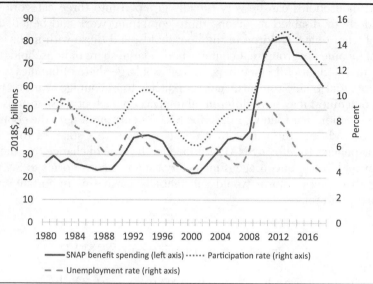

SNAP benefit spending (left axis) ······ Participation rate (right axis)

— — Unemployment rate (right axis)

month on an electronic benefits transfer (EBT) card that can be used in a check-out line like a debit card to purchase most foods that are intended to be taken home and prepared.

In 2017, 11.8 percent of U.S. households were food insecure at some point in the year. SNAP is designed to prop up families' purchasing power when their incomes are low and helps to buffer households' economic shocks due to job loss or other income declines. SNAP also has a stated goal of strengthening the agricultural economy, and every $5 increase in SNAP benefits has been shown to increase economic activity in the local economy by $9 (Hanson 2010). In addition, SNAP plays an important role as an automatic stabilizer, responding powerfully and quickly in times of economic downturns. During a recession, as unemployment rises, families' incomes fall, making more of them eligible for SNAP benefits (or making those already eligible for SNAP eligible for larger benefits).

Figure 1 presents SNAP participation (as a share of the population) and expenditures on benefits over time. Total expenditures (in inflation-adjusted 2018 dollars) were $27.2 billion in fiscal year (FY) 1990, peaking at $82.0 billion in 2013 in the aftermath of the Great Recession, then falling as the economy recovered. Over the same time period, SNAP participation has grown from 8.0 percent in 1990 to a high of 15.0 percent in 2013, falling back to 12.3 percent in 2018.

SNAP is the primary means-tested safety net program. Unlike most other major programs, it provides benefits based on need but does not have additional targeting to specific groups (such as the elderly, children, or workers). As a result, it serves a wide range of the population. It does this effectively because it works in conjunction with the market and normal economic decision-making. SNAP provides additional resources to purchase food through normal channels of trade, and families use those additional resources to decide what to purchase subject to the prices that they face and to their own tastes and preferences.

SNAP households can be very broadly grouped into three categories: those with elderly or disabled members; those combining work and benefit receipt, many of whom have children in the households; and those with no or very low levels of income—a group that contains both a large share of households without elderly, disabled, or child members, as well as a large share of families with children. Potential policy reforms, such as policies to encourage work or improve dietary outcomes, may have differential impacts on each of these groups.

In the section that follows, I describe SNAP's current design, the composition of its caseload, and the extent to which it varies across states. I then explore potential policies to reform SNAP, grouped by the type of change that the policymaker would like to encourage. Finally, I consider major reforms to SNAP, concluding that major reform would substantially harm this important universal safety net program.

Current Characteristics of SNAP

Under federal rules, to be eligible for SNAP a household's income and assets must meet three tests. First, their gross monthly income (before any deductions are applied) must be no higher than 130 percent of the poverty line, unless there is an elderly or disabled member in the household. Second, their net income, equal to total income less a series of deductions—including a standard deduction available to all households, some earned income, childcare expenses, legally obligated child support, housing costs that exceed half of the family's net income, and medical expenses for elderly or disabled household members—must be no higher than 100 percent of the poverty line.[1] Third, assets (which generally include bank accounts, but not retirement savings or most automobiles) must fall below $2,250, or $3,500 for households with an elderly or disabled member. States have the option to relax the gross income and asset limits. During normal economic times, unemployed, nondisabled childless adults are limited to three months of SNAP benefits every three years. The time limit can be waived at the state or substate level in areas with high and sustained unemployment.

SNAP benefits are calculated based on a federal formula that considers the resources a family has available to purchase food. In particular, the SNAP benefit formula assumes that 30 percent of a family's net income is available for food purchases. SNAP benefits are awarded as the difference between the cost of the U.S. Department of Agriculture's (USDA's) Thrifty Food Plan (a diet plan intended to provide adequate nutrition at a minimal cost) for a family of a given size and 30 percent of the family's net income (if net income is positive).

Figure 2 shows a stylized version of the relationship between income, SNAP benefits, and food spending for a family of a fixed size. The horizontal axis shows a family's net income, and the vertical axis measures SNAP benefits and food spending in dollars. The maximum SNAP benefit, shown as the dashed horizontal

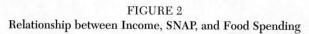

FIGURE 2
Relationship between Income, SNAP, and Food Spending

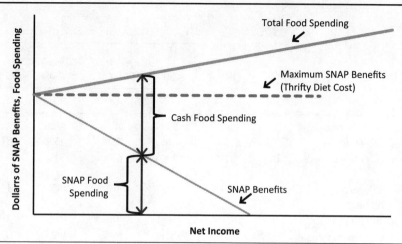

line, represents the minimum guaranteed food budget for participants. The downward-sloping line represents SNAP benefits received and is equal to the maximum benefit less 30 percent of the family's net income. A household of three with no net income would receive $505 in monthly SNAP benefits, while a household with $1,000 in net monthly income would receive $205 in benefits. The upward-sloping line represents a family's total food spending. As income increases, typically so does spending on food (and all other normal goods). As depicted in the graph, the majority of families spend more on food than the maximum SNAP benefit level, and also more than their monthly SNAP benefit amount (Hoynes, McGranahan, and Schanzenbach 2016). As family income increases, the share of total food spending coming from SNAP benefits declines. As a result, policies to use SNAP to alter a household's consumption bundle will have different leverage among those for whom SNAP represents a large part of the budget compared to those for whom it represents a more modest share.

SNAP serves a wide range of the population, including the elderly, disabled, children, employed adults, and unemployed adults. Table 1 presents characteristics of the SNAP caseload in 2017. Overall, the average monthly household benefit is $241. Children are present in 42 percent of households; and 44 percent have an elderly or disabled member; while 21 percent have no disabled, elderly, or child members. Overall, 31 percent have earnings, a fraction that has increased steadily over time from 23 percent in 1996 (Hoynes and Schanzenbach 2016). At the other extreme, 19 percent have no cash income (either earned or unearned).

The table also breaks up the characteristics of the caseload by income relative to the poverty threshold. As expected, average SNAP benefits are higher among lower-income households. The share of households with earnings increases across income-to-poverty bins. Fully half of SNAP households with incomes at or below 50 percent of the poverty threshold have no cash income of any type.

TABLE 1
Characteristics of Households on SNAP in 2017, Overall and by Income-to-Poverty Ratio

			By Income-to-Poverty Ratio		
	Overall	<50%	>50% to ≤100%	>100% to ≤130%	>130%
	(1)	(2)	(3)	(4)	(5)
Average monthly benefit	$241	$341	$212	$129	$57
Percent with children	42%	49%	35%	45%	31%
Percent with elderly or disabled member	44%	13%	67%	54%	58%
Percent with no disabled, elderly, or child members	21%	42%	6%	9%	14%
Percent without cash income	19%	50%	0%	0%	0%
Percent with any earnings[a]	49%	21%	89%	96%	97%
Share of SNAP caseload	100%	41%	41%	13%	5%

SOURCE: Authors' calculations based on 2017 SNAP Quality Control files.
NOTE: Children defined as younger than age 18. Elderly defined as age 60 or older.
a.Percent with any earnings calculated only for those households without an elderly or disabled member.

Among this poorest group of SNAP recipients, which comprises 41 percent of the households on SNAP, nearly half have children in the household, and 42 percent are childless and contain only nondisabled and nonelderly adults.

Table 2 shows how the characteristics of SNAP households have evolved over the past two decades. In 1996, nearly three in five SNAP households contained children; by 2017, that share fell to just over two in five. The share of households with elderly members increased from 16 to 24 percent over the same timeframe. The share of households not containing any elderly, disabled, or child members increased from 15 to 21 percent—and recall from Table 1 that the majority of these households have incomes below 50 percent of the poverty line. The table shows an increase in the share of households at both income extremes. Overall, an increasing share of the caseload has earnings and has incomes above the poverty threshold; at the same time, an increasing share has no cash income and an increasing share receives the maximum benefit, indicating that the household has no positive net income according to the SNAP benefit formula.

Participation rates among those eligible for SNAP are relatively high, estimated at 85 percent in 2016 (USDA 2019a). They have been steadily increasing in recent years, up from a low of 53 percent in 2001. Participation rates are estimated to be 100 percent for those with income levels below the poverty threshold and for families with children. Rates are lower for those with a lower expected benefit level, such as eligible households with income above the poverty

TABLE 2
SNAP Household Characteristics over Time

	1996	2005	2017
	(1)	(2)	(3)
HH with children	59%	54%	42%
HH with elderly or disabled members	34%	40%	44%
HH with no children, elderly, disabled	15%	16%	21%
Share with income below poverty	91%	88%	81%
Share with earnings	23%	29%	31%
Receive maximum benefit	25%	31%	37%
Have no cash income	10%	14%	19%

SOURCE: Author's calculations based on 2017, 2005 and 1996 SNAP Quality Control files.
NOTE: Children defined as younger than age 18. Elderly defined as age 60 or older.

threshold. The elderly also participate at low rates, and recent work finds that providing information on eligibility, or information plus application assistance, can meaningfully increase these rates (Finkelstein and Notowidigdo 2018).

While there is no variation across states in the SNAP benefit formula, there is nonetheless some variation across states in eligibility for and access to the program. One dimension along which state policies vary is on whether they have implemented a Broad-Based Categorical Eligibility (BBCE) policy, which confers categorical eligibility to households that are then able to apply for and receive SNAP benefits according to the usual benefits formula. In effect, these policies loosen or waive the gross income and asset tests. Note that states cannot further limit eligibility beyond federal requirements using BBCE. As shown in Table 3, forty-three states have adopted a BBCE policy that applies to all households; in two cases, BBCE policies are limited to households with children or households with earnings or dependent care expenses. Under BBCE, twenty-five states have raised the gross income limit to 185 percent of the federal poverty guideline or higher. Thirty-seven states have used BBCE to waive the asset test. It is worth emphasizing that these households only receive SNAP benefits if they qualify for them under the benefits formula based on their net income; in the absence of BBCE, they would be categorically ineligible for benefits even if the benefits formula would have awarded them positive SNAP amounts.

States vary widely in their participation rates among those eligible for SNAP, in 2016 ranging from 56 percent in Wyoming to essentially full participation in Illinois, Michigan, New Mexico, Oregon, Rhode Island, Vermont, and Washington (USDA 2019a). Some of this variation is influenced by states' adoption of agency policies that either promote or limit take-up. For example, states vary in terms of whether they have at least one outreach policy, whether they offer an online application to everyone in the state, whether they have adopted an allowable simplified reporting policy, and so on. Figure 3 shows the relationship between a

TABLE 3
State Variation in Access Policies

Has BBCE Policy	Number of States	Gross Income Limit (% Poverty Guidelines)[a]	Number of States	Asset Limit	Number of States
For all households (HH)	41	130	10	$5,000	5[c]
		160	2		
Only HH with at least one child	1	165	5	$25,000	1
		175	1		
Only HH with dependent care expenses or earned income	1	185	8	No limit	37[d]
		200	17[b]		

SOURCE: Economic Research Service (ERS), USDA, SNAP Policy Database, SNAP Policy Data Sets, available from https://www.ers.usda.gov/data-products/snap-policy-data-sets/.
NOTE: Policies in effect as of December 2016.
a. Gross income limits for households without an elderly or disabled member.
b. New York has a gross income limit of 200% for HH's with dependent care expenses, but 150% for those without earnings or dependent care expenses.
c. Michigan excludes one vehicle from the asset test but includes other vehicles with fair market value over $15,000. Texas excludes one vehicle up to $15,000 and includes excess vehicle value.
d. Thirteen states limit access among households with an elderly or disabled member and incomes over 200 percent of the FPT to fewer than $3500 in assets.

state's participation rate and its use of what I code as "expansive" SNAP policies.[2] On average, the state's SNAP participation rate among those eligible is 3 percentage points higher for every expansive policy adopted by the state.

It is widely documented that SNAP participants, like other Americans, have dietary intakes that fall far short of the goals set in dietary guidelines (Condon et al. 2015; Institute of Medicine and National Research Council 2013). SNAP participants score worse on measures of dietary quality and are more likely to be obese than nonparticipants. Bitler (2016) documents that much of these differences are driven by the fact that those who are financially worse off are the ones who participate in SNAP, and the differences in average outcomes do not represent causal impacts of the program.

Review of Research on SNAP

There is an active literature on the impact of SNAP on the short-term outcomes for beneficiaries, such as consumption, food insecurity, and labor supply. There is also a good deal of work on the longer-term impact of SNAP on children's health and economic outcomes and on the determinants of the SNAP caseload. This brief summary is a subset of the broader review of the literature over the past few decades, published in Hoynes and Schanzenbach (2016).

FIGURE 3
Relationship between Expansive SNAP Policies and Participation, 2016

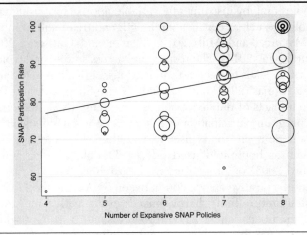

Number of Expansive SNAP Policies

Determinants of the SNAP caseload

As illustrated in Figure 1, participation in and expenditures on SNAP have varied significantly over time. At a macro level, this has generally aligned with fluctuations in the unemployment rate. While the macroeconomy is the largest contributor to changes in SNAP caseloads, SNAP and welfare policies have also played a role. For example, welfare reform and reductions in the length of SNAP certification periods led to reductions in SNAP caseloads in the 1990s (Currie and Grogger 2001; Ziliak, Gundersen, and Figlio 2003; Figlio, Gundersen, and Ziliak 2000). Changes in immigrant access to the safety net during the welfare reform period also led to reductions in SNAP participation (Borjas 2004; Haider et al. 2004; Kaestner and Kaushal 2005; Bitler and Hoynes 2013). Ganong and Liebman (2018) find that state policy changes explain a share of the increase in participation in the early 2000s.

There has been particular interest in the sharp increase in the caseload during the Great Recession. Ganong and Liebman (2018) find that unemployment explains most of the increase, estimating that a 1 percentage point increase in the state unemployment rate increases enrollment by 15 percent. Ziliak (2015) confirms a large role for unemployment and investigates a wider range of policies, finding a larger impact of policy, perhaps accounting for 30 percent of the caseload increase. Bitler and Hoynes (2016) find that the countercyclical effect of SNAP as measured by the effect of the unemployment rate on the SNAP caseload was larger during the Great Recession compared to the early 1980s recession (although the difference was not statistically significant).

Impacts of SNAP on food insecurity

An important goal of SNAP is to address food insecurity—that is, having inadequate or uncertain access to enough food for an active, healthy lifestyle. It has been a challenge to identify the causal impact of SNAP on food insecurity, and the literature is characterized by a wide range of estimates.

Several studies employ instrumental variable approaches, using as instruments state SNAP policies such as certification length and treatment of immigrants (Yen et al. 2008; Mykerezi and Mills 2010; Shaefer and Gutierrez 2013; Ratcliffe, McKernan, and Zhang 2011). The results vary across studies and typically find that SNAP participation leads to decreases in food insecurity, but many are not statistically significant. Borjas (2004) and Schmidt, Shore-Sheppard, and Watson (2016) investigate the impacts of public assistance, including SNAP and other programs, and find that program participation or higher benefit amounts lead to statistically significant reductions in food insecurity. Other, less credible studies using approaches such as household fixed effects (DePolt, Moffitt, and Ribar 2009; Wilde and Nord 2005) or propensity score matching (Gibson-Davis and Foster 2006) have found a positive association between SNAP and food insecurity.

Overall, the literature finds sharply mixed results, with some studies finding a positive association between SNAP and food insecurity, some finding a negative association, and some finding insignificant results. Gregory, Rabbitt, and Ribar (2015) recently reviewed this literature and conducted a replication exercise, implementing propensity score matching, longitudinal, and instrumental variables approaches in one sample. They find a range of estimates, illustrating well the difficulty in finding a way to isolate the causal impact of SNAP on outcomes, such as food security.

Impacts of SNAP on labor supply

By providing unearned income in the form of benefits, SNAP is predicted to have work disincentive effects. The (sparse) empirical literature using strong identification strategies tends to find that these work disincentives are modest.

East (2018b) examines SNAP's impact on labor supply, leveraging variation across states and over time in immigrants' eligibility for SNAP in the years after a 1996 rule that removed them from the program. She finds that SNAP causes single women immigrants to reduce their employment rates by 2 to 5 percentage points—a relatively modest impact among a group in which 65 to 70 percent are employed. While married male immigrants do not reduce their probability of employment in response to SNAP access, they do measurably reduce the number of hours that they work—on average, they work about 1.5 fewer hours per week when eligible for SNAP and are 4 to 4.5 percentage points less likely to work full time (on a base rate of 72 percent). There are no detectable impacts on the labor supply of unmarried male immigrants.

Hoynes and Schanzenbach (2012) use county variation in the rollout of the program to identify its impact on labor supply. They find no significant impacts on the overall sample, but among single-parent households with a female head—a group with high SNAP participation rates—they find that access to SNAP (then called the Food Stamp Program) in one's county of residence reduces employment by 183 hours annually. They find no significant impacts of the program on earnings or family income, though the estimates are imprecise.

Impacts of SNAP on consumption

Since SNAP increases the total resources that a family has to purchase food, economic theory predicts that it should increase food spending and, in most cases, nonfood spending as well. The empirical literature confirms that SNAP increases food spending and appears to increase the variety and quality of recipients' diets (Anderson and Butcher 2016). The literature is unsettled about the magnitudes of the increases in food and nonfood spending. Some studies find that recipients treat the additional resources in the same manner as they would an equivalent cash transfer (Hoynes and Schanzenbach 2009; Schanzenbach 2007), while others find that participants are especially more likely to purchase food with SNAP (Beatty and Tuttle 2014; Hastings and Shapiro 2018).

SNAP serves as social insurance, propping up consumption when families face declines in or low levels of income. Studies show that SNAP reduces volatility in consumption and income (Blundell and Pistaferri 2003; Gundersen and Ziliak 2003). Shaefer and Gutierrez (2013) also find that SNAP receipt reduces a family's likelihood of experiencing types of economic distress, such as falling behind on bills or forgoing medical care due to cost.

SNAP's impacts on long-term health and economic outcomes

The additional resources provided by SNAP likely would be expected to also improve a range of health and education outcomes. In general, studies find improvements in children's health and education in both the short and long run due to SNAP. The literature is more mixed on the short-run impact on adult obesity.

There is a small set of studies that examine the effect of SNAP on birth outcomes. Currie and Moretti (2008) use cross-county introduction of the program in California and find that SNAP is associated with a *reduction* in birth weight, a surprising result driven by increased births among teens and by birth weight declines in Los Angeles County. Almond, Hoynes, and Schanzenbach (2011) examine the effects of the program rollout across all counties in the United States, finding that SNAP improves infant outcomes, especially at the bottom of the birth weight distribution. East (2018a) utilizes changes in immigrants' eligibility across states and over time and finds that the mother's access to SNAP during pregnancy improves health at birth. In addition, she finds that increases in SNAP access during early life improve parent-reported health at ages 6 to 16 (with suggestive evidence of reductions in school days missed, doctor visits, and hospitalizations).

Hoynes, Schanzenbach, and Almond (2016) use the cross-county rollout to estimate the relationship between childhood access to the program and adult health and human capital outcomes. They find that early childhood access to SNAP leads to a large and statistically significant reduction in the incidence of "metabolic syndrome" (obesity, high blood pressure, heart disease, diabetes) as well as an increase in the share reporting to be in good health. They also find for women, but not men, that access to food stamps in early childhood leads to an increase in economic self-sufficiency. Bailey et al. (2019) use data from the Social

Security Administration and Census Bureau and the same identification strategy, finding positive impacts of early life access to SNAP on a number of outcomes including human capital, self-sufficiency, neighborhood quality, longevity, and a reduction in the likelihood of being incarcerated.

The predictions of SNAP's impact on body weight are ambiguous. If SNAP improves the quality of family diets, we might expect SNAP to reduce body mass index (BMI) or obesity outcomes. On the other hand, if SNAP causes participants to purchase more calorie-dense foods, then it may worsen these outcomes. The literature on this topic is unsettled. Schmeiser (2012) uses an instrumental variables approach, using state SNAP policies as instruments, and finds that SNAP reduces BMI among children for most gender-age groups. Kreider et al. (2012) address selection into SNAP and measurement error using a bounding approach, finding rather wide bounds that generally cannot rule out positive or negative effects of SNAP on BMI for children. Turning to adults, Fan (2010) uses a combination of fixed effects and propensity score matching and finds no significant effect of SNAP on obesity, being overweight, or BMI. Meyerhoefer and Pylypchuk (2008) combine individual fixed effects and an instrumental variables approach and find SNAP increases obesity among women but has no significant impact on men. Kaushal (2007) finds insignificant effects of SNAP on obesity among immigrants in the postwelfare reform era.

Potential Reforms within the Current Structure

Overall, extant evidence tells us that SNAP is an effective and efficient program that is well designed to work with the market, target benefits, and provide a phase-out that minimizes cliffs and other nonlinearities that may induce participants to respond to the program in suboptimal ways. Nonetheless, there are a number of potential reforms to SNAP that are often discussed in policy circles and are worth exploring further. Below, I outline a series of potential policy reforms organized around problems to be addressed and analyze them in terms of theory and research. Of course, policy in practice includes not only questions of evidence, but also of politics. I will leave discussions of the latter to those more skilled in that arena.

Reforms aimed at reducing food insecurity

While SNAP increases families' resources available for food purchases, nonetheless 31 percent of those reporting SNAP participation also experienced food insecurity in 2017. There are several types of policies that can address high levels of food insecurity, including providing more resources (through increased benefit levels or higher participation rates) or helping families to better smooth their consumption between paychecks or benefits payments.

One type of policy to attempt to reduce food insecurity is to increase benefit levels broadly among SNAP participants so that they have more money to spend on food. One way to do this is to increase the maximum SNAP benefit. As Ziliak (2016) explains, the USDA's Thrifty Food Plan (TFP) has become increasingly out of line with actual consumption patterns and assumes an unreasonable amount of time spent preparing meals from scratch. To address these shortcomings, he concludes that a 20 percent increase in SNAP's maximum benefit is needed in the short term and that, in the longer run, an evidence-based SNAP benefit would likely justify a similar maximum benefit level.[3] A $30 monthly benefit increase is predicted to decrease food insecurity by approximately 1 percentage point and improve the quality of diets consumed by SNAP participants (Anderson and Butcher 2016). Broad changes to SNAP payments are expensive; for example, Ziliak's proposal would increase SNAP spending by 24 percent but would also have additional spillover benefits to the macroeconomy as well as to dietary quality. Others have proposed replacing the USDA's TFP as the basis of SNAP benefits with its low-cost food plan, which costs about 30 percent more for a family of four (Food Research and Action Center 2012).

An alternative approach would be to increase benefits in a more targeted manner, aimed at families experiencing temporary increases in food costs. For example, families of the 22 million children who receive free or reduced-price school lunches (and the 12.5 million who receive free or reduced-price school breakfasts) on an average day typically lose access to these programs when school is out of session in the summer months. To offset these losses, currently the USDA offers the Summer Food Service Program, which provides free meals to children in low-income areas when school is out. The program is funded by the USDA and run by nonprofit community organizations (schools, camps, faith-based groups, hospitals, etc.) that can ensure that children receive meals in a supervised environment. Access to summer meals varies widely across locations, and on average only 2.7 million children participated in the program each day in July 2018 (USDA 2019b). One option to increase coverage would be to temporarily increase SNAP benefits to families with children during summer months. The USDA ran a series of high-quality randomized experiments to test the impact and feasibility of providing additional benefits to families with children during summer months through a Summer EBT program and found that benefits significantly reduce levels of children's food insecurity and very low food security (VLFS) (Collins et al. 2016). When families were provided an additional $60 in electronic benefits similar to SNAP payments, children's food insecurity declined by 20 percent, and VLFS declined by one-third. The following summer, they tested additional policies, including a $30 per month benefit and a Women, Infants, and Children (WIC)–based benefit, which is prescriptive on the types of food purchased. Comparing families who received $60 per month to those who received $30 per month demonstrated that the higher benefit level reduced food insecurity by an additional 10 percent but had no marginal impact on the rate of VLFS (suggesting that $30 per month was sufficient to ameliorate VLFS). The WIC model had better improvements in dietary quality for children, and similar impacts on food insecurity despite lower take-up rates. Which model (the SNAP-based or WIC-based) to expand would depend on the relative administrative costs at scale, as well as other policy preferences. In either case, increased summer food support benefits to families with children reaches a higher share of children than is currently served by the summer meals program. Of course, such a program would not convey the same community benefits (i.e., benefits from camps or other enrichment activities paired with the community summer meals), so a hybrid model of community-based and SNAP-based (or WIC-based) resources could be designed in a straightforward manner.

Another way to structure a targeted benefit increase would be to temporarily increase benefits to families with teenagers. Children's dietary requirements and food intake both increase during their teen years (U.S. Department of Health and Human Services 2015; Anderson and Butcher 2016), and families with teenagers experience higher rates of food insecurity than those with only younger children (Anderson et al. 2016). Note that these impacts are similar whether the teen is a male or female. Increasing SNAP benefits to families with teenagers would offset the increased costs of feeding older children and would help to reduce food insecurity among this group.

Studies have documented the so-called monthly SNAP cycle in which at the end of the benefits month dietary quantity or quality declines, or food insecurity increases, as participants run out of resources and await their next benefit payment (Todd 2015; Whiteman, Chrisinger, and Hillier 2018).[4] This has detrimental impacts on other outcomes as well, including children's test scores (Gassman-Pines and Bellows 2018) and emergency department visits among diabetics (Basu, Berkowitz, and Seligman 2017). Some advocate for breaking up SNAP payments from once to twice per month to encourage participants to smooth their consumption across the month. Recent work by Zaki and Todd (2019) find that SNAP participants obtain better value per dollar spent closer to the payment date, for example, by searching for bargains more effectively and purchasing larger item sizes that come with volume discounts. It is an empirical question whether more frequent payments, and how frequent they are, encourages more smoothing overall and whether there are particular groups made better or worse off. For example, Zaki (2016) finds sharp declines in consumption at the end of a two-week pay period. An experimental pilot program may be worth pursuing to study the trade-offs.

Reforms aimed at improving dietary quality

Another line of proposed reforms attempts to use the program to help improve the dietary quality of participants. In considering this issue, it is useful to think about the economic model of how SNAP works in conjunction with prices and individuals' tastes and preferences. In the absence of SNAP, consumers choose how much to spend on food and which mix of items they want to purchase subject to the prices that they face, as well as their own tastes and preferences.[5] For participants to change what they purchase fundamentally requires changing one of these: the prices that they face, their total food budget, or their underlying tastes and preferences.

How does SNAP impact consumer choice, then? As illustrated in Figure 2, by providing additional resources for food, SNAP is predicted to increase the purchase of food (and, to the extent that SNAP benefits are fungible, to increase the purchase of all normal goods). Theory predicts not only the quantity but also the quality of food purchased to increase, because when a household is consuming at subsistence level, it typically prioritizes calories over variety; but as income increases, consumption bundles shift toward more variety and less calorie-dense foods.

One way to increase families' total food budgets, which in turn improves the variety and quality of their diets, is to increase benefits levels. Anderson and Butcher (2016) simulate the expected impact of a $30 increase in SNAP benefits and predict increases in consumption of milk, grains, and vegetables, and a decrease in fast food consumption. Applicable lessons also can be drawn from the summer EBT program described above, which found that additional benefits improved dietary quality for children, increasing consumption of fruits and vegetables, dairy, and whole grains, and reducing consumption of added sugars.[6]

A different approach would be to decrease the relative prices of healthy foods through subsidies or other mechanisms, which would be predicted to cause families to shift their consumption toward the foods with now lower prices. Targeted price subsidies for healthy foods have been shown to be effective in the USDA's randomized controlled trial of the Healthy Incentives Pilot in Massachusetts—a program that gave SNAP recipients an immediate 30-cent rebate for every dollar they spent on a narrowly defined group of fruits and vegetables (Olsho et al. 2016). In response to this price rebate, consumption of the targeted healthy foods increased by 25 percent. In recent years, many local areas and a few states have taken a similar approach by awarding bonus dollars for benefits used at farmers' markets, allowing recipients to stretch their food budget further when they buy fresh produce. This approach would raise many difficult policy decisions, including which foods should be eligible for subsidies and what level of subsidy is best; without question, more research is needed into these issues. Nonetheless, the concept of subsidizing healthy foods has many merits, is a market-based solution that respects consumers' decision-making, and is feasible through SNAP.

Another option that garners support from some policy analysts is to disallow the purchase of soft drinks or sweetened beverages with SNAP benefits. Proponents hypothesize that by banning the purchase of sweetened beverages with SNAP, participants would curtail or even eliminate their purchase and consumption of these goods. Recall that SNAP benefits are modest—approximately $4.50 per person per day—and nearly all families supplement their SNAP purchases with groceries purchased from their cash income. At the same time, spending on sweetened beverages is also relatively low, averaging $12 per month (McGranahan and Schanzenbach 2011). Economic theory thus predicts that banning purchase of sweetened beverages would not change consumption of these goods, because the policy does not alter prices or consumers' tastes and preferences, and typically does not alter the budget constraint. A typical family that spends a modest amount on sweetened beverages, and importantly supplements their SNAP spending with cash resources that exceed the amount spent on sweetened beverages, would be expected to continue to purchase the identical basket of goods regardless of the ban—but they would have to make certain to pay for the soft drinks out of their own cash resources instead of their SNAP benefits. In other words, a sweetened beverage ban would be expected to increase the administrative costs of the program to both the USDA and retailers as they would be required to categorize sweetened beverages and monitor their purchase, and it could increase the stigma faced by recipients when they use the benefits, but it would not be expected to induce behavioral changes or dietary improvements.

In general, it is difficult to substantially improve dietary quality because dietary intake is based on tastes and preferences that are hard to alter. Policies that change prices or budget constraints show some promise to improve dietary quality through market mechanisms. Other more drastic reforms, such as moving to a more restrictive basket of goods, undermine many of the strengths of SNAP and are discussed further below.

Reforms aimed at encouraging work

Economic theory demonstrates that providing unearned income such as SNAP benefits is expected to reduce an individual's work effort, though in practice the effects of SNAP on work effort tend to be modest (East 2018b; Hoynes and Schanzenbach 2012). The SNAP benefit formula already attempts to reduce the disincentive to work by providing a 20 percent earned income deduction, and one way to further promote work is to increase this deduction (Schanzenbach 2013). Another way that SNAP reduces the disincentive to work is through waiving the gross income test under BBCE policies. Waiving the gross income test allows households to participate in SNAP that have higher levels of income but also high levels of allowable deductions such as childcare expenses and work deductions. Schanzenbach (2017) finds that SNAP families with gross incomes above standard gross income test level make up a small share of recipients— approximately 4 percent of households receiving 1.3 percent of total SNAP payments—but that 97 percent of them have earnings. Preserving such families' access to SNAP through waiving the gross income test reduces the benefit tax rate that they would otherwise face, promotes work, and provides needed support to these families.

Some analysts advocate for changing the current work requirement rules to further encourage work among SNAP participants.[7] The changes most frequently discussed include (1) expanding the groups that are subject to work requirements; (2) alternatively, eliminating work requirements for those currently exposed to them; and (3) changing the eligibility criteria under which states may request temporary waivers from the work requirements.

Under current law, able-bodied adults without dependents (known as ABAWDs, who are those between ages 18 and 49 who have no dependents and are not receiving disability benefits) may only receive SNAP for three months in a three-year period if they do not meet work requirements after this time limit. To be eligible after the time limit, an ABAWD must work at least 80 hours per month or participate in a state-approved workfare program. States may request temporary waivers from these time limits when unemployment is high or when there are insufficient jobs available in an area. Congress temporarily expanded the circumstances under which an area could qualify for a waiver during the Great Recession and suspended the time limit nationwide for part of 2009 and 2010, though states had the option to retain the time limit if they offered work opportunities to those subject to the rule.

Economists generally think about the effectiveness of work requirements and incentives—that is, carrots or sticks approaches to encouraging work—in the context of the local labor market. If individuals can increase their employment through exerting more effort, such as by searching for a job more diligently, or being willing to accept a lower-paying job, or working more hours, then incentives and/or requirements can potentially be quite effective. For example, the mid-1990s increase in the Earned Income Tax Credit (EITC) substantially increased earnings among the targeted group of unmarried mothers. On the other hand, the EITC likely had less of an incentive value during the Great Recession because unemployment was more of a function of factors outside of the individual's control such as macroeconomic conditions (Bitler and Hoynes 2010; Bitler, Hoynes, and Kuka 2017). The effectiveness of work requirements in SNAP will similarly vary by factors that influence whether participants can obtain a job, including the local labor market conditions and the individual's work readiness.

Bauer, Schanzenbach, and Shambaugh (2018) investigate labor market patterns that inform the likely impact of current SNAP work requirements and potential expansions of work requirements that were under debate in the 2018 Farm Bill. They demonstrate that variability in employment and hours among SNAP participants is high; and as a result, a large share of those who would be sanctioned under SNAP work requirements themselves have substantial work histories and may be falling below the required number of hours due to fluctuations on the low-wage labor market that are out of their direct control (see also Butcher and Schanzenbach 2018). Some of the sanctions against workers could be ameliorated by expanding the time period covered (e.g., instead of a monthly requirement, set a requirement for quarterly or annual hours) or otherwise smoothing across time periods, but such reforms would add complexity to an already complicated policy area.[8] Reforms to SNAP's employment and training programs are another approach to promoting work among SNAP participants. The USDA has commissioned several high-quality randomized-controlled trials of reforms to these programs, and results are expected in fall 2019.

Reforms aimed at targeting benefits or controlling costs

Economic growth is often described as the "right way" to reduce program costs. As shown in Figure 1, SNAP costs in large part vary with macroeconomic conditions, going down during economic expansions when more individuals are working and in turn fewer families require the assistance of the safety net. There are several additional policy options that could be adopted to reduce SNAP spending, including reducing eligibility or participation or further improving program integrity.

As shown in the previous section and the discussion of Table 3 above, many states have used BBCE to increase eligibility among households with gross incomes above 130 percent of the poverty threshold. Nationally in 2017, as shown in Table 1, SNAP families with gross incomes above 130 percent of the poverty threshold make up approximately 5 percent of households and receive 1.2 percent of total SNAP payments, and they are disproportionately families that have earnings; have child, elderly, or disabled members; or both. The CBO estimates that limiting eligibility to those with gross incomes at or below 200 percent of the poverty line (for households with an elderly or disabled member) or 130 percent of the poverty line (for households without an elderly or disabled member) would remove eligibility for 400,000 households and reduce spending by $5 billion over 10 years (Congressional Budget Office 2018).[9] Preserving such families' access to SNAP through waiving the gross income test reduces the benefit tax rate that they would otherwise face, promotes work, and provides needed support to these families.

Other states have used BBCE to extend SNAP access to those with assets above the federal limit of $2,250 in countable assets (excluding the value of vehicles).[10] The asset test reduces the population eligible for SNAP by 14 percent (Ratcliffe et al. 2016). Low-income households with assets above the test limit tend to have assets substantially above the limits, with median liquid asset levels of $36,000, and are more likely to include elderly members. Eliminating waivers to the asset test in SNAP would reduce participation, although the increased administrative cost burden associated with collecting asset data would offset potential savings.

As described above, participation rates are currently at 85 percent of the eligible population. Policies to reduce participation rates include adding administrative hurdles to application or renewal, or introducing policies that increase stigma on participants. The literature suggests that such policies will discourage the neediest from participating (Mills et al. 2014; Ribar and Edelhoch 2008).

Another way to reduce costs without limiting eligibility or take-up is to reduce fraud and error, although SNAP already performs well on this dimension. One approach is to improve monitoring for dual enrollment in SNAP across multiple states, which may, for example, occur if parents living in different states and sharing custody each claim the same children on their SNAP application, or if a participating family moves across state lines and enrolls in SNAP in the new state but fails to discontinue enrollment from the prior state. The National Accuracy Clearinghouse (NAC) currently monitors for dual SNAP enrollment across multiple states, and a recent demonstration project in southeastern states showed that the NAC could reduce the approximately two thousand cases per month of dual enrollment identified. If implemented nationwide, the NAC is predicted to save $114 million per year in erroneous payments.

Reforms aimed at improving SNAP's role in stimulating the economy

A stated goal of SNAP is to strengthen the agricultural economy. Since SNAP benefits are quickly spent by recipients, they provide a rapid fiscal stimulus to the economy. During normal economic times, moderately higher benefit levels that are still quickly spent would do more to stimulate the economy, as well as address food insecurity and related issues as described above. SNAP plays a particularly important stimulus role during economic downturns, with caseloads and spending expanding rapidly along with need. According to the Congressional Budget Office, SNAP is one of three programs that constitute the majority of the automatic stabilization aspect of federal spending, along with Unemployment Insurance and Medicaid (Russek and Kowalewski 2015). SNAP reaches a different population than is served by Unemployment Insurance, including those who do not meet minimum thresholds of hours or wages prior to job loss (Anderson, Butcher, and Schanzenbach 2015). Reforms that harm the program's ability to expand rapidly in times of economic downturns, such as block grants or broad work requirements, would blunt the program's effectiveness as a countercyclical stimulus.

SNAP's stabilization impact could be even greater if the benefits schedule is increased during recessions. This was demonstrated in the aftermath of the Great Recession, when for five years Congress temporarily increased maximum benefits and also awarded states additional administrative funds to serve an increased caseload (Keith-Jennings and Rosenbaum 2015). For example, maximum benefits to a family of four were increased by 13.6 percent, from $588 to $668. Blinder and Zandi (2015) estimate that every dollar of increased SNAP benefits spurred $1.74 in economic activity in the first quarter of 2009, and $1.22 in the first quarter of 2015—the highest multiplier of any of the policies adopted during the Great Recession.

Potential Major Reforms

As described in the previous sections, SNAP is a well-designed program that props up family food spending and stabilizes the economy when negative shocks occur. The program works with the market, providing resources that allow participants to obtain food from our highly efficient retail food system through normal channels. Proposals for major reforms to SNAP almost all make the program worse—in terms of being less effective or efficient—and not better. Some commonly proposed major reforms are considered below.

Block granting the program

There is some discussion of block granting the program, which would provide a set amount of funding to states and give them more flexibility on how to administer the program. Some lessons can be drawn from the 1996 block grant of Temporary Assistance to Needy Families (TANF), the cash welfare program. After the block grant, there were dramatic decreases in participation (which has been explained by a combination of macroeconomic strength and policy reforms). States shifted their TANF spending away from core supports (basic assistance, work activities and supports, and childcare) and toward a wider range of programs, some of which serve families that are not low income. The program's ability to respond to changes in need—due to economic downturns or to shifts in low-income populations across states—was blunted (Bitler and Hoynes 2016).

Block granting SNAP would harm its ability to serve its core purposes. As discussed above, a crucial role of SNAP is to serve as an automatic fiscal stabilizer in times of economic downturn. Its current structure allows the program to expand quickly, providing benefits to families that become eligible for the program due to job loss or other economic shocks. If the program were block granted and the funds were not promptly increased in proportion to economic downturns, some families made eligible during downturns may not be able to receive benefits. This would fundamentally undermine its stabilizing impact on the macroeconomy. Even though Congress could allocate additional resources in times of economic need, this would necessarily come with delays, reducing the ability to quickly stimulate the economy. More complicated block grant structures are possible, such as tying the block grant to population shifts and to inflation, or automatically increasing the grant during economic downturns. Such a structure would mitigate some of the drawbacks of a TANF-style block grant.

The Trump administration has proposed that SNAP be converted to a matching grant, where states must pay for a portion of benefits. This would also be expected to dampen its countercyclicality, depending on how the match is set, since states that are worse hit by the recession would struggle to meet their share of benefits at the same time that need is highest in those states. Many states have balanced budget requirements, which would exacerbate their inability to provide adequate matching funds during economic downturns.

Switching to a WIC- or commodities-based model

In their desire to improve the nutritional intake of participants, some advocate for replacing the current SNAP with a program that is more closely aligned with WIC, restricting benefits use for a specific bundle of goods. There are many ways to design this. For example, one could retain the basic SNAP system, in which participants receive benefits in the form of a dollar-value electronic voucher payment that can be redeemed at regular retail outlets at the regular prices charged. In this case, the list of permissible goods to purchase would be (dramatically) narrowed. Another option would be to adopt a model like the current WIC program, in which participants are given vouchers for quantities of particular goods (e.g., four gallons of milk per month). In this case, participants still use regular grocery stores, but no longer face prices. A third option would be for the government to directly provide goods to consumers.[11] Each of these approaches would require difficult policy choices about which items should be included that would be sufficient to serve the wide range of people who participate in SNAP. It is worth noting that WIC participation rates drop dramatically after age one, when the infant formula benefit discontinues, and range from 33 to 15 percent (Schanzenbach and Thorn 2019).

A key reason for SNAP's success is that it relies on the private sector to provide efficient access to food, through grocery stores and other retail outlets. Each of these proposals would dramatically reduce the efficiency of the program by raising administrative costs. To the extent that they move the procurement of goods away from a market-based system where consumers face prices, there will be new administrative inefficiencies and moral hazards as well. Such proposals would also diminish or eliminate the program's ability to act as a local economic stimulus. Students of economics will recognize that these reforms would also be expected to decrease participants' utility.

Replacing SNAP with a cash transfer

Others question the need for restricting SNAP benefits to purchasing food, arguing that these resources should be available to purchase other necessary goods such as housing and medical care. Some argue that it would be preferable to pay out benefits in cash, which can be spent on any good that the consumer wants to purchase. As described above, economists generally argue that if in-kind benefits like SNAP are paid at relatively modest levels, and most participants would like to spend at least as much on food as their SNAP benefits are worth, then the potential consumption distortion caused by providing benefits in-kind is modest.[12] Since the vast majority of participants spend more on food than their SNAP benefits are worth, replacing the program with an equivalent cash transfer would have only a small impact, with a small share of households getting more fungibility. As suggested by Table 1, many of these households are extremely disadvantaged, with little or no cash income. Barriers to work and mental health problems are also high among this population (Anderson et al. 2016). While it is clear that the very poor are not adequately served by the current structure of the safety net, in my opinion this likely would not be improved by replacing SNAP with cash. Having resources earmarked for food among this population likely has benefits that outweigh the efficiency loss in constraining their choices.

Conclusion

As currently structured, SNAP is an effective and efficient program. Its strength lies in its structure, which is based on a classic means-tested income transfer program as outlined by Milton Friedman (1962) in his negative income tax proposal and is now part of the economics canon. The program makes use of the highly efficient private market for distributing and obtaining food. It provides additional resources for food, while respecting consumer sovereignty in making decisions subject to their incomes, prices, and their own tastes and preferences. Its structure and efficiency allow the program to quickly respond to increased need during economic downturns, stimulating and stabilizing the economy. The inefficiencies caused by its being an in-kind transfer that can only be used to purchase food are modest and, in fact, likely serve to protect the most vulnerable.

This basic structure has enabled it to serve a wide range of participants, from the elderly to infants, workers and those not employed, across the entire nation. It has been able to adapt to broad macroeconomic trends, including our aging demography, increasing labor force participation among women, and stagnating wages for workers with lower education levels. To be sure, there are ways to modestly improve the program as described above. For example, policies to reduce food insecurity among families with children, especially during the summer months, are worth pursuing. There are also market-based approaches to improving dietary quality, for example by subsidizing healthy foods, that show promise. Straightforward changes to the benefits formula during economic downturns would also strengthen the program's ability to stabilize the economy during recessions. However, any potential reforms need to be carefully weighed so that they do not inadvertently reduce the many strengths of the program. The major reforms considered here generally move the program away from a market-based program that can quickly respond to changes in need and are not advisable. SNAP has been effective for the past half century, and with its current structure it should also be well-suited to meet the challenges of the next half century.

Notes

1. All SNAP households are eligible for the standard deduction, 69 percent claim the shelter deduction, and 31 percent claim the earnings deduction. Childcare, child support, and medical expense deductions are claimed by 4, 2, and 6 percent, respectively (CBPP, A Quick Guide to SNAP Eligibility and Benefits; see https://www.cbpp.org/research/food-assistance/a-quick-guide-to-snap-eligibility-and-benefits.).

2. The horizontal axis represents the number of the following policies adopted by the state: the use of BBCE, all SNAP benefits in state paid via EBT, online application available throughout the state, at least one outreach policy, simplified reporting, no households with earnings have a recertification period of three months or fewer, no asset test, and no fingerprint requirement. The modal state has adopted seven of these policies, one state (WY) has adopted four policies, and sixteen states (CA, CO, CT, DE, FL, IL, MN, MT, NC, NV, OH, OR, RI, SC, VT, WA) have adopted all eight.

3. These arguments apply to modest increases in maximum benefits. If benefits were to be raised dramatically (e.g., if they were to be doubled), many fewer families would be inframarginal, as described in Figure 2, and the impacts on spending and consumption would be hard to predict. Another way to increase benefits broadly without altering the maximum benefit would be to increase allowable deductions in the SNAP benefit formula, though this approach would not impact those currently receiving maximum SNAP benefits.

4. Note that benefits are not paid to all recipients on the same day, and instead are staggered across different days of the months in most states.

5. Nowhere is this more apparent than in the grocery store. Most consumers will acknowledge that there are items for sale at the grocery store that they have never consumed and will never opt to consume. But the reason they are stocked at the grocery store is, of course, that someone else demands those items. Our very efficient food supply system optimizes what products to sell based on consumer demand and their available shelf space.

6. The WIC-based summer EBT model had a larger impact on nutrition outcomes than the SNAP-based model.

7. In general, all adult SNAP participants must meet the following work requirements: registering for work, not voluntarily quitting a job or reducing hours, taking a job if offered, and participating in employment and training programs if assigned by the state.

8. A related issue is that under current policy, SNAP work requirements for ABAWDs may be temporarily waived during bad economic times either statewide or in certain areas. Some argue that these waivers are too generous and should be limited to times with higher unemployment rates. See Hoynes and Schanzenbach (2019) for further discussion of this issue.

9. Because SNAP recipients are eligible for free school meals, an estimated 265,000 children would also lose access to free meals.

10. The limit is higher for households with an elderly or disabled member.

11. The modern Food Stamp Program replaced such a system, called the Commodity Distribution Program (CDP). The switch from CDP to food stamps improved a number of outcomes, including birth outcomes and later-life outcomes for children who were given access to food stamps (Almond, Hoynes, and Schanzenbach 2011; Hoynes, Schanzenbach, and Almond 2016).

12. Behavioral economists argue that the distortion caused by in-kind transfers is larger than the neoclassical model predicts; see Hastings and Shapiro (2018).

References

Almond, Douglas, Hilary W. Hoynes, and Diane Whitmore Schanzenbach. 2011. Inside the war on poverty: The impact of food stamps on birth outcomes. *Review of Economics and Statistics* 93 (2): 387–403.

Anderson, Patricia M., and Kristin F. Butcher. 2016. *The relationships among SNAP benefits, grocery spending, diet quality, and the adequacy of low-income families' resources*. Policy Futures. Washington, DC: Center on Budget and Policy Priorities.

Anderson, Patricia M., Kristin F. Butcher, Hilary Hoynes, and Diane Whitmore Schanzenbach. 2016. Beyond income: What else predicts very low food security among children? *Southern Economic Journal* 82 (4): 1078–1105.

Anderson, Patricia M., Kristin F. Butcher, and Diane Whitmore Schanzenbach. 2015. Changes in safety net use during the Great Recession. *American Economic Review* 105 (5): 161–65.

Bailey, Martha, Hilary Hoynes, Maya Rossin-Slater, and Reed Walker. 2019. Is the social safety net a long-term investment? Large-scale evidence from the food stamps program. Goldman School of Public Policy Working Paper, Berkeley, CA.

Basu, Sanjay, Seth A. Berkowitz, and Hilary Seligman. 2017. The monthly cycle of hypoglycemia: An observational claims-based study of emergency room visits, hospital admissions, and costs in a commercially-insured population. *Medical Care* 55 (7): 639–45.

Bauer, Lauren, Diane Whitmore Schanzenbach, and Jay Shambaugh. 2018. *Work requirements and safety net programs*. Washington, DC: The Hamilton Project.

Beatty, Timothy K. M., and Charlotte Tuttle. 2014. Expenditure response to increases in in-kind transfers: Evidence from the Supplemental Nutrition Assistance Program. *American Journal of Agricultural Economics* 97 (2): 390–404.

Bitler, Marianne P. 2016. The health and nutrition effects of SNAP: Selection into the program and a review of the literature on its effects. In *SNAP matters: How food stamps affect health and well-being*, eds. J. Bartfeld, C. Gundersen, T. Smeeding, and J. Ziliak, 134– 60. Redwood City, CA: Stanford University Press.

Bitler, Marianne P., and Hilary W. Hoynes. 2010. The state of the safety net in the post-welfare reform era. *Brookings Papers on Economic Activity* 2:71–127.

Bitler, Marianne, and Hilary W. Hoynes. 2013. Immigrants, welfare and the U.S. safety net. In *Immigration, poverty, and socioeconomic inequality*, eds. David Card and Steven Raphael, 316–80. New York, NY: Russell Sage Foundation.

Bitler, Marianne, and Hilary Hoynes. 2016. *Strengthening Temporary Assistance to Needy Families*. Washington, DC: The Hamilton Project Policy Proposal.

Bitler, Marianne, Hilary Hoynes, and Elira Kuka. 2017. Do in-work tax credits serve as a safety net? *Journal of Human Resources* 52 (2): 319–50.

Blinder, Alan S., and Mark Zandi. 2015. *The financial crisis: Lessons for the next one*. Policy Futures. Washington, DC: Center on Budget and Policy Priorities.

Blundell, Richard, and Luigi Pistaferri. 2003. Income volatility and household consumption: The impact of food assistance programs. *Journal of Human Resources* 38:1032–50.

Borjas, George J. 2004. Food insecurity and public assistance. *Journal of Public Economics* 88 (7): 1421–43.

Butcher, Kristin F., and Diane Whitmore Schanzenbach. 2018. *Most workers in low-wage labor market work substantial hours, in volatile jobs*. Policy Futures. Washington, DC: Center on Budget and Policy Priorities.

Collins, Ann M., Ronette Briefel, Jacob Alex Klerman, Anne Wolf, Gretchen Rowe, Chris Logan, Ayesha Enver, Sydea Fatima, Anne Gordon, and Julia Lyskawa. 2016. *Summer Electronic Benefit Transfer for Children (SEBTC) demonstration: Summary report*. Cambridge, MA: Abt Associates. Available from https://fns-prod.azureedge.net/sites/default/files/ops/sebtcfinalreport.pdf.

Condon, Elizabeth, Susan Drilea, Carolyn Lichtenstein, James Mabli, and Katherine Niland. 2015. *Diet quality of Americans by SNAP participation status: Data from the National Health and Nutrition Examination Survey, 2007–2010*. Washington, DC: USDA.

Congressional Budget Office. 2018. Agriculture and Nutrition Act of 2018, H.R. 2.

Currie, Janet, and Jeffrey Grogger. 2001. Explaining recent declines in food stamp program participation [with comments]. *Brookings-Wharton Papers on Urban Affairs* 2001:203–44.

Currie, Janet, and Enrico Moretti. 2008. Did the introduction of food stamps affect birth outcomes in California? In *Making Americans Healthier: Social and Economic Policy as Health Policy*, eds. R. Schoeni, J. House, G. Kaplan, and H. Pollack. New York, NY: Russell Sage Foundation.

DePolt, Richard A., Robert A. Moffitt, and David C. Ribar. 2009. Food stamps, Temporary Assistance for Needy Families and food hardships in three American cities. *Pacific Economic Review* 14 (4): 445–73.

East, Chloe N. 2018a. The effect of food stamps on children's health: Evidence from immigrants' changing eligibility. *Journal of Human Resources*. doi:10.3368/jhr.55.3.0916-8197R2.

East, Chloe N. 2018b. Immigrants' labor supply response to food stamp access. *Labour Economics* 51:202–26.

Fan, Maoyong. 2010. Do food stamps contribute to obesity in low-income women? Evidence from the National Longitudinal Survey of Youth 1979. *American Journal of Agricultural Economics* 92 (4): 1165–80.

Figlio, David N., Craig Gundersen, and James P. Ziliak. 2000. The effects of the macroeconomy and welfare reform on food stamp caseloads. *American Journal of Agricultural Economics* 82 (3): 635–41.

Finkelstein, Amy, and Matthew J. Notowidigdo. 2018. Take-up and targeting: Experimental Evidence from SNAP. NBER Working Paper 24652, National Bureau of Economics Research, Cambridge, MA.

Food Research and Action Center. 2012. *Replacing the Thrifty Food Plan in order to provide adequate allotments for SNAP beneficiaries*. Washington, DC: Food Research and Action Center.

Friedman, Milton. 1962. *Capitalism and freedom*. Chicago, IL: University of Chicago Press.

Ganong, Peter, and Jeffrey B. Liebman. 2018. The decline, rebound, and further rise in SNAP enrollment: Disentangling business cycle fluctuation and policy changes. *American Economic Journal: Economic Policy* 10 (4): 153–76.

Gassman-Pines, Anna, and Laura Bellows. 2018. Food instability and academic achievement: A quasi-experiment using SNAP benefit timing. *American Educational Research Journal* 55 (5): 897–927.

Gibson-Davis, C. M., and E. M. Foster. 2006. A cautionary tale: Using propensity scores to estimate the effect of food stamps on food insecurity. *Social Service Review* 80 (1): 93–126.

Gregory, Christian, Matthew P. Rabbitt, and David C. Ribar. 2015. The Supplemental Nutrition Assistance Program and food insecurity. In *SNAP matters: How food stamps affect health and well being*, eds. J. Bartfeld, C. Gundersen, T. Smeeding, and J. Ziliak, 74–106. Redwood City, CA: Stanford University Press.

Gundersen, Craig, and James P. Ziliak. 2003. The role of food stamps in consumption stabilization. *Journal of Human Resources* 2003:1051–79.

Haider, Steven J., Robert F. Schoeni, Yuhua Bao, and Caroline Danielson. 2004. Immigrants, welfare reform, and the economy. *Journal of Policy Analysis and Management* 23 (4): 745–64.

Hanson, Kenneth. 2010. *The Food Assistance National Input-Output Multiplier (FANIOM) model and stimulus effects of SNAP*. ERR-103, Economic Research Service. Washington, DC: U.S. Department of Agriculture.

Hastings, Justine, and Jesse M. Shapiro. 2018. How are SNAP benefits spent? Evidence from a retail panel. *American Economic Review* 108 (12): 3493–3540.

Hoynes, Hilary W., Leslie McGranahan, and Diane W. Schanzenbach. 2016. SNAP and food consumption. In *SNAP matters: How food stamps affect health and well-being*, eds. J. Bartfeld, C. Gundersen, T. Smeeding, and J. Ziliak, 107–33. Redwood City, CA: Stanford University Press.

Hoynes, Hilary W., and Diane Whitmore Schanzenbach. 2009. Consumption responses to in-kind transfers: Evidence from the introduction of the Food Stamp program. *American Economic Journal: Applied Economics* 1 (4): 109–39.

Hoynes, Hilary W., and Diane Whitmore Schanzenbach. 2012. Work incentives and the Food Stamp program. *Journal of Public Economics* 96 (1): 151–62.

Hoynes, Hilary, and Diane Whitmore Schanzenbach. 2016. U.S. food and nutrition programs. In *Economics of means-tested transfer programs in the United States*, vol. 1, ed. Robert A. Moffitt, 219–301. Chicago, IL: University of Chicago Press.

Hoynes, Hilary, Diane Whitmore Schanzenbach, and Douglas Almond. 2016. Long-run impacts of childhood access to the safety net. *American Economic Review* 106 (4): 903–34.

Institute of Medicine and National Research Council. 2013. *Supplemental Nutrition Assistance Program: Examining the evidence to define benefit adequacy*. Washington, DC: The National Academies Press.

Kaestner, Robert, and Neeraj Kaushal. 2005. Immigrant and native responses to welfare reform. *Journal of Population Economics* 18 (1): 69–92.

Kaushal, Neeraj. 2007. Do food stamps cause obesity? Evidence from immigrant experience. *Journal of Health Economics* 26 (5): 968–91.

Keith-Jennings, Brynne, and Dottie Rosenbaum. 2015. *SNAP benefit boost in 2009 recovery act provided economic stimulus and reduced hardship*. Washington, DC: Center on Budget and Policy Priorities.

Kreider, Brent, John V. Pepper, Craig Gundersen, and Dean Jolliffe. 2012. Identifying the effects of SNAP (Food Stamps) on child health outcomes when participation is endogenous and misreported. *Journal of the American Statistical Association* 107 (499): 958–75.

McGranahan, Leslie, and Diane W. Schanzenbach. 2011. Who would be affected by soda taxes? Chicago Fed Letter Number 284. Chicago, IL: The Federal Reserve Bank of Chicago.

Meyerhoefer, Chad D., and Yuriy Pylypchuk. 2008. Does participation in the Food Stamp program increase the prevalence of obesity and health care spending? *American Journal of Agricultural Economics* 90 (2): 287–305.

Mills, Gregory, Tracy Vericker, Heather Koball, Kye Lippold, Laura Wheaton, and Sam Elkin. 2014. *Understanding the rates, causes, and costs of churning in the Supplemental Nutrition Assistance Program (SNAP)—Final report*. Washington, DC: Urban Institute for the U.S. Department of Agriculture.

Mykerezi, Elton, and Bradford Mills. 2010. The impact of food stamp program participation on household food insecurity. *American Journal of Agricultural Economics* 92 (5): 1379–91.

Olsho, Lauren W. E., Jacob A. Klerman, Parke E. Wilde, and Susan H. Bartlett. 2016. Financial incentives increase fruit and vegetable intake among Supplemental Nutrition Assistance Program participants: A randomized controlled trial of the USDA Healthy Incentives Pilot. *American Journal of Clinical Nutrition* 104 (2): 423–35.

Ratcliffe, Caroline, Signe-Mary McKernan, Laura Wheaton, Emma Kalish, Catherine Ruggles, Sara Armstrong, and Christina Oberlin. 2016. *Asset limits, SNAP participation, and financial stability*. Washington, DC: Urban Institute.

Ratcliffe, Caroline, Signe-Mary McKernan, and Sisi Zhang. 2011. How much does the Supplemental Nutrition Assistance Program reduce food insecurity? *American Journal of Agricultural Economics* 93 (4): 1082–98.

Ribar, David C., and Marilyn Edelhoch. 2008. Earnings volatility and the reasons for leaving the food stamp program. In *Income volatility and food assistance in the United States*, eds. Dean Jolliffe and James P. Ziliak, 63–102. Kalamazoo, MI: WE Upjohn Institute for Employment Research.

Russek, Frank, and Kim Kowalewski. 2015. How CBO estimate automatic stabilizers. Working Paper 2015-07, Congressional Budget Office, Washington, DC.

Schanzenbach, Diane Whitmore. 2007. What are food stamps worth? Working Paper, University of Chicago, Chicago, IL.

Schanzenbach, Diane Whitmore. 2013. Strengthening SNAP for a more food-secure, healthy America. *Discussion Paper* 2013-06. Washington, DC: The Hamilton Project.

Schanzenbach, Diane Whitmore. 2017. *The future of SNAP: Continuing to balance protection and incentives*. America Boondoggle Series. Washington, DC: American Enterprise Institute.

Schanzenbach, Diane Whitmore, and Betsy Thorn. 2019. Food support programs and their impacts on very young children. Health Policy Brief, March 28. *Health Affairs*.

Schmeiser, M. D. 2012. The impact of long-term participation in the Supplemental Nutrition Assistance Program on child obesity. *Health Economics* 21 (4): 386–404.

Schmidt, Lucie, Lara Shore-Sheppard, and Tara Watson. 2016. The effect of safety net programs on food insecurity. *Journal of Human Resources* 51 (3): 589–614.

Shaefer, H. Luke, and Italo A. Gutierrez. 2013. The Supplemental Nutrition Assistance Program and material hardships among low-income households with children. *Social Service Review* 87 (4): 753–79.

Todd, Jessica E. 2015. Revisiting the Supplemental Nutrition Assistance Program cycle of food intake: Investigating heterogeneity, diet quality, and a large boost in benefit amounts. *Applied Economic Perspectives and Policy* 27 (3): 437–58.

U.S. Department of Agriculture. 2019a. *Reaching those in need: Estimates of State Supplemental Nutrition Assistance Program participation rates in FY 2016.* Washington, DC: U.S. Department of Agriculture.

U.S. Department of Agriculture. 2019b. Summer Food Service Program. Food and Nutrition Services. Washington, DC: United States Department of Agriculture. Available from https://fns-prod.azureedge .net/sites/default/files/resource-files/sfsummar-4.pdf.

U.S. Department of Health and Human Services. 2015. *Dietary guidelines for Americans 2015– 2020.* Washington, DC: United States Department of Agriculture.

Whiteman, Eliza D., Benjamin W. Chrisinger, and Amy Hillier. 2018. Diet quality over the monthly Supplemental Nutrition Assistance Program cycle. *American Journal of Preventative Medicine* 55 (2): 205–12.

Wilde, Parke, and Mark Nord. 2005. The effect of food stamps on food security: a panel data approach. *Applied Economic Perspectives and Policy* 27 (3): 425–32.

Yen, Steven T., Margaret Andrews, Zhuo Chen, and David B. Eastwood. 2008. Food Stamp Program participation and food insecurity: An instrumental variables approach. *American Journal of Agricultural Economics* 90 (1): 117–32.

Zaki, Mary. 2016. Access to short-term credit and consumption smoothing within the paycycle. FEEM Working Paper No. 007.2016, FEEM, Milan.

Zaki, Mary, and Jessica E. Todd. 2019. Does it pay to pay less frequently? White Paper, University of Maryland, College Park, MD.

Ziliak, James P. 2015. Why are so many Americans on food stamps? The role of the economy, policy, and demographics. In *SNAP matters: How food stamps affect health and well being,* eds. J. Bartfeld, C. Gundersen, T. Smeeding, and J. Ziliak, 18–48. Stanford, CA: Stanford University Press.

Ziliak, James P. 2016. *Modernizing SNAP benefits.* Policy Proposal 2016-06. Washington, DC: The Hamilton Project.

Ziliak, James P., Craig Gundersen, and David N. Figlio. 2003. Food stamp caseloads over the business cycle. *Southern Economic Journal* 69 (4): 903–19.

When One Size Does Not Fit All: Modernizing the Supplemental Security Income Program

By
MARY C. DALY
and
MARK DUGGAN

The federal Supplemental Security Income (SSI) program is an important part of the safety net in the United States, paying means-tested benefits to children with disabilities, nonelderly adults with disabilities, and elderly individuals. In this article, we describe the eligibility criteria for the program, how these have changed over time, and the impact of these changes on SSI enrollment. We also show that over time, SSI has grown to serve a heterogenous population, with an array of life experiences and needs. In this context, we discuss potential reforms intended to modernize the program and increase its ability to achieve its goals. These include a proposal to raise the generosity of benefits for elderly SSI recipients, increase the incentive to work among nonelderly adult SSI recipients, and harmonize disability decision-making across medical examiners and administrative law judges.

Keywords: social policy; welfare; labor market; disability; reform; implementation; Security Disability Insurance

Supplemental Security Income (SSI) is a national means-tested transfer program for aged, blind, and disabled individuals with low incomes and assets. The federal SSI program was enacted in 1972 and began paying cash benefits in 1974, replacing a patchwork of state-run entitlement programs that were created under the Social Security Act of 1935 and its subsequent amendments in 1950. The establishment

Mary C. Daly is the president and chief executive officer of the Federal Reserve Bank of San Francisco. Her research focuses on labor market dynamics and the aggregate and distributional impacts of monetary and fiscal policy.

Mark Duggan is the Trione Director of the Stanford Institute for Economic Policy Research and The Wayne and Jodi Cooperman Professor of Economics at Stanford. His research focuses on the health care sector and the effects of government expenditure programs such as Medicare, Medicaid, and Social Security.

Correspondence: mary.daly@sf.frb.org

DOI: 10.1177/0002716219884072

of SSI was the culmination of a four-year debate over a more ambitious welfare reform proposal—the Family Assistance Plan (FAP)—that was intended to extend the federal social safety net to all low-income Americans. While Congress eventually rejected the universality of FAP, it passed SSI, a categorical welfare program based on the same negative income tax principles as FAP but targeted on a much smaller subset of low-income individuals who were not expected to work—the aged, blind, and disabled.[1]

SSI is funded by the federal government and administered by the federal Social Security Administration (SSA), following federally determined income, asset, and medical eligibility criteria (for those with disabilities). Benefits are set at the federal level and rise each year with inflation (using the Bureau of Labor Statistics Consumer Price Index). States are allowed to provide supplemental funding for SSI benefits, with all but four states supplementing the federal benefit for some or all of their SSI beneficiaries. In eleven states and the District of Columbia, the federal government administers state SSI supplements (SSA 2018c). In the other thirty-five states, SSI supplements are paid directly by state governments to SSI recipients.[2]

SSI began as a relatively small program providing benefits to a largely elderly population. For example, in 1974, more than 60 percent of the program's 4.0 million beneficiaries were aged 65 and up. Since that time, SSI has grown to be one of the largest federal means-tested cash assistance programs in the United States, with a caseload that is now dominated by children and working-age adults with disabilities.[3] In December 2017, 8.2 million people—the vast majority under age 65—received federal SSI benefits. Total SSI benefits paid in 2017 exceeded $54 billion, reflecting an average annualized benefit of about $7,000. Figure 1 shows trends in program enrollment and expenditures since SSI's inception in 1974. Total SSI expenditures are comparable to spending on the Earned Income Tax Credit (EITC) and Supplemental Nutrition Assistance Program (food stamp program) and substantially larger than the amount spent on the Temporary Assistance to Needy Families (TANF). An additional $127 billion was paid for SSI recipients' health insurance through the Medicaid program in 2014.[4]

Rapid program growth, the changing composition of SSI beneficiaries, and increasing pressure to better integrate traditional "nonworkers" into the labor market all have raised questions about the role that SSI plays in the broader U.S. social welfare system. While there have been various attempts to improve the economic outcomes of SSI recipients over time, for example, by encouraging current SSI recipients to return to work or by assisting child SSI recipients in transitioning off the program and into gainful employment in adulthood, SSI remains an absorbing state for most recipients. In other words, once individuals go on the SSI program and begin to draw benefits, relatively few will later exit the program to work.

NOTE: The views expressed here are the authors' and not necessarily those of others at the Federal Reserve Bank of San Francisco or in the Federal Reserve System. The article draws heavily from prior work including Burkhauser and Daly (2002, 2011); Daly and Burkhauser 2003; and Duggan, Kearney, and Rennane (2016). We thank our prior coauthors for many useful discussions on these issues, along with Robert Moffitt, James Ziliak, and many conference participants for their helpful feedback.

FIGURE 1
SSI Program Growth, 1974–2017

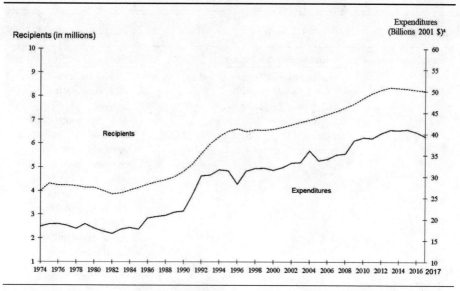

SOURCE: SSA (2018b, Tables 2 and 4).
NOTE: Annual expenditures estimated from monthly amount from December of each year.

In this article, we review the evolution of the SSI program, the determinants of caseload growth, and the evidence about its impacts on the targeted populations. We conclude with potential policy reforms. The article proceeds as follows. In the next section, we review the basic eligibility criteria for the program, and how some of those criteria have evolved over time. Then we describe trends in SSI caseloads and discuss their determinants. We go on to present a brief review of the economic issues associated with the program design and discuss the evidence regarding the impact of SSI on the targeted populations. Finally, we use what we have learned from the preceding sections to present reform ideas for SSI, and we end with conclusions.

SSI Eligibility Criteria

SSI is an income support program that provides benefits to three distinct low-income populations: the aged, the blind, and the disabled. As such, SSI eligibility is a function of three program-based categorical criteria—age, disability, or blindness—as well as more general requirements associated with income and asset limits and citizenship and residency rules. The SSA is responsible for screening applicants and making awards for SSI. Table 1 summarizes the SSI eligibility requirements that are described in detail in the remainder of this section.

TABLE 1
SSI Eligibility Requirements in 2019

Requirement	Definition	Exceptions/Exclusions
Limited income[a]	Countable income must be: ☐ below $750 a month for single adult or child ☐ below $1,125 a month for couple (In states that pay SSI supplements, countable income can be higher)	Not all income counts. Some exclusions are: ☐ $20 per month of most income ☐ $65 per month of earnings and one-half of earnings over $65 ☐ Supplemental Nutrition Assistance Program (SNAP) benefits, formerly known as food stamps ☐ home energy/housing assistance
Limited resources[a] (property and other assets a person owns)	☐ $2,000 for single adult or child ☐ $3,000 for couple (limit applies even if only one member is eligible)	Not all resources count. Some exclusions are: ☐ the home a person lives in ☐ a car, one per household ☐ burial plots for individual and immediate family ☐ burial funds up to $1,500; additional $1500 allowed for spouse ☐ life insurance with face value of 1,500 or less
Citizenship/residence[b]	☐ resides in one of the 50 states, Washington, D.C. or the Northern Mariana Islands; and ☐ U.S. citizen or national; or ☐ American Indians and Alaska Natives; or ☐ lawful permanent resident with 40 work credits; or ☐ certain noncitizens with a military service connection; or ☐ certain refugee or asylee-type noncitizens for up to seven years; or ☐ certain noncitizens in the U.S. or receiving SSI on August 22, 1996.	Exception to residence: certain children of U.S. armed forces personnel stationed abroad

(continued)

TABLE 1 (CONTINUED)

Requirement	Definition	Exceptions/Exclusions
Categorical: 65 or older, blind or disabled Blind Disabled	Meet only one of these: ☐ age 65 or older ☐ vision cannot be corrected to better than 20/200 or; ☐ visual field is less than 20 degrees ☐ physical or mental impairment that keeps a person from performing any "substantial" work and is expected to last 12 months or result in death ☐ a child's impairment must result in "marked and severe functional limitations" and must be expected to last 12 months or result in death	Person whose visual impairment is not severe enough to be considered blind may qualify under the non-blind disability rules: ☐ a job that pays $750 per month ($2,040 if blind) is generally considered substantial work ☐ special work incentives allow some income and resources to be excluded and permit payment of special cash benefits or continuation of Medicaid coverage even when a blind or disabled person is working

a.If only one member of a couple is eligible, the income and resources of both are considered in determining eligibility. If a child under age 18 is living with parents, the parents' income and resources are considered.

b.If a noncitizen has a sponsor who signed a legally unenforceable affidavit of support (INS Form I-134), the sponsor's income and resources are considered in determining eligibility and payment amount for three years following the date of lawful admission. (This rule does not apply to noncitizens who become blind or disabled after legal admission for permanent residence or to noncitizens who are not lawful permanent residents.) If the sponsor signed the new legally enforceable affidavit of support (INS Form I-864), the sponsor's income and resources are considered until the noncitizen acquires 40 work credits or becomes a citizen. (This rule applies to noncitizens who become blind or disabled after admission for permanent residence and to noncitizens who are not lawful permanent residents.)

Because SSI is a means-tested program, all applicants must meet basic income and asset tests. Applicants over the age of 65 who meet these tests automatically qualify for SSI benefits. Individuals also may receive SSI benefits for the blind if they have 20/200 (or worse) vision with the use of a correcting lens in their better eye, or if they have tunnel vision of 20 degrees or less (SSA 2018e). The criteria for nonelderly adults and children with disabilities are stricter and are subject to more judgment among evaluators. Below, we describe the process of disability determination for both nonelderly adults and children applying for SSI disability benefits.

Disability determination for nonelderly adults

Nonelderly adults apply for SSI benefits through one of the approximately twelve hundred SSA field offices in the United States.[5] SSA employees determine whether each applicant meets nonmedical requirements, including that he or she has sufficiently low income and assets. If monthly earnings exceed SSA's definition of substantial gainful activity (SGA), the applicant is deemed categorically ineligible.[6]

Applications that meet these financial criteria are then forwarded on to a state agency, where the disability determination process is typically carried out by a two-person team (Duggan, Kearney, and Rennane 2016). The first person is a state disability examiner, who assembles both medical and nonmedical evidence and requests a consultative exam when the medical evidence is not sufficient to make a disability determination. The examiner also prepares (or assists in preparation for more complicated cases) an assessment of the applicant's residual functional capacity. The second person on the team is a medical consultant who reviews the available medical evidence provided by the applicant and acquired through one or more additional consultative exams. The examiner prepares the paperwork for the final determination, which is subsequently signed by the medical consultant.

To qualify for SSI benefits, a nonelderly adult applicant must provide evidence of a medically determined physical or mental disability that limits her or his ability to engage in substantial gainful activity. Furthermore, the applicant must demonstrate that this condition will persist for at least 12 months or will result in death. If the condition passes a severity threshold and is on SSA's list of medical impairments, then the applicant has passed the disability determination. If the impairment is not on this list, then SSA considers whether the applicant can perform labor market tasks that she or he previously performed. If this is possible, then the applicant is found ineligible. If the applicant is unable to do past work, then the disability examiner considers whether there are other occupations in the economy that she or he could perform. In this case, the examining team considers not only the applicant's medical condition but also her or his age, education, and work experience.[7]

The medical eligibility criteria used by the SSI program do not vary across states and are the same as those used by the Social Security Disability Insurance (SSDI) program. Previous research has shown that there is variation across geographic areas in award rates, as one would expect if the applicant pools varied across states (Gruber and Kubik 1997). Furthermore, the disability determination is made by individual examiners and will inevitably involve some subjective judgments. Indeed, recent research (Maestas, Mullen, and Strand 2013) has shown that there is substantial variation across examiners in disability award rates even after controlling for the characteristics of applicants.

Applicants who are rejected on this "first round" may appeal the decision, which is considered by a second team of examiners. More than half of individuals rejected at the first round do file an appeal. Applicants denied on this second round then have the option to appeal to an administrative law judge (ALJ), and approximately 80 percent of those rejected at stage two do this. The assignment to ALJs is "essentially random" (Daub et al. 2006) and is determined based on the field office where the application was initially made (French and Song 2014). At this stage, the applicant is often joined by a lawyer or some other representative when appearing before the ALJ. One striking feature of these hearings is that only one side is represented—the SSA does not have representation to explain the reason for the initial decisions. Recent research has shown significant variation in award rates at this stage as well (French and Song 2014). Applicants denied at this second appeal can try again by appealing to the Social Security Appeals Council and then one more time to their district court.

During the past 10 years, accounting for decisions at all stages of the process including appeals, between 45 and 50 percent of nonelderly adult SSI applicants with a medical decision have been awarded benefits (SSA 2018a).[8] The average time from the initial application to the first decision is four months, while those appealing to the ALJ level or higher typically wait more than two years for the decision (Office of the Inspector General [OIG] 2008).

Disability determination for children

Screening children for SSI eligibility is in some respects even more complex than adult disability screening. Under the original legislation, Congress wrote that a child should be considered disabled if "he suffers from any medically determinable physical or mental impairment of comparable severity" to a disabling impairment in an adult (SSA 1997). In practice, children originally qualified for SSI if they had "a medically determinable physical or mental impairment which results in marked and severe functional limitations, and which can be expected to result in death, or which has lasted or can be expected to last for a continuous period of not less than 12 months." Between 1974 and 1989, the child disability determination process did not include a functional assessment or take into account the equivalent of adult vocational factors.

This changed in 1990 when the Supreme Court decided the case of *Sullivan v. Zebley* (493 U.S. 521 [1990]). The Court ruled that to meet the standard of equal treatment, a functional limitation component parallel to that of adults must be included in the initial disability determination process for children. In response, in 1990, SSA added two new bases for finding children eligible for benefits: (1) functional equivalence, which was set at the medical listing level of the disability determination process; and (2) an individual functional assessment (IFA), which was designed to be parallel with the functional and vocational assessment provided for adults. By allowing applicants who did not meet the medical listing to be found disabled if their impairments were severe enough to limit their ability to engage in age-appropriate activities, such as attending school, the IFA relaxed the eligibility criteria for children to be eligible for SSI benefits (U.S. General Accounting Office [GAO] 1994, 1995).

During the several years after this 1990 Supreme Court decision, SSA's use of the IFA, along with the new criteria that emphasized functioning when determining mental disabilities, led to a large expansion in the number of children determined to be categorically eligible for SSI. Many of these children had less severe disabilities than did those children awarded SSI benefits in the 1970s and 1980s. In the years prior to the Supreme Court decision, the number of children receiving SSI benefits was growing by about 3 percent per year and stood at 264,000 in

1989. In the seven years following the decision, the number of children on SSI rose to 955,000, an increase of 260 percent from 1989 to 1996. During this same period, the share of children receiving SSI benefits more than tripled from 0.4 percent to 1.4 percent (Duggan and Kearney 2007).

Perhaps partly because of this rapid growth in SSI enrollment, Congress changed the SSI eligibility rules for children as part of its well-known 1996 welfare reform legislation. The new regulations no longer used an individual functional assessment but retained the spirit of the functional limitation notion. To be found categorically eligible, a child had to demonstrate "a medically determinable physical or mental impairment or combination of impairments that causes marked and severe functional limitations, and that can be expected to cause death or that has lasted or can be expected to last for a continuous period of not less than 12 months" (SSA 2008). As a result of this change, nearly 100,000 children were terminated from the program in 1997, and the share of children receiving SSI remained steady at 1.2 percent from late 1997 through 2000. The new regulations also required children who reached the age of 18 to be evaluated again to determine whether they would continue to receive SSI benefits as adults.

The current determination process for children to receive SSI benefits is significantly less restrictive than it was before the *Sullivan v. Zebley* Supreme Court decision (493 U.S. 521 [1990]) but somewhat more restrictive than it was during the early 1990s (Berkowitz and DeWitt 2013; Wittenburg 2011; Wiseman 2010). SSI enrollment among children has risen substantially among children since 2000, with 1.6 percent of children receiving SSI benefits in 2017.[9]

The changes in child disability determination since the early 1990s has meant that a child's disability status is frequently determined by a subjective determination about performance in school, relative to age-appropriate peers. This has led to concerns that the program eligibility criteria may lead to an increase in diagnosing children with learning or behavioral disabilities, potentially leading to inappropriate medical treatment (Wen 2010; Wittenberg 2011). Recent research, while far from definitive, is consistent with this hypothesis. Leckman-Westin et al. (2018) found that children receiving SSI benefits due to a mental disorder were twice as likely as other children to be treated with higher-than-recommended dosage amounts of antipsychotic medications.[10]

SSI Program Caseloads

To make meaningful suggestions for improving SSI it is important to understand the characteristics of program beneficiaries. In this section, we describe the evolution of SSI caseloads, paying particular attention to participation among the three targeted populations. We also consider variation in program usage across states and for nonelderly adults and children with disabilities—the diagnoses that ultimately qualified them for the program.

As noted previously, SSI enrollment has grown substantially since the program's inception. Figure 2 shows that the composition of the program has also changed. The number of elderly recipients has remained relatively constant at

FIGURE 2
SSI Caseload Trends, 1974–2017

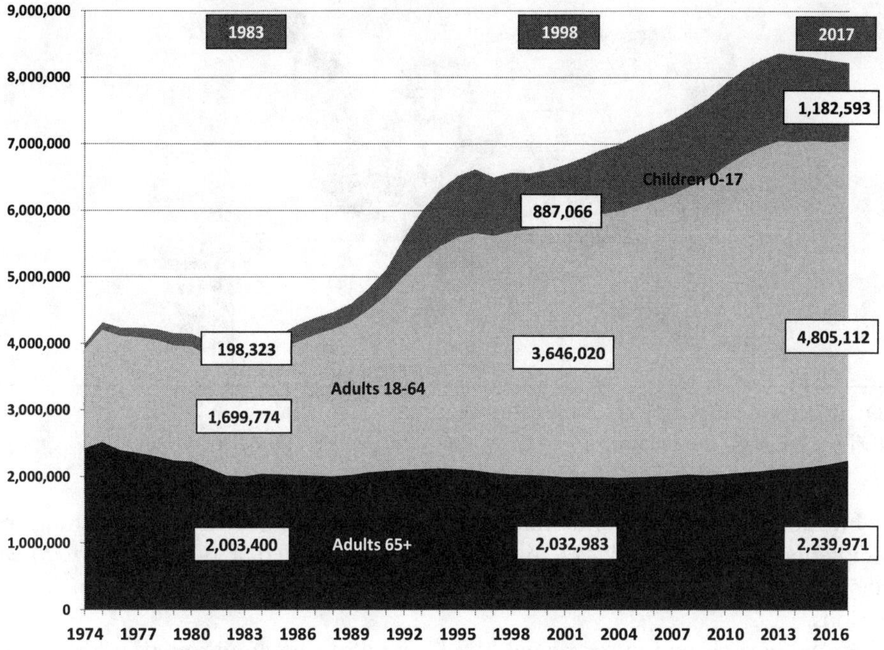

SOURCE: SSA (2018c, Table 7.A9).
NOTE: Includes blind persons and disabled persons aged 65 or older.

approximately 2.1 million during the entire life of the program. In contrast, the number of children and nonelderly adults has more than tripled, from 1.9 million in 1983 to 6.0 million by 2017.[11] As a result, elderly (aged 65 and up) beneficiaries currently account for less than 30 percent of all SSI recipients, compared to 60 percent in 1974.

As a result of these trends, the fraction of elderly individuals receiving SSI benefits has steadily fallen over time, from 7.0 percent in the early 1980s to just 4.4 percent in 2017. In contrast, the fraction of nonelderly adults receiving SSI has risen substantially (from 1.5 to 2.4 percent over the same period) and by even more among children (from 0.4 to 1.6 percent).

For the elderly, the decline in SSI enrollment relates to increased coverage under the Social Security (Old Age, Survivors, and Disability Insurance, or OASDI) program. Part of SSI's original goal was to supplement OASDI benefits for low-income individuals and households or to provide a minimum benefit for those individuals and households not eligible for Social Security benefits. As enrollment in OASDI has risen, the need for the SSI elderly program has declined. OASDI benefits are indexed to average wage growth in the economy. As OASDI benefit amounts have increased, the gap between the SSI supplement amount and OASDI has closed thereby reducing the need for the SSI supplement.

FIGURE 3
Nonelderly Adult SSI Population as Percentage of State Adult Population, 2017

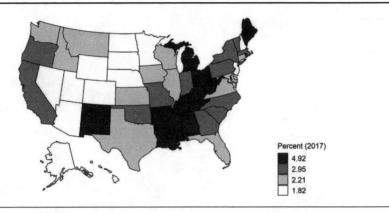

Percent (2017)
4.92
2.95
2.21
1.82

SOURCE: SSA (2018d); U.S. Census Bureau (2018).
NOTE: Colors on the map represent quartiles of the participation distribution.

For nonelderly adults and children with disabilities, growth in the number of recipients reflects material changes, as we discussed, that relaxed the medical eligibility criteria and made it easier to qualify for SSI benefits relative to earlier periods.

As the next three figures reveal, the fraction of people enrolled in SSI varies substantially across states, ranging from a low of 1 percent in North Dakota to a high of more than 5 percent in West Virginia.[12] Some of this is accounted for by differences across states in income levels and in health, for which we do not attempt to adjust in the figures that follow.

Figures 3 through 5 group states into quartiles of the targeted group's SSI participation rate distribution. Figure 3 shows that among the nonelderly adult SSI population, states with the highest rates of SSI enrollment tend to be in the South, while many of those with relatively low enrollment are in the West. Participation in the child SSI program also exhibits substantial geographic variation, as displayed in Figure 4. While most of the states with high adult SSI participation also have high child participation, there are some differences. For example, while Texas is in the top quartile of child SSI participation, it is below the median for nonelderly adult SSI participation. The elderly caseload—mapped in Figure 5—has a similar range and geographic pattern with the exception of two outliers: California and New York. In these two states, the elderly SSI caseload was approximately 13 and 9 percent of the total elderly population, respectively, which are the two highest state-specific enrollment rates. This likely reflects the more generous supplementation of SSI benefits in these states so that Social Security benefits are less likely to fully phase out the SSI benefits.

Another important aspect of the SSI program for the nonelderly adult and child populations is the composition of qualifying diagnoses. As shown in Figure 6, this varies considerably across the age distribution. The figure plots

FIGURE 4
Child SSI Population as Percentage of State Child Population, 2017

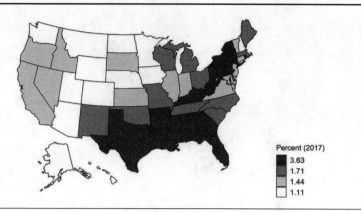

Percent (2017)
3.63
1.71
1.44
1.11

SOURCE: SSA (2018d); U.S. Census Bureau (2018).
NOTE: Colors on the map represent quartiles of the participation distribution.

the percentage of recipients who qualify for the program based on a physical impairment. The data reveal a u-shaped pattern in qualifying diagnoses. A majority of the youngest and oldest beneficiaries become eligible primarily on the basis of a physical disability—nearly 70 percent of children under age 5 and 65 percent of adults age 60 to 64. In contrast, less than 30 percent of recipients between the ages of 5 and 39 had a physical disability as their primary diagnosis. Mental and intellectual disabilities accounted for 57 percent of the total nonelderly adult SSI caseload in 2017. Most of these diagnoses are for conditions other than intellectual disabilities. These include mood disorders along with schizophrenic and other psychotic disorders.

The trends in SSI caseloads, variation in participation across states, and heterogeneity of diagnosis by age underscore the complexity of the SSI program. Below, we discuss how this complexity produces economic incentives at odds with stated program goals because the program is still administered with a one-size-fits-all approach that was created 45 years ago.

Economic Issues and Research Evidence

SSI differs in several important ways from other means-tested transfer programs in the United States. First and perhaps most importantly, nonelderly individuals must have a demonstrated disability that impedes labor market activity and/or educational performance to qualify. Second, SSI benefits are generous relative to other programs, such as TANF and food stamps. Third, the vast majority of SSI benefits are paid for with federal dollars. Because of this, relatively poor states are significantly subsidized by states with higher incomes. And finally, SSI payments are not intended to be temporary, which implies that any

FIGURE 5
Elderly SSI Population as Percentage of Elderly Adult Population, 2017

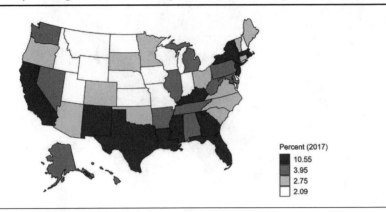

Percent (2017)
■ 10.55
■ 3.95
■ 2.75
□ 2.09

SOURCE: SSA (2018d); U.S. Census Bureau (2018). See https://www.census.gov/programs-surveys/popest.html.
NOTE: Colors on the map represent quartiles of the participation distribution.

program-induced distortions in behavior can be long-lasting (Burkhauser and Daly 2011; Duggan, Kearney, and Rennane 2016).

These program features introduce an important set of issues that have been highlighted by previous work. First, medical eligibility screening is a form of "tagging," in which the government imposes requirements that target funds to groups with especially high needs (Akerlof 1978). This tag allows the government to redistribute more resources on a per-recipient basis than would be possible if all individuals were potentially eligible for the benefit. It can also, however, introduce an incentive for individuals to overstate the severity of their medical condition(s) in an effort to qualify for benefits. Second, the SSI program introduces the standard trade-off between income protection and distortions to the labor supply and savings decisions of those receiving benefits. More specifically, individuals may work or save less when applying for SSI or to retain SSI benefits once receiving. Third, because the SSI program is funded by the federal government, there can be an incentive for state and local governments to shift current or potential future beneficiaries of their programs (e.g., TANF) to SSI (Kubik 2003).

Despite the relatively large size of the means-tested SSI program in terms of both enrollment and expenditures, there has been relatively little research examining its effects on outcomes such as savings and labor supply. Previous research using administrative data has found that the SSI program does reduce the labor supply of near-elderly individuals (Neumark and Powers 2005). Relatedly, more recent work (Deshpande 2016b) finds that in families with a child who becomes ineligible for SSI, parents fully offset the loss in income with additional earnings. In contrast, recent research suggests that the effects on labor supply on young adults who become ineligible for the program at age 18 after a medical eligibility screen are relatively small (Deshpande 2016a), with those losing SSI eligibility earning just one dollar for every three dollars in lost benefits as young adults. The variation in find-ings in these and a few other studies underscores the heterogeneity of the groups being served and the complexity of the SSI program to be a single service provider to three very different groups (children, nonelderly adults, and the elderly).

There has been even less research on the effects of potential reforms to the SSI program. One interesting recent study by the U.S. Government Accountability Office (GAO 2017) found that a number of the provisions designed to encourage labor supply among SSI recipients and their families are not well-understood. For example, children and young adults under the age of 22 on SSI and enrolled in school can—through the student earned income exclusion (SEIE)—preserve more of their SSI benefits and retain their Medicaid eligibility even if they have substantial earnings. However, virtually no SSI recipients make use of this benefit that could lead to greater work incentives and economic well-being. This is espe-cially troubling since many of these individuals will lose their SSI eligibility when they are reevaluated for the adult program and could benefit from greater work attachment now and in the future. More efforts by SSA to inform SSI recipients about these incentive provisions could have beneficial effects for recipients.

Related research (Hemmeter, Kauff, and Wittenberg 2009) has found that SSI recipient children who reach age 18 while in the program are typically not pre-pared for life without SSI (if they lose eligibility). This is especially true for child SSI recipients with mental disorders other than intellectual disabilities (formerly known as mental retardation), who are at much higher risk than other SSI recipi-ents of losing benefits at or soon after age 18. Taken together, this research sug-gests that targeted interventions in the years leading up to and immediately following age 18 for those SSI recipients who have work capacity could have a high payoff for them for many years in the future. The bang-for-the-buck of reforms at these younger ages seems likely to be much higher than for the near-elderly adults identified by Neumark and Powers (2005) as being affected by SSI disincentives.

Reforms to the SSI program's medical eligibility criteria, changes in the level of benefits, and changes in the phase-out rates could also strengthen the pro-gram. It is not obvious that the same monthly benefit should be paid to low-income elderly as to families with children who have a disability. Some straightforward first steps for the medical eligibility criteria would involve more efficiently targeting continuing disability reviews while also reducing the varia-tion across disability examiners and ALJs in their decision-making about awards.

Many of these changes would involve complicated trade-offs, in some cases reducing the various distortions inherent in any means-tested program while pos-sibly also lowering the insurance value of benefits or vice versa. It is noteworthy that state supplements to monthly SSI benefits have been falling in real terms over time, suggesting that few states consider the benefits to be far below where they optimally should be. It also seems likely that the recent reduction in enroll-ment is partially driven by tighter medical eligibility standards that are being employed by ALJs. These changes may have partly resulted from numerous accounts in the press of ALJs who appealed their SSDI application rejections.

For example, a *Wall Street Journal* article from May 2011 pointed out that one judge awarded 1,280 of the 1,284 appeals that came before him and that there were many other judges with similarly high award rates.[13]

More research is needed to estimate the effect of past and likely future changes in program generosity—both in the level of monthly benefits and in the stringency of the disability screen—on the health[14] and economic well-being of current and potential future recipients. Much more could be learned from pilot studies that can target interventions at specific populations to increase self-sufficiency for those with work capacity and economic well-being in the long run.

Potential Reforms

As we discussed, the SSI program currently serves three very different populations.

Elderly SSI recipients

The simplest of the three is the group of recipients above the age of 65, most of whom qualify purely due to low income rather than because of a medical condition. We see little reason to reform the basic structure of the program for this group since both the labor supply and savings incentive effects are likely small and because the share receiving benefits from this program has been steadily falling over time.

That said, it is noteworthy that the share of elderly Americans in poverty is twice as large as the share on SSI (9 percent versus 4.5 percent; see Figure 5). Indeed, if SSI benefits are the only source of income for an elderly individual, the ratio of his or her income to the poverty line would be just 73 percent. A modest increase in SSI benefits above the (2017) maximum of $735 per month would likely lead to significant reductions in poverty among the elderly. Alternatively, states could be encouraged to supplement the federal benefit for elderly recipients, moving them above the poverty line. In contrast to federal SSI benefits, state supplements to SSI benefits have, in inflation-adjusted terms, generally been falling over time. For example, in the State of California (which has a relatively generous SSI supplement), the state supplement for a nonelderly adult fell from $171 in 2011 to $161 in 2019. In inflation-adjusted terms, this represents a drop of 18 percent.

Related to this, with an asset test of just $3,000, many elderly individuals may have incomes far below the poverty line but assets above this threshold. This threshold has not changed since 1989. During that 1989 to 2018 time period, the consumer price index (CPI) has more than doubled (from 124.0 to 250.5). Inflation adjusting this threshold on an annual basis along with other thresholds (e.g., the amount of income that a person can earn before SSI benefits start to fall) would synchronize these program features with program benefits.

Nonelderly adult SSI recipients

For nonelderly adults, the case for revising some key features of the program seems even stronger. At present, the program provides all-or-nothing benefits that substantially lower a recipient's incentives to work (or save). This occurs for two reasons. First, once earnings reach a certain level, SSI benefits fall by one dollar for every two dollars in earnings. Second, if an individual shows substantial work capacity, it is more likely that benefits will be terminated. Allowing SSI recipients to keep more of their earnings, both through a higher earnings disregard (the amount one can earn before taxes kick in) and a lower phase-out rate, could increase work effort for this group. Given the low exit rate from the program, the budgetary costs of this are likely to be minimal, since SSI receipt is largely an absorbing state.

Related to this, one concern that SSI recipients may have had for the first 40 years of the programs was that, if they were to return to work, they would lose health insurance through the Medicaid program (Yelowitz 2000).[15] But as of 2014, individuals with incomes below 133 percent of the poverty line were made eligible for Medicaid as a result of the Affordable Care Act. However, not all states elected to expand their Medicaid program. Currently, there are thirty-seven states (including D.C.) that have expanded their Medicaid programs and fourteen states that have not. This creates variation across states in the effective SSI incentive effects. One way to reduce these inequities would be to provide a grace period for SSI recipients in these fourteen states to retain their Medicaid health insurance coverage if they were to return to work.[16]

SSI benefits are all-or-nothing—either an individual is deemed fully disabled or not disabled at all. One possible reform that accounted for the considerable heterogeneity across individuals in the severity of their disability would be to introduce partial disability benefits for those on the margin of qualifying. A similar system is used for the Veteran's Association's Disability Compensation program, through which disabled veterans can receive benefits reflecting disability of 10 percent all the way up to 100 percent (Autor et al. 2016). The effects of any such change on SSI expenditures, employment, and economic well-being among SSI applicants and their families would of course depend on the details. For example, the costs of the program would almost certainly increase if partial disability benefits were awarded primarily to individuals who, under the current system, would be rejected.

An additional desirable reform to the SSI program would be to provide more benefits at the "front end" so that SSI applicants who have some work capacity can avoid significant skill atrophy. For many individuals, the SSI application process takes a long time. This is especially true for applicants whose health is on the margin for qualifying, since they may not be disabled enough to be awarded benefits on the first round and so may then enter a lengthy appeals process. Indeed, more than half of rejected applicants in the 18 to 64 age range appeal the decision, and this process typically takes more than a year to complete. This group likely includes many with substantial work capacity that can be nurtured with an appropriate mix of rehabilitation (physical and/or mental) services.

Reforms to the SSI application process could also improve program efficiency and equity. It is noteworthy that more than half of applicants rejected at the first stage appeal this decision. Of those appealing this initial decision, nearly three in four are ultimately awarded benefits at the reconsideration, ALJ, or later stage. Because of this, nearly 40 percent of SSI awards to nonelderly individuals are made on appeal. Taken together, this suggests that the criteria used at later stages of the process differs from the criteria used on the front end. Synchronizing those criteria (perhaps making the criteria more lenient on the first stage) could reduce the uncertainty and wait time in the process while giving rejected applicants more confidence that the first-stage decision was the correct one. It is especially unfortunate if a person spends multiple years out of the workforce hoping to qualify for SSI and the application is ultimately denied.

A final possible proposal that is related to the previous one is that these early interventions should be tailored to the unique circumstances of each applicant. For example, it may be the case that physical therapy can help some SSI applicants to address musculoskeletal problems such as severe back pain. Alternatively, periodic visits with mental health professionals may allow many with mental disorders to better manage obstacles to realizing their potential in the workforce.

Perhaps the group that is most well positioned to spearhead these efforts is the SSI recipient's health insurer. In recent years, many state Medicaid programs have shifted their SSI populations from fee-for-service Medicaid into managed care plans (Kaiser Family Foundation 2019).[17] These private insurers often have detailed information about the individual's medical history and treatment effectiveness. However, they have little financial incentive to help an SSI recipient return to the workforce, since their payments do not increase if their beneficiaries' earnings rise. The insurer actually has the opposite financial incentive, since if a person returns to work, she or he may become ineligible for Medicaid. Revising Medicaid managed care plans' incentives so that they are rewarded as their recipients increase their work effort could lead to better outcomes both for current (or potential future) SSI recipients and for taxpayers.[18] A substantial body of previous research has shown that there are substantial health benefits to working and so the benefits to the recipient would often not be purely financial (Fitzpatrick and Moore 2017).

Child SSI recipients

We propose a somewhat different set of reforms for children who are receiving SSI benefits (Figure 4). One very innovative recent proposal by Wittenburg (2011) suggested tying the payment of a child's SSI benefits to his or her attendance in school. This ensures that family members and local school systems will continue to invest in the human capital of their child. A potential concern is that overstretched schools would not have the services necessary to foster learning for SSI children. As such, we suggest broadening the requirement to include school or a similar investment-oriented activity, the key idea being to tie benefits for SSI

FIGURE 6
Percentage of 2017 SSI Disability Caseload Diagnosed with a Physical Disability

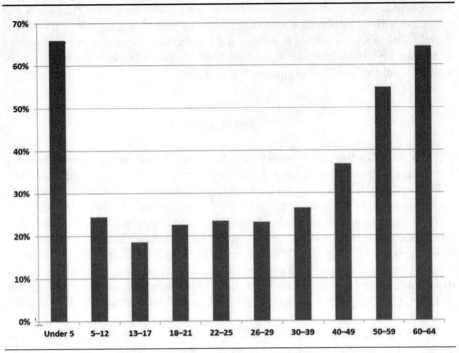

SOURCE: SSA (2018b, Table 35).

children to investments in their human capital that maximize their chances of
working as adults.

As with adults, we propose creating stronger financial incentives for private
insures that administer Medicaid managed care plans to children. If private
insures provide treatments focused on outcomes, more children will reach their
full potential. For child SSI recipients, the quality of mental health care will
clearly be very important, since more than 70 percent of child SSI recipients have
a mental disorder as their primary qualifying condition.

The disincentive to save that the program creates is a related issue that may
be especially important for families with children on SSI. Many families with a
disabled child may want to save money for his or her education in the future,
especially if they do not have to pay for private school during K–12 years. But
given SSI's means test, a parent who saves a nontrivial amount each year may
cause the child to lose SSI benefits. This discourages saving for higher education
or, for example, a private high school. Relaxing the asset requirement for qualified savings, for example, educational expenses, would allow families receiving
SSI to plan for and invest in their child's future without fear of losing benefits.

One final set of reforms that would apply for both children and adults in the
SSI program would be to improve the efficiency of program administration. One

area that warrants particular attention is the application process. Recent research has uncovered substantial variation across both disability examiners and ALJs in their decisions about benefit awards. This implies that—for a large fraction of SSI applicants—their application outcome depends somewhat on the "luck of the draw." While SSA is aware of this issue and has made some progress in addressing it, further efforts to leverage the benefits of "big data" to harmonize decision-making would substantially improve the program.

Conclusion

SSI is a program that serves more than 8 million of the nation's most disadvantaged individuals. It plays a key role in alleviating poverty among millions of individuals with disabilities while giving families additional resources that can cushion the financial and emotional costs of having a family member with a disability.

After rising steadily for decades through 2013, SSI enrollment has actually fallen among the nonelderly over the last few years. For example, the number of children receiving benefits fell from 1.32 million in 2013 to 1.15 million by 2018.[19] Similarly, the number of nonelderly adults on the program declined from 4.93 million in 2013 to 4.71 million in 2018. Whether this reflects the effects of tighter medical eligibility criteria for the program, improving health in the population, or the effects of a strong economy are important questions for future research.

But whatever the drivers of this change may be, reform of the SSI program could lead to substantial improvements in efficiency and increased benefits for program recipients. For the elderly, we propose an increase in the generosity of SSI benefits and a less stringent asset test. This would ensure that those who qualify for benefits are able to live above the poverty line and for those in poverty that they are not excluded from cash support due to asset valuations above the $3,000 limit. For nonelderly adults with disabilities, we propose changes that will increase their incentive to work while on SSI. Related to this, we encourage increases in the asset test for children on SSI so that their families can save for future educational expenses. For both adults and children with disabilities, we advocate greater efforts to harmonize disability decision-making among medical examiners and ALJs. And finally, given the substantial increase in Medicaid managed care enrollment among SSI recipients with disabilities, reforms to increase Medicaid managed care plans' incentives to help both groups realize their potential could have a very high payoff.

When SSI was enacted in 1972, the U.S. economy and social norms were different. At that time, those not expected to work included individuals aged 65 and older, the blind, and people with disabilities. These categories were always difficult to establish and assess, particularly with regard to disability, but these challenges have grown worse over time as social expectations over who should work and who should be entitled to income transfers have changed.

In addition, the role of SSI in the broader social safety net has evolved. The normal retirement age for Social Security benefits is increasing, welfare reforms have placed limits on the number of years single mothers with children may receive benefits in lieu of working, and poverty rates among children remain high. These circumstances suggest that income maintenance programs such as SSI will play an increasingly important role in the U.S. social safety net. All these factors will impact the politically determined boundaries of the only remaining federal cash-based means-tested entitlement program without time limits available to both adults and children.

Notes

1. See Berkowitz and DeWitt (2013) for a historical review of the genesis of the SSI program.

2. Supplements accounted for approximately 16 percent of SSI benefits paid in 2017 in the eleven states (and D.C.) with federally administered supplements. We were unable to locate data on SSI supplements paid in the other thirty-five states.

3. In 2017, approximately one in seven SSI recipients was under the age of 18, one in four was 65 or older, and the remaining 58 percent were between the ages of 18 and 64.

4. This is the most recent year for which Medicaid spending data by eligibility category are available. CMS (Centers for Medicare & Medicaid Services) reports $275 billion for 18.4 million aged and disabled Medicaid recipients. Because this exceeds the number of SSI aged and disabled recipients, we scale this down by the ratio of SSI aged and disabled to CMS aged and disabled.

5. SSA data indicate that there are currently 1,230 field offices; see https://www.ssa.gov/open/data/field-office-visitors-average-daily.html (accessed 19 April 2019).

6. The monthly substantial gainful activity amount increased from $500 to $700 in 1999 and has been indexed to inflation since. For 2019, SGA is $1,220 for nonblind individuals. For more information, see https://www.ssa.gov/oact/cola/sga.html.

7. See Wixon and Strand (2013) and Duggan, Kearney, and Rennane (2016) for a more detailed explanation of the process.

8. See final column of Table 69 at https://www.ssa.gov/policy/docs/statcomps/ssi_asr/2017/sect10.pdf.

9. During this same 2000 to 2017 period, the fraction of children in families with incomes below the poverty line also increased slightly, from 16.2 percent to 17.1 percent. While this may have contributed to the increase in child SSI enrollment, recent research suggests that changes in poverty do not have a significant effect on SSI enrollment (Aizer, Gordon, and Kearney 2013).

10. See https://www.jmcp.org/doi/full/10.18553/jmcp.2018.24.3.238.

11. See Table 7.A9 at https://www.ssa.gov/policy/docs/statcomps/supplement/2018/7a.pdf.

12. There is also substantial within-state variation in SSI enrollment. County-level data from the SSA are available for various years, for example, at https://www.ssa.gov/policy/docs/statcomps/ssi_sc/.

13. See https://www.wsj.com/articles/SB10001424052748704681904576319163605918524.

14. Recent research for the SSDI program did find that more generous benefits lead to a reduction in mortality, suggesting that there are effects of the programs on health as well as economic outcomes (Gelber, Moore, and Strand 2018).

15. SSI applicants and recipients are often eligible for other government programs, and SSA does provide some information to assist both applicants and recipients. For example, SSA field offices make available applications for SNAP (food stamp) benefits. See https://www.ssa.gov/ssi/text-other-ussi.htm.

16. The fourteen states that have not yet expanded Medicaid are Alabama, Florida, Georgia, Kansas, Mississippi, Missouri, North Carolina, Oklahoma, South Carolina, South Dakota, Tennessee, Texas, Wisconsin, and Wyoming.

17. See https://www.kff.org/medicaid/issue-brief/10-things-to-know-about-medicaid-setting-the-facts-straight/.

18. Nationally, more than 40 percent of disabled Medicaid recipients are enrolled in comprehensive managed care plans (Medicare Payment Advisory Commission [MedPAC] 2017). This includes, for example, two-thirds of disabled Medicaid recipients in both California and Texas. However, in most states, less than 10 percent of disabled Medicaid recipients are in a comprehensive Medicaid Managed Care (MMC) plan, including North Carolina at 0 percent and Missouri at 2 percent.

19. Data are for December in each year.

References

Aizer, Anna, Nora Gordon, and Melissa Kearney. 2013. Exploring the growth of the child SSI caseload. NBER Disability Research Center Paper no. NB 13–02, National Bureau of Economic Research, Cambridge, MA.

Akerlof, George A. 1978. The economics of "tagging" as applied to the optimal income tax, welfare programs, and manpower planning. *American Economic Review* 68 (1): 8–19.

Autor, David, Mark Duggan, Kyle Greenberg, and David Lyle. 2016. The impact of disability benefits on labor supply: Evidence from the VA's disability compensation program. *American Economic Journal: Applied Economics* 8 (3): 31–68.

Berkowitz, Edward D., and Larry DeWitt. 2013. *The other welfare: Supplemental Security Income and U.S. social policy.* Ithaca, NY: Cornell University Press.

Burkhauser, Richard V., and Mary C. Daly. 2002. Policy watch: U.S. disability policy in a changing environment. *Journal of Economic Perspectives* 16 (1): 213–24.

Burkhauser, Richard V., and Mary C. Daly. 2011. *The declining work and welfare of people with disabilities: What went wrong and a strategy for change.* Washington, DC: AEI Press.

Daly, Mary C., and Richard V. Burkhauser. 2003. The Supplemental Security Income program. In *Economics of means-tested transfer programs in the United States*, vol. 2, ed. Robert A. Moffitt, 79–139. Chicago, IL: University of Chicago Press.

Daub, Hal, Dorcas R. Hardy, Barbara B. Kennelly, David Podoff, and Sylvester J. Schieber. 2006. *Improving the Social Security Administration's hearing process.* Washington, DC: Social Security Advisory Board.

Deshpande, Manasi. 2016a. Does welfare inhibit success? The long-term effects of removing low-income youth from the disability rolls. *American Economic Review* 106 (11): 3300–3330.

Deshpande, Manasi. 2016b. The effect of disability payments on household earnings and income: Evidence from the SSI children's program. *Review of Economics and Statistics* 98 (4): 638–54.

Duggan, Mark, and Melissa Kearney. 2007. The impact of child SSI enrollment on household outcomes. *Journal of Policy Analysis and Management* 26 (4): 861–86.

Duggan, Mark, Melissa Kearney, and Stephanie Rennane. 2016. The Supplemental Security Income program. In *Economics of means-tested transfer programs in the United States*, vol. 2, ed. Robert A. Moffitt, 1–58. Chicago, IL: University of Chicago Press.

Fitzpatrick, Maria D., and Timothy J. Moore. 2017. The mortality effects of retirement: Evidence from Social Security eligibility at age 62. NBER Working Paper no. w24127, National Bureau of Economic Research, Cambridge, MA.

French, Eric, and Jae Song. 2014. The effect of disability insurance receipt on labor supply. *American Economic Journal: Economic Policy* 6 (2): 291–337.

Gelber, Alexander, Timothy Moore, and Alexander Strand. 2018. Disability insurance income saves lives. Stanford Institute for Economic Policy Research (SIEPR) Working Paper no. 18–005, Stanford, CA.

Gruber, Jonathan, and Jeffrey D. Kubik. 1997. Disability insurance rejection rates and the labor supply of older workers. *Journal of Public Economics* 64 (1): 1–23.

Hemmeter, Jeffrey, Jacqueline Kauff, and David Wittenburg. 2009. Changing circumstances: Experiences of child SSI recipients before and after their age-18 redetermination for adult benefits. *Journal of Vocational Rehabilitation* 30 (3): 201–21.

Kaiser Family Foundation. 2019. 10 things to know about Medicaid: Setting the facts straight. Available from https://www.kff.org/medicaid/issue-brief/10-things-to-know-about-medicaid-setting-the-facts-straight.

Kubik, Jeffrey D. 2003. Fiscal federalism and welfare policy: The role of states in the growth of child SSI. *National Tax Journal* 56 (1): 61–79.

Leckman-Westin, Emily, Molly Finnerty, Sarah Hudson Scholle, Riti Pritam, Deborah Layman, Edith Kealey, Sepheen Byron, Emily Morden, Scott Bilder, Sheree Neese-Todd, Sarah Horwitz, Kimberly Hoagwood, and Stephen Crystal. 2018. Differences in Medicaid antipsychotic medication measures among children with SSI, foster care, and income–based aid. *Journal of Managed Care & Specialty Pharmacy* 24 (3): 238–46.

Maestas, Nicole, Kathleen Mullen, and Alexander Strand. 2013. Does disability insurance receipt discourage work? Using examiner assignment to estimate causal effects of SSDI receipt. *American Economic Review* 103 (5): 1797–1829.

Medicare Payment Advisory Commission (MedPAC). 2017. *Report to the Congress: Medicare payment policy*. Washington, DC: MedPAC.

Neumark, David, and Elizabeth T. Powers. 2005. The Supplemental Security Income program and incentives to take up Social Security early retirement: Empirical evidence from the SIPP and Social Security administrative data. *National Tax Journal* 58 (1): 5–26.

Office of the Inspector General (OIG). 2008. Disability claims overall processing times. U.S. Social Security Administration Report no. A-01-08-18011. Washington, DC: OIG.

U.S. Census Bureau. 2018. State population totals and components of change: 2010–2018. Washington, DC. Available from https://www.census.gov/data/datasets/time-series/demo/popest/2010s-state-total .html (accessed 5 March 2019).

U.S. General Accounting Office (GAO). 1994. *Rapid rise in children on SSI disability rolls follows new regulations*. Report no. GAO/HEHS-94-225. Washington, DC: GAO.

U.S. General Accounting Office (GAO). 1995. *New functional assessments for children raise eligibility questions*. Report no. GAO/HEHS-95-66. Washington, DC: GAO.

U.S. Government Accountability Office (GAO). 2017. *SSA could strengthen its efforts to encourage employment for transition–age youth*. Report no. GAO-27-485. Washington, DC: GAO.

U.S. Social Security Administration (SSA). 1997. *The definition of disability for children*. SSA Publication no. 05-11053. Washington, DC: SSA.

U.S. Social Security Administration (SSA). 2008. *Disability evaluation under Social Security*. SSA Publication no. 64-039. Washington, DC: SSA.

U.S. Social Security Administration (SSA). 2018a. *Annual report of the Supplemental Security Income Program*. Baltimore, MD: Office of the Chief Actuary.

U.S. Social Security Administration (SSA). 2018b. *SSI annual statistical report, 2017*. SSA Publication no. 13-11976. Washington, DC: Office of Research, Evaluation and Statistics.

U.S. Social Security Administration (SSA). 2018c. *SSI annual statistical supplement, 2018*. SSA Publication no. 13-11700. Washington, DC: Office of Research, Evaluation and Statistics.

U.S. Social Security Administration (SSA). 2018d. *SSI recipients by state and county, 2017*. SSA Publication no. 13-11976. Washington, DC: Office of Research, Evaluation and Statistics.

U.S. Social Security Administration (SSA). 2018e. *2018 red book*. SSA Publication no. 64-030. Washington, DC: SSA.

Wen, Patricia. 12–14 December 2010. The other welfare. *The Boston Globe*.

Wiseman, Michael. 2010. Supplemental Security Income for the second decade. Prepared for *Reducing poverty and economic distress after ARRA: The most promising approaches*. Washington, DC: The Urban Institute.

Wittenburg, David. 2011. Testimony for hearing on Supplemental Security Income benefits for children. Submitted to Committee on Ways and Means, U.S. House of Representatives. Washington, DC: Mathematica Policy Research.

Wixon, Bernard, and Alexander Strand. 2013. Identifying SSA's sequential disability determination steps using administrative data. Social Security Administration, Research and Statistics Note 2013–01. Washington, DC: SSA.

Yelowitz, Aaron. 2000. Using the Medicare buy-in program to estimate the effect of Medicaid on SSI participation. *Economic Inquiry* 38 (3): 419–41.

This article reviews current federal housing assistance policies and briefly summarizes research evidence about the efficacy of the different programs. We identify three key challenges that these programs face in meeting their stated objectives and suggest strategies for addressing them. The first challenge is the large variation in market conditions across the country, which makes it difficult to design assistance programs that are universally appropriate. We call for adjusting the type of assistance across markets, allowing for a greater match between subsidies and needs. The second set of challenges concerns subsidy generosity, structure, and targeting. The current system provides large subsidies to a small number of low-income households while providing nothing to most. Assuming limited government resources, we call for exploring the impact of more modest or time-limited subsidies to serve more people with more attention to targeting. The third challenge is the relatively poor location of housing in current assistance programs. We suggest strategies to help more assisted families reach high-opportunity areas.

Keywords: housing; neighborhoods; subsidies; targeting

Reforming Housing Assistance

By
ROBERT COLLINSON,
INGRID GOULD ELLEN,
and
JENS LUDWIG

Federal low-income housing policy tries to do a lot. It tries to improve the quality of the homes in which low-income families live, to help low-income households reach a broader range of neighborhoods, to reduce homelessness, and to alleviate housing cost burdens. It is asked to do this in an environment in which housing is expensive, slow, and difficult to build (particularly in high-cost urban areas) and neighborhoods continue to be highly segregated by income and race. Our aim here is to identify ways that the current system falls short

Robert Collinson is the Wilson Family LEO Assistant Professor in the Department of Economics at University of Notre Dame.

Correspondence: jludwig@uchicago.edu

DOI: 10.1177/0002716219877801

in meeting its objectives, to present some proposals for reform, and to assess the reform options that are most promising.

We start with an overview of current housing policy and then briefly summarize what existing research tells us about the efficacy of different programs. We then identify three key challenges that housing assistance programs face in meeting the goals stated above and suggest some strategies for addressing those challenges.

First, we describe the large variation in market conditions across the country, which makes it difficult to design housing programs and policies that are appropriate across all areas. We call for adjusting the type of assistance across markets, allowing for a greater match between subsidies and needs.

Second, we highlight the fact that the existing system of housing assistance provides sizable subsidies to a small number of low-income households but provides nothing to most of them. This is not likely to be the optimal approach if, as seems plausible, there are diminishing marginal benefits of additional subsidy dollars to program recipients. Absent large infusions of additional resources into housing programs that would allow a greater number of needy households to receive the relatively generous subsidies that are currently provided, there would seem to be value in exploring the impact of modest, time-limited subsidies to serve more people.

Finally, we document the relatively poor location of housing in current assistance programs. Many program participants wind up in very disadvantaged neighborhoods, which seem to have adverse impacts on a range of important outcomes, such as physical and mental health, well-being, and children's long-term life chances. We suggest some strategies to help more assisted families reach high-opportunity areas.

Overview of Current Housing Policy

Key programs

Federal low-income housing programs can be broadly divided into three categories: (1) public housing; (2) privately owned, subsidized housing; and (3) tenant-based vouchers.

Public housing, established by the Housing Act of 1937, was the federal government's first major low-income housing program. Although the federal

Ingrid Gould Ellen is the Paulette Goddard Professor of Urban Policy and Planning at New York University and a faculty director at the NYU Furman Center.

Jens Ludwig is the Edwin A. and Betty L. Bergman Distinguished Service Professor at the University of Chicago, research associate of the National Bureau of Economic Research, director of the University of Chicago Crime Lab, and codirector of the Urban Education Lab.

NOTE: We thank Robert Moffitt and James Ziliak, as well as others participating in the authors' conference for *The ANNALS of the American Academy of Political and Social Science* on entitlement reform, for helpful insights and suggestions. All opinions and any errors are our own.

government provided most of their funding, public housing developments are owned and operated by housing authorities established by local governments, which have control over siting, management, and tenant selection. Today, close to three thousand local public housing agencies own and operate public housing under the supervision of the U.S. Department of Housing and Urban Development (HUD).

Congress initially expected that the federal government would pay for construction costs, while local housing authorities would cover operating costs through rental revenues. Over time, however, buildings aged, and both maintenance and utility costs rose. In response, the federal government started to provide substantial subsidies to cover the gap between the rents tenants pay and the costs of operating and maintaining developments (HUD 1974). The federal government also helps to fund renovations and capital improvements through the public housing capital fund. Both of these federal subsidy streams have long been funded at less than the formula's promise, and housing authorities have had to defer needed capital repairs. HUD released a study in 2010 estimating that the 1.1 million public housing units around the country face a backlog of more than $25 billion in unmet capital needs (Finkel et al. 2010).

The second key category of federal housing programs includes those that subsidize the creation of privately owned, low-income housing. First emerging in the 1960s and continuing until the mid-1980s, these programs offered upfront mortgage subsidies or long-term rental assistance contracts to private developers who would agree to provide housing with reduced rents for a specified number of years. These programs generally aimed to house a slightly higher income set of households than those served by public housing. The largest of these programs was the Section 8 New Construction and Substantial Rehabilitation program, simply referred to as "project-based Section 8." As with the case of public housing, the government provides ongoing rent subsidies to these developments to cover the gap between the rents tenants pay and the cost of operating developments.

Today, the largest project-based subsidy and the only major source of support for new production of subsidized rental housing in the United States is a tax credit administered by the Treasury Department: the Low Income Housing Tax Credit (LIHTC). Created by the Tax Reform Act of 1986, tax credits are allocated annually to states on a per capita basis, and states in turn award credits to developers to support the construction and rehabilitation of low-income, rental housing. Projects are eligible for tax credits if at least 20 percent of their tenants have incomes below 50 percent of the local area median income (AMI) or at least 40 percent have incomes below 60 percent of AMI. (For reference, the annual poverty level is approximately 40 percent of the average AMI [Collinson, Ellen, and Ludwig 2016]). While LIHTC developments can be mixed income, in practice, the vast majority contain only units affordable to households earning under 60 percent of AMI or lower, with 95 percent of units in tax credit projects qualifying as low-income units (Collinson, Ellen, and Ludwig 2016).[1] Projects must meet these requirements for a minimum of 30 years to qualify for a 10-year stream of tax credits.

The third category of federal housing assistance is tenant-based vouchers. The housing choice voucher program is the only tenant-based program that is currently active. Voucher recipients generally pay 30 percent of their income toward rent, while the federal government covers the difference between this payment and the rent, up to a specified maximum payment standard. To qualify for the voucher program, housing units must meet certain quality and size standards, and participation by landlords is voluntary, though fourteen states and several localities have now passed discrimination laws that prohibit landlords from discriminating against voucher holders.[2] (Owners of LIHTC housing are also prohibited from discriminating against voucher holders.) The voucher program is currently HUD's largest housing subsidy program for low-income households.

Number of recipients

Figure 1 charts the number of federally assisted households or units by program from the start of federal low-income housing assistance to the present. The stock of public housing grew steadily from the early 1950s to the mid-1970s. The late 1970s saw a shift toward programs that subsidized units in private market housing through the creation of the project-based Section 8 and tenant-based Section 8 voucher programs. Vouchers continued to grow through the 1990s, while public housing and project-based Section 8 declined or plateaued. The 1990s and 2000s saw a steady rise in the LIHTC program, which was created through the Tax Reform Act of 1986. Figure 2 plots federal spending on low-income housing per capita over time. Low-income housing spending grew mostly uninterrupted from the 1960s through the late 1990s. Spending on low-income housing has largely plateaued since 2000.

The three main HUD programs, public housing, housing vouchers, and project-based Section 8, serve roughly 4.5 million households and nearly 10 million persons each year. The LIHTC, meanwhile, subsidizes 2.2 million units, though some of the households in these units also receive HUD rental assistance. Table 1 shows the characteristics of households subsidized through these various programs. As shown, HUD-assisted households are quite disadvantaged, with average incomes of $12,000 to $15,000. More than 70 percent of these households earn less than 30 percent of their AMI. Tenants in LIHTC developments appear to have higher incomes, but still more than 80 percent earn less than half of the local AMI. Nearly 45 percent of housing voucher households are families with children, compared to just 38 percent of public housing tenants, 36 percent of LIHTC households, and 28 percent of households in project-based Section 8 developments. A large share of HUD-assisted households are headed by an elderly member or contain a member with disabilities. Across HUD programs, about 24 percent of HUD-assisted households have earned income; this number is slightly higher for public housing and vouchers, as those households include more working-age adults.

Housing voucher participants tend to be younger than those receiving other forms of assistance. Only a quarter of voucher households are headed by an adult

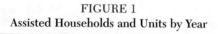

FIGURE 1
Assisted Households and Units by Year

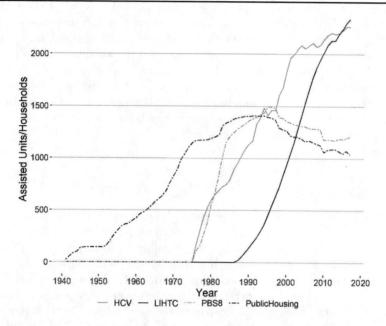

SOURCE: Public Housing, Tenant-Based Voucher, and Project-Based Section 8 come from HUD's Annual Performance Report 1999–2013. See https://www.hud.gov/program_offices/spm/appr. Pre-1998 numbers for HUD programs come from Olsen (2003).
NOTE: LIHTC counts are low-income units placed in service from HUD's Low Income Housing Tax Credit Database. PBS8 = project-based Section 8. HVC = Housing choice voucher.

over the age of 62, compared to roughly a third of households in public housing and LIHTC developments and nearly half of tenants in project-based Section 8 developments. Tenants in project-based Section 8 developments tend to be older (and whiter) relative to participants in other HUD programs or LIHTC, since some project-based Section 8 contracts provide rental assistance to Section 202 developments.[3] Public housing households live in relatively more impoverished neighborhoods on average than either housing voucher or project-based Section 8 households.

(Recent) Research on Efficacy

In this section, we review the best available recent research about the efficacy of different means-tested housing programs: public housing, publicly subsidized project-based housing, and tenant-based housing vouchers.[4]

FIGURE 2
Low-Income Housing Spending by Year

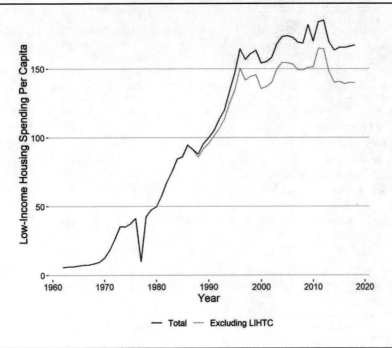

SOURCE: Data on federal outlays are compiled from OMB historical tables, Table 8.7: outlays for discretionary programs; see https://www.whitehouse.gov/omb/historical-tables. Data on tax expenditures costs of the LIHTC are from the Joint Committee on Taxation, Estimates of Federal Tax Expenditures 1988–2018; see https://www.jct.gov/publications.html?func=select&id=5.

NOTE: The figure plots real per capita federal spending on low-income housing. Dollar values are U.S. dollar 2018 values adjusted using the U.S. Bureau of Economic Analysis (BEA) Personal Consumption Expenditures (PCE) Price Deflator.

Public housing

Means-tested housing programs for many people probably conjure up images of high-rise public housing projects of the sort that were built during the 1950s and 1960s, which have become synonymous with terrible living conditions and high rates of crime and racial segregation. But the assumption of very difficult living conditions in these projects overlooks the fact that most public housing projects are not so distressed, and the worst of them have been torn down in recent years through HUD's HOPE VI program. Perhaps even more importantly, it is easy to forget the terrible slum conditions that public housing families left behind when the developments were initially built.

Historically, America's public housing program reinforced residential segregation by race and income, in part through reserving some housing developments for blacks and some for whites. Data from the 1960s showed that 72 percent of

TABLE 1
Characteristics of Households Receiving Housing Assistance

| | HUD Programs, 2017 | | | Treasury |
Program	Public Housing	Housing Choice Vouchers	Project-Based Section 8	LIHTC (2013/2014)
Subsidized units (thousands)	1,041	2,489	1,280	2,210
Subsidized people (thousands)	2,071	5,288	2,058	NA
Average household income/year	14,753	14,454	12,505	17,152
% with earned income	30	31	19	NA
% of local median (household income)	25	23	23	NA
% very low income (less than 50% AMI)	90	94	96	81
% extremely low income (less than 30% AMI)	71	73	75	47
% with children	38	44	28	36
% female head with children	34	40	25	NA
% with disability, among all persons in households	21	23	17	12
% 62 or more (head or spouse)	33	25	49	32
% minority	67	69	55	NA
% black non-Hispanic	43	48	34	NA
% Native American non-Hispanic	1	1	1	NA
% Asian or Pacific Islander	3	3	5	NA
% white non-Hispanic	33	31	42	NA
% Hispanic	21	17	15	NA
Poverty rate (census tract)	33	24	27	
% minority (census tract)	61	56	51	

SOURCE: A Picture of Subsidized Housing (2017). LIHTC: HUD Data on LIHTC Tenants 2013/2014. See https://www.huduser.gov/portal/datasets/assthsg.html.

public housing projects at the time were inhabited by people of a single race (Bonastia 2006, 74). Part of the issue also stemmed from the role that local politicians played in deciding where housing developments would be built.[5] Opposition to new public housing was weakest in those communities where initial housing conditions were most distressed, and so projects were disproportionately likely to be built in predominantly low-income and minority neighborhoods (see, for example, Hunt 2009). Newman and Schnare (1997, Table 3) show that in the mid-1990s, public housing units were much more concentrated in extreme-poverty areas than were the units occupied by other low-income people (defined in their study as other welfare recipients).[6] More recent evidence suggests that households in place-based, assisted housing live in neighborhoods with low-performing public elementary schools (Horn, Ellen, and Schwartz 2014).

Unfortunately there is no experimental or "natural experiment" evidence that we know of on the effects of public housing on residential mobility.[7] However, the evidence we have suggests that public housing tenants tend to remain in their units for longer than other renters, though the typical public housing resident does not stay as long as many think. Lubell, Shroder, and Steffen (2003) find that the average public housing resident stays in his or her unit for 8.5 years and the median resident stays for 4.9 years. As a comparison, the median renter in the United States had lived in her or his home for 2.2 years in 1998 (Hansen 1998). Of course, at least part of this difference here could be due to differences in the types of families who are in public housing, that is, selection bias.

One of the rationales for providing assistance to low-income families in the form of in-kind housing benefits instead of cash is the possibility that housing consumption has positive externalities on labor supply. (That said, it bears repeating that about two-thirds of HUD subsidy recipients are either elderly or disabled.) While one of the major reviews of the empirical literature written a dozen years ago argued that "housing assistance is not persuasively associated with any effect on employment" (Shroder 2002, 381, 410), a growing body of evidence since that time provides a stronger basis for concluding there is some decline in work effort at least as a result of HUD programs. Perhaps the best available empirical evidence on the effects of public housing on labor supply is the study by Susin (2005), who uses data from the Survey of Income and Program Participation (SIPP) to compare public housing residents with unsubsidized SIPP respondents who are matched on observable characteristics. While this research design may be susceptible to bias from omitted variables, the estimates suggest public housing reduces earnings of adult participants by 19 percent (see also Olsen et al. 2005).

Advocates also sometimes point to positive effects of housing on children's outcomes as another type of externality and justification for in-kind housing programs. While the research is limited, two of the more rigorous studies do find benefits for children. First, Currie and Yelowitz (2000), whose research design takes advantage of the fact that the number of bedrooms to which a family would be entitled within a housing project depends on the gender mix of children in the family. Specifically, children of the same gender have to share a bedroom, but those of opposite genders do not. So a family with one adult and two children will be eligible for a three-bedroom apartment if the household has a boy and a girl but just a two-bedroom if the children are of the same sex. Using child gender composition as an instrument for the likelihood of being in public housing (families eligible for larger apartments are 24 percent more likely to live in housing projects), Currie and Yelowitz find beneficial impacts of public housing on a number of different outcomes: public housing reduces the likelihood a family is overcrowded by 16 percentage points, a finding that holds for both blacks and whites;[8] has no detectable effects for whites on schooling outcomes (as measured by grade retention in their Census data); but reduces grade retention by 19 percentage points for blacks. The one important potential limitation with this finding is the reliance on grade retention as a measure of schooling outcomes, since schools in relatively higher-poverty areas may (all else equal) be less likely to hold children back.[9]

Second, Andersson et al. (2018) use a sibling-difference design to explore the effects of public housing, which asks whether siblings with different public housing exposure during childhood had different outcomes later in life. They find that longer stays in public housing during adolescence are associated with increased earnings in adulthood. Their estimates imply that each additional year in public housing as a teenager increases earnings at age 26 by 4 to 5 percent. They also find longer stays in public housing during childhood are associated with lower rates of adult incarceration. Their estimates suggest that each year of public housing participation in childhood increases lifetime earnings by more than $40,000. The challenge with studies using this design is the difficulty of knowing whether differences in outcomes might be due to other unmeasured differences between the siblings or unmeasured changes in the family circumstances that affect the length of assistance spells.

Privately owned, place-based subsidized housing

Unfortunately, despite becoming the largest federal place-based housing program, there is remarkably limited research of which we are aware that examines the effects of the LIHTC on low-income families. For example, relatively little is currently known about the effects of the LIHTC on housing affordability. LIHTC rent limits mean that the program tends to reach low-income households but not the very poorest households (Desai, Dharmapala, and Singhal 2010). There is research documenting the number of units produced under the program (see, for example, Cummings and DiPasquale 1999; Desai, Dharmapala, and Singhal 2010) and research showing that the LIHTC increases the total number of rental units in an area (Baum-Snow and Marion 2009).[10] All else equal, we would expect an outward shift in rental housing in these areas to reduce rents, but the magnitude of this effect is, as far as we are aware, not currently known. O'Regan and Horn (2013) report that tenants in LIHTC-supported housing who earn less than 30 percent of the AMI face lower rent burdens than unassisted renters but far higher burdens than households with similar incomes who are participating in HUD programs.

Nor do we have much sense for the effects of the LIHTC on neighborhood conditions of families. LIHTC developments receive more tax credits if they are located in census tracts in which at least half of households are LIHTC-eligible, which incentivizes developers to build housing in such areas (Baum-Snow and Marion 2009). But states adopt other siting priorities as well. Nonexperimental evidence shows that LIHTC tenants, on average, live in neighborhoods that have nearly identical poverty rates, slightly higher minority concentrations, and higher average crime rates as those lived in by poor households as a whole (Lens, Ellen, and O'Regan 2011). But we do not know what the neighborhood conditions would have otherwise been for the type of families served by the program.

There is more robust evidence on the spillover effects of LIHTC developments on the surrounding neighborhood. Recent work from Diamond and McQuade (2019) finds that LIHTC developments have very different effects on the surrounding neighborhood depending on the existing neighborhood conditions. In low-income neighborhoods, the LIHTC appears to boost neighboring housing values, lower property and violent crime, and increase entry of nonminority home buyers. In high-income, predominately white neighborhoods, the LIHTC lowers housing values modestly and attracts lower-income home buyers but has no effect on racial composition or crime. This is consistent with earlier work from Baum-Snow and Marion (2009), who find that the construction of LIHTC units increase the median value of nearby homes in low-income areas. Similarly, Schwartz et al. (2006) assess the impact of city-assisted subsidized housing investments on abandoned lots in New York City on surrounding property values and find that these investments substantially increased the value of neighboring properties. Spillover effects appear to be heterogeneous across neighborhood and local economic conditions, as well as the particular program studied (Diamond and McQuade 2019; Briggs, Darden, and Aidala 1999).

Little is currently known about the effects of the LIHTC on labor supply. Unlike HUD programs like public housing or housing vouchers, the LIHTC uses a system of flat rents that should not generate a substitution effect on labor supply. However, to the degree to which the LIHTC subsidizes low-income households, we would expect there to still be an income effect that depresses work effort, potentially countervailed to some unknown degree by whatever the effects are of improved and more stable housing conditions on labor market success.

Housing vouchers

We have very strong evidence that housing vouchers (relative to not receiving any government subsidy at all) improve a number of housing-related outcomes for recipients. Housing vouchers substantially reduce the likelihood of experiencing homelessness and other forms of housing instability. Two multisite random assignment studies provide the best available evidence. HUD's recent Family Options Study randomized priority for housing assistance, including housing vouchers, to families living in emergency shelters. At the 37-month follow-up, being randomized into the voucher group reduced the probability of living unsheltered, doubled up, or in emergency shelters by 21 percentage points relative to the control group, or 55 percent of the control mean; and reduced the number of days experiencing this instability in the previous 6 months by about 29 days, or 60 percent of the control mean (Gubits et al. 2016). Families randomized to the voucher priority group were also less likely to be overcrowded and reported fewer addresses in the previous six months (Gubits et al. 2016). These results closely mirror the effects found in HUD's Welfare to Work (WtW) experiment a decade earlier, which provided vouchers to recent Temporary Assistance to Needy Families (TANF) recipients. Families receiving vouchers through the WtW allocation were 9 percentage points less likely to be living on the street or in shelter (compared to a control mean of 12 percent) and 35 percentage points less likely to have experienced housing insecurity (compared to a control mean of 44 percent) five years after random assignment (Wood, Turnham, and Mills 2008).

Housing vouchers also significantly increase housing consumption while reducing housing costs for assisted households. In a voucher study in Chicago carried out by Jacob and Ludwig (2012) that capitalized on a randomized waitlist lottery, the average family at baseline (without a subsidy) was paying about 58 percent of their reported income toward rent. Voucher receipt enables families to reduce their out-of-pocket spending on rent to about 27 percent of reported income.[11] Similarly in HUD's WtW experiment, the average control group family spends about $529 on rent per month (including utilities), equal to roughly one-quarter of reported monthly income.[12] Welfare receipt reduces out-of-pocket spending on rent by $211 per month, or about 40 percent (Mills et al. 2006, 139, Exhibit 5.3).

Measuring gains in housing consumption is complicated by the fact that land-lords might be aware of the rent limits in the voucher program and may artificially raise the rent of a unit to meet the tenant's new ability to pay (Mallach 2007; Collinson and Ganong 2018). With that caveat in mind, it is very clear that the market rents of the housing units in which people reside are dramatically higher for people with vouchers compared to similar people without them. For example, Jacob and Ludwig's (2012) study of housing vouchers in Chicago shows that vouchers enable recipients to live in units with rents that are about 50 percent higher than the rents for the units in which they would otherwise live (this change in unit rent is equal to 25–30 percent of average income for these households). The HUD WtW study by Mills et al. (2006) shows that vouchers also affect direct measures of housing quality, such as increased housing unit quality and size.[13] Vouchers also increase by more than 20 percentage points the rate at which recipients and their children live on their own rather than with other relatives, which may reduce crowding and enable people to get away from difficult, or even abusive, relationships. Many voucher recipients report in qualitative interviews that they value this independence for its own sake as well. Similarly, HUD's Family Options Study provided vouchers to families in emergency shelters and found reductions in the chance of homelessness (21 percentage point reduction in chance of being homeless or doubled up at least once, 17 versus 38 percent) as well as reduced crowding (Gubits et al. 2016).

Another potential goal for the voucher program is to reduce residential instability, although in the short-term vouchers may increase the number of moves as families use their new subsidy to relocate to a new unit. The WtW voucher experiment by Mills et al. (2006) found that the average control group family in their study moved roughly twice over the five-year follow-up period; voucher receipt reduced the total number of moves by about 0.9 (the treatment-on-the-treated, or TOT effect). About 53 percent of the control group had moved out of their baseline census tract in the Mills et al. study; voucher receipt increased that by 11 percentage points. In contrast, the Chicago voucher study by Jacob and Ludwig (2012) finds the average number of moves over the follow-up period was about 2.7 for the control group; the effect of moving with a voucher (TOT) was to increase the number of moves by 0.12. Vouchers may do more to reduce instability among those likely to be highly unstable. In the Family Options Study, vouchers relative to status quo for families initially living in emergency shelters reduced the number of places lived in six months from 1.6 to 1.3 (Gubits et al. 2016).

Another goal is to improve access to better neighborhoods. Jacob and Ludwig (2012) find that the average unsubsidized family who applied for a housing voucher in the late 1990s in Chicago was living in a tract with a poverty rate of 26 percent; those families randomly assigned good positions on the voucher program waitlist who moved with a voucher were in tracts with poverty rates that were just 1 percentage point lower (the "control mean" for share black was 78 percent, with a TOT effect also of about 1 percentage point). Similarly, the control group in the Mills et al. (2006) study of HUD's WtW voucher experiment were in tracts with an average poverty rate of 27 percent; the TOT effect was 2 percentage points (Exhibit 3.6).[14] As for the quality of local schools, in a reanalysis of data from HUD's WtW study, Horn, Ellen, and Schwartz (2014) find that the families randomly assigned vouchers reached neighborhoods with schools that had the same proficiency rates as the schools near to control group families.

A few studies have rigorously examined the effects on work effort from the voucher program. The study of the HUD WtW voucher experiment by Mills et al. (2006) found sizable reductions in quarterly employment rates (3 or 4 percentage points, or 6–8 percent of the control mean of 53 percent), but these were only statistically significant during the first year following random assignment. The Mills et al. study also found persistent increases in TANF receipt rate, equal to 4 percentage points during the first year (about 7 percent of the control mean of 56 percent) and equal to about 7 percentage points three years out (nearly 20 percent of the control mean). Jacob and Ludwig's (2012) study of housing vouchers in Chicago found that voucher receipt reduces quarterly employment rates by 4 percentage points (6 percent of the control mean), quarterly earnings by $330 (10 percent decline), and increased TANF receipt by 2 percentage points (15 percent). All of these effects appear to persist through 8 years after random assignment (so more persistent than in Mills et al. 2006), although updated data for this sample suggest the effects eventually do fade out after 14 years (Jacob, Kapustin, and Ludwig 2015).

We also see mixed evidence about whether the housing voucher program as it normally operates substantially improves children's outcomes. Jacob, Kapustin, and Ludwig (2015) use administrative data on a large sample of children in Chicago combined with a random lottery design and find no statistically significant effects on various measures of children's schooling outcomes, criminal involvement (as measured by arrest records), or health (as measured by Medicaid claims data). With statistically insignificant findings, a key issue always is the precision of the estimates, since null findings can often come with 95 percent confidence intervals that are so wide that they cannot rule out medium-size or even large effects. But in the Chicago voucher lottery, the estimates can rule out effects of voucher receipt on children's test scores that are any larger than about 0.06 to 0.09 standard deviations. These findings are similar to those found by the WtW experiment study by Mills et al. (2006), which relied on a smaller sample and parent reports of child outcomes.

Yet in New York City, Cordes et al. (forthcoming) find that children whose families receive vouchers perform 0.05 standard deviations better on both English language arts and mathematics tests in the years after they receive a voucher. The analysis finds significant racial differences in impacts, with small or no gains for black students but significant gains for Hispanic, Asian, and white students. Similarly, the Family Options Study suggests that families living in emergency shelters who receive vouchers may see improvements in child outcomes such as executive functioning, behavior problems, and sleeping problems (Gubits et al. 2016).

Most of the results discussed in this section implicitly answer a policy question: What happens to low-income families if we expand the scale of the voucher program and begin to subsidize families who had previously been living unsubsidized in the private housing market? A different policy question that is also relevant is, What happens if we shift the mix of housing subsidies that are provided in the form of housing vouchers at the expense of fewer units of public housing, which, as noted above, tends to concentrate poor families in high-poverty, racially segregated areas?

The best evidence we have on this question to date comes from HUD's Moving to Opportunity (MTO) demonstration, which randomly assigned public housing residents in very high-poverty neighborhoods in the early 1990s to receive either regular housing vouchers or vouchers that are constrained to be used in low-poverty neighborhoods (tracts with 1990 poverty rates below 10 percent). MTO shows that a variety of direct measures of housing quality improved as a result (Orr et al. 2003; Sanbonmatsu et al. 2011), although it should be noted that many of the baseline housing projects from which MTO families were drawn were among the most distressed in the nation and have subsequently been torn down as part of the HOPE VI program. The switch from public housing to either type of voucher (standard or location-constrained) led to changes in neighborhood conditions such as lower poverty rates, although with small effects on racial composition.

The switch to regular housing vouchers from public housing in MTO had no detectable effects on adult earnings outcomes but did have important effects on adult physical and mental health and overall self-reported well-being (Ludwig et al. 2011, 2012). We also see evidence that children benefit from moving into the voucher program from very distressed public housing projects in high-poverty neighborhoods. In the interim (five-year) MTO follow-up, relative to the control group (that did not receive help moving out of public housing), girls experienced improvements in mental health (0.19 standard deviations), declines in risky behavior (0.13 standard deviations), and a decline of about 40 percent in lifetime arrest prevalence (Kling, Ludwig, and Katz 2005; Kling, Liebman, and Katz 2007; see also Orr et al. 2003). However, voucher receipt relative to distressed public housing may have, if anything, led to worse outcomes for boys with respect to outcomes like risky behavior (by 0.21 standard deviations). We see a similar pattern, although somewhat more muted, in the long-term MTO follow-up that followed families for 10 to 15 years after the time of random assignment with respect to risky or antisocial behaviors (Sanbonmatsu et al. 2011), but sizable effects on mental health outcomes that—as of the 5-year follow-up—go in opposite directions for boys versus girls (Kessler et al. 2014).[15]

MTO also produced significant improvements in adult outcomes for young children whose families were given vouchers to move to lower-poverty neighborhoods. Chetty, Hendren, and Katz (2015) show that children who move when they are very young to a lower-poverty area experience long-term gains in earnings in adulthood. These children saw 31 percent higher earnings, amounting to an estimated lifetime gain of $302,000, relative to young children whose families were not provided a voucher.

This work suggests that reforms to low-income housing policy might focus on improving the neighborhood conditions to which children in assisted households, particularly young children, are exposed. MTO improved neighborhood conditions because it relocated public housing tenants from several of the most impoverished neighborhoods in the country and placed restrictions on the poverty levels of the neighborhoods to which families relocated. This unique context and policy difference generated large changes in neighborhood conditions. That said, voucher holders often face difficulty in finding suitable units and landlords who will accept their vouchers, especially in low-poverty neighborhoods. Audit studies have documented high levels of landlord discrimination against voucher holders, especially in low-poverty neighborhoods (Perry 2009; Phillips 2017; Cunningham et al. 2018). The latest national study of voucher success rates showed that only three out of every ten households that received a voucher in 2000 failed to rent a unit through the program. In tight markets, the failure rate was four in ten (Finkel and Buron 2001).

In short, while we have learned a lot about housing programs, there is much we still need to know. We know that households receiving housing subsidies enjoy lower rents and rent burdens and are at lower risk of homelessness. Some quasi-experimental research suggests that children see improved educational and later job market outcomes from living in subsidized housing as well. But the research on impacts on nonhousing outcomes is decidedly mixed, and we have virtually no information about the impacts of the LIHTC, which is now the largest source of support for subsidized housing construction. That said, research has offered important insights into some of the shortcomings of housing programs and suggests ample opportunities for reform.

Existing Proposals to Expand and Reform Federal Housing Assistance

Several 2020 presidential candidates have offered proposals to substantially expand housing assistance (Hartley et al. 2019). Two of the most detailed proposals call for creating a renter tax credit that would provide assistance to a broad swath of renters: the HOME Act proposed by Senator Cory Booker and the Rent Relief Act proposed by Senator Kamala Harris. Each of the proposals contains elements that we think would be good use of public funds, as well as features that raise some concerns.

Eligibility

Eligibility for these plans is limited to renters, which we think is wise. Renters are much more likely to be in poverty, have fewer assets, and spend a greater fraction of their income on housing. But the proposals are poorly targeted within the renter population and would provide assistance to high-income renters. The HOME Act includes no income-eligibility restrictions at all, while the Rent Relief Act has very high income ceilings ($100,000).[16] We are in favor of tighter income restrictions to ensure that scarce resources are devoted to those who need it most. Without such eligibility criteria, these proposals would direct considerable resources to relatively high-income households. For example, a single individual earning $70,000 a year renting in the highest fair market rent (FMR) zip codes in the Washington, D.C., metro would likely receive more than $5,000 in assistance annually under the HOME Act plan. Using existing low-income housing eligibility guidelines, which adjust for household size and local costs, would be a simple improvement.

Benefit amount

The proposed HOME and Rent Relief Acts define the benefit amount as the difference between HUD's FMR and 30 percent of a tenant's income, but the HOME Act proposes to use the Small Area FMR (SAFMR). As we detail below, we think that low-income housing policy should both enable and encourage families with young children to live in higher-opportunity neighborhoods, so we prefer the use of SAFMRs to set benefit levels. However, without narrower income eligibility restrictions, using SAFMRs would likely direct more generous subsidies to less needy households. Therefore, we prefer a benefit calculation using SAFMRs paired with tighter income eligibility.

While we prefer SAFMRs for families with children, the policy rationale for using SAFMRs for single adults or households without children is less compelling. Neighborhoods have less transformative effects on adults. Therefore, we favor using conventional metro-area FMR values for households without children.

The HOME Act and Rent Relief Act use actual housing expenditures to calculate benefit amounts, but such a structure can potentially encourage overconsumption of housing. We are concerned about the spillover effects on rental prices of such a large-scale expansion of subsidy. As discussed below, setting the benefit level at expected rents will encourage households to economize on rent and not accept overpriced rentals. It would also simplify administration of the credit.

The advantage of this general approach is that it embeds a gradual phasing out of assistance. As incomes rise, the value of assistance falls, so that households with the highest incomes derive no benefit from receipt of assistance. This may discourage work, as we discuss below, but avoids sharp eligibility cliffs likely to distort behavior.

Finally, the HOME Act, as well as Senator Elizabeth Warren's housing platform, include provisions to incentivize states and local communities to develop new inclusive zoning policies, programs, or regulatory initiatives to create more affordable housing supply. President Obama also proposed $300 million for such incentive grants in his FY 2016 budget, though they were not included in the final budget (Furman 2015). We strongly endorse policies and incentives that allow housing supply to be more responsive to increases in demand and help to ensure that substantial expansions of housing assistance principally benefit tenants. But such incentives will be far less effective if they require land use reforms for funding sources that higher-income, exclusionary communities rarely use (like Community Development Block Grants).

Housing Challenges and Reforms

We build on the proposals discussed above to make our recommendations for reform. We prioritize reforms that address three key housing policy challenges: divergent housing market needs, the limited share of low-income households receiving assistance and the distortions current subsidies may create, and the concentration of assisted households in low-income neighborhoods.

Divergent housing market needs

Varying market conditions. Over the past 50 years or so, low- and moderate-income households have seen their rents rise more rapidly than their incomes. The result has been increasing rent burdens. Figure 3 divides renters into five groups, depending on where they fall in the overall distribution of incomes in the United States, and shows that rent burdens for households in each of the income quintiles rose between 2000 and 2015. The figure makes clear how much higher rent burdens are for the lowest-income renters. In 2015, more than 80 percent of renters in the bottom income quintile paid more than 30 percent of their income on rent, up from 72 percent in 2000. Indeed, 54 percent of renters in the bottom income quintile paid more than *half* of their income on rent in 2015 (not shown on figure), up from 45 percent in 2000. But while affordability problems are most serious for the lowest-income renters, affordability challenges have climbed up the income ladder in recent years. Between 2000 and 2015, the share of moderate-income renters (those with incomes in the second lowest quintile) paying more than 30 percent of their income for rent jumped from 26 to 43 percent. Among middle-quintile households, the rent-burdened share rose from 7 to 17 percent. In short, renters across the board are paying more of their incomes on rent now than they were in earlier decades, and for those with below-median income, this translates into less money left over for other goods.

Notably, every large metropolitan area in the United States has seen an increase in rent burdens over the past few decades as incomes have stagnated and rents have risen (Ellen and Lubell 2019). But the underlying drivers of this

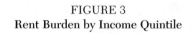

FIGURE 3
Rent Burden by Income Quintile

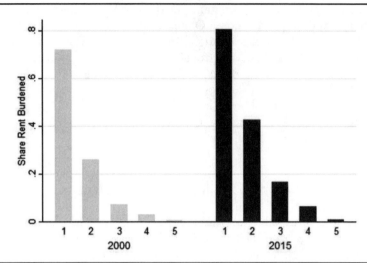

SOURCE: Authors' calculations using data are from Integrated Public Use Microdata Series (IPUMS) American Community Survey (ACS) 2000, 2015 (Ruggles et al. 2019).
NOTE: The figure displays the fraction rent burdened by income quintile for renters in 2000 and 2015.

affordability crisis have differed in different places. Figure 4 shows the change between 1980 and 2018 in rents and median renter incomes for each of the four census regions of the country. Although the regions are internally heterogeneous, we still see significant differences among them. Rents and incomes have risen most dramatically in the Northeast and West, but rent growth has significantly outpaced renter income growth since 2000. In the Midwest and South, by contrast, rents and incomes have grown significantly less quickly over this period, and income growth has not substantially lagged rent growth.

Looking at vacancy rates, we also see substantial variation across regions. In 2018, the housing vacancy rate in the West region was just 5.1 percent, while it hovered at 7.6 and 8.7 percent in the Midwest region (U.S. Census Bureau 2018). An examination of specific metropolitan areas shows even sharper contrasts. Among metropolitan areas above one million people in 2015, the rental vacancy rate varied from 2.4 percent in San Francisco to 9.6 percent in Las Vegas (NYU Furman Center 2017).

The simple story is that the rising rent burdens in coastal cities have resulted more from rent growth due to growing demand and limited land and supply restrictions, while in the heartland, the challenge has been more about falling incomes and rents failing to fall to match that decline. A single federal policy or program is likely to be ill-suited to address this broad range of market conditions. Efforts to expand the supply of housing affordable to low-income households may be critical in parts of the country experiencing growth in population and

FIGURE 4
Changes in Income and Rent (indexed to 100 for 1983)

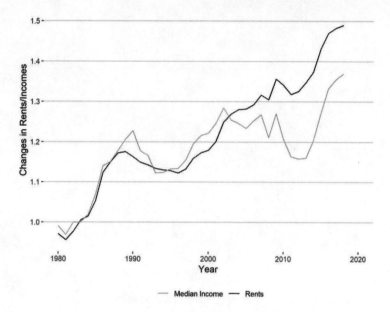

Northeast: Changes in Income & Rents (Base=1983)

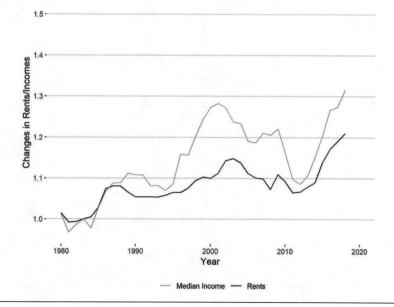

Midwest: Changes in Income & Rents (Base=1983)

FIGURE 4 (continued)

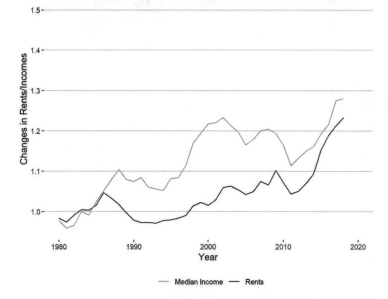

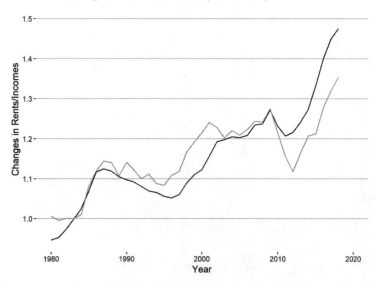

SOURCES: Rent Series: Consumer Price Index, Residential Rent index and Less-Shelter Index. Bureau of Labor Statistics. https://www.bls.gov/cpi/data.htm Income Series: Authors' calculation: Data are from Integrated Public Use Microdata Series (IPUMS) Current Population Survey (CPS) 1980–2017 (Flood et al. 2018).

incomes, while demand-side strategies are more appropriate in declining areas with high vacancy rates. Similarly, it may be appropriate to adjust the rent formula across local economies, depending on the local joblessness rate (Austin, Glaeser, and Summers 2018). In areas in the eastern heartland with extraordinarily high rates of joblessness, it may make sense to reduce the implicit tax on earnings embedded in most housing assistance programs to encourage more work.

Targeting assistance to meet market needs. While the United States is characterized by very heterogeneous market conditions, our current housing policies do little to account for this diversity. The most egregious example of this is the LIHTC, which supports the construction and rehabilitation of low-rent housing and provides the same per capita supply-side subsidy in supply-constrained states like Massachusetts, where the rental vacancy rate was 2.4 percent in the first quarter of 2019, as it does in high-vacancy states like Alabama, where the rental vacancy rate was 15.8 percent during the same quarter.[17] In many parts of the country, the LIHTC simply subsidizes the construction of market-rate rental housing (Green 2011).

Some economists have called for the wholesale elimination of the LIHTC and replacing it with more funding for demand-side subsidies (Olsen 2016). To be sure, the LIHTC is inefficient and poorly targeted. But in coastal, supply-constrained parts of the country, simply providing additional demand-side subsidies could fuel demand and put upward pressure on rents (Susin 2002). This is especially concerning in a world in which only one in four income-eligible households actually receives a federal housing subsidy. Further, the LIHTC can help to break through community resistance to new housing in supply-constrained areas, where residents appear to be more open to new subsidized and mixed-income rental housing in their backyard than new market rate housing (Hankinson 2018). Even in a first-best world in which housing regulations are relaxed in supply-constrained places, the availability of land is limited, and it takes decades for new housing to filter down to levels affordable for low-income households. Further, as noted above, voucher holders face a difficult time finding affordable units and landlords who will accept their vouchers, especially in tight markets.

It is worth reiterating that we strongly endorse efforts to reform restrictive land use regulations that make building difficult and add to the price of housing in coastal regions of the country. But these land use regulations are controlled by state and local governments, and the federal government has few politically viable tools to reform them. As noted above, policy-makers could condition grants on land use reforms, but they should make reforms conditional on funds that higher-income communities value.

One natural reform is to afford states and localities more flexibility to tailor the housing assistance they provide to their individual market needs. Most notably, Congress might transform the LIHTC into a stream of flexible funds that states and localities could use for either supply-side or demand-side subsidies. The LIHTC currently costs the federal government about $9 billion per year, which could support over a million additional housing choice vouchers. Given the popularity of place-based assistance among developers and politicians, it is possible that state and local governments would still favor place-based assistance even in slack markets. The federal government might restrict the use of the LIHTC in high-vacancy markets, limiting it to moderate rehabilitation projects only or developments in high-opportunity areas. An arguably even better (though more politically challenging) approach might be for the federal government to allocate vouchers to metropolitan areas with rental vacancy rates above some threshold and allow for flexibility only in tighter markets.

There would clearly be political challenges to changing the tax credit to an on-budget expense. But there is at least some precedent to allowing such a conversion: during the housing crash, the market for tax credits all but disappeared as financial institutions found themselves without taxable income to offset. The American Recovery and Reinvestment Act of 2009 authorized the Tax Credit Exchange Program (TCEP) to allow state housing finance agencies to exchange unused or returned 9 percent credits from 2007 through 2009 for a grant from the U.S. Treasury. A similar mechanism could be used going forward to allow states and localities to convert LIHTCs into more flexible funds. An alternative would be to allow states to sell their tax credits to other states. Given that demand for tax credits tends to be higher in high-growth areas, such a market would tend to move supply subsidies to higher-growth areas.

Subsidy availability, structure, and generosity

Scarcity, inequity, and targeting. Housing assistance is unique among the major forms of means-tested transfers in the United States in the high degree of rationing. Unlike other in-kind transfers, such as food stamps, housing assistance is not an entitlement. Only about one-in-four eligible households receives some type of housing assistance. But housing is expensive, and those who are lucky enough to get a housing voucher receive an average of more than $8,000 per year. This is comparatively generous relative to other social programs in the United States. Consequently, the existing system of housing assistance provides a small number of households sizable transfers, while many receive nothing at all.

The rationale for providing a large amount of assistance to a small number of households is not clear. Some advocates argue that landlords in many markets would resist renting to poor households with shallow subsidies, viewing them as too risky. A different argument is that housing is lumpy and made lumpier by local housing and building codes. As a result, shallower subsidies could still leave poor families paying unsustainable shares of their rents or living in poor housing. But most economists believe in declining marginal utility of income, which implies potential utility gains from spreading less generous assistance across more eligible households.

Certainly, the existing system of assistance is inequitable: using the American Housing Survey and Survey of Income and Program Participation, we calculate a Gini Index for housing assistance of 0.41, compared to 0.29 for the Supplemental Nutrition Assistance Program (SNAP). This suggests a fundamental unfairness of the existing system; however, if the households that receive assistance are substantially needier than other eligible households, it could, in principle, be justifiable. Therefore, the targeting of assistance among eligible households is of first order importance to understanding the benefits of reforms to the existing system of housing assistance.

It remains unclear how current rationing practices affect the targeting of assistance. Since demand for housing assistance vastly outstrips the supply of housing assistance, most assistance is allocated to households from lengthy local waitlists. Available data suggest that as many as 6.5 million households are on a waitlist for either public housing or housing vouchers at any given time (Collinson, Ellen, and Ludwig 2016). And in many areas these waitlists are closed (that is, not open to receiving additional applications). Local housing authorities select applicants using a variety of mechanisms, such as first-come first-served, random lottery, or special preferences. How these mechanisms affect the characteristics of who receives scarce housing subsidies is unknown. In some economic models, waiting times can act as a price that allocates housing units to those who want it most (Leshno 2017). In practice, waiting tolerance might be only weakly correlated with need for housing assistance. For example, households that apply for assistance, but are unable to secure a stable address while they wait for housing, may be particularly difficult to locate or contact when they finally arrive near the top of the waitlist. Moreover, waiting could also deter those with the most immediate need for housing from applying for assistance altogether. In practice, we do not have much empirical evidence on how waiting for assistance affects who receives assistance. Finally, while young children could arguably benefit the most from assistance, long waitlists mean that families with children are unlikely to receive assistance until their children are older.

Reducing inequity and increasing the responsiveness of assistance. As documented above, the current system of housing assistance is extremely inequitable, and thus an important question is whether low-income families would be better served by a program that provides time-limited or more modest subsidies to a larger share of income-eligible households (see, for example, Olsen 2016).

One potential argument for such a switch is the standard idea of diminishing marginal utility; that is, the benefits to recipients and society as a whole from the marginal subsidy dollar may be declining as the size of the housing subsidy increases. It seems implausible that the benefits of housing subsidy are strictly convex in the subsidy amount. However, nearly all housing markets exhibit a minimum price to rental housing that raises the possibility that smaller, more widely available subsidies may be insufficient to lift households out of homelessness and allow them to find stable housing. Whether shallower subsidies would hinder other objectives of housing assistance, such as deconcentrating poverty, is unclear. Understanding more about this question is critical given that, as noted above, our current system of federal means-tested subsidy programs reaches such a small share of eligible households.

A different justification for smaller or time-limited subsidies is that while the current system of providing large, long-term subsidies might help to address the problem of low levels of permanent income, it does little to help poor families with a different and perhaps equally important problem: income volatility (see, for example, Moffitt and Zhang 2018; Morduch and Schneider 2017). Because income "shocks" are by definition transitory, the ideal solution would involve rapid delivery of a temporary housing subsidy at the right time. There is some evidence that short-term rental assistance, such as emergency cash grants to households at risk of losing their apartment, is effective at preventing homelessness (Evans, Sullivan, and Wallskog 2016). Whether a widespread system of housing subsidies that targets more immediate needs, such as evictions or job loss, could be more effective than existing programs at reducing housing instability is still largely untested, but it holds promise. Unfortunately, the current system, which produces long waits, is not very helpful to families who, for example, experience income shock due to job loss, divorce, or a health problem and need short-term help right away. Compared to a system that provides a larger share of households with either smaller or more time-limited subsidies, the current system may inadvertently contribute to relatively more evictions and spells of homelessness.

Whether smaller, more widely available subsidies are an improvement relative to the existing system depends on the effectiveness of these subsidies relative to larger subsidies as well as the targeting efficiency of these programs. If housing authorities or other program administrators can effectively predict which households would have the most costly counterfactual outcomes, if left unassisted, then focusing narrowly targeted assistance to these households could be justifiable. Of course, this presumes that not all income-eligible low-income households are equally in need of housing assistance. This assumption seems defensible given that there are 7.5 million unassisted households earning less than 30 percent AMI, compared to about 1.4 million adults and children in homeless shelters each year. However, if housing program administrators have few methods to credibly distinguish which low-income households are in greatest need of assistance, then smaller, more broad-based subsidies may be sensible.

At the very least, we see a need for more experimentation with shallower subsidies that can test whether they are sufficient to lift households out of homelessness and allow them to find stable housing in a diverse set of neighborhoods, even in tight markets.

Housing programs versus using the tax code. A different question that is somewhat related to that of whether to provide fewer, larger subsidies or more, less costly subsidies is the programmatic vehicle for delivering subsidies: through housing programs like vouchers, or instead through the tax code. A number of proposals made leading up to the 2020 presidential election suggest providing tax credits to low-income renters for the portion of their rents that exceed 30 percent of gross income (see Hartley et al. [2019] for details). Once we open up the possibility of using the tax code, which, unlike existing housing programs, would be available to all eligible households, we can in principle modify the subsidy (tax credit) amount to provide as deep or shallow a subsidy as society would like. One potential advantage of relying on the tax code rather than housing vouchers is to increase the willingness of landlords to rent units to subsidized households since the subsidy would be invisible to the landlord. This is not an inconsequential benefit, given the apparent unwillingness of many landlords in audit studies to rent units to families that are receiving housing vouchers (Perry 2009; Moore 2018; Phillips 2017; Cunningham et al. 2018).

The potential downside of relying on the tax code rather than voucher programs stems from the loss of the inspections required by the voucher program, which may generate some social value to low-income households. Another potential downside is that liquidity-constrained low-income families may prefer voucher subsidies that are distributed over the course of the year rather than tax credits. Little is known about the relative merits of these different issues, but this would be an important question to learn more about in the future. Finally, some of the proposals are not means-tested and would provide subsidies to high-income households choosing to live in high-rent neighborhoods.

Expanding housing assistance. The recent tax proposals analyzed by Hartley and colleagues (2019) entail dramatic expansions of housing assistance, which would substantially cut poverty. Housing is expensive, and renters are relatively poor, so transferring resources to renters to pay for housing reduces material poverty significantly. Hartley et al. estimate that these proposals would reduce poverty (as measured by the Supplemental Poverty Measure) by 2.5 to 3 percentage points. These proposals, which would make housing assistance an entitlement for renters below a certain income threshold, also carry sizable budgetary costs of $90 to $135 billion, annually.

A key concern with sweeping expansions of assistance is that landlords will raise rents in response to the policy change. The textbook public economic result is that the incidence of a tax or subsidy will depend crucially on the elasticities of supply and demand for the taxed/subsidized good. If supply is less than perfectly elastic, and demand is at all elastic, then a demand-side (tenant) subsidy will be passed through in part to the supply side (landlords) through increases in equilibrium prices. Recent research has found that landlords capture some of the incidence of existing housing voucher subsidies through rent increases (Collinson and Ganong 2018; Eriksen and Ross 2012; Susin 2002). These concerns are magnified considerably with a housing subsidy that is universal, since the magnitude of the demand response is likely to be much larger than existing programs.

Understanding the spillover effects of a major expansion of housing subsidies on rental prices is critical to evaluating these proposals. However, convincingly estimating these effects is quite difficult. In the 1970s, HUD ran an ambitious research demonstration that attempted to evaluate the market-level effects of a significant expansion in tenant-based housing subsidies. The Housing Assistance Supply Experiment was motivated precisely by the concern that landlords would capture the benefits of the subsidy expansion through increased rents (Lowry 1982).

The ideal experiment would randomly saturate some housing markets with housing subsidies while leaving others unchanged, but this would be extremely costly by the standards of social experiments.[18] Instead, HUD selected two small metropolitan housing markets—Brown County, Wisconsin (Green Bay) and St. Joseph County, Indiana (South Bend)—with differing market conditions and rapidly rolled out large, new housing assistance programs in each. Both communities were surveyed extensively before and after implementation and compared to regional trends.

The Housing Assistance Supply Experiment produced a number of notable findings, but the headline result was that the introduction of a large new housing assistance program did *not* produce large increases in rents or housing prices. There were two major reasons for this: (1) the program did not produce a particularly large increase in housing demand, and (2) the housing stock proved to be fairly responsive in accommodating growing demand. The increase in housing demand from the program was only modest, as only about one-third of eligible households took up assistance, and many recipients of assistance were inframarginal, using the subsidy to reduce their rent burdens rather than increase housing consumption (Rydell 1982).[19] The housing markets in Green Bay and South Bend were also able to accommodate increased demand through upgrading vacant units and, over time, new construction.

There are a number of design features of the housing assistance certificate, which may have further contributed to the small effects on prices. First, the size of the housing assistance payment did not depend on the actual rent of the unit; rather, it was the difference between a predetermined prevailing market rent (similar to an FMR) and 25 percent of the household's income. Other than a unit meeting a minimum quality standard, there was no minimum (or maximum) rent, so recipients remained price sensitive as they bore the cost of the marginal dollar in housing expenses. This meant that there were strong incentives for recipients to negotiate FMRs. Second, unlike the current housing voucher program, assistance payments were made to tenants rather than directly to landlords. If landlords price discriminate against subsidized renters, as in Collinson and Ganong (2018), then making subsidies "invisible" to landlords could limit their ability to raise rents. Third, assistance was made available to all income-eligible households regardless of whether they were homeowners or renters. This meant that renters could look to purchase housing, thus expanding the pool of eligible housing.

How these results from two relatively soft markets during the 1970s generalize to today's housing market and recent proposals to expand housing assistance is unclear. We would expect landlords in the most supply-constrained markets to be most successful at capturing the incidence of a subsidy expansion. The tighter housing market setting in the Housing Assistance Supply Experiment—Green Bay—is probably not comparable to the most supply constrained, high-demand metros today. The recent proposals considered above call for refundable tax credits available to all renters below a given income threshold paying more than 30 percent of income toward rents. These credits would be expected to have higher take-up, and hence larger impacts on housing demand, than the housing assistance in the Housing Assistance Supply Experiment, which required housing inspections and greater administrative hurdles.

We prefer setting subsidy amounts at the difference between a predetermined subsidy ceiling and 30 percent of income regardless of the actual rent amount. Currently, the Housing Assistance Payment (HAP) for a family with a voucher is equal to the lesser of the gross rent minus 30 percent of the tenant's income, or the payment standard (PS) minus 30 percent of the tenant's income:[20]

$$\begin{array}{c} \textit{Housing Assistance} \\ \textit{Payment } (HAP) \end{array} = \min \left(\begin{array}{l} \textit{Gross Rent} - 30\% \times \textit{Income,} \\ PS - 30\% \times \textit{Income} \end{array} \right)$$

We would simplify this to just the PS minus 30 percent of the tenant's income ($HAP = PS - 30\% \times \textit{Income}$), regardless of the actual rent of the unit. This would allow households that rent for less than the typical rent to keep any residual subsidy. This would minimize the effects of housing assistance expansions on market rents. Further, this policy would encourage tenants to economize on housing and find landlords offering a fair rent. It would also simplify administration by not requiring verification of annual rent amounts.

We acknowledge that setting benefit amounts based on expected rent expenditure rather than actual expenditures could be criticized that it less directly targets "rent burdens."

This highlights a tension in program design: program features designed to encourage households to economize on their housing spending will buffer the demand response and reduce the risk of landlords raising rents, but they will also undermine the motivation for using in-kind transfers rather than cash. A common economic motivation for using in-kind transfers rather than a cash transfer is to encourage households to spend relatively more on the transferred good than they otherwise would with a simple cash transfer. As we discuss below, structuring the subsidy schedule using small-area FMRs in the neighborhood in which the tenant resides would still preserve incentives to locate in higher-opportunity neighborhoods, an important policy objective.

Mitigating work disincentives. A final issue that is also related to subsidy amounts and structures has to do with efforts to mitigate potential work disincentive effects of housing subsidy programs. Since families in existing housing programs like housing vouchers or public housing pay rents that are a fixed share of their adjusted income (unlike unsubsidized households where rent is rent, and does not change as income changes), the result is to increase the effective marginal tax rate on earnings. Jacob and Ludwig (2012), for instance, find that compared to unsubsidized households containing able-bodied working-age heads, those receiving a housing voucher have labor force participation rates that are 6 percent lower and earnings that are 10 percent lower. By contrast, Mills et al. (2006) report that while voucher holders in a larger set of cities initially saw reduced earnings, this effect disappeared after the first year in the program. But the standard errors grow over time, so their estimates in out years are imprecise.

As part of HUD's Moving to Work (MtW) demonstration program, local housing authorities are being given the chance to experiment with different modifications to these rent rules, including the following:

- Counting income in "tiers" instead of as a continuous income measure, so that rent does not change as income changes within a tier, but then would take a bigger jump once income changes enough to put the family into a higher income tier. Whether creating more "lumpy" measures of income like this (such as tiers) for purposes of calculating rent requirements will reduce work disincentives depends in part on the degree to which program participants are forward-looking and understand the structure of the rent payment schedule.

- Raising rents at a constant rate per year (3 percent or 5 percent of FMR) regardless of what happens to a family's income. The effect of this change on labor supply would not necessarily be expected to be the opposite of what is found by Jacob and Ludwig (2012) because families would still experience a large income effect that under standard economic theory would reduce work effort. Also unknown is the extra hardship this might impose on families whose incomes do not increase year to year, as well as how, in practice, housing authorities do or do not choose to grant hardship exemptions to the rent increases.
- Work requirements, where the effects of these on work effort would depend in part on local labor market conditions combined with the specific choices local housing authorities make in enforcing them and what they count as work.

Put differently, the net effects of these proposed changes on work are unclear as a conceptual matter. HUD has several large-scale randomized control studies out in the field right now that will provide useful evidence on the relative merits of these different candidate policy changes.

Neighborhood access

Poor locational outcomes for assisted households. The Housing Act of 1949 espoused the goal of "a decent home and a suitable living environment" for all Americans. Yet our subsidized housing programs have historically fallen short in delivering on this goal. By 1990, more than a third of public housing tenants lived in census tracts with poverty rates above 40 percent, as compared to just 12 percent of other low-income households (Newman and Schnare 1997). In more recent years, place-based subsidized housing has been built in a somewhat more diverse but still disadvantaged set of neighborhoods. For example, LIHTC units are typically built in neighborhoods with lower levels of poverty compared to public housing but higher levels of poverty compared to the average rental unit (see Rohe and Freeman 2001; Freeman 2005; McClure 2008; Ellen, O'Regan, and Voicu 2009; McClure and Johnson 2015). More recent evidence suggests that households in place-based, assisted housing live in neighborhoods with public elementary schools that are ranked well below the median within their state (Ellen and Horn 2018).

Perhaps most surprising, despite that one of the original motivations for establishing the voucher program was its potential to help low-income families reach neighborhoods that offer better schools and greater opportunities for economic advancement, voucher holders generally live in very disadvantaged neighborhoods. Research shows that on average, voucher holders live in less disadvantaged neighborhoods than the residents of public or other HUD-assisted housing (Devine et al. 2003; Hartung and Henig 1997; Pendall 2000), but only in slightly less disadvantaged neighborhoods than the average poor household (Galvez 2010; Pendall 2000; Wood, Turnham, and Mills 2008). More recent data suggest little change: only about one in five voucher households lived in low-poverty neighborhoods in 2010, down slightly from 2000 (McClure, Schwartz, and Taghavi 2015). Families with vouchers continue to live near schools that are lower performing than those close to other poor families (Ellen and Horn 2018). As discussed above, experimental studies suggest that receipt of a voucher leads to only small improvements in neighborhood quality (Eriksen and Ross 2012; Jacob and Ludwig 2012; Mills et al. 2006).

Improving neighborhood access for families with children. Most vouchers are given to tenants in private rental housing and the neighborhoods where they use their vouchers are observably similar to those where they were previously living. A series of reforms could make housing vouchers more successful at capturing the types of improvements in child outcomes found in MTO.

Previous work has documented that neighborhood effects function in part through the duration of exposure, with benefits eroding as children approach adulthood (Chetty, Hendren, and Katz 2015; Chetty and Hendren 2018). An implication of this is that young children can realize the largest gains from relocating to less impoverished, higher-opportunity neighborhoods. Currently the voucher program is poorly suited to capture these benefits; most families that receive assistance do so after several years on a waitlist, so their children often spend their most formative years in more impoverished neighborhoods waiting for the possibility of relocating with housing assistance. Housing assistance for families could target housing vouchers to families with very young children, who not only may benefit more from assistance but also may be more likely to move to higher-opportunity neighborhoods because their children have not yet developed strong ties to their existing community and school (Ellen, Horn, and Schwartz 2016). This could be operationalized as a general preference or limited preference applied by housing authorities in drawing from their waitlist. General preference would move households with qualifying children to the top of the waitlist immediately upon application, while a limited preference would set aside some vouchers specifically for families with young children. Both policies have the potential to distort fertility or household composition, but if housing assistance continues to be heavily rationed—even within preference groups—then the effects may be small.

A recent approach to improving the locational outcomes for voucher holders is to allow the voucher to pay more in higher-rent neighborhoods and reduce its value in low-rent neighborhoods by setting SAFMR. This policy appears to be a cost-effective approach to moving families to better neighborhoods in Dallas, Texas (Collinson and Ganong 2018), and more recently in five other demonstration communities (Finkel et al. 2017). This policy is currently being expanded to over twenty metropolitan areas, but it could be rolled out nationwide.

There are several policies that could complement an expansion of SAFMRs. The first is to include source of income as a protected class under federal law. Currently, discrimination on the basis of race, ethnicity, religion, national origin, sex, disability, and familial status is illegal in the United States. However, there are no federal protections for households on the basis of how they pay their rent.

Even with greater legal protections for voucher tenants, it is possible that landlords, frustrated by the administrative burden of the voucher program, may screen out tenants using other means. Therefore, policy should also seek to ease administrative burdens associated with the voucher program, which could improve landlord participation and ultimately tenant locational choices. These include allowing for less frequent, risk-based inspections of voucher units, permitting housing authorities to fund vacancy losses and paying out damage claims from landlords. HUD could create a fund to insure landlords against missed payments from tenants or late payment from local housing authorities.

Another important reform is to expand mobility counseling and housing search assistance to help families successfully move to lower-poverty areas. MTO participants who were restricted to leasing up in low-poverty census tracts were about 10 to 14 percentage points less likely to successfully use their voucher, even with housing search assistance (Galiani, Murphy, and Pantano 2015; Shroder 2002). Historically, HUD has only sporadically funded housing counseling, leading to a great range in availability and quality of counseling services available to tenants (Cunningham et al. 2010). To prioritize improving the neighborhood environments for children in assisted households, HUD could fund housing mobility counseling for all voucher households with a child under the age of 12 living in neighborhoods with poverty rates exceeding 20 percent. The average cost of mobility counseling for a household that successfully leased up in MTO was roughly $3,800 (Goering et al. 1999), which is less than the tax revenue generated by increases in the future earnings of children in the typical MTO family (Chetty, Hendren, and Katz 2015). The 2019 funding bill for HUD included $28 million for a new housing choice voucher mobility demonstration to help families with children access neighborhoods that offer them a richer set of opportunities.

It may be difficult for the federal government to guess what policy or administrative changes would be most effective at moving voucher holders to neighborhoods with greater opportunities. For this reason, it could be more effective to aggressively incentivize public housing authorities to achieve desired locational outcomes for their tenants. Currently, housing authority performance is graded on fourteen indicators, ranging from accurate income verification and rent reasonableness determinations to tenant selection processes. Only one indicator concerns the locational outcomes of voucher tenants. The corresponding performance metric for deconcentrating voucher households does not affect the funding levels of the housing authority. This means that housing authorities have only weak incentives to place tenants in high-opportunity neighborhoods. One way to change this would be to tie the administrative fees paid to public housing authority to their performance on a robust set of indicators of voucher location quality. This would create a pay-for-performance approach for local housing authorities to improve the locational outcomes of their tenants.

Finally, voucher tenants may lack information about the availability of affordable rental units in low-poverty communities. While the federal government likely could not legally host its own apartment listing service, it could increase technical assistance funding for local housing authorities to partner with real estate listing providers to ensure that tenants have better information about the full set of available units.

Conclusion

To be sure, federal housing programs currently assist a lot of people and help them to remain stably housed. But as we have described, they also fall short of their promises, and it is useful to consider ways to improve them so they can provide assistance that is better tailored to local needs, serve more households at the time when they most need assistance, and help more young children to reach neighborhoods where they can thrive.

To better tailor housing assistance to local market conditions, we recommend that the federal government prioritize tenant-based assistance and renovation subsidies in metropolitan areas with high rental vacancy rates and allow for more flexibility to subsidize *new* place-based subsidized housing in tight markets with rental vacancy rates below some threshold level. To help more voucher families with children reach high-opportunity neighborhoods, we recommend that Congress add source of income as a protected class under federal law, provide additional support for mobility counseling and housing search assistance, and offer funding to local housing agencies to partner with real estate listing providers. In addition, even without congressional action, HUD could mandate broader adoption of SAFMR, reduce administrative burdens of the voucher program to encourage more landlords to participate, and incentivize local housing agencies to improve the locational outcomes of the voucher families with children whom they serve.

As for subsidy generosity and targeting, we call for more experimentation with shallower subsidies that can test whether they are sufficient to lift households out of homelessness and allow them to find stable housing in a diverse set of neighborhoods, even in tight markets. If the political environment allows more households to be awarded deep rent subsidies, we recommend moving to a subsidy structure in which renters can pocket the difference between the maximum subsidy and some share of their income to limit impacts on market rents. Assuming that politics continue to limit the number of low-income households who are served, we call for greater attention to targeting. The political hurdles are significant, but we hope advocates and policy-makers will continue to explore ways to stretch these dollars further and use them to provide the greatest benefit.

Notes

1. The amount of tax credits available for a project increases with the share of units that charge affordable rents.

2. For a list of these states and localities and a description of the laws, see Poverty and Race Research Action Council 2005, updated 2014.

3. The Section 202 program provides capital subsidies for developments that serve low-income seniors.

4. For more thorough discussions of the literature on each of these points, see Collinson, Ellen, and Ludwig (2016)

5. Hunt (2009) provides an excellent account for the City of Chicago. More generally, for a public housing project to be built in a political jurisdiction, it must establish a public housing authority (PHA). Many jurisdictions chose not to create one. Furthermore, because the PHA had to obtain the local government's cooperation, the local government had veto power over the location of the projects.

6. Fully 36 percent of public housing tenants lived in census tracts with poverty rates over 40 percent, versus just 12 percent of other low-income households. In addition, 38 percent of public housing residents were in census tracts with minority shares over 80 percent, compared to 18 percent of other low-income households.

7. The data used by Currie and Yelowitz (2000) do not allow them to apply their natural-experiment (IV) research design to measures of residential mobility. However, they do present some ordinary least squares (OLS) results that show that residence in public housing is correlated with a higher rate of changing schools by children in public housing families relative to their non–public housing counterparts. (We recognize that changing schools mixes together the effects of residential moves with other reasons why children might change schools over time.) In any case, Currie and Yelowitz argue that OLS results are likely to be biased in the direction of overstating any negative effects of public housing, so, as the authors note, it is not clear what to make of that correlation.

8. The sample mean for the census overcrowding measure they use in their paper is about 1 percent for whites and 10 percent for blacks (Currie and Yelowitz 2000, Table 6), but these sample means are not quite the right benchmark for judging the size of the public housing effects, since the relevant mean would be the one for the set of families who would have been in public housing had the gender mix of children in the home been different (or in the language of Angrist, Imbens, and Rubin [1996], the "compliers").

9. For example, Jacob and Lefgren (2009) find that in the Chicago Public School system in the early 1990s, retention rates for students in grades 3, 6, and 8 were on the order of 1 or 2 percent. In 1996–97, CPS enacted a policy to end "social promotion" and tie promotion to performance on a standardized achievement test. The performance standard was set to equal about the 15th to 20th percentile of the national achievement distribution, with about 30 to 40 percent of students failing to meet the standard after the policy and about 10 to 20 percent each year retained in grade. A different observational study, Newman and Harkness (2002), use data from the 1997 National Survey of America's Families to estimate that children who lived in public housing for more years between 1968 and 1982 had somewhat higher employment rates and labor earnings as young adults.

10. Baum-Snow and Marion (2009) find more crowd out of new LIHTC units (that is, LIHTC units displace some private-market housing that would have been built anyway) in gentrifying areas. Malpezzi and Vandell (2002) do not find a detectable effect of the LIHTC on the supply of rental housing, but their research design is not nearly as convincing as that of Baum-Snow and Marion.

11. It is possible that some, or perhaps even many, families have unreported income (see, for example, Edin and Lein 1997). Because the same income denominator is used to calculate the share of spending on housing for families both with and without vouchers, this means the Jacob and Ludwig (2012) study should still be getting the sign of the effect of vouchers on housing affordability correct. But because the denominator will be too small under both the voucher and no-voucher conditions, the "levels" (share of income spent on housing) will be too low in both cases, and the percentage point change in share of income spent on housing will be too large.

12. Exhibit 4.16 of Mills et al. (2006) reports monthly TANF cash benefits during the first period after random assignment of $1,325 for the control group, while Exhibit 4.10 reports quarterly earnings of $1,863, or about $621 per month.

13. For example, the share of families in the control group that live in crowded housing conditions (more than one person per bedroom) at the time of their follow-up survey is about 39 percent, while the effect of voucher use (the treatment on the treated effect) is minus 22 percentage points ($p < .05$); see Table 5.3 of Mills et al. (2006, 139). Similarly, the share of control group families reporting two or more housing problems is 13.5 percent, and the TOT is again about one-half that (minus 7 percentage points), although it is not quite significant.

14. Carlson et al. (2012) use a propensity-score matching design and find that housing voucher recipients are not living in significantly different neighborhoods from nonrecipients in the short term; the effect is only about one-half a percentage point in tract poverty four years postreceipt.

15. Compared to the control group, girls in families assigned to the traditional voucher group in MTO had lower rates of major depression (6.5 percent vs. 10.9 percent) and conduct disorder (0.3 percent versus 2.9 percent), while for boys there were higher rates of post-traumatic stress disorder from the traditional voucher treatment (4.9 percent versus 1.9 percent).

16. The benefit calculation does implicitly cap assistance for higher income households once 30 percent of income exceeds the relevant FMR.

17. Vacancy rates from the quarterly Current Population Survey/Housing Vacancy Survey estimates from the U.S. Census Bureau. See https://www.census.gov/housing/hvs/data/rates.html.

18. It is worth noting that even this experiment would suffer from concerns over migration and spatial spillovers across treated and untreated units.

19. Low take-up of assistance appeared to be driven in part by failure to meet minimum quality standards but also from low assistance payment amounts for eligible households with higher incomes.

20. Income is adjusted income after deducting certain allowable expenses.

References

Andersson, Fredrik, John C. Haltiwanger, Mark J. Kutzbach, Giordano Palloni, Henry O. Pallakowski, and Daniel H. Weinber. 2018. Childhood housing and adult earnings: A between-siblings analysis of housing vouchers and public housing. NBER Working Paper 22721, National Bureau of Economic Research, Cambridge, MA.

Angrist, Joshua, Guido Imbens, and Donald Rubin. 1996. Identification of causal effects using instrumental variables. *Journal of the American Statistical Association* 91 (434): 444–55.

Austin, Benjamin, Edward Glaeser, and Lawrence Summers. 2018. Jobs for the heartland: Place-based policies in 21st century America. *Brookings Papers on Economic Activity* 49 (1): 151–255.

Baum-Snow, Nathaniel, and Justin Marion. 2009. The effects of low income housing tax credit developments on neighborhoods. *Journal of Public Economics* 93 (5–6): 654–66.

Bonastia, Christopher. 2006. *Knocking on the door: The federal government's attempt to desegregate the suburbs.* Princeton, NJ: Princeton University Press.

Briggs, Xavier de Souza, Joe Darden, and Angela Aidala. 1999. In the wake of desegregation: Early impacts of scattered-site public housing on neighborhoods in Yonkers, New York. *Journal of the American Planning Association* 65 (1): 27–49.

Carlson, Deven, Robert Haveman, Thomas Kaplan, and Barbara Wolfe. 2012. Long term effects of public low-income housing vouchers on neighborhood quality and household composition. *Journal of Housing Economics* 2:101–20.

Chetty, Raj, and Nathaniel Hendren. 2018. The impacts of neighborhoods on intergenerational mobility II: County-level estimates. *Quarterly Journal of Economics* 133 (3): 1163–1228.

Chetty, Raj, Nathaniel Hendren, and Lawrence F. Katz. 2015. The effects of exposure to better neighborhoods on children: New evidence from the Moving to Opportunity experiment. NBER Working Paper 21156, National Bureau of Economic Research, Cambridge, MA.

Collinson, Robert A., Ingrid Gould Ellen, and Jens Ludwig. 2016. Low-income housing policy. In *Economics of means-tested transfer programs in the United States*, vol. II, ed. Robert A. Moffitt, 59–126. Chicago, IL: University of Chicago Press.

Collinson, Robert, and P. Ganong. 2018. How do changes in housing voucher design affect rent and neighborhood quality? *American Economic Journal: Economic Policy* 10 (2): 62–89.

Cordes, Sarah, Ingrid Gould Ellen, Keren Horn, and Amy Ellen Schwartz. Forthcoming. Do housing vouchers improve academic performance? Evidence from New York City. *Journal of Policy Analysis and Management*.

Cummings, Jean L., and Denise DiPasquale. 1999. The low-income housing tax credit: An analysis of the first ten years. *Housing Policy Debate* 10 (2): 251–307.

Cunningham, M., M. Galvez, C. L. Aranda, R. Santos, D. Wissoker, A. Oneto, R. Pittingolo, and J. Crawford. 2018. *A pilot study of landlord acceptance of Housing Choice Vouchers*. Washington, DC: Urban Institute.

Cunningham, M. K., M. Scott, C. Narducci, S. Hall, and A. Stanczyk. 2010. *Improving neighborhood location outcomes in the Housing Choice Voucher program: A scan of mobility assistance programs*. Washington, DC: Urban Institute.

Currie, Janet M., and Aaron Yelowitz. 2000. Are public housing projects good for kids? *Journal of Public Economics* 75 (1): 99–124.

Desai, Mihir A., Dhammika Dharmapala, and Monica Singhal. 2010. Tax incentives for affordable housing: The Low Income Housing Tax Credit. In *Tax policy and the economy*, vol. 24, ed. Jeffrey R. Brown, 181–205. Chicago, IL: University of Chicago Press.

Devine, Deborah J., Robert W. Gray, Lester Rubin, and Lydia B. Taghavi. 2003. *Housing Choice Voucher location patterns: Implications for participant and neighborhood welfare*. Washington, DC: U.S. Department of Housing and Urban Development, Office of Policy Development and Research.

Diamond, Rebecca, and Timothy McQuade. 2019. Who wants affordable housing in their backyard? An equilibrium analysis of low income property development. *Journal of Political Economy*. Available from https://doi.org/10.1086/701354.

Edin, Kathryn, and Laura Lein. 1997. *Making ends meet: How single mothers survive welfare and low-wage work*. New York, NY: Russell Sage Foundation Press.

Ellen, Ingrid Gould, and Keren Horn. 2018. *Housing and educational opportunity: Characteristics of local schools near families with federal housing assistance*. Washington, DC: Poverty and Race Research Action Council.

Ellen, Ingrid Gould, Keren Horn, and Amy Ellen Schwartz. 2016. Why don't housing choice voucher recipients live near better schools? Insights from experimental and big administrative data. *Journal of Policy Analysis and Management* 35:884–905.

Ellen, Ingrid Gould, and Jeff Lubell. 2019. *The rent is too damn high: The growing cost of shelter in America*. Policy Focus Report. Cambridge, MA: Lincoln Land Institute.

Ellen, Ingrid Gould, Katherine O'Regan, and Ioan Voicu. 2009. Sitting, spillovers, and segregation: A re-examination of the Low Income Housing Tax Credit Program. In *Housing markets and the economy: Risk, regulation, policy; essays in honor of Karl Case*, eds. E. Glaeser and J. Quigley, 233–367. Cambridge, MA: Lincoln Institute for Land Policy.

Eriksen, Michael, and Amanda Ross. 2012. The impact of housing vouchers on mobility and neighborhood attributes. *Real Estate Economics* 41 (2): 255–77.

Evans, William N., James X. Sullivan, and Melanie Wallskog. 2016. The impact of homelessness prevention programs on homelessness. *Science* 353 (6300): 694–99.

Finkel, Meryl, and Larry Buron. 2001. *Study on Section 8 voucher success rates*, vol. I: *Quantitative study of success rates in metropolitan areas*. Washington, DC: U.S. Department of Housing and Urban Development.

Finkel, Meryl, Samuel Dastrup, Kimberly Burnett, Thyira Alvarez, Carissa Climaco, and Tanya de Sousa. 2017. *Small area fair market rent demonstration evaluation: Interim report*. Washington, DC: U.S. Department of Housing and Urban Development.

Finkel, Meryl, Ken Lam, Christopher Blaine, R. J. de la Cruz, Donna DeMarco, Melissa Vandawalker, and Michelle Woodford. 2010. *Capital needs in the Public Housing Program*. Cambridge, MA: Abt Associates.

Flood, Sarah, Miriam King, Renae Rodgers, Steven Ruggles and J. Robert Warren. 2018. Integrated Public Use Microdata Series, Current Population Survey: Version 6.0 [dataset]. Minneapolis, MN. Available from https://doi.org/10.18128/D030.V6.0.

Freeman, Lance. 2005. Household composition and housing assistance: Examining the link. *Cityscape* 8 (2): 49–68.

Furman, Jason. 2015. Barriers to shared growth: The case of land use regulation and economic rents. Prepared Remarks. Washington, DC: The Urban Institute. Available from https://obamawhitehouse .archives.gov/sites/default/files/page/files/20151120_barriers_shared_growth_land_use_regulation_ and_economic_rents.pdf.

Galiani, Sebastian, Alvin Murphy, and Juan Pantano. 2015. Estimating neighborhood choice models: Lessons from a housing assistance experiment. *American Economic Review* 105 (11): 3385–3415.

Galvez, Martha. 2010. *What do we know about Housing Choice Voucher program location outcomes? A review of recent literature*. Washington, DC: Urban Institute.

Goering, John, Joan Kraft, Judith Feins, Debra McInnis, Mary Joel Holin, and Huda Elhassan. 1999. *Moving to opportunity for fair housing demonstration program: Current status and initial findings*. Washington, DC: U.S. Department of Housing and Urban Development.

Green, Richard. 2011. Thoughts on rental housing and rental assistance. *Cityscape: A Journal of Policy Development and Research* 13 (2): 39–55.

Gubits, Daniel, Marybeth Shin, and Michelle Wood, et al. 2016. *Family options study: 3-year impacts of housing and services interventions for homeless families*. Washington, DC: HUD.

Hankinson, Michael. 2018. Why do renters behave like homeowners? High-rent, price anxiety and NIMBYism. *American Political Science Review* 112 (3): 473–93.

Hansen, Kristen A. 1998. *Seasonality of moves and duration of residence*. Current Population Reports. Washington, DC: U.S. Census Bureau.

Hartley, Robert Paul, Sophie Collyer, Sara Kimberlin, and Christopher Wimer. 26 February 2019. Progressive tax credit proposals for addressing U.S. poverty in the upcoming 2020 elections. Poverty & Social Policy Brief 3 (2). New York, NY: Columbia University.

Hartung, John M., and Jeffrey R. Henig. 1997. Housing vouchers and certificates as a vehicle for deconcentrating the poor: Evidence from the Washington, D.C., metropolitan area. *Urban Affairs Review* 32 (3): 403–19.

Horn, Keren Mertens, Ingrid Gould Ellen, and Amy Ellen Schwartz. 2014. Do Housing Choice Voucher holders live near good schools? *Journal of Housing Economics* 23:28–40.

Hunt, D. Bradford. 2009. *Blueprint for disaster: The unraveling of Chicago public housing*. Chicago, IL: University of Chicago Press.

Jacob, Brian A., Max Kapustin, and Jens Ludwig. 2015. The impact of housing assistance on child outcomes: Evidence from a randomized housing lottery. *Quarterly Journal of Economics* 130 (1): 465–506.

Jacob, Brian A., and Lars Lefgren. 2009. The effect of grade retention on high school completion. *American Economic Journal: Applied Economics* 1 (3): 33–58.

Jacob, Brian A., and Jens Ludwig. 2012. The effects of housing assistance on labor supply: Evidence from a voucher lottery. *American Economic Review* 102 (1): 272–304.

Kessler, Ronald C., Greg J. Duncan, Lisa A. Gennetian, Lawrence F. Katz, Jeffrey R. Kling, Nancy A. Sampson, Lisa Sanbonmatsu, Alan M. Zaslavsky, and Jens Ludwig. 2014. Associations of housing mobility interventions for children in high-poverty neighborhoods with subsequent mental disorders during adolescence. *Journal of the American Medical Association* 311 (9): 937–47.

Kling, Jeffrey R., Jeffrey B. Liebman, and Lawrence F. Katz. 2007. Experimental analysis of neighborhood effects. *Econometrica* 75 (1): 83–119.

Kling, Jeffrey R., Jens Ludwig, and Lawrence F. Katz. 2005. Neighborhood effects on crime for female and male youth: Evidence from a randomized housing voucher experiment. *Quarterly Journal of Economics* 120 (1): 87–130.

Lens, Michael C., Ingrid Gould Ellen, and Katherine O'Regan. 2011. Do vouchers help low-income households live in safer neighborhoods? Evidence on the Housing Choice Voucher program. *Cityscape: A Journal of Policy Development and Research* 13 (3): 135–59.

Leshno, Jacob. 2017. Dynamic matching in overloaded waiting lists. Available from https://papers.ssrn.com/sol3/papers.cfm?abstract_id=2967011.

Lowry, Ira. 1982. *Looking back on the Housing Assistance Supply Experiment*. The Rand Paper Series: P-6785. Santa Monica, CA: RAND Corporation.

Lubell, M. Jeffrey, Mark Shroder, and Barry Steffen. 2003. Work participation and length of stay in HUD-assisted housing. *Cityscape* 6 (2): 207–23.

Ludwig, Jens, Greg J. Duncan, Lisa A. Gennetian, Lawrence F. Katz, Ronald C. Kessler, Jeffrey R. Kling, and Lisa Sanbonmatsu. 2012. Neighborhood effects on the long-term well-being of low-income adults. *Science* 337 (6101): 1505–10.

Ludwig, Jens, Lisa Sanbonmatsu, Lisa A. Gennetian, Emma Adam, Greg J. Duncan, Lawrence F. Katz, Ronald C. Kessler, Jeffrey R. Kling, Stacy Tessler Lindau, Robert C. Whitaker, and Thomas W. McDade. 2011. Neighborhoods, obesity and diabetes: A randomized social experiment. *New England Journal of Medicine* 365 (16): 1509–19.

Mallach, Alan. 2007. Landlords at the margins: Exploring the dynamics of the one to four unit rental housing industry. Working Paper RR07-15, Joint Center for Housing Studies, Harvard University, Cambridge, MA.

Malpezzi, Stephen, and Kerry Vandell. 2002. *Does the Low-Income Housing Tax Credit increase the supply of housing?* Madison, WI: Center for Urban Land Economics Research.

McClure, Kirk. 2008. Deconcentrating poverty with housing programs. *Journal of the American Planning Association* 74:90–99.

McClure, Kirk, and Bonnie Johnson. 2015. Housing programs fail to deliver on neighborhood quality, reexamined. *Housing Policy Debate* 25 (3): 463–96.

McClure, Kirk, Alex F. Schwartz, and Lydia B. Taghavi. 2015. Housing Choice Voucher location patterns a decade later. *Housing Policy Debate* 25 (2): 215–33.

Mills, Gregory, Daniel Gubits, Larry Orr, David Long, Judie Feins, Bulbul Kaul, Michelle Wood, and Amy Jones & Associates, Cloudburst Consulting, and the QED Group. 2006. *The effects of housing vouchers on welfare families*. Washington, DC: U.S. Department of Housing and Urban Development, Office of Policy Development and Research.

Moffitt, Robert A., and Sisi Zhang. 2018. Income volatility and the PSID: Past research and new results. NBER Working Paper 24390, National Bureau of Economic Research, Cambridge, MA.

Moore, Kathleen M. 2018. "I don't do vouchers": Experimental evidence of discrimination against housing voucher recipients across fourteen metro areas. Working Paper.

Morduch, Jonathan, and Rachel Schneider. 2017. *The financial diaries: How American families cope in a world of uncertainty*. Princeton, NJ: Princeton University Press.

Newman, Sandra, and Joseph Harkness. 2002. The long-term effects of public housing on self-sufficiency. *Journal of Policy Analysis and Management* 21 (1): 21–43.

Newman, J. Sandra, and Ann B. Schnare. 1997. ". . . And a suitable living environment": The failure of housing programs to deliver on neighborhood quality. *Housing Policy Debate* 8:703–41.

NYU Furman Center. 2017. *2017 national rental housing landscape: Renting in the nation's largest metropolitan areas*. New York, NY: NYU Furman Center.

Olsen, Edgar O. 2003. Housing programs for low-income households. In *Means-tested transfer programs in the United States*, ed., Robert Moffitt. Chicago, IL: University of Chicago Press.

Olsen, Edgar O. 2016. Alleviating poverty through housing policy reform. In *A safety net that works: Improving federal programs for low-income Americans*, ed. Robert Doar, 87–106. Washington, DC: American Enterprise Institute.

Olsen, Edgar O., Catherine A. Tyler, Jonathan W. King, and Paul E. Carrillo. 2005. The effects of different types of housing assistance on earnings and employment. *Cityscape* 8 (2): 163–88.

O'Regan, M. Katherine, and Keren M. Horn. 2013. What can we learn about the Low-Income Housing Tax Credit program by looking at the tenants? *Housing Policy Debate* 23 (3): 597–613.

Orr, Larry, Judith D. Feins, Robin Jacob, Erik Beecroft, Lisa Sanbonmatsu, Lawrence F. Katz, Jeffrey B. Liebman, and Jeffrey R. Kling. 2003. *Moving to Opportunity for Fair Housing Demonstration Program: Interim impacts evaluation*. Report prepared by Abt Associates Inc. and the National Bureau of Economic Research. Washington, DC: U.S. Department of Housing and Urban Development, Office of Policy Development and Research.

Pendall, Rolf. 2000. Why voucher and certificate users live in distressed neighborhoods. *Housing Policy Debate* 11 (4): 881–910.

Perry, J. 2009. *Housing choice in crisis*. Technical report. New Orleans, LA: Greater New Orleans Fair Housing Action Center.

Phillips, D. C. 2017. Landlords avoid tenants who pay with vouchers. *Economics Letters* 151:48–52.

Poverty and Race Research Action Council. 2005. Appendix B, Updated 2019. Washington, DC. Available from https://prrac.org/pdf/AppendixB.pdf.

Rohe, William M., and Lance Freeman. 2001. Assisted housing and residential segregation: The role of race and ethnicity in the siting of assisted housing developments. *Journal of the American Planning Association* 67 (3): 279–92.

Ruggles, Steven, Sarah Flood, Ronald Goeken, Josiah Grover, Erin Meyer, Jose Pacas and Matthew Sobek. 2019. IPUMS USA: Version 9.0 [dataset]. Minneapolis, MN: IPUMS. Available from https://doi.org/10.18128/D010.V9.0.

Rydell, C. Peter. 1982. *Price elasticities of housing supply*. Santa Monica, CA: RAND Corporation. Available from https://www.rand.org/pubs/reports/R2846.html.

Sanbonmatsu, Lisa, Jens Ludwig, Lawrence F. Katz, Lisa A. Gennetian, Greg J. Duncan, Ronald C. Kessler, Emma Adam, Thomas W. McDade, and Stacy Tessler Lindau. 2011. *Moving to Opportunity for Fair Housing Demonstration Program: Final impacts evaluation*. Washington, DC: U.S. Department of Housing and Urban Development, Office of Policy Development and Research.

Schwartz, Amy, Ingrid Gould Ellen, Ioan Voicu, and Michael Schill. 2006. The external effects of subsidized housing. *Regional Science and Urban Economics* 36:679–707.

Shroder, D. Mark. 2002. Does housing assistance perversely affect self-sufficiency? A review essay. *Journal of Housing Economics* 11 (4): 381–417.

Susin, Scott. 2002. Rent vouchers and the price of low-income housing. *Journal of Public Economics* 83 (1): 109–52.

Susin, Scott. 2005. Longitudinal outcomes of subsidized housing recipients in matched survey and administrative data. *Cityscape* 8 (2): 189–218.

U.S. Census Bureau. 2018. *Quarterly residential vacancies and homeownership, third quarter 2018*. Washington, DC: U.S. Department of Commerce.

U.S. Department of Housing and Urban Development (HUD). 1974. *Housing in the seventies*. Washington, DC: HUD.

Wood, Michelle, Jennifer Turnham, and Gregory Mills. 2008. Housing affordability and family well-being: Results from the housing voucher evaluation. *Housing Policy Debate* 19 (2): 367–412.

The Temporary Assistance for Needy Families Program: Time for Improvements

The 1996 welfare reforms imposed major changes on the nation's means-tested benefits, including a requirement that states place at least half of their cash welfare caseload in work or related activities. Congress also increased both cash and in-kind subsidies for low-income working families. Between the mid-1990s and 2000, work and wages among low-income women increased and poverty declined. The recessions of 2001 and 2007–2009 caused rising employment to falter, but after 2014, women's employment rose again, and poverty declined. The impacts of welfare reform on these outcomes have been disputed, with many on the Left charging that states have used welfare funds inappropriately and many on the Right arguing that welfare reform played a major role in the improvements in work, wages, and poverty. We review reforms that have been proposed by one or both parties in recent years, including focusing spending on benefits and work. We conclude with lessons of these reform experiences for future reforms of entitlement programs.

Keywords: Temporary Assistance for Needy Families; work requirements; labor force participation rate; supplemental poverty rate; welfare dependency; Earned Income Tax Credit

By
RON HASKINS
and
MATT WEIDINGER

After a long and sometimes bitter debate, on August 22, 1996, President Clinton signed bipartisan legislation that repealed the Aid to Families with Dependent Children (AFDC) program, originally enacted during the New Deal, and replaced it with the Temporary Assistance for Needy Families (TANF) program

Ron Haskins is a senior fellow and holds the Cabot Family Chair in Economic Studies at the Brookings Institution, where he codirects the Center on Children and Families.

Matt Weidinger is a resident fellow in poverty studies at the American Enterprise Institute (AEI), where his work is focused on safety net policies, including cash welfare, child welfare, disability benefits, and unemployment insurance.

Correspondence: rhaskins@brookings.edu

DOI: 10.1177/0002716219881628

ANNALS, *AAPSS*, 686, November 2019

(Haskins 2006; DeParle 2004). There have now been a host of excellent reviews of the nature of reforms introduced by TANF as well as the impacts of the legislation associated with an array of outcomes, including employment, wages, child well-being, and many others (Ziliak 2016; Bitler and Hoynes 2010; Blank 2002; Blank and Haskins 2001; Grogger and Karoly 2005). There is agreement among reviewers about many of these impacts, especially on employment, earnings, and poverty and especially before the recessions of 2001 and 2007–2009. Here we first summarize the changes in cash welfare policy introduced by TANF and then turn to a review of its impacts. We then examine problems with the TANF program before reviewing proposals now being made to reform the program.

TANF Program Description

The purposes of the TANF program are to (1) provide assistance to needy families so children can be cared for at home, (2) end the dependence of families on government assistance, (3) reduce nonmarital pregnancies, and (4) promote the formation and maintenance of two-parent families. To accomplish those tasks, states have broad flexibility in spending TANF funds (Falk 2019).

In 2017, the average household receiving TANF included three persons and was headed by a single mother. Benefits vary by state but average $425 per month nationwide. As of January 2019, of the roughly 1.2 million households on TANF,[1] 429,000 were in California and 128,000 were in New York. These figures on caseload size are somewhat misleading because many states conduct what are called separate state programs (SSP) that are supported solely with state and local funds and thus operate under less rigorous rules than their regular TANF programs that are supported with federal funds. Further complicating matters is that TANF spending on families can be divided into assistance and nonassistance. Assistance is cash and cash equivalents, some child care funds, and payments for transportation and job search for an unemployed family. Nonassistance includes nonrecurrent short-term benefits, case management, employment-related services that do not provide basic income support, and other services. Under the Department of Health and Human Services (HHS) regulations, state reports on TANF, including work participation rates, include only families receiving assistance.

The TANF program is a $16.5 billion per year block grant, meaning annual federal funding is fixed and not subject to change as open-ended entitlement programs are. In contrast, the prior AFDC program—like other major means-tested benefit programs including Medicaid, food stamps, and Supplemental Security Income—provided open-ended federal funds, resulting in significant increases in federal funding as caseloads increased over time.

To receive their full share of federal block grant funds, states must satisfy "maintenance-of-effort" (MOE), or state spending, requirements that collectively total about $10.3 billion per year. The basic MOE requirement is 80 percent of the annual state block grant but is reduced to 75 percent if the state meets its work requirement (see below).

The TANF block grant is not adjusted for inflation, meaning the federal block grant and effectively the state MOE requirement have remained fixed at the value enacted in 1996. In real terms, the value of the federal block grant has dropped by 37 percent since 1996 due to inflation. During the same period, the number of individuals receiving assistance under TANF fell by even more, most notably in the early years following enactment of the 1996 law.

The TANF block grant includes a "sunset date," requiring Congress to regularly review the program and extend its authorization. The original sunset date was the end of Fiscal Year (FY) 2002, and TANF's authorization has been extended more than three dozen times since, with the only long-term reauthorization law enacted in 2006 and effective through FY2010. With minor exceptions, the provisions of the 2006 version of the law are still in effect.

TANF included several funding streams designed to address specific goals, including (1) a "contingency fund"—originally a fund equal to $2 billion and later an annual grant of over $600 million—designed to assist states experiencing economic distress; (2) "supplemental grants" totaling $800 million over a four-year period (1998–2001) for seventeen states with historically high poverty rates or experiencing significant population growth (these grants were extended before lapsing in 2011); (3) $100 million per year in bonuses for states that successfully reduced out-of-wedlock births—a key driver of poverty and welfare dependence—without increasing the number or rate of abortions (this bonus fund was replaced by a research, demonstration, and technical assistance fund in 2006); and (4) $200 million per year in bonus funds for certain "high-performance" states (this bonus fund was repealed in 2006, with the savings used to provide additional child care).

States can reserve unspent TANF funds from year to year, in effect creating "rainy day" funds in anticipation of rising needs due to a recession or other causes. As of the end of FY2017, states had collectively reserved $3.3 billion in this way.

TANF includes work participation requirements for both adults receiving assistance and states operating the program (Congressional Research Service 2017). States generally are expected to engage at least 50 percent of households with a work eligible individual in one or more of twelve "work activities" (or nine activities in the case of single-parent families with a child under age six). The list includes private sector employment and job search, participation in employment and training, and other activities. Failure to meet this 50 percent standard can result in loss of some or all federal TANF funds, but states receive credit for caseload reduction toward this work participation rate target. As a result of this credit, the steep caseload decline, and a work requirement phase-in rate, states had little trouble satisfying their work participation requirement in the early years after enactment, often without placing very many recipients in work programs. For this reason, the 2006 reauthorization law rebooted the caseload reduction credit to use more recent—and much lower—caseloads as a baseline, raising the work participation rate requirement back to 50 percent for most states. However, many states have since used other loopholes in TANF law and regulation to keep from directly engaging 50 percent of adults on assistance in work or related activities, which has led to calls for further reforms. Even states that violate the work requirement have the opportunity to avoid penalties by signing a "corrective compliance plan," and most have done so.

TANF assistance is generally limited to no more than five years per adult recipient, although states may make limited exceptions for hardship or use state funds to pay benefits beyond this limit. States may also choose to shorten the maximum duration individuals may collect federal TANF funds to fewer than five years, and some twenty states have opted to do so.

Understanding TANF Work Requirements

Whether welfare benefits should be accompanied by work requirements and how strong the requirements should be has been a central issue in the debate over welfare for more than three centuries (Himmelfarb 1984). In the Democratic campaign for the 1992 presidential nomination, Bill Clinton of Arkansas—a state that had created its own welfare reform program that emphasized work (Friedlander et al. 1985)—frequently spoke out on the need to help welfare recipients obtain jobs. Republicans had always supported this policy but were surprised to hear a prominent Democrat emphasize work. After the election of Clinton to the presidency in 1992 and Republicans to the majority in both the House and Senate in 1994, both parties backed legislation that would place strong work requirements on welfare recipients. Although it took two years of negotiations over work requirements and many other issues related to welfare reform (Haskins 2006), the two parties worked out a bill that passed Congress on a large bipartisan majority, was signed by President Clinton in August 1996, and replaced the former AFDC program with the TANF program and made many other reforms.

The work requirements in the 1996 legislation appeared on their face to be stronger than anything even contemplated by Congress in the past. When fully implemented, states were required to have 50 percent of their welfare caseload in work or education and training programs for at least 30 hours per week, although the states' ability to count education and training toward fulfilling the work requirement was limited. There are two major ways states could lower the 50 percent requirement. When the TANF program was first enacted in 1996, states could subtract the percentage reduction in their caseload relative to 1995 from the 50 percent requirement. For example, if a state reduced its caseload by 30 percent between 1995 and 2000, it would have to meet a 50 percent minus 30 percent or only 20 percent requirement. Eventually, as the TANF caseload dropped precipitously (Figure 1), this caseload reduction provision meant that most states had to meet a zero percent participation standard. To address this problem, in the Deficit Reduction Act of 2005, Congress changed the year from which the caseload decline was calculated from 1995 to 2005. This reform greatly increased the share of recipients who would be required to work for states to meet the work requirement. A second way to reduce the work requirement, as

FIGURE 1
Number of Family AFDC/TANF Cases, 1980–2018

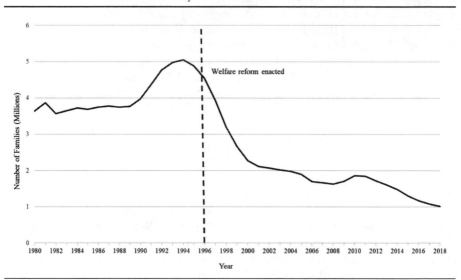

SOURCE: Office of Family Assistance, Administration for Children & Families, U.S. Department of Health & Human Services. See https://www.acf.hhs.gov/ofa/programs/tanf/data-reports.

established by TANF regulations, was for the state to spend more money on their TANF program than required by the state's MOE requirement.

In addition to the 50 percent work requirement for single-parent families, there is a separate work requirement of 90 percent for the TANF two-parent program. Few states have managed to meet the 90 percent requirement. For example, in 2017, of the 133,172 work-eligible families in the two-parent caseload, only 69 percent met the work requirement for the nation as a whole.

Effects: Changes in Economic Measures Associated with TANF

What happened to the TANF caseload after the 1996 reforms? Figure 1 shows the number of families on AFDC and TANF from 1980 to 2018. Except for a large increase in 1981, a recession year, the number of families on AFDC increased only slightly between 1980 and 1989. Then in the five years after 1989, the average monthly caseload jumped by more than 25 percent, from under 4 million to 5 million, one of the greatest short-term increases in the program's history. This increase was widely noted and gave a boost to Republican claims that welfare needed to be reformed to emphasize work.

The caseload began declining in 1995, even before enactment of welfare reform in 1996. It then declined for 14 consecutive years, from 5.05 million

FIGURE 2
Labor Force Participation Rate for Select Groups of Women, Age 18–54, 1990–2018

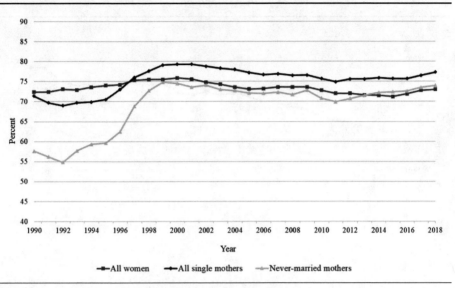

SOURCE: Current Population Survey, U.S. Census Bureau and the Bureau of Labor Statistics.
See https://cps.ipums.org/cps/sda.shtml.

families in 1994 to 1.63 million families in 2008, an unprecedented drop of nearly 70 percent. Thus, the welfare rolls were declining throughout the period immediately before and following welfare reform. Meanwhile, what was happening to work rates among females with children? Figure 2 suggests that mothers who left welfare and similar low-income mothers with backgrounds that could have led to spells on welfare increased their work rates and then maintained a historically high level of work. The data in Figure 2 are labor force participation (LFP) rates, defined by the Department of Labor as the share of mothers either employed or actively looking for work. The seven-year period leading up to 2000 saw strong increases in the LFP rates of all single mothers, never-married single mothers (the most disadvantaged group and the most likely to be on welfare), and married mothers. After the recession of 2001 and the deep recession of 2007–2009, neither the groups of all single mothers nor never-married mothers returned to the very high LFP rates that they had achieved in 1999 and 2000, but they remained well above their averages prior to welfare reform.

Turning to income, Figure 3 shows the wage and salary income of never-married and married mothers ages 18 to 54 (adjusted for inflation using the Consumer Price Index research series CPI-U-RS). The chart shows that the wage and salary income of never-married mothers rose sharply after the 1996 reforms and remains above prereform levels today. Married mothers as a group earn more than never-married mothers. Their incomes rose even more than those of never-married mothers, suggesting that welfare reform was not the only

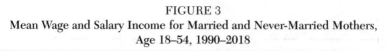

FIGURE 3
Mean Wage and Salary Income for Married and Never-Married Mothers,
Age 18–54, 1990–2018

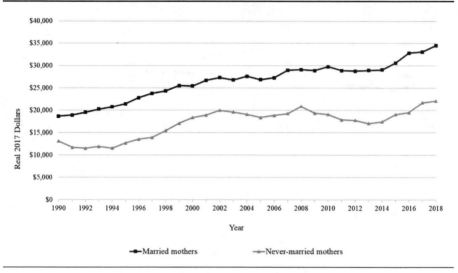

SOURCE: Current Population Survey, U.S. Census Bureau and the Bureau of Labor Statistics.
See https://cps.ipums.org/cps/sda.shtml.

factor that contributed to rising income among mothers and their children. Even so, the rise in income by never-married mothers is a major development in the goal of helping single mothers to improve their financial status.

Given the increases in work and income by unmarried mothers, there is little surprise that the poverty rates of children have been declining in most years since the enactment of welfare reform in 1996 (Figure 4), depending on what measure of poverty is being used. Under the official poverty measure, 20.8 percent of children were in poverty in 1995. But the rate fell continuously over the next five years to around 16.2 percent in 2000. It then rose following the recession of 2001, stayed nearly constant until the recession that began in 2007, and then rose continuously to 22 percent in 2010. Child poverty has declined since 2012 to about 18 percent in 2016 under the official measure.

The picture of child poverty in the United States is remarkably different under a newer Census Bureau measure called the Supplemental Poverty Measure (SPM). An important insight for understanding child poverty and changes in poverty during the welfare reform era is that the official measure does not count a host of government benefits such as those delivered through the tax code as well as housing, food stamps, and other noncash benefits. Many of these benefits, especially the ones delivered through the tax code, increased at about the same time as welfare reform was enacted and have continued to grow since then. The Earned Income Tax Credit (EITC), the biggest income supplement that has the biggest impact on poverty, goes to millions of

FIGURE 4
Child Poverty Rates Using Two Measures of Poverty, 1990–2016

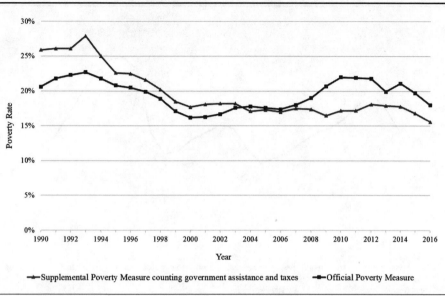

SOURCE: Center on Budget and Policy Priorities analysis of Columbia University Population Research Center, see https://www.cbpp.org/child-poverty-has-fallen-to-record-low-once-government-aid-is-counted; U.S. Census Bureau data, see https://www.census.gov/topics/income-poverty/poverty.html.

low-income working families; the Child Tax Credit, another major supplement to the income of working families, was enacted in 1997 and has been expanded since (Marr et al. 2015). These two benefits go only to individuals or families that work and have earnings.

Without making claims about causality, the SPM shows that much more progress has been made against child poverty since enactment of welfare reform than under the official measure (Figure 4). In every year since 2003, poverty as measured by the SPM is lower than under the official measure. Under both measures, child poverty declined between 1992 and 2000. But child poverty declined under the SPM almost every year after 1993, falling from about 27 percent to about 15 percent in 2015, one of its lowest rates ever. Both measures of poverty show that the nation made progress after the 1996 reforms, but the progress is much more impressive under the SPM measure, in large part because the benefits triggered by earnings, such as the EITC and the Child Tax Credit (CTC), are so much more generous for disadvantaged families when they work.

As is the case in all major social reforms, there are serious issues of causation raised by both the scope of the founding legislation and the many contextual factors that influence most of the outcomes related to various provisions in the legislation (Grogger and Karoly 2005; National Academies of Sciences, Engineering, and Medicine [NAS] 2019). In the case of welfare reform, the central outcomes we use to examine the effects of the legislation are rates of welfare receipt, work

FIGURE 5
Unemployment Rate for Women, Age 16 Years and Over, 1990–2018

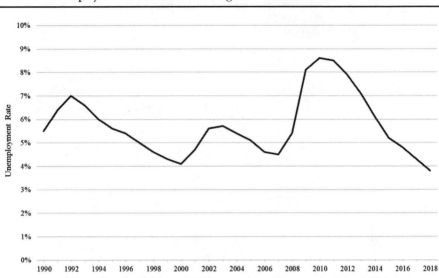

SOURCE: Labor Force Statistics from the Current Population Survey, U.S. Bureau of Labor Statistics. See https://data.bls.gov/timeseries/LNS14000002.

rates, income, and poverty rates. All improved in the years following the 1996 reforms. Nonetheless, the state of the economy is bound to influence all of these measures as well. In addition, other programs designed to increase the income and reduce the poverty rates of low-income families, especially families with children, changed around the time of welfare reform, complicating this picture further. Perhaps for this reason, many reviewers across the political spectrum (Blank 2009; Haskins 2017; Grogger and Karoly 2005) have attributed improvements in the rates of work, income, and poverty following the 1996 reforms to a combination of a strong economy, other reforms like the increases in the EITC, and welfare reform policies themselves.

The unemployment rate is perhaps the most important of the economic factors influencing the measures reviewed here, in large part because the others are greatly impacted by employment. The initial impacts of the economy and employment were helpful for stimulating the earnings of mothers leaving welfare. As demonstrated by the female unemployment rate (Figure 5), when welfare reform was implemented beginning in 1997, the economy was in the fifth year of a recovery that saw the unemployment rate fall from 7.0 percent in 1992 to 5.0 percent in 1997. The fall in female unemployment continued for another three years during the initial years of implementation of the 1996 legislation, declining to 4.1 percent in 2000, the then-lowest rate since 1969. After 2000, the rate moved up and then down before beginning a three-year rise at the time of the deep recession of 2007–2009 that saw the rate more than double to 8.6 percent in 2010, a historically high unemployment rate. Thereafter the rate declined every year for eight years to 3.8 percent in 2018. Thus, the American economy played an important role in helping women to find jobs in the initial years of welfare reform and in many—but not all—the years since. There can be no question that the economy plays an important role in the earnings of mothers leaving welfare and mothers who have low incomes but avoid welfare.

Issues with TANF

Even though there have been positive developments associated with TANF in terms of increased work and earnings and decreased poverty and dependence, there are concerns about the program, several of them becoming more pronounced over time. Our goal in this section is to review several of the major issues, with an eye toward proposing policy changes in the next section.

Failure to engage recipients in work activities

A key concern with the current TANF program is that caseload reduction credits, along with loopholes like excess MOE credits and "token checks,"[2] are allowing states to satisfy the work participation rate without actively engaging a significant share of adults in work activities. A related concern is the nature of the work participation requirements themselves, insofar as states are expected to engage current recipients in work and other activities without being held accountable for longer-term outcomes, such as whether former recipients are entering, staying in, or advancing in work. An obvious step in the right direction would be to measure the success of TANF work requirements in helping recipients to get jobs, keep the jobs, and move up the income ladder. But for 20 years, it has proven difficult to maintain high TANF work participation rates, especially because states have exploited ways to undermine the participation rates. Congress tried to fix the participation problems in the 2006 reauthorization, but so far this has not been successful, as states have used a combination of further case reductions and loopholes like excess MOE credits and token checks to drive down the share of current TANF recipients they are expected to engage in work activities.

Problems with TANF spending

Large declines in TANF dependency—a key goal of the 1996 law—have left many states relatively flush with federal and state TANF funds previously spent on welfare checks. The dependency declines have been achieved in part by accounting "tricks" that many states employ to meet the work participation standard. Some states have responded by increased spending on "other services" such as foster care, adoption, child welfare services, and efforts to prevent out-of-wedlock pregnancies. For example, according to the Congressional Research Service, in FY2017 several states reported using more than half of federal and

FIGURE 6
Spending on TANF, 1995, 2000–2017

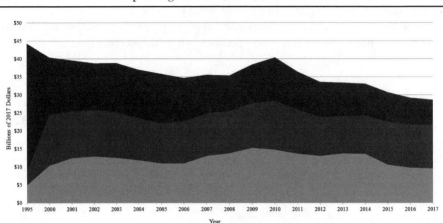

SOURCE: Office of the Administration for Children & Families, U.S. Department of Health and Human Services. Available from https://www.acf.hhs.gov/ofa/programs/tanf/data-reports. NOTE: This series includes fifteen TANF expenditures assigned to three categories for the year 2000 to 2017: Cash Aid (basic assistance), Work Support (work, education, and training activities; child care [spent or transferred]; refundable tax credits; work supports and supportive services; pre-kindergarten/Head Start), and Other (program management, child welfare services, transferred to Social Services Block Grant [SSBG], out-of-wedlock pregnancy prevention, nonrecurrent short term benefits, services for children and youth, authorized solely under prior law, fatherhood and two-parent programs, and other). In 1995, Aid to Families with Dependent Children accounts for cash aid spending, the Job Opportunities and Basic Skills Training program accounts for work support expenditures, and the Emergency Assistance program is categorized as other spending. Due to limited spending data around the time that TANF was enacted, the figure excludes the years 1996 to 1999.

state TANF funds for child welfare (e.g., Georgia and North Dakota), pre-K/ Head Start (e.g., Arkansas), child care (e.g., Delaware and Illinois), or "other" services (e.g., Michigan); only Alaska and Kentucky spent more than half of program funds for basic assistance, and no state spent that much on work, education, and training (Falk 2019). In fact, as shown in Figure 6, TANF funding priorities changed substantially over the years between 1995 and 2017. While TANF cash assistance declined substantially, except for a brief period during the recession of 2007–2009, spending on work supports and other programs such as child welfare increasingly became part of overall TANF spending.

Despite these positive developments, some argue that real declines in the value of the TANF block grant, especially when coupled with data about the number of families in deep poverty, warrant increasing federal TANF funds in the block grant. We address caveats about the number of families in deep poverty. We also argue that a more prudent policy than increasing federal funds

FIGURE 7
Federal and State Spending of TANF Funds on Core vs. Noncore TANF Activities

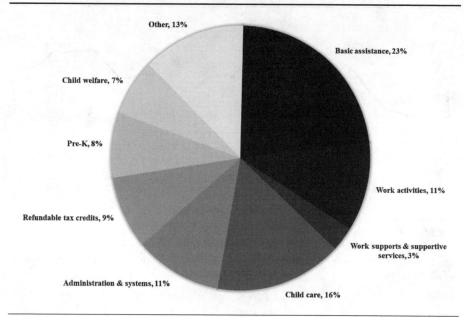

SOURCE: Figure created using data in the CBPP analysis of Department of Health and Human Services 2017 TANF Financial data. In Schott, Floyd, and Burnside (2019).

would be to first require states to contribute their full MOE funds to TANF by closing several loopholes that have already resulted in the program becoming more federally funded than Congress intended in the 1996 law.

Beyond using the flexibility afforded by TANF to spend program funds directly on "other services," some states have opted to divert funds altogether or use those funds to supplement other state spending and free up resources for non-TANF purposes. For example, about half the states currently avoid the separate and higher work requirement for two-parent families by putting these cases in a solely state-funded program where the work requirement does not apply. Also, in 2015 sixteen states counted third-party spending as if it were state spending toward satisfying the MOE requirement, something states are permitted to do under TANF rules.[3] In three of those states (Georgia, Alabama, and Missouri), third-party funds accounted for more than a third of state MOE; and in another eight states, it accounted for between 10 and 33 percent of state MOE. This factor both directly reduces the amount such states need to contribute from state funds and could also allow these states to claim excess MOE credits toward the work participation requirement. And where state TANF spending has been rising—such as on child care and refundable tax credits (included in the "work support" category in Figure 6)—it is impossible to know whether such increased spending has been in addition to what states would have otherwise spent for those purposes.

FIGURE 8
Share of Population in Deep Poverty (Less than 50 Percent Poverty Line), 1975–2017

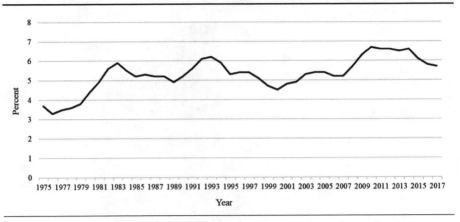

SOURCE: U.S. Census Bureau, Current Population Survey, Annual Social and Economic Supplements, Table 5: Percent of People by Ratio of Income to Poverty Level: 1970 to 2017. See https://www.census.gov/data/tables/time-series/demo/income-poverty/historical-poverty-people.html.

If not, the flexibility inherent in TANF has allowed states to claim this spending as TANF program spending, freeing state resources that would have otherwise been required for those uses to be spent on non-TANF purposes.

Data based on new reporting requirements imposed on states by HHS show how states use TANF dollars. The spending data for 2017 were carefully examined in a study by Schott, Floyd, and Burnside (2019) of the Center on Budget and Policy Priorities (CBPP) (Figure 7). These data show that only 23 percent of TANF funds were spent on basic assistance (cash payments to families) in 2017. Another 11 percent was spent on work activities and 3 percent on work supports. Even if the 16 percent spent on child care is included under work supports, only a total of 53 percent of TANF funds is spent on activities directly related to basic assistance and work.

A possible outcome of the reduced TANF spending on benefits could be an increase in the rate of deep poverty. As shown in Figure 8, the share of Americans in deep poverty (or poverty under one-half the poverty level: $9,552.50 in 2017) rose in an uneven pattern from between 3 percent and 4 percent in the mid-1970s to between 6 percent and 7 percent from 2005 to 2009. It then fell to a little under 6 percent in 2017 (U.S. Census Bureau 2018, Table 5). However, just as the Official Poverty Level (OPM) leaves out many means-tested benefits from the calculation of the poverty level, the deep poverty measure also leaves these same means-tested benefits out of the accounting (Hall and Rector 2018). Recent research by Bruce Meyer and his colleagues (2019) suggests that more than 90 percent of those considered to be in extreme poverty are not once the value of in-kind transfers are added to income, survey reports of earnings and transfer receipt are replaced with administrative records that are more accurate, and the ownership of assets are accounted for.

FIGURE 9

Number of Families Receiving AFDC/TANF for Every 100 Families with Children in Poverty, 1980–2017

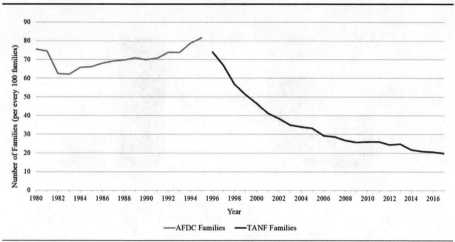

SOURCE: Administration for Children and Families (ACF) Office of Family Assistance, see https://www.acf.hhs.gov/ofa/programs/tanf/data-reports; U.S. Census Bureau Historical Data: Families, Table 4: Poverty Status, by Type of Family, Presence of Related Children, Race and Hispanic Origin, see https://www.census.gov/data/tables/time-series/demo/income-poverty/historical-poverty-people.html.

A decline in TANF spending on benefits for single mothers may have played a role in the increase in deep poverty under the OPM. As shown in Figure 9, the ratio of poor families receiving a TANF benefit has declined consistently since TANF was enacted in 1996, from 74 per 100 in 1996 to 20 per 100 in 2017 (Floyd, Burnside, and Schott 2018). Even so, we have already seen that poverty as measured by the SPM has been declining or stable in nearly all years throughout this period. Perhaps the rates would have declined more if more people had received TANF (although TANF alone does not usually remove people from poverty), but parents were able to make up for at least some of the loss of income from TANF by other means, among them wages and public benefits from work programs such as the EITC as well as other means-tested programs, especially Food Stamps (Tiehen, Jolliffe, and Smeeding 2015).

There are other public programs that have also been increasing the income of disadvantaged families with children. We have referred to expansions of the EITC and the creation of the CTC in 1997. According to an estimate from the CBPP (Horton 2016), taken together the EITC and the CTC lifted 9.8 million people, including 5.1 million children, out of poverty in 2015.

We also note that the number of families receiving a cash benefit under TANF does not include those receiving other forms of TANF assistance (called "nonassistance") like short-term assistance or services that fall under the rising "other" category displayed in Figure 6. TANF gathers almost no data on the number of people receiving such forms of help.

Another program that has had an important impact on the income of single parents is the child support enforcement program, which was reformed and

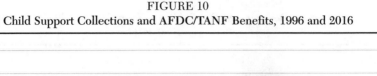

FIGURE 10
Child Support Collections and AFDC/TANF Benefits, 1996 and 2016

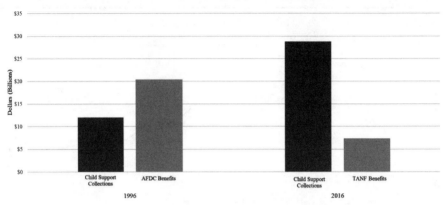

SOURCE: Office of Child Support Enforcement, Preliminary Report FY2016, Table P-1. See https://www.acf.hhs.gov/sites/default/files/programs/css/2016_preliminary_report.pdf.

greatly strengthened by the same legislation that created the TANF program in 1996. The child support program collects money from parents (usually the father) who do not live with their children to help the custodial parent maintain a home and pay for the child's expenses. Figure 10 shows that in 1996 when TANF was enacted, child support collections were $12 billion, and the AFDC program paid out $20.4 billion in benefits. But in 2016, two decades later, the child support program collected $28.8 billion in child support payments, mostly from fathers, over 95 percent of which was paid to families, while TANF cash benefits had declined to only $7.4 billion (Williams 2017). The child support program enrolls and collects funds for both poor and nonpoor families, so the numbers in Figure 10 do not provide a fully accurate picture of how much child support has picked up the slack in TANF payments to poor and near-poor families while TANF payments declined over the years, but a major portion of the child support funds went to poor and near-poor families. In addition, many families that were above poverty in 2016 had previously been below poverty but are now helped to stay above the poverty line by child support payments.

In any case, we cannot take the decline in federal and MOE funds being spent on TANF cash benefits as a fully accurate indicator of the extent to which government funds are helping the poor. There are many sources of government spending on the poor, some of which provide them with cash while others provide them with services.

Possible Reforms of TANF

To address these problems and concerns, TANF reform proposals have been put forward by a number of individuals and groups. These efforts have included a comprehensive five-year reauthorization bill crafted by senior Republicans on the House Committee on Ways and Means, which has jurisdiction over TANF, as well as by a senior House Democrat who subsequently became a member of the committee. The Republican legislation was approved on a partisan vote in Ways and Means in May 2018 but was never considered on the House floor. Similar legislation was introduced in early 2019 by senior Republicans in the House and Senate but has not been acted on in either body. The Democrat bill, titled the "RISE Out of Poverty Act," introduced by Rep. Gwen Moore (D-WI), would significantly expand TANF and child care funding; replace the current Contingency Fund with one modeled after the Emergency Contingency Fund included in the 2009 stimulus law; and make a number of changes in work requirements, time limits, and other policies that would tend to increase TANF caseloads and spending. In each case, the legislation provides an indication of key TANF issues under debate.

What follows is an overview of possible reforms that respond to most of the problems and concerns that we have outlined. Most have at least some promise of attracting bipartisan support.

Strengthening TANF work requirements

The original TANF legislation required states to engage at least 50 percent of adult recipients in work and related activities while receiving assistance. Various credits and exceptions have reduced that requirement, including in an estimated twenty states, to zero,[4] effectively absolving such states of the need to engage any adults in work and other activities. The Republican bill would address these flaws in a number of ways, including by transitioning to an outcome-focused measurement system. In addition, it would phase out by 2023 the ability of states to count third-party spending as state spending, which would minimize the degree to which "excess MOE credits" could reduce the target work rate. This policy is bolstered by 2012 research conducted by the Government Accountability Office, which found that in 2009 "16 of 45 states that met the TANF work participation rate would not have done so without the credit they received for excess state MOE spending" (Government Accountability Office 2012). Even liberal organizations have recognized that the availability of such credits may entice states to "claim as MOE certain existing expenditures they hadn't previously claimed" (Schott, Floyd, and Burnside 2019, 17).

If reforms result in the retention of the work participation rate system, we propose strengthening the system for current recipients by also explicitly ending excess MOE credits as well as updating the baseline for calculating caseload reduction credits on an annual basis for the latest caseload. These reforms will better ensure that a significant share of current work-eligible adults engage in work and other productive activities and that states are held accountable for that result, as current law intends.

There is also merit, and potentially bipartisan support, for holding states more accountable for helping TANF recipients enter, remain, and advance in employment, as the Ways and Means bill would do. As CBPP has noted, "The primary measure of TANF's success should be whether families leave the program with employment and are on a path to earn enough to provide for their families, not simply whether they participate in a pre-defined set of activities that may or may not prepare them for employment and help them move out of poverty. The measure should . . . align TANF with other workforce programs under the Workforce Innovation and Opportunity Act" (Floyd, Burnside, and Schott 2018, 9). Separately, HHS recently began exploring use of employment data in the National Directory of New Hires to assist states in administering this proposed change to measuring outcomes of entering, retaining, and advancing in employment (Carter 2019).

The 1996 law encouraged adults to participate in work or other activities defined by the state within 24 months of coming into the program and similarly authorized, but did not require, the development of plans by states to ensure families are making progress toward program goals. The Republican bill would strengthen current law by requiring states to engage all work-eligible individuals in work and activities (as defined by the state), and consistent with individual plans required, and regularly updated, for each household. Others see risks in expecting states to engage more adults in work and related activities (Schott 2019). The Democrat "RISE Act" moves in the opposite direction by adding new exceptions to the work requirements (such as for those applying for disability benefits), removing restrictions on the counting of vocational education as work, and reducing to 20 the number of hours of participation required to be counted as "working," among other changes. Given states' proven capacity to minimize— even to the point of eliminating—any effective work requirement for adults on TANF, renewing that fundamental feature of the TANF program, as the Republican bill would do, seems an overdue improvement to ensure more families are making progress toward work, and states are held accountable for that result.

Focus funding on core activities

To counteract concerns about TANF funds being diffused on purposes other than the core goals of paying benefits and promoting work, a number of reforms could be made. For example, the Republican bill requires a minimum of 25 percent of federal and state TANF funds to be spent on core purposes, including assistance, work supports and supportive services, work, wage subsidies, and nonrecurring short-term benefits. Depending on the details, this policy could have bipartisan support, as CBPP has noted: "Congress should require states to spend a specific share of their state and federal TANF funds on these core purposes" (Floyd, Burnside, and Schott 2018, 9). Policy-makers should review whether a 25 percent floor is sufficient in the context of the overall reform proposal, or a higher floor is merited, but some reform that guarantees that some percentage of TANF funds are spent on core activities seems reasonable and consistent with both the basic intent of TANF and changes needed to better satisfy that intent in the future.

Ensuring a focus on poor families

Some concerns about insufficient TANF spending on poor families seem to reflect little more than a desire for mandating the payment of basic cash assistance, hearkening back to the former AFDC program. For example, the Democrat "RISE Act" mandates that TANF benefits be "sufficient to meet the basic economic needs (including food, clothing, shelter, utilities, household goods, personal care items, and general incidental expenses) of a family"; it also proposes what amounts to a $150-billion-plus increase in TANF funding over the next 10 years by adjusting the block grant for past and future inflation and changes in child population by state. While it is difficult to imagine Republican support for such expensive changes, there are other possible reforms that could promote more poverty reduction. For example, the Republican bill would add as a program purpose "to reduce child poverty by increasing employment entry, retention, and advancement of needy parents." The Democrat "RISE Act" would similarly make the first program purpose of TANF to "reduce poverty among children." The Republican bill also would target program spending on families with incomes below 200 percent of poverty. In addition, the bill would take various steps to tighten program spending on the core purposes of work and basic assistance, which could be expected to increase incomes and reduce poverty as well. These seem reasonable—and potentially bipartisan—changes.

The recent report on cutting child poverty by half in 10 years from NAS (2019) presents and analyzes a menu of policies and programs that could be used in case Congress decides to enact policies that would reduce child poverty. Based on careful analysis and program simulation, the committee that wrote the report expected expansions of the EITC, the Child and Dependent Care Tax Credit, a new child allowance, and a boost in the minimum wage, among others, to be the approaches that had the biggest impacts on poverty. Many of the report's approaches to reducing child poverty would have the effect of increasing work by parents. One approach, which featured expansion of the EITC, expansion of the Child and Dependent Care Tax Credit, an increase in the minimum wage, and the roll out of a new work program that featured training and help finding a job that matched the training, would induce a net increase in jobs of slightly more than 1 million. Thus, the NAS recommendations represented a combination of new public benefits and additional income from work.

Better assisting states in economic emergencies

The original TANF legislation contained a provision called the "Contingency Fund," which provided $2 billion for additional assistance to states experiencing economic distress. These funds were depleted by the Great Recession of 2007–2009. Congress then appropriated in the 2009 economic stimulus law $5 billion in an "Emergency Contingency Fund" (ECF) for states to use in FY2009 and FY2010 to conduct activities to recover from or mitigate the effects of the recession (Falk 2017, 14). Since 2013, approximately $600 million per year has been appropriated for the contingency fund, with funds broadly available to and spent by states even as unemployment has continued to decline (Falk 2017).

There are several practical concerns with the current contingency fund, including that the triggers for states to access funds do not accurately reflect real need for additional funding. Meanwhile, concerns about the effectiveness of the 2009 stimulus law and recent dysfunction in Congress reflected in the prolonged government shutdown that began in 2018 have caused some prominent former Obama administration officials to question whether future "temporary" stimulus measures like the ECF could be enacted in the event of another serious national recession (Weidinger 2019). That concern may be why the Democrat "RISE Act" would permanently append a modified version of the ECF to the TANF program (providing up to $2.5 billion per year to states whose unemployment rates exceed 6.5 percent) as well as add a new open-ended entitlement program to provide federal employment subsidies, which would involve significant expenses. Especially in the context of legislation that would better focus TANF spending on core purposes, increase real state MOE spending, and promote continued state savings for a "rainy day,"[5] a reasonable compromise would be to provide contingency funds only when needed during a national recession, while reducing or eliminating this funding when the economy is strong. Key features, such as requiring states to have increased their own spending (without receiving credit for spending by third parties), should be part of a potential bipartisan agreement, with any additional federal funds fully offset.

TANF performance measures

There is widespread agreement among researchers that measures of performance are usually superior to measures of process. Yet the required measures in the TANF program do not focus on performance. To fully evaluate the TANF program, measures of outcomes are necessary. The Office of Planning, Research & Evaluation (OPRE) at HHS has made progress in studying the impacts of welfare reform. In 2015, it created the Employment Strategies for Low-Income Adults Evidence Review (ESER), a systematic review of research on employment and training programs published between 1990 and 2014 (Administration for Children and Families 2018). That project reviewed more than three hundred studies and rated the quality of their designs. Few of the studies show impacts on outcomes.

While OPRE was working to establish the ESER, Congress enacted the Consolidated Appropriations Act of 2017, which required HHS to establish information about research projects that had used "proven or promising" approaches to help welfare recipients find jobs. HHS used many of the definitions and procedures used in the ESER to build the new clearinghouse. Although ESER did not assess the effectiveness of the interventions, studies included had to measure the effectiveness of programs that had the primary aim of improving employment-related outcomes; be targeted primarily on low-income adults; and have taken place in the United States, Canada, or the United Kingdom. In addition, the outcome measures had to include employment, earnings, public benefit receipt, or education and training. Clearly, the ESER provides a solid foundation on which the new clearinghouse is now being constructed.

Based on data from the ESER, the new clearinghouse can include the types of studies that provide the high-quality, experimental data from random-assignment studies needed to accurately determine the impacts of programs that are similar to welfare reform on the outcomes that Congress wants examined. It would be a relatively straightforward matter for Congress, in cooperation with OPRE and the firm helping HHS build the new clearinghouse (Mathematica Policy Research), to write language setting the requirements for providing uniform outcomes across states that would allow Congress to more fully assess the impacts of welfare reform. This approach resembles the proposal in the Republican bill.

It would also be important for HHS by regulatory policy or Congress by new legislation to encourage high-quality studies, especially randomized controlled trials, on major issues being raised about TANF. One of the most important issues with the TANF program is that the emphasis on random-assignment studies prior to passage of the 1996 legislation has all but disappeared. HHS should focus funding on exploring the questions now being raised by the data and studies released by the ESER, including whether families leaving welfare are better off financially than families on welfare, whether the training programs being used by states are helping families improve their earnings, and whether children leaving welfare are less or more likely to be poor and to be better off in other ways than children on welfare.

Alleviating marriage penalties

Two of the four purposes of the original TANF legislation concerned family composition because, according to Republicans, promoting marriage and the formation of two-parent families would likely have the effect of diminishing the need for families to rely on welfare benefits. Thus, Republicans included provisions designed to increase marriage rates and reduce nonmarital births, despite that research on earlier efforts to promote marriage had been at best modestly encouraging (Lundquist et al. 2014; Haskins 2015). There have now been several reviews of the evidence on whether work requirements or other features of the TANF legislation had the effect of increasing marriage or reducing nonmarital births. Arguably, the two best and most thorough reviews of this literature are by Klerman (2005) on the studies before approximately 2003 and Blank (2009) on the studies before 2008.

The Klerman review is based on thirteen studies published between 1999 and 2002 (see Appendix A, Table A.5 in Grogger and Karoly 2005). The studies were both experimental and observational and included the impacts of specific reforms as well as packages of reforms. Although there are a few scattered positive effects on some aspects of family composition, there is no consistent pattern of impacts. Klerman's conclusion is typical: that "mandatory work requirements have no impact on marriage" (2005, 183). Blank's review focused on three studies published between 2004 and 2006. Based on state panel data from Vital Statistics,

Current Population Survey data on children under age 16 over the years 1989 to 2000, and data on low-income families between 1999 and 2001 from the Three-City Study, Blank summarizes the three studies as showing, respectively, fewer new divorces and fewer new marriages, "little effect of welfare reform," and a small increase in children living with two adults but no increase in children living with biological fathers (Blank 2009, 38 and Table 1.4).

Thus, the welfare reforms implemented as a result of the 1996 legislation have not had major impacts on family composition. Even so, given the positive impacts on financial well-being and children's development of increases in two-parent families, it seems wise to include at least modest efforts to promote the formation of two-parent families in TANF reforms. These should include provisions to remove current programmatic marriage penalties, such as the separate and higher work participation rate that applies to two-parent households; such changes are included in the Republican and Democrat bills and have received bipartisan support in the past. And given the centrality of strong families and the desire of many low-income parents to marry, other policies that temporarily overcome financial disincentives to marry inherent in means-tested programs like TANF merit consideration as well (Zirger 2018).

Lessons for Entitlement Reform

The creation and operation of the TANF program offers important process lessons as well as negative and positive lessons for entitlement reform more generally.

Process lessons of TANF start with the challenge of achieving major changes in important entitlement programs like cash welfare. The replacement of AFDC with TANF marked the culmination of a major national discussion that included a presidential election in which the winner promised to "end welfare as we know it"; and when that did not happen, a historic congressional realignment unfolded, in part because opposition Republicans pledged to follow through with welfare reform. And still it took the passage of three major welfare reform bills (the first two were vetoed by President Clinton) before the 1996 welfare reform law was enacted. Key process lessons include that major entitlement reform is difficult, requires political tenacity, and depends on popular support to get across the finish line.

Negative lessons are evident from experience as TANF has been implemented. While it was fashionable to "trust the states" when TANF was created, the program included specific programmatic "strings" that required states to engage recipients in work and other productive activities. In practice, however, many states have exploited loopholes and gimmicks to minimize the actual engagement of recipients in work activities in keeping with federal law. For example, the Congressional Research Service (2017) noted that "more than half" of recent "improvements" in the national work participation rate resulted from the establishment of California's earnings supplement program, which offered small "token" welfare checks to individuals who were already working so they could be counted toward meeting the state's work participation rate. Still other states have replaced state spending with third-party spending and claimed "excess spending credits" that reduced the expectation they engage recipients even more. This experience suggests that the authors of the 1996 reform law were right to include a programmatic sunset in the TANF program that requires regular review to ensure the program continues to fulfill its mission. Even so, actual updates to the TANF program have been rare, resulting in a status quo of low work participation for over a decade. States have formed a powerful block in favor of maintaining if not increasing federal program funding, minimizing state spending requirements, and maintaining low expectations when it comes to engaging recipients in constructive activities. Reformers targeting other entitlement programs should heed this experience, especially if they presume state compliance with the text and spirit of new federal program requirements. The cooperation of states should not be assumed; Congress must include provisions that give states strong incentives to cooperate, including penalties that are imposed if they fail to cooperate.

Still, the positive lessons of TANF outweigh the negative and offer hope for broader entitlement reforms in other programs. The first and perhaps most important lesson from TANF is that significant reform to entitlement programs is possible. The former open-ended AFDC entitlement program was replaced with a capped block grant that has not been adjusted even for inflation now for more than 20 years. It would have been hard to imagine in 1996, but TANF continues to be regularly reauthorized with bipartisan support[6]—even with modest annual funding cuts due to this lack of an inflation adjustment, which has reduced the real value of the block grant by 37 percent since 1996. Even sharper declines in TANF receipt have muted the appeal of calls for increased federal program funding; if anything, reform should focus on ensuring states actually contribute their fair share of funds to the program. Even as this and other program reforms are under discussion, the basic structure of TANF remains intact and is likely to endure. The TANF program's combination of fixed but flexible funding, work requirements, time limits, and other programmatic features have limited receipt of welfare checks and at the very least promoted additional work and earnings that contributed to subsequent reductions in poverty. Further reforms to TANF should be about strengthening, not replacing, those key program features. Reformers in other programs would do well to mimic these sorts of outcome-oriented features if they seek to achieve similar results elsewhere.

Notes

1. Around 200,000 of the TANF cases get only token payments so states can count them in their work calculation.

2. Some states have taken steps to satisfy the work participation requirement by providing small "earnings supplements" to some working individuals, so they could be counted toward the program's work participation requirement at little expense. The Congressional Research Service notes that the reported increase in the national average TANF work participation rate from 2011 (29.5 percent) to 2017 (53.0

percent) "stems mostly" from such earnings supplements, along with caseload reduction credits. See https://fas.org/sgp/crs/misc/RL32760.pdf.

3. Some of the most egregious examples include states' counting as "state TANF spending" the imputed value of Girl Scout troop leaders' volunteer time and aid regularly offered by private food banks.

4. For twenty states, see https://republicans-waysandmeansforms.house.gov/uploadedfiles/jobs_toolkit.pdf.

5. For example, the Ways and Means bill would allow states to set aside up to 15 percent of annual program funds in a "rainy day" fund for later use. See https://gop-waysandmeans.house.gov/wp-content/uploads/2018/05/JOBS-for-Success-Act-Bill-Text-Introduction-1.pdf.

6. See http://www.aei.org/publication/while-congress-differs-on-border-wall-house-and-senate-bills-agree-on-trimming-welfare-block-grant/.

References

Administration for Children and Families. 2018. *Employment strategies for low-income adults evidence review, 2013–2018*. Washington, DC: U.S. Department of Health and Human Services. Available from https://www.acf.hhs.gov/opre/research/project/employment-and-training-evidence-review.

Bitler, Marianne, and Hilary W. Hoynes. 2010. The state of the social safety net in the post-welfare reform era. *Brookings Papers on Economic Activity* 2:71–127.

Blank, Rebecca M. 2002. Evaluating welfare reform in the United States. *Journal of Economic Literature* 40 (4): 1105–66.

Blank, Rebecca M. 2009. What we know, what we don't know, and what we need to know about welfare reform. In *Welfare reform and its long-term consequences for America's poor*, ed. James Ziliak, 22–58. New York, NY: Cambridge University Press.

Blank, Rebecca M., and Ron Haskins, eds. 2001. *The new world of welfare*. Washington, DC: Brookings Institution.

Carter, Clarence. 1 March 2019. Potential new employment outcomes measures of TANF work-eligible individuals. Memorandum to Steven Wagner, Principal Deputy Assistant Secretary, Administration for Children and Families.

Congressional Research Service. 2017. *Temporary Assistance for Needy Families (TANF): The work participation standard and engagement in welfare-to work activities*. Washington, DC: Congressional Research Service. Available from https://fas.org/sgp/crs/misc/R42768.pdf.

DeParle, Jason. 2004. *American dream: Three women, ten kids, and a nation's drive to end welfare*. New York, NY: Penguin Group.

Falk, Gene. 2017. *Temporary Assistance for Needy Families (TANF) block grant: A legislative history*. Washington, DC: Congressional Research Service. Available from https://fas.org/sgp/crs/misc/R44668.pdf.

Falk, Gene. 2019. Temporary Assistance for Needy Families (TANF) block grant: Responses to frequently asked questions. Washington, DC: Congressional Research Service. Available from https://fas.org/sgp/crs/misc/RL32760.pdf.

Floyd, Ife, Ashley Burnside, and Liz Schott. 2018. *TANF reaching few poor families*. Washington, DC: Center on Budget and Policy Priorities. Available from https://www.cbpp.org/sites/default/files/atoms/files/6-16-15tanf.pdf.

Friedlander, Daniel, Gregory Hoerz, Janey Guint, James Riccio, Barbara Goldman, Judith Gueron, and David Long. 1985. *Arkansas final report on the WORK Program in two counties*. New York, NY: MDRC.

Government Accountability Office. 2012. Temporary Assistance for Needy Families: State maintenance of effort requirements and trends. Testimony before the Subcommittee on Human Resources, Committee on Ways and Means, House of Representatives, 112th Cong. (statement of Kay E. Brown, Director, Education, Workforce, and Income Security).

Grogger, Jeffrey, and Lynn A. Karoly, eds. 2005. *Welfare reform: Effects of a decade of change*. Cambridge, MA: Harvard University Press.

Hall, Jamie, and Robert Rector. 2018. *Examining extreme and deep poverty in the United States*. Washington, DC: The Heritage Foundation. Available from https://www.heritage.org/poverty-and-inequality/report/examining-extreme-and-deep-poverty-the-united-states.

Haskins, Ron. 2006. *Work over welfare: The inside story of the 1996 welfare reform law*. Washington, DC: Brookings Institution.

Haskins, Ron. 2015. The family is here to stay—or not. *Future of Children* 25 (2): 129–53.

Haskins, Ron. 2017. *Using government programs to encourage employment, increase earnings, and grow the economy*. Arlington, VA: George Mason University, Mercatus Center. Available from https://www.mercatus.org/publications/federal-fiscal-policy/using-government-programs-encourage-employment-increase-earnings.

Himmelfarb, Gertrude. 1984. *The idea of poverty*. New York, NY: Alfred A. Knopf.

Horton, Emily. 2016. *EITC, CRC together lifted 9.8 million out of poverty in 2015*. Washington, DC: Center on Budget and Policy Priorities. Available from https://www.cbpp.org/blog/eitc-ctc-together-lifted-98-million-out-of-poverty-in-2015.

Klerman, Jacob A. 2005. Family structure. In *Welfare reform: Effects of a decade of change*, eds. Jeffrey Grogger and Lynn A. Karoly, 173–99. Cambridge, MA: Harvard University Press.

Lundquist, Erika, JoAnn Hsueh, Amy E. Lowenstein, Kristen Faucetta, Daniel Gubits, Charles Michalopoulos, and Virginia Knox. 2014. *A family-strengthening program for low-income families: Final impacts from the Supporting Healthy Marriage Evaluation*. OPRE Report 2014-09A. Washington, DC: Office of Planning, Research and Evaluation, Administration for Children and Families, U.S. Department of Health and Human Services. Available from https://www.acf.hhs.gov/sites/default/files/opre/shm2013_30_month_impact_reportrev2.pdf.

Marr, Chuck, Chye-Ching Huang, Arloc Sherman, and Brandon Debot. 2015. *EITC and Child Tax Credit promote work, reduce poverty, and support children's development, research finds*. Washington, DC: Center on Budget and Policy Priorities. Available from https://www.cbpp.org/research/federal-tax/eitc-and-child-tax-credit-promote-work-reduce-poverty-and-support-childrens.

Meyer, Bruce D., Derek Wu, Victoria R. Mooers, and Carla Medalia. 2019. The use and misuse of income data and extreme poverty in the United States. National Bureau of Economic Research Working Paper 25907, Cambridge, MA.

National Academies of Sciences, Engineering, and Medicine. 2019. *A roadmap to reducing child poverty*. Washington, DC: The National Academies Press.

Schott, Liz. 2019. *Rigid "universal engagement" TANF bills would hurt vulnerable families*. Washington, DC: Center on Budget and Policy Priorities. Available from https://www.cbpp.org/blog/rigid-universal-engagement-tanf-bills-would-hurt-vulnerable-families.

Schott, Liz, Ife Floyd, and Ashley Burnside. 2019. *How states use funds under the TANF block grant*. Washington, DC: Center on Budget and Policy Priorities. Available from https://www.cbpp.org/sites/default/files/atoms/files/1-5-17tanf.pdf.

Tiehen, Laura, Dean Jolliffe, and Timothy M. Smeeding. 2015. The effect of SNAP on poverty. In *SNAP matters: How food stamps affect health and well-being*, eds. Judi Bartfeld, Craig Gundersen, Timothy Smeeding M., and James P. Ziliak, 49–53. Stanford, CA: Stanford University Press.

U.S. Census Bureau. 2018. Historical poverty tables: People and families – 1959 to 2018. Washington, DC: U.S. Census Bureau. Available from https://www.census.gov/data/tables/time-series/demo/income-poverty/historical-poverty-people.html.

Weidinger, Matt. 2019. *A look at the consequences of the 2009 stimulus law as Congress contemplates "automatic stimulus" legislation*. Washington, DC: American Enterprise Institute. Available from http://www.aei.org/spotlight/consequences-2009-stimulus-law/.

Williams, Robert G. 2017. *A proposal for modernizing TANF distribution in the child support program*. Denver, CO: Veritas HHS. Available from https://docs.wixstatic.com/ugd/50e240_413d85fdbe7742219 5d39412c3b56eaf.pdf.

Ziliak, James. 2016. Temporary Assistance for Needy Families. In *Economics of means-tested transfer programs in the United States*, vol. 1, ed. Robert A. Moffitt, 303–93. Cambridge, MA: National Bureau of Economic Research and University of Chicago Press.

Zirger, Jeffrey M. 2018. Criteria for evidence of effectiveness to be applied to projects identified for inclusion in the What Works Clearinghouse of Proven and Promising Projects to move welfare recipients into work. *Federal Register* 83 (109): 26290–93.

Child Care and Child Care Policy: Existing Policies, Their Effects, and Reforms

By
V. JOSEPH HOTZ
and
MATTHEW WISWALL

We analyze policies that support and affect the provision and costs of child care in the United States. These policies are motivated by at least three objectives: (1) improving the cognitive and social development of young children, (2) facilitating maternal employment, and (3) alleviating poverty. We summarize this policy landscape and the evidence on the effects they have on the development of children and parents. We provide a summary of the use and costs of nonparental child care services; and we summarize existing policies and programs that subsidize child care costs, provide child care to certain groups, and regulate various aspects of the services provided in the United States. We then review the evidence on the effects that child care policies have on these objectives. We go on to discuss the existing evidence of their effects on various outcomes. Finally, we outline three reform proposals that will both facilitate work by low-income mothers and improve the quality of child care that their children receive.

Keywords: child care; early childhood education; policy reforms

The early educational experiences and care of America's children have become major focuses of public policy over the last 40 years. This increasing focus is motivated by at least three separate issues. First, there is growing evidence that exposure of young children, especially infants and toddlers, to enriching child care has important impacts on both children's cognitive, personal, and social development; and their readiness for successful entry into primary school (K–6). In addition, increasing evidence indicates that such exposure has impacts on individuals' success in college,

V. Joseph Hotz is the Arts & Sciences Professor of Economics at Duke University and a faculty research associate of the National Bureau of Economic Research. He is an applied microeconomist who conducts research on education, the family, and social policy; and on the development of applied econometric methods.

Correspondence: v.joseph.hotz@duke.edu

DOI: 10.1177/0002716219884078

ANNALS, *AAPSS*, 686, November 2019

careers, and a range of other later life outcomes. Second, access to nonparental child care for young children has become a requirement for the labor force participation of women with young children. In 2017, for example, 65.3 percent of the 22.9 million children in the United States under the age of six had mothers who were in the labor force.[1] Finally, and related to the first two, it appears that access to child care and early education, especially that which is of high quality, ameliorates the short- and long-term consequences of poverty in the United States for the some 20 percent of America's children who live in poverty,[2] as well as for their parents, especially single mothers.

In this article, we analyze the main policies that support and affect the provision and costs of child care in the United States.[3] We summarize this policy landscape and the evidence on the effects these policies have on maternal employment, child poverty, and child development. As we discuss, federal child care policy has focused primarily on facilitating maternal employment of low-income families and on alleviating poverty. But other child care policies have focused primarily on improving the quality of child care that children from disadvantaged backgrounds receive, based on increasing evidence of the developmental benefits of early childhood education. An important theme of our analysis is the tensions and trade-offs in designing and implementing public policies for child care and early education. Finally, based on existing evidence, we consider possible reforms, including expansions of the existing Head Start program and the provision of universal child care in the United States; expansions of existing child care subsidies and tax credits for child care expenses; and ways to improve information that parents, especially those in low-income families, have about the quality of child care services available to them, and how they can use this information to make their child care decisions.

In the next section, we provide a brief summary of evidence on child care use and costs in the United States, emphasizing differences across the income distribution of families. We then provide an overview of existing child care policies that directly provide child care services, ones that subsidize their costs, state programs that regulate the provision and quality of child care services, and more recent state quality rating improvement systems (QRISs) that seek to improve information on the quality of child care providers in local markets. We go on to summarize the evidence on the impacts of the direct-provision and subsidy programs, for state child care regulations, and for QRISs.

We focus on how these programs and policies affect maternal labor supply, poverty, and child development. Finally, we discuss proposals for three different sets of child care policy reforms, some of which entail expansions of existing

Matthew Wiswall is the Juli Plant Grainger Professor of Economics at the University of Wisconsin–Madison and a faculty research associate at the National Bureau of Economic Research. He is an applied microeconomist who conducts research on child development, education, and applied econometric methods.

NOTE: We thank Jim Ziliak and Robert Moffitt for comments on earlier drafts, Janet Currie and Melissa Kearney for their comments, and especially Aaron Sojourner for his extensive comments on an earlier draft of the article.

programs and others that are modeled after those in other countries. We outline the specifics of these reforms and their likely costs and critically evaluate their likelihood for improving the well-being of low-income families and their children's development.

Child Care Use, Its Costs, and Licensed Facilities

In this section, we briefly summarize patterns of child care use, expenditures, and the number and capacity of licensed child care facilities in the United States.

Use of child care

Here, we examine the use of different types of child care, using the 2012 National Survey of Early Care and Education (NSECE).[4] Figure 1 displays the average hours of care in different care types for each household child. Average hours are constructed for a 40-hour "regular" work week, allowing a focus on the child care most relevant for parental work schedules. For children in their first year, on average about 16 of the 40 hours are spent in various forms of child care, and not with parents. Of that 16 hours of care, about 3 hours on average are in child care centers, 4.5 hours with a regular paid individual caregiver (e.g., a nanny), 5.5 hours with a regular unpaid individual caregiver (e.g., a grandparent), and a remaining nearly 3 hours are in irregularly provided care.

As children age, they spend less time in the care of their parents. At age four, nonparental child care peaks at about 25 hours on average, with on average only 15 hours of the 40 regular work week hours spent with parents. The fraction of households using regular center-based care in particular rises from less than 10 percent of households in the first year to the majority of households by age four. This increase in center-based care is due in part to the increase in pre-K usage among households. Even after K–12 school entry (ages 6–8), nonparental care still is substantial with about 10 hours of child time spent in various forms of nonparental child care, representing mainly after-school care.

One of the key considerations for a policy reform that would subsidize child care or otherwise change its availability or desirability is the potential take-up or demand for child care. This demand could come from households that are not using nonparental arrangements to care for their children or ones that have their children in some form of nonparental care. To provide some evidence on this potential demand, Figure 2 displays the mean weekly hours of nonparental child care, where nonparental hours is the sum of all hours spent in various forms of formal and informal childcare, but not with parents. Across all ages, the highest-income households (those with annual incomes greater than $75,000) use more nonparental care hours, and for the youngest children (in the first year), the highest-income households use twice as much nonparental care as the lowest income households.

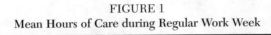

FIGURE 1
Mean Hours of Care during Regular Work Week

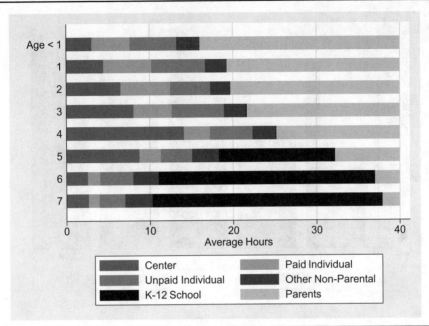

SOURCE: Authors' calculations from 2012 National Survey of Early Care and Education (NSECE) public-use data files.
NOTE: Each household child is counted separately. Household-level sample weights are used to compute all statistics. Hours of each care type is the sum over of all hours reported. Parent hours are the residual hours assuming a 40-hour "regular" work week for all households. Center care is home or non-home-based care in which the child participates at least 5 hours per week and includes Head Start and pre-K. Paid and unpaid individual care is care provided by a single individual (e.g., nanny or grandmother) in which the child typically spends at least 5 hours per week. Other nonparental care includes irregular care (less than 5 hours per week) or unknown type care.

Household expenditures

We next turn to examining recent patterns in household expenditures on child care. We examine household "out-of-pocket" expenditures on child care, net any subsidies they receive.[5] Figure 3 reports expenditures as a percentage of household income only for those households that report positive expenditures. These figures illustrate the regressivity of costs facing families. Focusing first on child care for the youngest children (aged 0–2), for the lowest-income households that are paying something out of pocket for child care, the median percentage of income paid on child care is about 30 percent of household income. For the high-income households, this figure is much lower, about 7 percent. As the children age, the percentage paid by the lowest-income households falls to about 20 percent, still several times higher than the high-income households.[6]

FIGURE 2
Mean Weekly Hours of Nonparental Care by Family Income

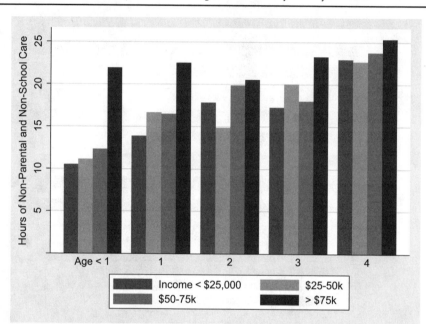

SOURCE: Authors' calculations from 2012 NSECE public-use data files.
NOTE: Each household child is counted separately. Household level sample weights are used to compute all statistics. Hours of nonparental care are trimmed at 60 hours.

Number and Capacity of Licensed Child Care Facilities

Figure 4 displays trends in the number and total capacity of licensed child care facilities by type in the United States over the period 2005 to 2014. The figure shows trends in three types of child care facilities: (1) child care centers, that is, child care services provided in a nonresidential setting that involve multiple staff (directors, teachers, assistants, etc.) with multiple children; (2) family child care homes, that is, a single individual providing child care to children in their own home; and (3) group child care homes, that is, child care provided to children in a provider's home but where there is more than one individual providing the care. Over this period, the number of licensed child care facilities has actually declined, due to declines in the number of family child care homes (–30.6 percent) and group child care homes (–11.4 percent), even though the number of child care centers increased slightly (4.5 percent). At the same time, the capacity of child care facilities has increased by 15 percent, largely because the average licensed child care center became 26 percent larger over this period. This increased capacity of licensed child care centers is likely to benefit the development of young children, given the evidence that we discuss below that licensed child care centers tend to

FIGURE 3

Median Percentage of Household Income Spent on Child Care (if positive expenditure)

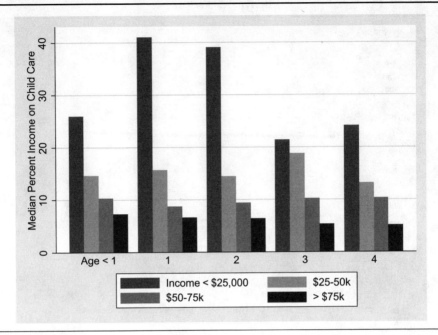

SOURCE: Authors' calculations from 2012 NSECE public-use data files.
NOTE: Each household child is counted separately. Household-level sample weights are used to compute all statistics. This statistic is computed only if expenditure on the child is positive. For the low-income households ($0–50k household income), the median expenditure across all households is 0.

provide more developmentally enriching environments than informal modes of child care. It is important to note, however, that even with this growth in capacity, as of 2014, the existing capacity in licensed child care centers only would have accommodated 33 percent of the children in the United States under the age of 6.

Child Care Policies, Regulations, and Information Provision

In this section, we discuss the major U.S. policies related to child care, with a focus on those that subsidize child care, assist directly in its provision, and regulate the services and settings of its providers.[7]

Child Care Development Fund

The Child Care Development Fund (CCDF) authorized under the Child Care Development Block Grant (CCDBG) Act provides grants to states to

FIGURE 4
Number and Capacity of Licensed Child Care Facilities in the United States,
by Type, 2005–2014

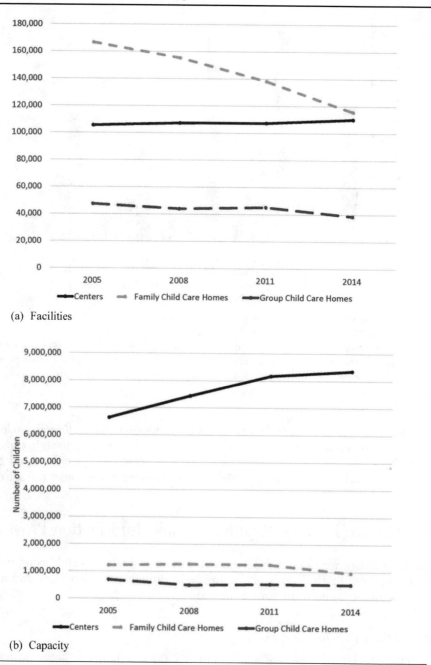

(a) Facilities

(b) Capacity

SOURCE: National Association for Regulatory Administration (NARA; 2006, 2010, 2013, 2014). *Child Care Licensing Studies*.

subsidize the child care expenses of low-income working parents with young children. In fiscal year (FY) 2018, the federal appropriation was $5.23 billion, with a state match of $2.92 billion, bringing the combined funding under the CCDF program to $8.1 billion. CCDF subsidies are provided in the form of vouchers to eligible families, which can then be used to defray the cost of child care at private providers. In FY2017, approximately 1.32 million children and 796,000 families received child care assistance under the CCDF, with 74 percent of those families having incomes less than 150 percent of the federal poverty level (Administration for Children and Families 2019). States have discretion over setting the eligibility requirements, including thresholds for family income and the maximum age of children covered by these subsidies,[8] and which work- and education-related activities (e.g., work, job search, training, and education) qualify for these subsidies (Stevens, Blatt, and Minton 2017). States also have discretion over setting requirements and policies that apply to child care providers that qualify for CCDF subsidies, including reimbursement rates for CCDF subsidized care and licensing regulations.

The 2014 reauthorization of the CCDBG Act included two key components to reorient the provision of child care assistance to low-income populations. The first set aside CCDF funds to improve the quality of child care services available to eligible children, and the second helped states to fund child care quality rating and information systems to help low-income families be more informed and, thus, better consumers of child care services. We discuss the latter component below.

Child and dependent care tax credit and exclusion of child care expenses benefits

There are two tax benefits that offset families' work-related child care expenses.[9] The first and largest, the Child and Dependent Care Tax Credit (CDCTC), provides a credit worth between 20 percent and 35 percent of a family's work-related child care expenses for children under age 18. Eligible care expenses are limited to $3,000 per child ($6,000 for two or more dependents), and credits vary by a family's adjusted gross income (AGI).[10] A key feature of this credit is that it is nonrefundable, so it can only offset income taxes that the filer owes. Thus, low-income families with no or low incomes get no or little benefit from the CDCTC. In addition to the federal credit, twenty-four states currently have a version of the CDCTC, and ten of these states have credits that are partially or fully refundable.[11]

Tax filers can also make use of dependent care flexible spending accounts (FSAs), provided through their employer and similar to FSAs used for health care expenses, that allow employees to set aside a portion of their pretax income to pay for child care expenses. Employees with children also may have access to subsidized workplace-provided child care as a nontaxable fringe benefit. Both of these provisions tend to benefit full-time, higher-income workers and are not available to individuals who do not work.[12] As shown in Figure 5, 6.2 million

FIGURE 5
Families Benefiting and Amount of Benefit from the CDCTC and the Tax Exclusion of
Child Care Benefits by Adjustable Gross Income, Tax Year 2016

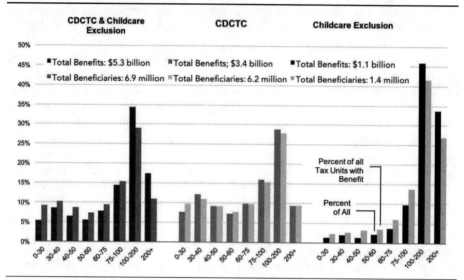

SOURCE: U.S. Department of Treasury, Office of Tax Analysis, *Child Care Tax Benefits in 2016*, Tables 1–3, https://www.treasury.gov/resource-center/tax-policy/tax-analysis/Documents.

families (tax filers) claimed the CDCTC for a total of $3.4 billion in tax year 2016, while 1.4 percent benefited from child care FSAs for a $1.14 billion tax benefit, for a combined tax benefit of $5.3 billion to 6.8 million families. As can be seen in this figure, these tax-related benefits are primarily used by and benefit high-income families.

Head Start and Early Head Start programs

Head Start is a federal program providing direct funding for child care centers to provide free care to eligible children, primarily from low-income households. In 2017, Head Start served about 1 million children, at an outlay of about $9 billion in federal government funding. Head Start primarily serves three- and four-year-old children, but about 20 percent of the children were younger than three and enrolled in the Early Head Start program (Administration for Children and Families 2017). In addition to child care, Head Start also provides an array of services to enrolled children and their families, including health services for children.

State regulation of child care providers

In the United States, regulation of child care providers is almost exclusively the domain of states. However, states do not regulate the quality of child care services directly; rather, they impose standards on the various aspects of these services. Existing state regulations of child care facilities and providers can be loosely organized into those regulating (1) labor intensiveness of care; (2) training and qualifications required of providers and their staff; (3) the health and safety of child care settings and staff obligations; and (4) strategies for verifying compliance, that is, inspections.[13] These dimensions of child care services are what developmental psychologists refer to as "structural quality" (Yoshikawa et al. 2013).

With respect to regulating the labor intensiveness of care, all states impose minimum child/staff ratios for center-based facilities, and the majority of states impose maximum group size restrictions. These regulations differ by the age of children. State regulations for the training and education of child care staff include minimum educational and experience requirements and periodic ongoing training that differ by staff position (directors vs. teachers vs. aides). While both of these types of regulations vary across states, on average their stringency has not changed much over the past 20 years. Some previous research has indicated that regulations of the labor intensiveness of care and the educational qualifications of providers are associated with objective measures of child care quality (e.g., the cognitive, emotional, and social development of young children),[14] other research questions these findings (Blau 2000, 2003b). More recently, states have been developing regulations to address the health and safety of child care providers, including safety features of facilities and requiring criminal background checks of child care staff, which have resulted from heightened concerns about staff with histories of child abuse. Finally, most states conduct periodic inspections of child care facilities, especially child care centers, and some states conduct unannounced inspections.

Child care resource and referral (CCR&R) services and QRISs

The CCDBG Act, with CCDF grants, also seeks to improve the quality of child care and the information consumers have by helping to fund state and local CCR&R agencies and, more recently, states' QRISs. State CCR&R networks provide assistance to child care providers and parents in developing and locating high-quality child care programs at the local level. These agencies provide business development assistance to child care providers and have developed databases on child care programs that meet certain standards that parents can use to identify child care programs in their local markets. Since 1980, the federal government has mandated that states maintain such databases as a condition for receiving funding under the CCDF and provide guidelines, technical assistance, and grants for their operation and development. At the same time, these databases do not collect or distribute detailed information about the quality of individual providers.

As part of the 2014 reauthorization of the CCDBG Act, the federal government has "incentivized" states to develop QRISs that do provide information to parents and others about the developmental, safety, and health dimensions of child care facilities and providers. In particular, the 2014 reauthorization envisioned systems in which ratings of the quality of child care providers that would stimulate increased availability and use of high-quality child care.[15] Figure 6 displays the "logic model" envisioned for these systems. As noted in Cannon et al. (2017), this logic views QRISs as market-oriented systems in which information provided via ratings of programs improves parents' ability to judge the quality of alternative child care providers and to use this information in making their choices. Better-informed parents are presumed to be more likely to choose higher-rated and higher-quality care. As a result, lower-rated providers are motivated to improve the quality of their programs. State-level systems then help providers, both existing and new entrants, to develop "business plans" to improve their curricula, facilities, workforces, and management practices to achieve higher ratings and better compete in the child care marketplace (see also Zellman and Perlman 2008).

Evidence on the Effects of Child Care Subsidies

Child care subsidies can take several forms: in-kind subsidies of an offer of a tuition subsidized spot at a government funded child care center like Head Start or vouchers that households could use to subsidize the costs of using nongovernment providers of their choice. In addition, child care is subsidized via tax credits that tax-paying households can use to defray their child care expenses.

An important consideration in assessing the impacts of programs that provide or subsidize child care services is that they may not be used (or taken up) by all households eligible for them. Some households may prefer their current child care arrangements, even when the subsidy is substantial, or prefer parental care over any nonparental form of care. Still other households may prefer their current child care center and not want, for example, to travel farther for their children to attend a government funded care center. How take-up is affected by the particular program structure is an important consideration for evaluating the impacts of different policies.

Another important consideration is that an offer of subsidized care, although it may facilitate parental employment and improve household finances, will not necessarily benefit children and their development. If the take-up of the care causes the household to substitute away from higher-quality forms of care toward lower-quality care, then the care subsidy may harm children's development. A leading example of this possibility is a government program offering free but low-quality care, which causes some households to substitute away from higher-quality care. This possibility highlights the salience of the quality of the care being subsidized, and the particular restrictions and regulations associated with the policy.

Small-scale demonstration programs

A number of small-scale demonstration programs—most prominent among them Perry Preschool Project (began 1962), Carolina Abcedarian Project (1972),

FIGURE 6
The QRIS Logic Model

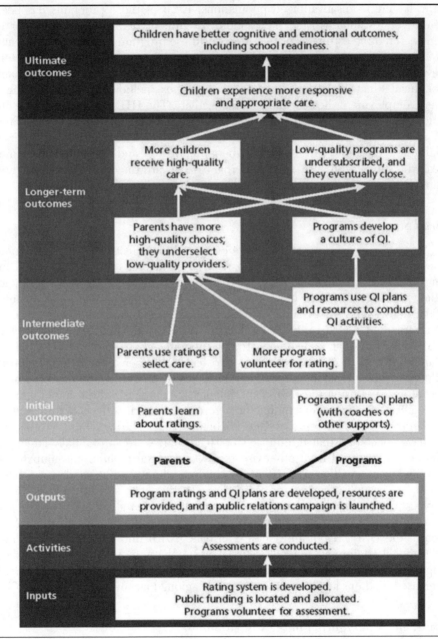

SOURCE: Zellman and Perlman (2008). Permissions to reprint granted from RAND Corporation. See https://www.rand.org/pubs/monographs/MG795.html and https://www.rand.org/pubs/perspectives/PE235.html

and the Infant Health and Development Program (IHDP) (1985)—have provided evidence of the short- and long-term effects of offering free center-based care, largely to disadvantaged populations. Each of these programs has been extensively evaluated using the random assignment of the treatment offer to provide credible estimates of the effects of these programs. Elango, García, and Heckman (2016) provide a recent review of evidence on their effects on child development and conclude that they had positive effects on short-run IQ and beneficial effects on various longer-term outcomes, including educational attainment, employment, health, and criminal activity. The IHDP program stands out among these programs in that it did not restrict program eligibility based on family income, and provided evidence that the offer of free center-based care to children ages one to three primarily benefited lower- and middle-income families, who substituted away from maternal care toward the center-based program care (Duncan and Sojourner 2013; Chaparro and Sojourner 2015).

Head Start

A number of previous studies have evaluated the effect of Head Start. Some use nonexperimental methods (comparison of participants to nonparticipant siblings and discontinuities in program rules); others, like the Head Start Impact Study (HSIS), are based on random assignment designs (Currie and Thomas 1995; Ludwig and Miller 2007; Deming 2009; Bitler, Hoynes, and Domina 2014; Carneiro and Ginja 2014; Feller et al. 2016; Walters and Kline 2016; Morris et al. 2018). Like the small-scale demonstration programs, these studies find that Head Start improved short-run test scores and had a number of beneficial long-run effects on educational attainment, earnings, health, and crime. Some of the most recent analyses using the HSIS experiment have emphasized the importance of care substitution in understanding the heterogeneity in the effects of the program (Feller et al. 2016; Walters and Kline 2016; Morris et al. 2018). These recent studies have concluded that the impacts of Head Start were substantially larger for children who would have otherwise received parental or informal nonparental care and were small or nonexistent for children who would have otherwise been cared for through other center-based care. Positive effects of Early Head Start, serving younger children, have also been found (Love et al. 2002). The evidence of the effects of Head Start on parents is more mixed. Using experimental variation in the HSIS, Sabol and Chase-Lansdale (2015) find an effect on parental educational attainment but not their labor supply. A more recent unpublished paper using state-level changes in Head Start eligibility finds that Head Start increased mother's labor supply, particularly among black women (Russo 2017).

Pre-K and kindergarten in the United States

Prior evidence on the effects of child care policies comes from the U.S. experience with the expansion of public school kindergarten (typically children aged 5–6), beginning in the 1960s, and the more recent expansion of pre-K programs (typically aged 4–5).[16] Some evidence indicates that the introduction of public kindergarten in the 1960s and 1970s increased maternal employment, particularly among single mothers (Cascio 2009; Gelbach 2002). But evidence from recent pre-K introduction indicates there are small, if any, effects on maternal employment, possibly due to the availability of other child care subsidies (Fitzpatrick 2010). In a recent paper, Cascio (2017a) studies the recent expansion of pre-K in the United States, from only four states with public funding in the early 1980s to forty states by 2011, and finds substantial positive effects of attending universal pre-K on reading and mathematics scores of four-year-old children from low-income households, but smaller to no effects for high-income households.[17]

Child care subsidies

There is a fairly extensive literature on the effects of subsidizing child care costs on maternal employment summarized in Blau (2003a); Ziliak, Hokayem, and Hardy (2008); and Morrissey (2017). Past studies differ by the source of variation in child care prices and subsidies used, the demographic groups considered, and the statistical strategies used to identify their effects on maternal employment. Typically, studies present their findings in terms of elasticities, that is, the percentage change in an outcome (e.g., employment) due to a 1 percent change in the net hourly cost of child care. Studies reviewed by Blau (2003a) show elasticities with respect to maternal employment ranging from 0.06 to –0.34; those reviewed by Ziliak, Hokayem, and Hardy have slightly larger (in absolute value) elasticities; those by Morrissey have slightly smaller ones, while both of their ranges are less than 0.[18] Finally, Enchautegui et al. (2016) estimate employment elasticities of 0.05 for women with children ages 0 to 12 and 0.07 for women with children ages 0 to 3, using aggregate state-level employment data and changes in state CCDF subsidy rates. Taken together, these findings indicate that reductions in child care costs will result in fairly modest increases in maternal employment. Furthermore, by comparison, Ziliak, Hokayem, and Hardy note that subsidizing child care costs tends to produce larger maternal employment increases than does increasing the minimum wage but smaller ones than does increasing the EITC.

A series of papers (Herbst and Tekin 2010, 2016; Hawkinson et al. 2013; Johnson, Ryan, and Brooks-Gunn 2012) study the relationship between child outcomes and parents' report of receiving a subsidy for their child's care in the year before kindergarten, where most of the studies are based on temporal and across-state variation in CCDF-funded vouchers. These studies find that subsidy receipt reduces math and reading scores measured at kindergarten entry and increases reports of behavioral problems, among other measured deleterious effects.[19] But they also find that the adverse effects are mainly for children with mothers with high human capital, suggesting that the care subsidies, which are in general not restricted by quality, are inducing some households to switch from higher-quality maternal care to lower-quality paid care.

Evidence from outside the United States

A rich variety of child care policies in other countries provide potentially important evidence for evaluating policy reform in the United States. A number of recent studies have examined experiences with mainly universal child care programs, across a number of different countries and areas: Argentina (Berlinski and Galiani 2007), Israel (Schlosser 2010), Italy (Brilli, Del Boca, and Pronzato 2016; Biroli et al. 2018), Sweden (Lundin, Mörk, and Öckert 2008), England (Brewer et al. 2016), Spain (Felfe, Nollenberger, and Rodriguez-Planas 2015), Germany (Bauernschuster and Schlotter 2015), Norway (Havnes and Mogstad 2011a, 2011b, 2015; Andresen and Havnes 2018), and Québec (Baker, Gruber, and Milligan 2008, 2015). A few findings stand out.

First, the effect of universal child care programs depends on the existing usage of child care and the ages of children covered. In the Norwegian case for example, a universal child care program started in the 1970s covering children aged three to six is estimated to have had modest positive effects on maternal labor supply because the program mainly caused a substitution between different types of nonparental care, from unsubsidized care to subsidized care (Havnes and Mogstad 2011b). In contrast, a later Norwegian universal program started in 2002, covering children aged two and up, had a larger positive effect on maternal labor supply (Andresen and Havnes 2018).

Second, the issue of the quality of care offered in the universal program comes to the fore in understanding the results of a Québec universal child care program. Starting in the 1990s, the Canadian province of Québec provided universal care to children of all ages, with an out-of-pocket cost capped at CAN$5 per day. Using differences between Québec and other Canadian provinces, Baker, Gruber, and Milligan (2008, 2015) find that this program had substantial deleterious effects on child outcomes, such as anxiety, aggressiveness, motor and social skills, and health. However, it appears that the types of care subsidized under this program were of lower quality than the programs considered in the United States.[20] In addition, the take-up of the Québec program was twice as large for educated mothers (some college or more) than for less educated mothers (high school or less), likely because the low-income households already had access to some subsidized care at the time that the program began. Therefore, it is possible that the Québec program caused many households to switch from higher- to lower-quality care. Baker, Gruber, and Milligan (2015) conclude that in the case of the Québec program, "Our findings for young children clearly contrast with those of the Perry, Abecedarian, and Head Start studies. These latter programs both provide higher quality care and are targeted at less advantaged children" (p. 30).

Evidence on the Effects of Child Care Regulations and QRISs

The theoretical literature most relevant to assessing the effects of child care regulations is that of imposing minimum quality standards or licensing in a competitive product market (Leland 1979; Shapiro 1986; Klein and Leffler 1981). Assuming products/services vary in quality that is costly to produce and that consumers care about quality, but are uncertain ex ante about quality, imposing binding minimum quality standards would increase average product/service quality and increase consumers' willingness to pay for it, due to assurance of higher quality. But consumers will face higher prices for the higher-quality product/service, which will discourage their purchase. The net effect of these opposing forces on consumers—greater quality assurance versus higher cost of quality—is ambiguous. At the same time, they imply that the overall supply of child care services is likely to decline, although the available supply should be of higher quality.

But, as noted in the literature on the effects of child care regulation (Blau 2003b; Blau and Currie 2006; Blau 2007; Hotz and Xiao 2011), this simple theory does not adequately characterize key features of the child care market. First, the quality of child care services is not directly regulated; rather, states tend to regulate the quality of "inputs" used in the production of these services, such as the educational qualifications of staff or the number of staff per child in a center. Thus, there is the potential for input-substitution when some inputs are regulated and others are not. Second, in the presence of alternative modes of child care, imposing higher minimum quality standards on one mode can induce mode-substitution, for example, parents substitute from child care centers to unregulated (or less regulated) providers in response to more stringent regulations. Finally, child care services involve multiple dimensions beyond their developmental quality. This complicates the capacity for regulation to improve quality, since regulating this aspect of services will increase their cost but also may induce parents to substitute toward providers that are high in other dimensions, for example, are closer to their work or have more convenient hours, which will mitigate some of the regulation's impact on quality.

Effects of state regulations

We begin with the findings on the effects of child care regulations on use of regulated care and the substitution to nonregulated (or less regulated) modes of care. The evidence is mixed. Most studies (Chipty and Witte 1997; Gormley 1991; Lowenberg and Tinnin 1992; Currie and Hotz 2004) find that more stringent child/staff requirements for child care centers and other regulations reduce the incidence and hours of such care used by parents (Hotz and Kilburn 1997; Hofferth and Chaplin 1998). But other studies (Ribar 1992; Chipty 1995; Blau 2003b) either find no impacts or imprecisely estimated negative effects of more stringent regulations on use and hours of center-based care.

The evidence of more stringent regulations on how much parents spend on child care also is mixed. Hotz and Kilburn (1997) and Hofferth and Chaplin (1998) find that tougher regulations are associated with higher family expenditures per hour of child care among families paying for care. Chipty (1995) finds that stricter group size regulations increase family expenditures per hour on child care but stricter child/staff ratios reduce it.[21]

Several studies have examined the effects of more stringent child care regulations on maternal employment. Most studies (Ribar 1992; Blau 1993; Hotz and

Kilburn 1997) find either small negative or insignificant positive effects of more stringent regulations on maternal labor supply. More recently, Han and Waldfogel (2001) find that more stringent regulations lead single mothers to be less likely to be employed but increase the employment rates of married mothers. They argue this finding is consistent with married mothers, who are wealthier than single ones, being more sensitive to the improved quality arising from more stringent regulations, while the employment of single (and poorer) mothers is more affected by the higher costs that regulation produces.

The theory implies that more stringent regulations would reduce the available supply of child care but increase the quality of care of providers that remain in business. Early studies based on survey data of households (Gormley 1991; Chipty 1995; Lowenberg and Tinnin 1992) or, for example, of child care providers (Chipty and Witte 1997), found that stricter regulations reduce the number of slots in regulated facilities and result in higher turnover of providers. More recently, Hotz and Xiao (2011), using panel data on the universe of all child care centers,[22] also find that more stringent regulations reduce the number of child care centers or group child care homes in local markets.[23] They find that this crowd out of center care facilities is greater in local markets with higher concentrations of low-income parents.

Blau finds mixed evidence on the effects of more stringent regulations on the quality of child care services available to parents (Blau 1997, 2000, 2007), with results being sensitive to the statistical methods used to control for other state-level differences that may be correlated with state regulations. In contrast, Hotz and Xiao (2011), using panel data on child care providers and a more robust estimation strategy, find that more stringent regulations increase the fraction of centers that are of sufficient quality to be accredited by an external and independent accrediting agency, although these increases accrue disproportionately to higher-income markets. Finally, we note that Currie and Hotz (2004) find that more stringent regulations improve the safety of child care centers, reducing the incidence of accidents in child care centers requiring medical attention.

In summary, the evidence suggests that more stringent regulations provide mixed benefits. While such regulations do appear to reduce the exposure of children to providers with unacceptably low levels of quality, they also tend to induce substitutions on various margins that, on average, tend to benefit children and parents from more advantaged backgrounds. As such, regulating child care services appears to be, at best, a rather blunt policy instrument for improving the quality of child care, especially for disadvantaged children.

Effects of state QRISs

In a recent study, Herbst (2018) examined the effects of the presence of QRISs in states on child care choices, maternal employment, and the supply and compensation of child care workers. Using the variation in when states rolled out their QRIS over time to identify these effects, Herbst finds that the presence of a state QRIS increases the probability of parents using nonparental forms of child care, although he finds that high-income families are more likely to use formal modes of care (child care centers), while low-income households are more likely to use informal modes of care, that is, family child care homes. He also finds that the presence of a state QRIS increases weeks worked and hours of work of mothers, but these effects are only for high-skilled mothers. Finally, Herbst finds that the presence of state QRISs increases the qualifications of child care workers.

In another recent study, Bassok, Dee, and Latham (2019) more directly examine the effectiveness of QRISs in stimulating the improvement of quality of child care providers. Recall the QRIS logic model discussed above. It presumed that QRISs would incentivize lower-rated child care providers to improve the quality of their services in response to parental use of higher-rated providers. Using data for North Carolina, Bassok, Dee, and Latham (2019) find that lower-quality providers do experience declines in enrollment after the implementation of that state's QRIS and that these declines were larger in markets with greater concentrations of other providers.

While the findings of Herbst (2018) and especially Bassok, Dee, and Latham (2019) are promising for the potential of the QRIS logic model to improve the quality of child care services, more evidence is needed on the impacts of these systems on the supply and demand (by parents) of higher-quality child care services before one can draw reliable conclusions.

Finally, we note the cautionary nature of the findings of Quick et al. (2016) in their assessment of California's QRIS. As they note, California's ratings of providers did not include measures of "process quality," such as measures of child interactions with teachers and other children and the overall classroom environment. Research has found that such measures are more predictive of cognitive and behavioral outcomes than measures of structural quality (Sabol et al. 2013). Furthermore, Quick et al. find that parents were either unaware of the relevance of such developmentally based measures for child care or tended to place greater value on other dimensions of their providers, such as proximity to workplaces and convenience of hours. The latter findings suggest the need to educate parents on the benefits of developmentally enriched child care services and on how to use information in QRISs to identify facilities that provide them.

Options for Reforming Child Care Policies

Our discussion of reforms focuses on three kinds of policy interventions: (1) direct provision of child care services by government, (2) expanding and better targeting child care subsidies and tax credits, and (3) improving the information that parents have about the quality of child care provider services. For each, we evaluate specific policy reforms, assessing their promise and their potential drawbacks for addressing the major policy objectives discussed above: (1) increasing maternal employment among low-income families, (2) reducing the exposure of the young children in these families to poverty, and (3) improving the development of these children.

We do not include possible reforms to existing state regulations of child care providers. While reforms are possible in this domain, the existing evidence summarized above indicates that without coupling them with some combination of the reforms we do consider, increasing the stringency of regulations is not likely to significantly produce developmentally relevant improvements in quality and is likely to exacerbate low-income families' access to affordable child care.

Policy reform 1: Direct provision: Expanding Head Start or universal child care

We first consider policy reforms in which there is an active government role in providing child care, either through a targeted expansion of Head Start to all children in poverty or through an expansion to a universal program offered to all children, as in many other countries. With respect to targeted policies, our review of the existing evidence, both for the United States and elsewhere, indicates that low-income and disadvantaged families tend to benefit the most, both in terms of increasing maternal employment and child development. Thus, on economic efficiency grounds, targeting child care policies for such families clearly makes sense.

To calculate the cost of expanding Head Start to all 3.8 million children living in poverty in 2018,[24] we start with computing the per hour cost of the current Head Start program, which is not directly available from government statistics. We estimate that the hourly cost of Head Start is about $5.92 per hour.[25] This is an expensive per hour rate, higher than the median price paid per hour by high-income households on the private market.[26] The high cost likely reflects the relative high quality of Head Start care and the range of health and other services Head Start provides to their participating children and families. The cost of covering all children under age five living in poverty with a full-time (40 hours) and all year (52 weeks) offer of child care would then be $47.12 billion,[27] or a cost per child per year of $12,313. This is the total cost assuming that every child participates. Subtracting the funding Head Start already receives and funding from other state and federal programs that this program would replace, and taking into account that take-up would not be full, the new funding required could be between $10.5 to $25 billion, implying the expanded program would need between two and four times the current budget.[28]

If all 20 million children under the age of five in the United States were to be provided access to and took up a universally available program of child care at the cost of Head Start, the total cost would be approximately $246 billion. The new funding required would likely be between $100 and $175 billion, given that take-up would likely be less than 100 percent and netting out the cost of existing governmental programs (primarily Head Start, CCDF, and CDTC) that would no longer be needed. Even with these adjustments, this would be an expensive program. Furthermore, existing evidence suggests that many households, particularly higher-income ones, would not experience any increases in maternal employment nor improvements in child outcomes, as this program would simply substitute subsidized care for high-quality parental or nonparental care that high-income households already provide for their children. On the other hand, universal policies do have a number of potential advantages, even if they are not as efficient as targeted ones. For one, the administrative burden of checking eligibility is eliminated. In addition, universal programs would eliminate any incentives for households to reduce or stop working to qualify for means-tested assistance. Universal programs also may reduce the stigma of program participation, extending care to households who might otherwise be reluctant to enroll.

Policy reform 2: Subsidizing child care costs

An alternative to the direct provision of child care services is to subsidize these services through vouchers under CCDF-funded programs and the tax treatment of child care expenses through the CDCTC. The evidence reviewed above indicates that providing CCDF-funded vouchers to low-income families increases maternal employment, while the existing CDCTC also increases the labor supply of mothers in households with sufficient tax liabilities to be eligible for the credit. Recently, Ziliak (2014), Children's Defense Fund (2015), Hamm and Martin (2015), and Cascio (2017b) have proposed to expand the coverage for CCDF-funded subsidies or make the CDCTC refundable and better target its coverage to increase maternal employment of low-income families and thereby reduce poverty. We focus on proposals to reform these two subsidy programs evaluated in the National Academies of Sciences, Engineering and Medicine (2019)—hereafter the "Poverty Report"—to reduce childhood poverty in the United States. We briefly describe each.

The first proposal would expand child care subsidies under the CCDF to cover families with earnings less than 150 percent of the federal poverty threshold, while keeping state subsidy rates (and, thus, state copayment rates) at current levels. (Recall that states are currently given discretion in determining the income eligibility of CCDF-funded child care subsidies, and most states do not cover families up to the 150 percent poverty threshold.) Allowing for employment responses of families newly eligible for a child care subsidy, the report estimated that this proposal would reduce the child care expenses of working single mothers with children under 12 by 16.6 percent and by 0.6 percent for married mothers, and would increase the employment of single mothers by 237,000 (3.3 percent of this group's prereform employment) and 15,000 (0.11 percent) for low-income married mothers. This expansion of CCDF subsidies would increase annual net labor earnings of low-income families by $4.2 billion. However, this policy reform would have only a modest impact on child poverty, reducing the current childhood poverty rate of 13 percent by 0.6 percent. This very modest reduction in child poverty is due, in part, to the fact that the subsidy is only a partial one, with newly employed parents having to pick up any remaining costs of child care. Finally, this expansion of CCDF-funded subsidies would increase annual net costs to government by $6.9 billion.

The Poverty Report also examined making the CDCTC fully refundable and better targeting it to benefit low-income families. Their proposed reform would (1) increase the maximum credit for one child from $3,000 to $4,000, keeping the maximum credit for two or more children at $6,000; and (2) increase the credit rate to 100 percent of qualifying child care expenses for AGI under $25,000 among families with children under age five, and then reduce the credit by 10 percentage points for each $5,000 of additional income, eliminating the credit for AGIs above $70,000.[29] (Recall that the existing credit only credited 35 percent of qualifying expenses for AGI below $15,000; reduced the credit to 20 percent for AGI at or above $43,000; and, because the CDCTC is currently nonrefundable, only offset families' positive federal income tax liabilities.)

Again allowing for employment responses, the Poverty Report estimated that this reform would reduce the child care expenses of low-income single mothers by 42.6 percent and increase maternal employment by 8.5 percent. Although it also would reduce the child care expenses of low-income two-parent households by 16.6 percent, maternal employment for this group would actually decrease by 128,000 or 1 percent of this group's prereform employment level. This reduction in employment is due to the fact that some lower-income intact families would no longer be eligible for the CDCTC, given its phase-out for AGIs above $70,000. Nonetheless, labor earnings of all low-income families would increase by $9.3 billion, producing a modest reduction in child poverty of 1.2 percentage points. The net cost to government of this reform would be $5.1 billion, which is substantially less than the increase in labor earnings it is projected to generate. In short, making the CDCTC refundable, more progressive, and better targeted to low-income families would significantly reduce the child care cost burden facing low-income families in the United States, facilitate maternal employment, and increase these families' capacity to provide for themselves and their children.

Although making the CDCTC refundable and better targeted would raise maternal employment and labor earnings among low-income families, it need not improve the quality of the care received by the children in these families. This depends on whether parents use the subsidies to purchase higher-quality care. Recognizing that parents may not choose to invest in higher-quality care, several of the proposals for reforming the CDCTC also would change current qualifying child care expense provisions of the credit. For example, Ziliak (2014) has proposed to have a larger credit for parents who use licensed, center-based care, and a recent proposal by Hamm and Martin (2015) would require that CDCTCs only support expenses for child care facilities with high ratings in state QRISs.

Requiring or incentivizing low-income parents to purchase higher-quality care by such changes in the qualifying child care expenses for CDCTCs has some potential drawbacks. The Ziliak (2014) and Hamm and Martin (2015) proposals would require the IRS to verify the licensing or ratings status of child care providers from local administrative records, imposing additional administrative burdens on the IRS. These costs will be high in the short run, given that not all states have QRISs and most of them are relatively new. Also, as noted above, licensing requirements for centers or QRIS ratings may not yet be good measures of developmentally relevant quality. Finally, the findings of Hotz and Xiao (2011) that stringent regulations restrict the availability of high-quality child care in poor neighborhoods are likely to make it more difficult for low-income working families to qualify for CDCTCs that are limited to licensed or highly rated providers.

For all these reasons, changing the current definition of qualifying child care expenses for CDCTCs seems premature at best. However, in the next section, we discuss ways to foster parents' greater use of high-quality care by improving the information they have about the quality of care and the ways they use it.

Policy reform 3: Improving quality through better information

Finally, we consider the issue of improving the quality of child care used by low-income families beyond the direct provision of high-quality care discussed under reform 1. Recall one of the theoretical justifications for imposing minimum standards was to mitigate the presumed informational deficits parents have with respect to the quality of potential child care providers. An alternative way to address these deficits is to provide parents with credible information about the provider quality so that parents become more informed consumers. This is the logic model for QRISs (see Figure 6).

However, QRISs are at an early stage of development and face several challenges. First, as already noted, QRIS ratings are primarily based on measures of "structural" factors (e.g., child/staff ratios, staff education, group size) rather than measures of process quality, and only the latter have been found to be predictive of children's cognitive, emotional, and social development. That said, process quality measures have not been used to construct QRIS ratings of providers, in large part because they require professionals to visit and directly observe the interactions and environment of the child care facility. Second, there is a lack of consensus of what process measures to include in ratings. Third, currently, provider participation in state and local QRISs is voluntary and includes only a fraction of providers. Finally, the Quick et al. (2016) findings, and those by Cryer and Burchinal (1997) and Mocan (2007), show that parents' knowledge of and preferences for these developmentally based dimensions of child care services limit their likely impact on parents' child care decisions even if they were included in provider ratings.

Given these challenges, we do not recommend that our proposed reform of the child care tax credit (reform 2) require that low-income working families can only claim expenses from highly ranked child care providers. At least not initially. But we do see real merit in the QRIS logic model for improving the quality of child care that low-income children experience, even if programs, like Head Start or other publicly provided child care, are expanded (reform 1). Therefore, as the third element of our proposed reforms, we recommend that the federal government, presumably under the CCDBG Act, expand and sustain its support for the development of state and local QRISs but, in addition, include additional funding for research in two areas.

The first area for research is to develop and validate measures of process quality that can be implemented at the provider level in a cost-effective manner. This will require adaptation and subsequent revalidation of existing process quality measures[30] and exploration of alternative strategies for their reducing their costs of collection so that assessments can be conducted of existing and new child care providers regardless of their size or ownership structure.

The second area is to evaluate ways of increasing parents' awareness and understanding of the importance of early child development and, more importantly, about the relative effectiveness of different features of child care settings for facilitating such development, so that parents can make more informed child care choices and better monitor the providers they do choose. On the latter, recent studies, from Dechausay and Anzelone (2016) for example, which evaluated alternative strategies adapted from the behavioral sciences to help educate parents eligible for CCDF subsidies, should be expanded, and states should be encouraged to undertake formal evaluations of these strategies to improve the knowledge base of best practices in this area.

We are not able to provide estimates of the funding needed to support these lines of research. But we encourage the federal government to develop a sustained research program for each, incentivize states to undertake such studies, and require that credible methods be used to evaluate them.

Conclusion

Decades of research have provided strong evidence that programs, like Head Start, that provide high-quality child care to low-income households have positive effects on child development and long-term outcomes. Research also suggests that expansions of the existing child care vouchers (CCDF) and making the existing child care tax credits (CDCTC) refundable and better targeted to low-income families would significantly reduce the cost of child care for low-income families and facilitate maternal employment. However, expansions of these voucher and tax credit programs alone may have only small positive effects, and perhaps even negative ones, on child development if increasing the generosity of these programs causes households to switch away from higher-quality forms of care toward subsidized lower-quality ones. We therefore recommend the pairing of subsidy expansions with programs that increase the take-up of higher-quality forms of child care. Rather than directly increase regulatory stringency in a few domains, an alternative approach that seems promising is to expand and sustain support for the development of state and local QRISs to provide better information to parents on the quality of child care options and to better educate parents on its importance.

Notes

1. U.S. Census Bureau, American Community Survey, 2013–17 5-year estimates.

2. Annie E. Casey Foundation, Kids Count Data Center. The estimate is for children living in families with incomes below the federal poverty level.

3. Although very much related to child care, we omit discussion of policies related to workplace parental leave and general welfare programs, both of which can change the demand for child care and may be substitutes or complements to the child care policies we analyze.

4. The NSECE surveyed a U.S. nationally representative sample of 11,629 households that had at least one child under age 13. The survey contains one of the most detailed sources of information on the different forms of child care used by each household.

5. For this reason, out-of-pocket expenditures by households cannot be used to directly compute the cost of care for subsidy receiving households, as these expenditures do not represent the sticker price of the care provided.

6. The price of child care also has been increasing faster than the overall rate of inflation. See https://www.bls.gov/opub/ted/2016/college-tuition-and-fees-increase-63-percent-since-january-2006.html.

7. For discussions of theoretical justifications for subsidizing and/or regulating child care, see Blau (2003a) and Blau and Currie (2006).

8. States can set the income eligibility limit at or below the federal limit of 85 percent of state median income. In 2015, the eligibility thresholds ranged from $838 to $5,279 per month for a family of three (Stevens, Blatt, and Minton 2017).

9. We do not consider other provisions of federal and state tax code, such as the Child Tax Credit (CTC), the Additional Child Care Tax Credit (ACTC), and the Earned Income Tax Credit (EITC), as none of them is directly targeted to reduce families' child care costs.

10. Families below $15,000 qualifying for the full 35 percent credit, with rates falling by 1 percentage point for each additional $2,000 of AGI until it reaches 20 percent for family AGI of $43,000 or more.

11. See tabulations at http://www.taxcreditsforworkersandfamilies.org/state-tax-credits/#1468434107561-be99920d-11c4.

12. See Stoltzfus (2015) for more on these two tax-related subsidies for child care.

13. State child care regulations over the past 15 years are documented in the National Association for Regulatory Administration (NARA) Child Care Licensing Studies. See NARA (2006, 2010, 2013, 2016) for details.

14. See Ruopp et al. (1979) and Mocan et al. (1995) and studies summarized in Hayes, Palmer, and Zaslow (1990) and Blau and Currie (2006).

15. The development of QRISs was also encouraged by the "Race to the Top-Early Learning Challenge" (RTT- ELC), a $1 billion joint initiative of the U.S. Departments of Education and Health and Human Services. Some twenty states were awarded grants under the RTT-ELC.

16. See Duncan and Magnuson (2013) for an overview.

17. This is largely consistent with most of the other recent research, for example, Bartik and Hershbein (2018); Barnett et al. (2018); Yoshikawa, Weiland, and Brooks-Gunn (2016); Farran and Lipsey (2015).

18. While a positive employment elasticity, such as the 0.06 estimate in Blau (2003a), is theoretically possible, most studies find evidence that lowering child care costs increase mothers' employment.

19. One exception to this is Healy and Dunifon (2014), who do not find a negative relationship in a sample of working mothers. Bernal and Keane (2010) also find adverse effects of nonmaternal child care.

20. Based on an audit study of the centers involved, Japel, Tremblay, and Côté (2005) report that a majority, 61 percent, had only a "minimal" educational component, and an additional 12 percent were of "inadequate quality."

21. See Blau and Currie (2006) for an excellent further discussion of the latter findings and potential reasons for their differences.

22. Hotz and Xiao (2011) use data from U.S. Economic Censuses of the child care industry, which, in principle, cover all child care establishments in U.S. markets.

23. Hotz and Xiao (2011) find no evidence that those providers remaining in business increase their size, so that more stringent regulations do, on average, reduce the availability of child care center capacity in local markets.

24. See the 2018 Current Population Survey (CPS) Annual Social and Economic (ASEC) Supplement: https://www.census.gov/data/tables/time-series/demo/income-poverty/cps-pov/pov-02.html.

25. In 2018 (the last year of data), federal funding for Head Start was $9,127,241,683 and served 887,125 children, a cost of $10,288 per child. Given that only about 56 percent of enrollment was in center-based care with 5 days per week for more than 6 hours per day, we estimate that average annual hours of care is $52 \times ([0.56 \times 40] + [0.44 \times 25]) = 1,736.8$, assuming the remaining non-full-time hours were on average 25 hours per week. The average hourly cost then is $10,288/1,736.8 = $5.92 per hour. This calculation uses data for the standard Head Start program, for three- to four-year-olds, and does not adjust for the potentially higher cost of providing care to younger children.

26. In 2018, the median price of care paid by households with higher than $75,000 income was $5.15. Authors' calculations from the 2012 National Survey of Early Care and Education.

27. $5.92 \times (52 \times 40) \times 3.827$ million = $47.12 billion.

28. Assuming take-up is between 50 and 80 percent lowers the cost to $23.6 to $37.7 billion. Subtracting $9.1 billion of existing Head Start funding, and subtracting a further $4 billion in funding from the Child Care Development Fund, lowers the new funding required to $10.5 to $24.6 billion. Some of this new program offer would also likely overlap with pre-K programs, which are being increasingly offered in the United States.

29. The proposed reform would provide lower credits for children ages 5 through 12.

30. See, for example, the measures considered in Sabol et al. (2013).

References

Administration for Children and Families. 2017. *Head Start program facts fiscal year 2017*. Washington, DC: U.S. Department of Health and Human Services. Available from https://eclkc.ohs.acf.hhs.gov/about-us/article/head-start-program-facts-fiscal-year-2017.

Administration for Children and Families. 2019. *Characteristics of families Served by the Child Care and Development Fund (CCDF) based on preliminary FY 2017 data*. Washington, DC: U.S. Department of Health and Human Services. Available from https://www.acf.hhs.gov/occ/resource/characteristics-of-families-served-by-child-care-and-development-fund-ccdf.

Andresen, Martin Eckhoff, and Tarjei Havnes. 2018. Child care, parental labor supply and tax revenue. Discussion Paper 11576, IZA Institute for Labor Economics, Bonn, Germany.

Baker, Michael, Jonathan Gruber, and Kevin Milligan. 2008. Universal child care, maternal labor supply, and family well-being. *Journal of Political Economy* 116 (4): 709–45.

Baker, Michael, Jonathan Gruber, and Kevin Milligan. 2015. Non-cognitive deficits and young adult outcomes: The long-run impacts of a universal child care program. NBER Working Paper 21571, National Bureau of Economic Research, Cambridge, MA.

Barnett, W. Steven, Kwanghee Jung, Allison Friedman-Krauss, Ellen C. Frede, Milagros Nores, Jason T. Hustedt, Carollee Howes, and Marijata Daniel-Echols. 2018. State prekindergarten effects on early learning at kindergarten entry: An analysis of eight state programs. *AERA Open* 4 (2): 1–16.

Bartik, Timothy J., and Brad J. Hershbein. 2018. Pre-K in the public schools: Evidence from within U.S. states. Working Paper 18-285, W. E. Upjohn Institute for Employment Research, Kalamazoo, MI.

Bassok, Daphna, Thomas S. Dee, and Scott Latham. 2019. The effects of accountability incentives in early childhood education. *Journal of Policy Analysis and Management* 38 (4): 838–66.

Bauernschuster, Stefan, and Martin Schlotter. 2015. Public child care and mothers' labor supply? Evidence from two quasi-experiments. *Journal of Public Economics* 123:1–16.

Berlinski, Samuel, and Sebastian Galiani. 2007. The effect of a large expansion of pre-primary school facilities on preschool attendance and maternal employment. *Labour Economics* 14:665–80.

Bernal, Raquel, and Michael P. Keane. 2010. Quasi-structural estimation of a model of child-care choices and child cognitive ability production. *Journal of Econometrics* 156 (1): 164–89.

Biroli, P., D. Del Boca, J. J. Heckman, L. Pettler Yu Koh, S. Kuperman, S. Moktan, C. Pronzato, and A. Ziff. 2018. Evaluation of the Reggio approach to early education. *Research in Economics* 72 (1): 1–32.

Bitler, Marianne P., Hilary W. Hoynes, and Thurston Domina. 2014. Experimental evidence on distributional effects of Head Start. NBER Working Paper 20434, National Bureau of Economic Research, Cambridge, MA.

Blau, David M. 1993. The supply of child care labor. *Journal of Labor Economics* 11 (2): 324–47.

Blau, David M. 1997. The production of quality in child care centers. *Journal of Human Resources* 32 (2): 354–87.

Blau, David M. 2000. The production of quality in child care centers: Another look. *Applied Developmental Science* 4 (3): 136–48.

Blau, David M. 2003a. Child care subsidy programs. In *Means-tested transfer programs in the United States*, ed. Robert Moffitt, 443–516. Chicago, IL: University of Chicago Press.

Blau, David M. 2003b. Do child care regulations affect the child care and labor markets? *Journal of Policy Analysis and Management* 22 (3): 443–65.

Blau, David M. 2007. Unintended consequences of child care regulations. *Labour Economics* 14 (3): 513–38.

Blau, David M., and Janet Currie. 2006. Preschool, day care and after-school care: Who's minding the kids? In *Handbook of the economics of education*, vol. 2, eds. Eric A. Hanushek and Finis Welch, 1163–1278. New York, NY: Elsevier.

Brewer, Mike, Sarah Cattan, Claire Crawford, and Birgitta Rabe. 2016. Does more free childcare help parents work more? Discussion Paper 10415, IZA Institute of Labor Economics, Bonn, Germany.

Brilli, Y., D. Del Boca, and C. Pronzato. 2016. Does child care availability play a role in maternal employment and children's development? Evidence from Italy. *Review of Economics of the Household* 14 (1): 27–51.

Cannon, Jill S., Gail L. Zellman, Lynn A. Karoly, and Heather L. Schwartz. 2017. *Quality rating and improvement systems for early care and education programs: Making the second generation better.* Santa Monica, CA: RAND Corporation. Available from https://www.rand.org/pubs/perspectives/PE235.html.

Carneiro, Pedro, and Rita Ginja. 2014. Long-term impacts of compensatory preschool on health and behavior: Evidence from Head Start. *American Economic Journal: Economic Policy* 6 (4): 135–73.

Cascio, Elizabeth U. 2009. Public preschool and maternal labor supply: Evidence from the introduction of kindergartens in American public schools. *Journal of Human Resources* 44 (1): 140–70.

Cascio, Elizabeth U. 2017a. Does universal preschool hit the target? Program access and preschool impacts. NBER Working Paper 23215, National Bureau of Economic Research, Cambridge, MA.

Cascio, Elizabeth U. 2017b. Public investments in child care. In *The 51% driving growth through women's economic participation*, eds. Diane W. Schanzenbach and Ryan Nunn, 123–41. Washington, DC: The Brookings Institution.

Chaparro, Juan, and Aaron J. Sojourner. 2015. Same program, different outcomes: Under- standing differential effects from access to free, high-quality early care. Discussion Paper 9552, IZA Institute for Labor Economics, Bonn, Germany.

Children's Defense Fund. 2015. *Ending child poverty now*. Washington, DC: Children's Defense Fund. Available from https://www.childrensdefense.org/reports/2015/ending-child-poverty-now-2015-full-report.

Chipty, Tasneem. 1995. Economic effects of quality regulations in the day-care industry. *American Economic Review* 85 (2): 419–24.

Chipty, Tasneem, and Ann Dryden Witte. 1997. An empirical investigation of firms' responses to minimum standards regulations. NBER Working Paper 6104, National Bureau of Economic Research, Cambridge, MA.

Cryer, Debby, and Margaret Burchinal. 1997. Parents as child care consumers. *Early Childhood Research Quarterly* 12:35–58.

Currie, Janet, and V. Joseph Hotz. 2004. Accidents will happen? Unintentional childhood injuries and the effects of child care regulations. *Journal of Health Economics* 23 (1): 25–59.

Currie, Janet, and Duncan Thomas. 1995. Does Head Start make a difference? *American Economic Review* 85 (3): 341–64.

Dechausay, Nadine, and Caitlin Anzelone. 2016. *Cutting through complexity: Using behavioral science to improve Indiana's Child Care Subsidy Program*. OPRE Report 2016-03. Washington, DC: Office of Planning, Research and Evaluation, U.S. Department of Health and Human Services. Available from https://www.acf.hhs.gov/opre/resource/cutting-complexity-behavioral-science-improve-indianas-child-care-subsidy-program.

Deming, David. 2009. Early childhood intervention and life-cycle skill development: Evidence from Head Start. *American Economic Journal: Applied Economics* 1 (3): 111–34.

Duncan, Greg J., and Karen Magnuson. 2013. Investing in preschool programs. *Journal of Economic Perspectives* 27 (2): 109–32.

Duncan, Greg J., and Aaron J. Sojourner. 2013. Can intensive early childhood intervention programs eliminate income-based cognitive and achievement gaps? *Journal of Human Resources* 48 (4): 945–68.

Elango, Sneha, Jorge Luis García, and James J. Heckman. 2016. Early childhood education. In *Economics of means-tested transfer programs in the U.S.*, vol. 2, ed. Robert Moffitt, 235–97. Chicago, IL: University of Chicago Press.

Enchautegui, Maraí, Nina Chien, Kimberly Burgess, and Robin Ghertner. 2016. *Effects of the CCDF Subsidy Program on the employment outcomes of low income mothers*. Washington, DC: U.S. Department of Health and Human Services, Office of the Assistant Secretary for Planning and Evaluation. Available from https://aspe.hhs.gov/system/files/pdf/253961/EffectsCCSubsidiesMaternalLFPTechnical.pdf.

Farran, Dale C., and Mark W. Lipsey. 2015. Expectations of sustained effects from scaled up pre-K: Challenges from the Tennessee Study. *Evidence Speaks Reports* 1 (3).

Felfe, Christina, Natalia Nollenberger, and Núria Rodriguez-Planas. 2015. Can't buy mommy's love? Universal childcare and children's long-term cognitive development. *Journal of Population Economics* 28 (2): 393–422.

Feller, Avi, Todd Grindal, Luke Miratrix, and Lindsay C. Page. 2016. Compared to what? Variation in the impacts of early childhood education by alternative care type. *Annals of Applied Statistics* 10 (3): 1245–85.

Fitzpatrick, Maria Donovan. 2010. Preschoolers enrolled and mothers at work? The effects of universal prekindergarten. *Journal of Labor Economics* 28 (1): 51–85.

Gelbach, Jonah B. 2002. Public schooling for young children and maternal labor supply. *American Economic Review* 92 (1): 307–22.

Gormley, William T., Jr. 1991. State regulations and the availability of child-care services. *Journal of Policy Analysis and Management* 10 (1): 78–95.

Hamm, Katie, and Carmel Martin. 2015. *A new vision for child care in the United States: A proposed new tax credit to expand high-quality child care*. Washington, DC: Center for American Progress. Available from https://cdn.americanprogress.org/wp-content/uploads/2015/08/31111043/Hamm-Childcare-report.pdf.

Han, Wenjui, and Jane Waldfogel. 2001. Child care costs and women's employment: A comparison of single and married mothers with pre-school-aged children. *Social Science Quarterly* 82 (3): 552–68.

Havnes, Tarjei, and Magne Mogstad. 2011a. Money for nothing? Universal child care and maternal employment. *Journal of Public Economics* 95 (11): 1455–65.

Havnes, Tarjei, and Magne Mogstad. 2011b. No Child Left Behind: Subsidized child care and children's long-run outcomes. *American Economic Journal: Economic Policy* 3 (2): 97–129.

Havnes, Tarjei, and Magne Mogstad. 2015. Is universal child care leveling the playing field? *Journal of Public Economics* 127:100–114.

Hawkinson, Laura E., Andrew S. Griffen, Nianbo Dong, and Rebecca A. Maynard. 2013. The relationship between child care subsidies and children's cognitive development. *Early Childhood Research Quarterly* 28 (1): 388–404.

Hayes, Cheryl, John Palmer, and Martha Zaslow. 1990. *Who cares for America's children? Child care policy for the 1990s*. Washington, DC: National Academy Press.

Healy, Olivia, and Rachel Dunifon. 2014. Child-care subsidies and family well-being. *Social Service Review* 88 (3): 493–528.

Herbst, Chris M. 2018. The impact of quality rating and improvement systems on families' child care choices and the supply of child care labor. *Labour Economics* 54:173–90.

Herbst, Chris M., and Erdal Tekin. 2010. Child care subsidies and child development. *Economics of Education Review* 29 (4): 618–38.

Herbst, Chris M., and Erdal Tekin. 2016. The impact of child-care subsidies on child development: Evidence from geographic variation in the distance to social service agencies. *Journal of Policy Analysis and Management* 35 (1): 94–116.

Hofferth, Sandra, and Duncan Chaplin. 1998. State regulations and child care choice. *Population Research and Policy Review* 17:111–40.

Hotz, V. Joseph, and M. Rebecca Kilburn. 1997. Regulating child care: The effects of state regulations on child care demand and its cost. University of Chicago Working Paper, Chicago, IL.

Hotz, V. Joseph, and Mo Xiao. 2011. The impact of regulations on the supply and quality of care in child care markets. *American Economic Review* 101 (5): 1775–1805.

Japel, Christa, Richard E. Tremblay, and Sylvana Côté. 2005. Quality counts! Assessing the quality of daycare services based on the Quebec longitudinal study of child development. *IRPP Choices* 11 (5).

Johnson, Anna D., Rebecca M. Ryan, and Jeanne Brooks-Gunn. 2012. Child-care subsidies: Do they impact the quality of care children experience? *Child Development* 83 (4): 1444–61.

Klein, Benjamin, and Keith B. Leffler. 1981. The role of market forces in assuring contractual performance. *Journal of Political Economy* 89 (4): 615–41.

Leland, Hayne E. 1979. Quacks, lemons, and licensing: A theory of minimum quality standards. *Journal of Political Economy* 87 (6): 1328–46.

Love, John M., Ellen Eliason Kisker, Christine M. Ross, Peter Z. Schochet, Jeanne Brooks-Gunn, Diane Paulsell, Kimberly Boller, Jill Constantine, Cheri Vogel, Allison Sidle Fuligni, and Christy Brady-Smith. 2002. *Making a difference in the lives of infants and toddlers and their families: The Impacts of Early Head Start*, vol. 1: *Final technical report*. Washington, DC: U.S. Department of Health and Human Services. Available from https://www.acf.hhs.gov/opre/resource/making-a-difference-in-the-lives-of-infants-and-toddlers-and-their-families-0.

Lowenberg, Anton D., and Thomas D. Tinnin. 1992. Professional versus consumer interests in regulation: The case of the U.S. child care industry. *Applied Economics* 24 (6): 571–80.

Ludwig, Jens, and Douglas L Miller. 2007. Does Head Start improve children's life chances? Evidence from a regression discontinuity design. *Quarterly Journal of Economics* 122 (1): 158–208.

Lundin, Daniela, Eva Mörk, and Björn Öckert. 2008. How far can reduced childcare prices push female labour supply? *Labour Economics* 15 (4): 647–59.

Mocan, Naci. 2007. Can consumers detect lemons? An empirical analysis of information asymmetry in the market for child care. *Journal of Population Economics* 20 (4): 743–80.

Mocan, Naci, Margaret Burchinal, John Morris, and Suzanne Helburn. 1995. Models of quality in center child care. In *Cost, quality and child outcomes in child care centers*, ed. Suzanne Helburn, 141–90. Denver, CO: University of Colorado Press.

Morris, P. A., M. Connors, A. Friedman-Krauss, D. C. McCoy, C. Weiland, A. Feller, and H. Yoshikawa. 2018. New findings on impact variation from the Head Start Impact Study: Informing the scale-up of early childhood programs. *AERA Open* 4 (2): 1–16.

Morrissey, Taryn W. 2017. Child care and parent labor force participation: A review of the research literature. *Review of Economics of the Household* 5 (1): 1–24.

NARA. 2006. *2005 Child Care Licensing Study*. Minneapolis, MN: National Association for Regulatory Administration. Available from https://www.naralicensing.org/assets/docs/2005ChildCareLicensingStudy/2005_licensing_study_final_report_web.pdf.

NARA. 2010. *2008 Child Care Licensing Study*. Minneapolis, MN: National Association for Regulatory Administration. Available from http://www.naralicensing.drivehq.com/2008_Licensing_Study/1005_2008_Child%20Care%20Licensing%20Study_Full_Report.pdf.

NARA. 2013. *2011 Child Care Licensing Study*. Minneapolis, MN: National Association for Regulatory Administration. Available from https://www.naralicensing.org/assets/docs/ChildCareLicensingStudies/2011-2013_child%20care%20licensing%20study.pdf.

NARA. 2016. *2014 Child Care Licensing Study*. Minneapolis, MN: National Association for Regulatory Administration. Available from https://www.naralicensing.org/2014-cc-licensing-study.

National Academies of Sciences, Engineering and Medicine. 2019. *A roadmap to reducing child poverty*. Washington, DC: National Academies Press.

Quick, Heather E., Laura E. Hawkins, Aleksandra Holod, Jenifer Anthony, Susan Muenchow, Jill S. Cannon, Lynn A. Karoly, Gail L. Zellman, and Susannah Faxon-Mills. 2016. *Independent evaluation of California Race to the Top-Early Learning Challenge quality rating and improvement system: Cumulative technical report*. Washington, DC: American Institutes for Research and RAND Corporation. Available from https://www.cde.ca.gov/sp/cd/rt/documents/rttelcqrisevalreport.pdf.

Ribar, David C. 1992. Child care and the labor supply of married women: Reduced form evidence. *Journal of Human Resources* 27 (1): 134–65.

Ruopp, Richard, Jeffrey Travers, Frederic Glantz, and Craig Coelen. 1979. *Children at the center: Summary findings and their implications*. Cambridge, MA: Abt Books.

Russo, Anna. 2017. A head start for the whole family: Assessing the labor supply response of mothers of Head Start participants. Senior thesis, Yale University, New Haven, CT.

Sabol, Terri J., and P. Lindsay Chase-Lansdale. 2015. The influence of low-income children's participation in Head Start on their parents? Education and employment. *Journal of Policy Analysis and Management* 34 (1): 136–61.

Sabol, Terri J., Sandra L. Soliday Hong, Robert C. Pianta, and Margaret R. Burchinal. 2013. Can rating pre-k programs predict children's learning? *Science* 341:845–46.

Schlosser, Analia. 2010. Public preschool and the labor supply of Arab mothers: Evidence from a natural experiment. Unpublished Manuscript, Tel Aviv University.

Shapiro, Carl. 1986. Investment, moral hazard, and occupational licensing. *Review of Economic Studies* 53 (5): 843–62.

Stevens, Kathryn, Lorraine Blatt, and Sarah Minton. 2017. *Child care subsidies under the CCDF Program: An overview of policy differences across states and territories*. Report 2017-46 Office of Planning, Research and Evaluation. Washington, DC: U.S. Department of Health and Human Services. Available from https://www.acf.hhs.gov/opre/resource/child-care-subsidies-under-the-ccdf-program-an-overview-of-policy-differences-across-states-and-territories-as-of-october-1-2017.

Stoltzfus, Eric R. 2015. Access to dependent care reimbursement accounts and workplace-funded child-care. *Beyond the Numbers: Pay & Benefits* 4 (1).

Walters, Christopher R., and Patrick Kline. 2016. Evaluating public programs with close substitutes: The case of Head Start. *Quarterly Journal of Economics* 131 (4): 1795–1848.

Yoshikawa, Hirokazu, Christina Weiland, and Jeanne Brooks-Gunn. 2016. When does preschool matter? *The Future of Children* 26 (2): 21–35.

Yoshikawa, Hirokazu, Christina Weiland, Jeanne Brooks-Gunn, Margaret R. Burchinal, Linda M. Espinosa, William T. Gormley, Jens Ludwig, Katherine A. Magnuson, Deborah Phillips, and Martha J. Zaslow. 2013. *Investing in our future: The evidence base on preschool education*. Washington, DC: Society for Research in Child Development. Available from https://www.fcd-us.org/the-evidence-base-on-preschool/.

Zellman, Gail, and Michael Perlman. 2008. *Child care quality rating and improvement systems in five pioneer states: Implementation issues and lessons learned*. Report MG-795- AECF/SPF/UWA. Washington, DC: RAND Corporation. Available from https://www.rand.org/pubs/monographs/MG795.html.

Ziliak, James P. 2014. Proposal 10: Supporting low-income workers through the Refundable Child-Care Credits. In *Policies to address poverty in America*, eds. Melissa S. Kearney and Benjamin H. Harris, 109–17. Washington, DC: The Hamilton Project, Brookings Institution.

Ziliak, James P., Charles Hokayem, and Bradley Hardy. 2008. *Child care subsidies and the economic well-being of recipient families: A survey and implications for Kentucky*. Lexington, KY: University of Kentucky Center for Research on Poverty.

Reflections

Work, Family, and Community: A Framework for Fighting Poverty

The contributions to this volume make clear that the social safety net in the United States is large, complex, and robust. In this reflection, we offer insights into the adequacy of the existing safety net to reduce material hardship and meet the future challenges facing this nation. Our perspective is broad and moves from the effects of each individual program covered in this volume to the safety net's function as a whole and its relation to employment and earnings. We offer a framework for reform that we believe should guide policy-makers and analysts moving forward, and we comment on challenges and potential solutions offered in this collection of work. We conclude with some suggestions for how the safety net can better support employment as the cornerstone of an antipoverty agenda and, by extension, help to build strong families and communities. With this framework in mind, we challenge the next generation of social safety net reformers to reconsider the structure of the social safety net, so it is focused on work, strong families, and vibrant communities.

Keywords: safety net; poverty; means-tested programs; economic prosperity

By
ANGELA RACHIDI
and
ROBERT DOAR

A s of this writing, the American economy is on pace to experience its longest economic expansion in history. Unemployment rates across the country are at historic lows, with strong wage growth being driven by workers in the bottom half of the income distribution (Bureau of Labor Statistics [BLS] 2019).[1] At the same time, changes to family structure, a labor market that requires new and different

Angela Rachidi is a research fellow in poverty studies at the American Enterprise Institute (AEI), where she studies poverty and the effects of federal safety net programs on low-income people in America.

Robert Doar is the president of and Morgridge Scholar at the AEI. He previously led the poverty studies team at AEI and served in leadership positions in the social service programs of New York State and New York City.

Correspondence: angela.rachidi@aei.org

DOI: 10.1177/0002716219884867

skills, and an evolution in what individuals want from the labor market all present challenges for future generations. As we revisit the purpose of our social safety net, we assess its adequacy within this context.

Among the strengths of this volume is that it not only provides a comprehensive look at this country's social insurance and means-tested transfer programs; it also raises a number of important issues that too often get ignored in partisan policy debates, such as how program participation affects employment and family structure. We applaud the authors and editors for acknowledging the complexity of these issues, even though we do not always agree with their interpretations or with their proposed solutions.

Our reaction to the contributions to this volume centers on the goal of a safety net working in conjunction with a free and vibrant economy, which encourages employment as the best path out of poverty. Our safety net is clearly and rightly designed with this in mind: programs either support people while they work (for example, the Earned Income Tax Credit [EITC] and child care assistance) or offer a safety net during periods of unemployment (for example, Temporary Assistance for Needy Families [TANF], unemployment insurance [UI], Social Security Disability Insurance [SSDI], and Social Security).

With this in mind, the safety net performs well. The vast majority of poor families with children (87.4 percent) receives some cash support from the safety net, and when near-cash benefits through Supplemental Nutritional Assistance Program (SNAP) are considered, the share reaches 97 percent (Rachidi and Jin 2017). This does not even account for Medicaid, school lunch, and a host of other programs discussed in this volume. But the safety net works *best* to support low-income people and reduce hardship when combined with employment. A full-time working single parent of two children earning $8 per hour can expect more than $11,000 in refundable tax credits and SNAP benefits per year, which, when combined with earnings, brings her or him above the poverty line. Add to that the value of Medicaid and other potential benefits such as housing and child care assistance, and the safety net brings most full-time working families well out of poverty.

The work of researchers such as Dr. Bruce Meyer of the University of Chicago and Dr. James Sullivan of Notre Dame has borne this out. Using a consumption-based poverty measure, Meyer and Sullivan find that only 2.8 percent of people today are poor in the United States based on 1980s poverty thresholds, a decline of 11 percentage points over the last 35 years (Meyer and Sullivan 2017). Similarly, Meyer and colleagues recently found that extreme poverty in the United States is almost nonexistent when making adjustments to survey data to account for misreporting and underreporting (Meyer et al. 2019).

But assessing adequacy, in our view, involves more than just determining whether the social safety net reduces material hardship. This is where we depart from one of the main themes across this volume, which is that to address future challenges we need to expand existing programs. We believe that redistributing more income without consideration for how it affects work effort and family structure results in a number of negative consequences that undermine the over-arching goal of economic prosperity for all Americans. For example, some individual programs can discourage nonworkers from taking employment and discourage those already working from earning more, in direct conflict with the overall work-promotion aspects of the safety net. Transfer payments may ease the hardship of poverty, but sustained employment and strong families are the best path toward economic prosperity and human flourishing.

Reforming the social safety net for the next generation means revisiting it from this perspective, asking how it can better encourage employment and strong families collectively, while continuing to provide sufficient security for those who cannot provide for their families through employment.

The volume as a whole touches on many of these issues. The implications of the safety net for work and earnings are covered throughout, with some authors giving more attention and raising more concerns than others. Many authors acknowledge that, much like the benefits of individual programs for reducing material hardship, individual programs' negative effects on employment seem modest when considered in isolation. However, taken as a whole, the structure of the safety net and its effects on employment, earnings, and even the message it sends about work expectations may have profound implications.

The same is true for family formation. It is no secret that most government programs are more generous for unmarried families than married ones, suggesting a marriage disincentive or "penalty." Yet as a whole, this volume leaves the impression that the behavioral effects of safety net programs on marriage are small to nonexistent. One must wonder, however, about the collective impact on marriage and childbearing when families participate in more than one program at a time, a question facing methodological challenges not well addressed in the existing empirical research (see, for example, Wilcox, Price, and Rachidi 2016; Low et al. 2018). At the very least, the evidence is clear that having married parents benefits children (Kearney and Levine 2017). Our social safety net should, at a minimum, acknowledge this reality and be designed to support marriage and low-conflict coparenting.

But federal antipoverty policy is only one part of the equation. The volume as a whole downplays the role that states and cities play in addressing poverty among their residents, whether it be through state- or city-sponsored efforts or through the flexibility afforded to them by federal programs. States and cities must be viewed as partners in reforming the social safety net because they are policy laboratories and because they may best understand the needs of their residents.

Finally, we must acknowledge an understated but important point about the role of a healthy economy in fighting poverty. Free enterprise and a strong economy reduce poverty by increasing opportunities for employment, earnings gains, and mobility among low-income individuals and by generating wealth that can be used to help support those who cannot work. The chances greatly increase for all people to flourish when government, alongside private and philanthropic institutions, supports the most vulnerable and protects free enterprise. We therefore view the social safety net—inasmuch as it encourages work—not as a concession, but a complement to our economic system. We want this complementarity preserved for future generations.

The role of a strong economy in reducing poverty has perhaps never been clearer than in the moment that this volume is being assembled. Rising employment and wages, an extended period of a tight labor market, and the continued availability of government-provided supports for both employed and unemployed people have reduced poverty. Notwithstanding all the challenges we face in accurately measuring who is poor, these factors put together mean that poverty in America is the lowest it has been in at least the past 50 years (Meyer and Sullivan 2017). This important observation—that our best defense against poverty is a strong economy—should serve as the foundation of safety net reforms for future generations. The status of the economy may be cyclical, but public policies designed to maximize its potential are an important component of antipoverty policy.

The remainder of this review turns to the individual contributions to this volume and assesses them through the broader framework we identified above: work, family, and the role for state and local entities. We identify salient issues raised by each author as they assess program adequacy and potential reforms, with an eye to how the program contributes to positive and negative work effects of the safety net. We discuss some of the key challenges and the potential solutions laid out in the volume within the context of how each program relates to work and family. We conclude by presenting a few ideas of our own that we think warrant consideration as policy-makers embark on reforming the social safety net in coming years.

The Salient Issues

The contributions to this volume aptly reveal that the social safety net in this country serves a number of different purposes, which can sometimes conflict. This can make assessing adequacy difficult. As Haskins and Weidinger (this volume) show in their article on TANF, states use TANF money for a variety of worthwhile purposes that support the diverse interests of low-income families. But the flexibility given to states has resulted in some states moving away from providing cash assistance to poor families, one of the original purposes of the program, and instead funding things like tax credits for low-income working parents or child welfare services, for example. From the narrow view of providing cash aid to low-income families, TANF might appear inadequate. But as Haskins and Weidinger point out, TANF viewed more broadly has achieved some safety net goals: it has successfully led to lower poverty among children and higher work rates among never-married mothers.

Similarly, Hotz and Wiswall (this volume) acknowledge a tension within the country's child care assistance policy, with policies designed to increase the quality of child care driving up costs in conflict with policy aims to provide access to affordable child care. Tensions emerge across programs, too. Hoynes (this volume) describes the desire to support low-wage work as a key purpose of the EITC, yet Schanzenbach (this volume) acknowledges that SNAP can decrease work. Collinson, Ellen, and Ludwig (this volume) admit the same when it comes to housing assistance programs. In short, the safety net can occasionally get in its own way by prioritizing narrow policy goals (such as financial support) at the expense of the broader purpose of the safety net (increasing employment, for example), and vice versa.

With these tensions in mind, the authors in this volume identified a few key themes concerning adequacy. Those include, for means-tested programs, meeting the basic needs of low-income families, such as nutrition, housing, and health insurance; smoothing incomes for people temporarily or permanently unable to work either due to a weak labor market or disability; and, in some cases, the desire for the government to redistribute income from wealthier Americans to those with less. Among social insurance programs, the common purpose laid out in this volume without regard to income is for the government to help Americans protect against the loss of income due to temporary or permanent unemployment, including retirement.

Across this volume, the authors conclude that these programs are largely adequate in meeting these core purposes and, in many cases, describe substantial benefits beyond that core. A few highlights include Hoynes's article on refundable tax credits, which describes several benefits of the EITC and CTC for low-income working families, including increased employment rates for parents and healthy development for children. Schanzenbach offers a similarly positive assessment of SNAP, describing its benefits on both food security and economic stabilization. Haskins and Weidinger describe various benefits of TANF, including reduced welfare, increased employment, and lower child poverty.

Contributions to this volume also highlight the virtues of social insurance programs that are not means-tested, including SSDI and UI, in protecting Americans against the risk of lost earnings due to disability or non-disability-related unemployment. And few can argue with Burtless (this volume) on Social Security and Chandra and Garthwaite (this volume) when it comes to Medicare that both programs have met their core purposes of lowering poverty and improving health among older Americans. Of course, spending on seniors has dwarfed spending on children, as many commentators have pointed out, making the safety net's benefits for children even more impressive.

Although each individual contribution concludes that programs have achieved a base level of adequacy in reducing material hardship, we are left with several reservations. We wonder at what expense the social safety net has achieved these benefits—not monetary expense, necessarily, but rather social expense and depression of work effort—and whether their success can be sustained in the context of a changing social and economic environment. This brings us to the challenges identified by many of the authors of this volume.

Challenges and How to Address Them

In our view, the biggest challenge inherent in the design of the safety net is how to counteract forces that undermine the very things that lift families out of poverty, namely, work and having two married parents. Related questions surround solvency and sustainability given the rising costs associated with many of these programs. We view these challenges as related: if reforms can better lift families out of poverty by addressing the root causes, they reduce the need for ever-expanding expenditures on an increasingly poor population.

The contributors to this volume took a slightly different view. The common challenge offered by the authors across individual means-tested programs is that benefit levels or reimbursement rates are inadequate. Or, in the cases of TANF and housing assistance, that program expenditures have not kept pace with inflation. This assessment naturally leads many authors to propose increased spending. But this largely ignores how these programs work together; and in many cases it would raise effective marginal tax rates on dollars earned by those seeking to get out of poverty, exacerbating sustainability problems and undermining the overarching goal of reducing poverty.

For example, in their assessment of TANF, Haskins and Weidinger reprint a well-known chart showing that fewer than one out of every four poor families receive TANF, interpreting this to mean that TANF should spend more on cash aid to poor families. But this overlooks the fact that most poor families receive (alone or in combination) Supplemental Security Income (SSI), the EITC, unemployment insurance, SNAP, or Medicaid. In fact, our own research suggests that when all these safety net programs are considered, more than 95 percent of poor families with children receive some support from the government (Rachidi and Jin 2017). Though these families are classified as poor based on their earned income, when income from additional programs is factored in, these families often rise above the poverty line.

Instead of aiming to enroll more poor families in more government programs, or simply to increase benefit levels, we should focus on how to help them get out of poverty for good. This requires cohesion across safety net programs, especially in encouraging employment and self-reliance. We were encouraged to see that work disincentives were a common challenge mentioned across the means-tested program articles, especially those focused on disability, including SSDI and SSI. The issue was raised but emphasized less in the articles on SNAP, housing assistance, and Medicaid.

There are several good examples from this volume of proposed reforms that would focus means-tested programs on work and program exit while maintaining a robust support system for those who cannot work. Daly and Duggan's assessment of SSI is one. They describe an "absorbing state" created by SSI where beneficiaries must prove an inability to work to get assistance and for the most part, never work again to maintain eligibility. They describe incentives for states to divert low-income individuals to SSI from state-funded programs and for individuals to overstate their condition to secure assistance. They offer a number of proposed reforms, two of which we strongly support. Reformers should consider partial disability payments in SSI that recognize a person's inability to fully engage with the labor market, but also not fully disengage. And there is a strong case for Medicaid to reconsider the incentives it places on managed care companies to keep people sick and not working to maximize their enrollment.

Maestas makes similar points related to SSDI. She identifies disincentives to work as a key program challenge and recommends changing the way eligibility is determined. She describes SSDI, as currently designed, as partially linked to the business cycle and questions whether that is appropriate. Because eligibility is determined by functional disability and one's education, age, or skill level, more people become eligible when the economy is down. But when the economy recovers, few incentives exist to return to the labor market, and skill atrophy makes reentry more challenging. The federal government needs to revisit how disability claims are determined in SSDI, with an eye toward helping people with disabilities to remain in the labor market, even if in a limited capacity.

Across other articles, negative work impacts are also mentioned but deemphasized. In the article on SNAP, Schanzenbach mentions the research evidence that shows work disincentives, but she proposes increasing the program's "earned income disregard" to counteract the negative work effect. This can be part of the solution (though it will be costly), but not a solution in itself. Work expectations in exchange for benefits, when implemented properly, can have positive effects on employment and send a powerful message about the role of public assistance programs in a free society. Abandoning this principle erodes social trust and does little to help people become economically mobile.

Similarly, Collinson, Ellen, and Ludwig acknowledge the evidence from housing assistance programs showing that they can reduce work but describe the effects as modest and do not recommend program changes to address them. Currie and Duque make the same argument about Medicaid, dismissing any suggestion that Medicaid beneficiaries should be expected to work if they are capable. And while Hoynes describes work promotion within the EITC—which is one program that consistently shows positive work effects—she downplays the problem of the marriage penalty, which highlights the tension between working toward one goal (employment) while undermining another (strong families). Across these programs, we would like to see more emphasis on work, and in the case of the EITC we would like to see reforms that improve the integrity of the program and treat married couples equally, without reducing the overall positive work effects.

In contrast, Haskins and Weidinger recommend strengthening work requirements in TANF to address low levels of work among poor populations. We agree with their assessment to shift the program to an outcome-focused approach versus the current process-focused one. We also support giving states more flexibility to blend funding from other programs (for example, SNAP, workforce development, and child support enforcement) and more autonomy to decide the best services to provide to job seekers, while holding them accountable for low-income people finding and sustaining employment. For those uncomfortable with increased state autonomy, we propose a new round of state-led demonstration projects similar to those from the 1990s that led to welfare reform.

But as we have stressed, policy-makers must consider potential negative employment effects when families participate in more than one program at the same time. Hoynes mentions this potential problem in her article on the EITC, but it receives little attention in other articles. This is perhaps because the behavioral effects of marginal tax rates related to multiple program participation are empirically difficult to test, resulting in little evidence. Cross-program reforms, allowing more flexibility to states to blend funding sources, slower phase-out periods for benefit programs, or coordination of benefit phase-outs could offer solutions. States should be given more tools like these to better address this problem.

Beyond the challenges that affect work, the contributors to this volume identified other important challenges that limit the safety net's effectiveness. Currie and Duque highlight several challenges in Medicaid, particularly related to cost and access to care. But policy-makers should address the key problems with Medicaid as we see it: incentives built in for states to spend more rather than less, as well as declining quality and access to services because of the complicated nature of the Medicaid funding formula in a health care system that cannot control costs. We prefer reforms like those proposed by James Capretta (2017), such as changing the incentive structure in the funding formula by moving away from open-ended federal matching funds to more state control. He argues for creating two streams of funding—one for the elderly and disabled, and one for children and nondisabled adults—and giving states more incentive to manage the program efficiently and control the growth in spending. This solves the fundamental problem of access while providing a better opportunity to control costs.

Hotz and Wiswall identify a number of challenges with the child care assistance program that are also worth noting. The tension between funding high-quality care while also providing access to affordable child care can be addressed in a few ways. Hotz and Wiswall acknowledge that the evidence is thin for whether quality-improvement efforts, such as state regulations on child-to-staff ratios, actually work. But without question they drive up costs. Reforms should center on revisiting state regulations and requirements to ensure that policy-makers only impose those requirements that truly lead to safe and secure child care settings, as well as better-quality interactions between caregivers and children. We would also like to see more attention paid to how child care assistance programs can promote stability for children, including for children with parents who work different types of schedules. Nontraditional work schedules are crucial to the health of our economy in a global environment and many lower-skilled workers fill these jobs. Through public and private efforts, community leaders can better ensure that children experience stability in their child care settings even when their parents' work schedules must change.

Another common challenge identified throughout the volume involves the ability of federal programs to be responsive to local needs. Collinson, Ellen, and Ludwig aptly point out that our existing housing assistance programs have at times contributed to community decline by failing to account for variation in market conditions across the country, leaving many areas with poor-fitting programs that do not account for local needs. Housing assistance could be focused on more modest, time-limited vouchers, as the authors note, to support mobility to better neighborhoods—something research has shown to be critically important for economic mobility (Chetty and Hendren 2018).

Safety-net responsiveness to local needs comes up in other articles as well. The block grant structure of TANF and child care assistance through the Child Care Development Block Grant demonstrate how federal policy can be implemented with state-level flexibility responsive to local conditions. Giving more flexibility to states in programs such as SNAP and Medicaid is worth considering with the goal of returning some autonomy to states and local communities. This can happen by transforming the way programs are financed by using block grants, for example, but also by using existing mechanisms like approving state-level waivers to federal legislation.

One more challenge to highlight is related to SNAP and health, especially children's health. Schanzenbach identifies a number of purposes for SNAP but missed the expressly stated purpose from the authorizing legislation, which is "to safeguard the health and well-being of the Nation's population by raising levels of nutrition among low-income households" (U.S. Department of Agriculture [USDA], Food and Nutrition Service [FNS] 2008). SNAP has been largely inadequate in this regard. According to research from the USDA, the federal agency that operates SNAP, participants have higher rates of obesity, consume more sugary beverages, and have lower healthy eating scores than similar and higher income nonparticipants (USDA, FNS 2015), and grocery store transactions that involve SNAP include more sugary beverage purchases and fewer fruits and vegetables than those that do not involve SNAP (Leung et al. 2017). We believe it is time for federal lawmakers to place additional restrictions on what can be purchased with SNAP benefits by not allowing sugary beverages, similar to what they already do with other unhealthy products like alcohol and tobacco. This would be conducive to better health and increased employment.

A Framework for Moving Forward

We close with a few considerations for policy-makers as they seek to reform means-tested and social insurance programs for future generations. We outlined some reforms already that support the three pillars of our antipoverty agenda: work, family, and local autonomy. In practical, tangible terms, that would mean allowing partial disability payments in SSI and SSDI; changing how eligibility is determined in disability programs; and giving more autonomy to states in TANF, SNAP, Medicaid, and child care; while holding them accountable for helping benefit recipients find and keep work. But these are marginal reforms to expansive programs that likely will not address all the challenges that we identified above.

We believe that the broader concern about how the safety net impacts employment and family structure warrants more fundamental reforms. Policy-makers and analysts should, at times of economic health such as this one, revisit the principles underlying the social safety net and how they translate to current program design and funding priorities. Policy-makers must ask themselves: what is the safety net supposed to achieve? How does that goal fit into the legitimate function of government and allow space for institutions of meaning to play their proper role in American life?

We believe the safety net complements free enterprise by reducing material hardship for those in need and investing in the development of children, to maintain a strong, sustainable, free economy and a just society for future generations. However, the safety net is not, and cannot be, everything to everyone. It must facilitate, or at least remain compatible with, the primary values of work and family, the building blocks of a healthy, fair, and virtuous life. Government assistance should always be designed and funded with this crucial consideration in mind.

So while we laud the safety net for doing well what it does—reducing material hardship—we must take a critical eye to assessing its choice (often reflecting factional political influences and bureaucratic priorities) of *what to do*. For instance, our current system disproportionately invests in the elderly and spends the bulk of the money targeted to low-income families on health insurance and long-term care costs for the ill. In a world of limited resources, that kind of prioritization should not be taken for granted and may require difficult or even unpopular reallocation decisions, preferably ones that direct more programs to aiding and supporting children.

The answer to the paradox of reducing hardship while maintaining a strong focus on work and family cannot simply be to spend more money on programs for the poor, as some in this volume propose. Programs cannot grow indefinitely in a world where debt matters, and increasing expenditures on programs such as Medicaid creates new problems of market distortions and insufficient access to health care. Reforming Social Security, Medicare, and Medicaid with an eye toward controlling costs and increasing access to needed goods and services is necessary, both for the health of the programs and so that they do not crowd out further investments in employment and the development of children.

Rethinking the proper role and function of the safety net may mean better addressing the underlying conditions that lead to poverty. Policy-makers will have to confront, among others, such patterns as unhealthy lifestyles that lead to poor health (and translate to limited employment and marriage prospects), poor early care and education opportunities for young children, the breakdown of two-parent families, and cash aid programs that keep people poor for fear that increased earnings will come at the cost of what government support they get. A social safety net that promotes self-reliance and recognizes its proper role in American life can invest in communities and early childhood with the aim of preventing these underlying conditions from taking hold in the first place.

This, fundamentally, requires a close examination of how the safety net is structured and how programs work (or do not work) together. Health insurance programs, food assistance programs, and disability assistance programs need to work in concert to incentivize good health, proper nutrition, and active lifestyles (all of which are aided, it is worth noting, by employment and marriage). In concrete terms, this means revisiting the entire health care and food production systems in this country with an eye toward improving individual health and well-being. This will help to ensure that people can fully benefit from the virtues of our society, including education, employment, and civic opportunities.

The federal government has taken the lead in developing welfare-state infrastructure, but this reevaluation questions whether that need be the case. States need more flexibility to improve early care and education systems, improve the health and skills of their residents, and attract and retain jobs. Too often federal programs condition funding in ways that prevent states and local communities from doing what they believe is in their best interests. This, of course, does not mean states should not be held accountable, but federal policy-makers must recognize that a one-size-fits-all solution crafted in Washington, D.C., cannot possibly meet the demands of our nation's diverse population. States should be required to demonstrate effectiveness in their programming, and federal funding should only continue when results are achieved.

Now is a perfect time to revisit the structure of our social safety net with an eye toward work, family, and community autonomy, especially in light of the opportunities and challenges that we have summarized. But we recognize that fundamentally reforming the social safety net is not an easy task. Our AEI colleague Yuval Levin (2019) summarized the issue well when he said,

> The challenge facing welfare reformers is daunting: They have to find ways to help people who lack not only money but often also stable families, functional communities, and decent schools. They have to encourage work and responsibility while offering aid [which] often works best when it is accompanied by advice, by obligations, and by evident compassion at a personal level.

Notwithstanding these challenges, we take comfort in our belief that policy-makers are up to the task and can enact policies that reflect our deepest-held values and meet the needs of our future as a diverse, ambitious, free, and prosperous people.

Note

1. Federal Reserve Bank of Atlanta Wage Tracker 2019, available at https://www.frbatlanta.org/chcs/wage-growth-tracker.aspx (accessed 9 August 2019).

References

Bureau of Labor Statistics. July 2019. The employment situation. *News release*. Washington, DC: BLS.

Capretta, James C. 2017. Medicaid. In *A safety net that works: Improving federal programs for low-income Americans*, ed. Robert Doar, 47–62. Washington, DC: American Enterprise Institute Press.

Chetty, Raj, and Nathaniel Hendren. 2018. The impacts of neighborhoods on intergenerational mobility I: Childhood exposure effects. *Quarterly Journal of Economics* 133 (3): 1107–62.

Kearney, Melissa S., and Phillip B. Levine. 2017. The economics of nonmarital childbearing and the marriage premium for children. *Annual Review of Economics* 9:327–52.

Leung, Cindy W., June M. Tester, Eric B. Rimm, and Walter C. Willett. 2017. SNAP participation and diet-sensitive cardiometabolic risk factors in adolescents. *American Journal of Preventive Medicine* 52 (2): S127–37.

Levin, Yuval. 2019. Economic mobility: Is the American Dream in crisis? Testimony given at a hearing before the Subcommittee on Economic Policy, Senate Committee on Banking, Housing, and Urban Affairs, 116th Congress.

Low, Hamish, Costas Meghir, Luigi Pistaferri, and Alessandra Voena. 2018. Marriage, labor supply and the dynamics of the social safety net. National Bureau of Economic Research Working Paper, Cambridge, MA.

Meyer, Bruce D., and James X. Sullivan. 2017. *Annual report on US consumption poverty: 2016.* Washington, DC: AEI. Available from https://www.aei.org/wp-content/uploads/2017/09/meyer_sullivan_consumption_poverty_report_2016.pdf.

Meyer, Bruce D., Derek Wu, Victoria R. Mooers, and Carla Medalia. 2019. The use and misuse of income data and extreme poverty in the United States. National Bureau of Economic Research Working Paper, Cambridge, MA.

Rachidi, Angela, and Shijie Jin. 28 February 2017. *The reach of the cash-based safety net for poor families with children in America.* AEI Economic Perspectives. Available from https://www.aei.org/wp-content/uploads/2017/02/The-Reach-of-the-Cash-Based-Safety- Net.pdf.

U.S. Department of Agriculture, Food and Nutrition Service. 2008. Food and Nutrition Act of 2008 Provisions. Available from https://fns-prod.azureedge.net/sites/default/files/resource-files/Food%20And%20Nutrition%20Act%20Of%202008%20Enacted%20122018.pdf.

U.S. Department of Agriculture (USDA), Food and Nutrition Service. 2015. Diet quality of Americans by SNAP participation status: Data from the National Health and Nutrition Survey 2007–2010. Washington, DC: USDA. Available from https://fns-prod.azureedge.net/sites/default/files/ops/NHANES-SNAP07-10.pdf.

Wilcox, W. B., J. Price, and Angela Rachidi. 2016. *Marriage penalized: Does social welfare policy affect family formation?* Washington, DC: American Enterprise Institute and Institute for Family Studies Research Report.

The Economic Context for Reforming the Safety Net

By
KAREN DYNAN

As we wrestle with the future of our safety net and social insurance programs, it is important to understand not only the features and outcomes associated with individual programs but also the broader economic context. This reflection piece discusses several relevant aspects of the macroeconomy and of economic and financial conditions facing households: rising government debt, slower macroeconomic growth, limited tools to fight future recessions, greater income inequality, and the financial struggles of households. It goes on to draw lessons for how we should reform our system of entitlement programs.

Keywords: safety net; Social Security; recessions; government debt; inequality

Whether and how to reform our nation's safety net and social insurance programs have been topics of long-standing interest to policy-makers. As a group, these programs are designed to protect individuals from hardship, enhance the future prospects of beneficiaries and their children, and support overall economic activity. While most policy experts would agree that the programs advance these goals on net, many also believe that the programs could do better. Furthermore, some in the policy community argue that changes are necessary to reduce the budgetary costs of the programs. Given projections that fiscal pressures will rise significantly, this discussion is only likely to intensify.

The articles in this volume stand to inform the debate over potential changes to our safety

Karen Dynan is a professor of the practice of economics in the Harvard University Economics Department and a nonresident senior fellow at the Peterson Institute for International Economics. She served as assistant secretary for economic policy and chief economist at the U.S. Treasury Department from 2014 to 2017.

NOTE: I thank Jim Ziliak and Robert Moffitt for helpful comments.

Correspondence: kdynan@fas.harvard.edu

DOI: 10.1177/0002716219885605

net and social insurance programs. Each article describes a specific program (such as Social Security) or a set of programs that falls in a specific area (such as affordable housing). The articles discuss what research has shown to be the successes of the programs as well as their shortcomings. The articles then discuss proposals to change the programs, including options aimed at making them more effective at meeting their goals, reducing their costs, or some combination. Finally, the articles present the authors' own recommendations for how to proceed.

As we wrestle with the future of our safety net and social insurance programs, it is essential to understand not only the features and outcomes associated with individual programs but also relevant aspects of the macroeconomy and of economic and financial conditions facing households. These broader considerations help to inform the goals for reform, both because they bear on how these programs affect economic security at the household level and because the macroeconomic consequences of the programs are highly relevant for the programs' design. The piece begins by highlighting several important economic factors: rising government debt, slower macroeconomic growth, limited tools to fight future recessions, greater income inequality, and the financial struggles of many U.S. households. The piece then turns to the implications for policy.

Rising Government Debt

Over the past dozen years, the Great Recession, the slow economic recovery that followed, and (to a lesser extent) the 2017 tax cuts have contributed to more than a doubling of federal debt relative to gross domestic product (GDP). According to the Congressional Budget Office (CBO), federal debt amounted to 78 percent of GDP in 2019, up from 35 percent in 2007 (CBO 2019b). Prior to the recession, the CBO projected that this ratio would be just 17 percent in 2019 (CBO 2007).

Traditionally, such an increase in debt would be viewed as imposing considerable costs on the economy. But the recognition that various forces have led to a significant—and likely persistent—decline in real interest rates over the past several decades has begun to change this thinking.[1] An important recent literature (Summers 2016; Elmendorf and Sheiner 2017; Blanchard 2019) argues that lower interest rates imply that the costs of any given amount of government debt are lower now than they were previously. Lower interest rates are associated not only with more favorable debt dynamics because of reduced interest obligations but also with a higher optimal level of government debt because the opportunity cost of using loanable funds to finance the government (as opposed to private investment) is lower.

However, lower interest rates do not let the government off the hook from addressing the projected future excess of noninterest spending over revenue that will eventually cause federal debt to snowball. Even assuming that government borrowing rates remain fairly low, federal debt is projected to climb sharply in coming decades and reach 144 percent of GDP by 2049 under current law

FIGURE 1
Federal Debt Held by the Public

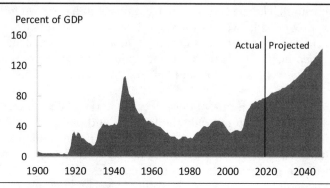

SOURCE: Data from CBO (2019b).

(Figure 1). Federal debt is projected to rise to 219 percent of GDP by 2049 if the law is changed to keep certain major policies—such as the individual tax cuts enacted in 2017—in place. There remains widespread agreement that debt cannot rise indefinitely relative to GDP without exposing the economy to significant harms and risks. But lower rates do create some room to be more selective about the timing and nature of the fiscal adjustment such that the changes also address other economic and social goals.

Slower Macroeconomic Growth

A second important background factor is slower macroeconomic growth. Since 2000, growth in real U.S. GDP has averaged only around 2 percent per year, down from more than 3 percent in the 1970s, 1980s, and 1990s. This slower pace of growth is widely expected to persist. When economic forecasters were asked in early 2019 about average real GDP growth over the next 10 years, the mean response was 2.1 percent (Survey of Professional Forecasters 2019). Some respondents had a considerably more pessimistic outlook, with the 10th percentile of responses forecasting average growth of just 0.5 percent per year.

Economic growth in the long run depends on the average pace of change in two factors: the amount of labor supplied and the amount of output that each unit of labor can produce (labor productivity). The former factor can more than account for the decline in trend GDP growth. A few decades ago, a steady flow of women entering the workforce supported robust labor supply growth. But that uptrend in female labor force participation ended around the turn of the century. More recently, the ongoing retirement of the Baby Boom generation has been substantially weighing on labor supply. A decades-long downtrend in the labor force participation rate of working-age men has also held down overall labor supply (Black and Powell 2017). The CBO (2019a) estimates that annual "potential"

FIGURE 2
Potential Labor Force Growth

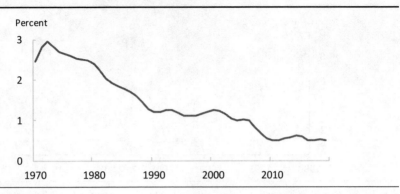

SOURCE: CBO (2019a).

labor supply growth fell from an average of almost 2 percent between 1970 and 1999 to an average of just 0.5 percent per year in the 2010s (Figure 2), with growth projected to be that low or lower over the next three decades.

The slowdown in real GDP growth has important negative consequences. When the economy is growing 3 percent per year, real GDP will double in 23 years; when it is growing 2 percent per year, it will take 35 years to double. Of course, the distribution of income matters for who will bear the brunt of the lower growth, but the lower trend is unlikely to be a positive one for the most vulnerable households. Slower overall economic growth is also contributing to the fiscal challenges faced by the United States. The CBO estimates that if GDP growth were 0.5 percentage point faster per year than expected, federal debt as a share of GDP would rise by 28 percentage points over the next 30 years instead of the 66 percentage points in the baseline forecast (CBO 2019b).

Limited Tools to Fight Future Recessions

Policy-makers interested in reforms to safety net and social insurance programs should also bear in mind the likely future limitations on the macroeconomic tools that have traditionally been used to stabilize the economy. Most notably, low real interest rates, together with subdued inflation, have produced very low nominal interest rates—and because nominal interest rates cannot be negative (or at least very negative), the Federal Reserve will have less room to cut policy rates in future downturns. Indeed, as of mid-2019, the nominal federal funds rate was below 2.5 percent, allowing for further cuts that would total less than half as much as the cumulative reduction in the federal funds rate in each of the past three recessions (Figure 3). More generally, Laubach and Williams (2016) conclude that persistent low interest rates mean that episodes of hitting the zero lower bound are likely to occur more often and be more severe in the future.

FIGURE 3
Federal Funds Rate

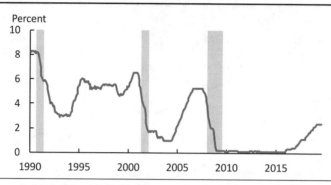

SOURCE: Board of Governors of the Federal Reserve System; see https://www.federalreserve
.gov/releases/h15/.
NOTE: Shaded areas denote recessions.

Of course, the Federal Reserve can turn to unconventional tools of monetary policy—such as quantitative easing and forward guidance—to help fight future downturns, as it did during the Great Recession. Such tools should be able to compensate for some of the reduced scope of conventional monetary policy. But many monetary policy experts have doubts about whether the collective current set of central bank tools will be enough to fully address a meaningful economic downturn (see, for example, Bernanke 2017).

The limitations on monetary policy suggest that fiscal policy will have a more important role to play combating future downturns. Countercyclical fiscal policy can be effective—for example, the American Recovery and Reinvestment Act of 2009 (ARRA) featured a set of tax cuts and spending measures that is estimated to have significantly reduced the severity of the Great Recession and to have hastened the ensuing recovery (Blinder and Zandi 2015). But this type of "discretionary" fiscal policy has its own limitations. One traditional concern is that the potentially substantial amount of time needed to develop, pass, and implement a big fiscal package delays needed support for a weak economy. Another concern that emerged after the onset of the Great Recession is the risk of political resistance to using expansionary fiscal policy to support aggregate demand. For example, Europe turned to fiscal austerity in the early 2010s amid still-weak economic conditions (Krugman 2015), and the United States put in place deficit-cutting measures that created a fiscal drag in 2011 when the unemployment rate remained above 8 percent (Furman 2018).

Without sufficiently vigorous monetary and fiscal policy, recessions may be more severe, last longer, and be associated with weaker and more fragile recoveries. In turn, they are likely to produce more individual hardship, with research suggesting that the groups hurt the most—minorities, young people, and those with low education—tend to be the ones who have lower incomes even when the economy is at full employment (Hoynes, Miller, and Schaller 2012). More severe recessions are also more likely to leave ongoing scars. There is growing evidence

FIGURE 4
Cumulative Growth in Real Market Income

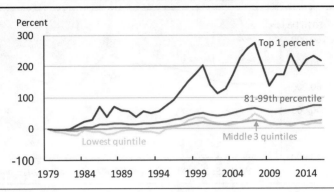

SOURCE: CBO (2019a).

that the Great Recession generated employment and income losses that persisted after the unemployment rate had normalized (see, for example, Yagan 2019), and research examining the severe U.S. recessions of the early 1980s found lower earnings for laid-off workers decades later (Davis and von Wachter 2011).

Greater Income Inequality

Higher income inequality should also change how we think about our safety net and social insurance programs. Over the past several decades, market incomes have grown rapidly for households at the very top of the income distribution, fairly strongly for other households in the top quintile, and only weakly for the rest of the distribution. According to the CBO (2019a), market incomes for the top 1 percent of U.S. households were up 218 percent over the 36 years between 1979 and 2016, while market incomes for others in the top quintile rose 74 percent, market incomes in the middle three quintiles rose 25 percent, and market incomes for the bottom quintile increased just 17 percent (Figure 4).[2] These patterns tell us that much of the U.S. population received little direct benefit from the overall growth in the economy over this period.

A major turnaround of these distributional trends seems unlikely in the future given the underlying causes. Technology evolved in a way that rewarded those with high skills and displaced middle- and lower-skill workers who do routine tasks. Changes in labor market institutions—such as the decline of unions and the rise of nontraditional work arrangements—weakened the bargaining power of workers. Globalization created larger markets, enhancing the incomes of top CEOs and superstars in various fields. None of these developments seems likely to reverse in coming decades, and some may get worse.

Among the concerns about growing income inequality is the potential for it to be self-reinforcing. Kearney (2014) highlights various findings suggesting that

FIGURE 5
Real Household Net Worth

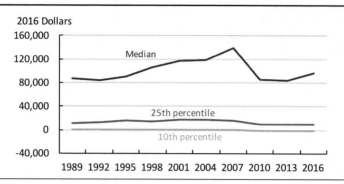

SOURCE: Survey of Consumer Finances; see https://www.federalreserve.gov/econres/scfindex .htm.

children from low-income areas are disadvantaged relative to children from high-income areas in ways that contribute to gaps in their future achievement. In line with this view, Chetty et al. (2014) show that areas with higher income inequality and income segregation tend to have lower rates of social mobility.

These trends not only can impede individuals from reaching their full potential; they likely have negative implications for the broader economy and society. They can be destructive for the social fabric and foster a sense that the system is not fair and that institutions are not to be trusted. In doing so, they may increase resistance for needed structural reforms and create support for populist policies like protectionism, reinforcing the lower trend in economic growth.

Financial Struggles of Many U.S. Households

Finally, discussions about changes to safety net and social insurance programs should consider the financial state of households, particularly in the middle and lower parts of the income distribution. Substantially fewer U.S. households are showing signs of acute financial distress, such as loan delinquency or bankruptcy, than they were a decade ago.[3] However, many households struggle to accumulate wealth, which may cause them harm (or at least present obstacles) over the longer run, and they look to be worse off in this regard than a few decades ago. According to the Survey of Consumer Finances, the net worth of the median household was $97,290 in 2016, down from $117,520 in 2001 (in 2016 dollars). At the 25th percentile, net worth was just $10,160 in 2016, down from $17,369 in 2001; and at the 10th percentile, net worth was –$1,030 in 2016, down from $135 in 2001 (Figure 5).

Perhaps relatedly, a literature pioneered by Lusardi, Tufano, and Schneider (2011) suggests that a material share of U.S. households are "financially fragile." These authors found that about one-quarter of households would not be able to come up with $2,000 in a month's time if needed. Along the same lines, a recent survey by the Federal Reserve found that 12 percent of adults would not be able to pay an emergency expense of just $400 by any means (Board of Governors of the Federal Reserve System 2019).

The apparent inability of many households to accumulate material amounts of wealth hampers economic and social mobility. It is more difficult for a household with low wealth to invest in higher education or start a new business. At the macroeconomic level, these obstacles may lead to a less-skilled workforce and less innovation and dynamism. Low wealth may also make households less resilient to shocks, which could lead to worse recessions and slower economic recoveries.

Of particular note are financial trends among households with members who are now nearing retirement age. Households in this group today are less likely than their earlier cohorts to have a defined-benefit pension to supplement their Social Security income. According to the Survey of Consumer Finances, 28 percent of households whose heads were between the ages of 50 and 59 in 2016 reported being covered by a defined-benefit pension, down from 49 percent of households in this age group in the mid-1990s. Yet households in this age group do not appear to have compensated for reduced coverage in defined-benefit pensions by doing more retirement savings—median household net worth in the 50 to 59 age group was $145,900 in 2016, 17 percent below the median in the mid-1990s after adjusting for inflation.

What These Trends Mean for Entitlement Reform

These considerations—together with the insights provided by the other articles in this volume—have several important implications.

Implication 1: The financing of the Social Security program will need to be fixed, and the fix should be progressive

As Burtless (this volume) notes, available estimates suggest that the Social Security program's resources (incoming revenues plus what is available in the trust fund) will begin to be insufficient to fund scheduled benefits sometime between 2030 and 2035. Addressing this problem is widely viewed as a central component of putting government debt on a sustainable trajectory. Indeed, under current law, Social Security is scheduled to contribute between 1 and 2 percentage points to annual federal budget deficits for the next 30 years (CBO 2019b). Burtless discusses various options for raising payroll taxes and reducing benefits in ways that would shore up the program finances.

The faster income growth experienced by the top of the distribution in recent decades implies that higher-income households are in a better position to bear cuts in benefits or increases in taxes than are lower-income households. This difference makes a case for progressive adjustments to the Social Security program; although, as is clear from the discussion in Burtless (this volume), the solvency issues are sufficiently big such that adjustments for top earners alone cannot solve the problems. Broader household financial security considerations reinforce the argument for cutting benefits less (if at all) for households low in the earnings distribution. Sizable cuts could undo the enormous decline in old-age poverty that Burtless credits to the program. Moreover, the greater struggles of more recent generations to accumulate retirement saving, together with the decline in private defined-benefit pensions, suggest that future cohorts of retirees may need the program even more than earlier cohorts to avoid poverty and other types of hardship.[4]

An important related issue flagged by Burtless (this volume) is that a disparity in mortality improvements undermines the argument that rising average life expectancy justifies an older full-benefit retirement age. Individuals in the bottom 40 percent of the income distribution appear to have experienced no increase in longevity on average in recent decades (National Academies of Sciences, Engineering, and Medicine 2015). This development strengthens the case for progressive adjustments to the program. Combining an older retirement age with younger full-benefit retirement ages for households lower in the income distribution might be one solution; another, suggested by Burtless, would be to combine an older full-benefit retirement age with more generous benefits at lower incomes, which would make it easier for lower-income individuals to make ends meet with the reduced payments that come with claiming early.

Implication 2: It is imperative that we curb growth in government spending on health care

Growth in government spending on health care is expected to be a key driver of higher future government debt, with the CBO (2019b) projecting that federal spending for the major health care programs will rise from 5.9 percent of GDP in 2019 to 10.7 percent of GDP in 2049. Given the fiscal sustainability challenges discussed earlier, we need to curb growth in this spending. If we do not, health care spending will increasingly crowd out other key types of government spending—including essential outlays done through many of the programs covered in this volume. As Currie and Duque (this volume) point out, this crowding out will occur not just at the federal level, but also at the state level, with higher state spending on Medicaid putting pressure, for example, on state education budgets.

A central tension is that we want more and better health care for Americans. Both Currie and Duque (this volume) and Chandra and Garthwaite (this volume) underscore the importance of providing adequate health insurance for Americans—not just because we want good health outcomes (with their beneficial spillovers, for example, to people's earnings) but also because insurance reduces the financial struggles associated with large medical expenses. Moreover, as our society grows older and richer, those who are already insured will need and want more care.

More than two-thirds of the expected rise in spending on the major federal health care programs relative to GDP over the next 30 years owes to federal health care costs per person growing in excess of the pace of growth of GDP (also known as "excess cost growth").[5] International comparisons suggest that we can get more value for our money—the United States spends about twice as much per person on health care as other high-income countries (Papanicolas, Woskie, and Jha 2018), and yet we have *worse* outcomes by a variety of metrics (Elmendorf 2018). The especially poor health outcomes for people lower in the income distribution—as evidenced, for example, by Case and Deaton's (2017) work on "deaths of despair"—reinforce concerns about growing income inequality.

Tackling excess health care cost growth will be difficult, but the Currie and Duque (this volume) and Chandra and Garthwaite (this volume) articles offer some policy ideas that would take us in the right direction. Medicare appears to be the priority given its large size. Reforms to the Medicare Advantage (MA) program could create more competition among private-sector MA insurers, putting downward pressure on prices. Then exposing the entire Medicare system to competitive bidding through a "premium support" feature could limit cost growth in the traditional fee-for-service part of Medicare. As Chandra and Garthwaite point out, restraining growth in drug prices in both Part B and Part D of Medicare is an important part of holding down costs; they propose a set of reforms that would primarily operate through market mechanisms so as to avoid some of the innovation-inhibiting distortions that occur when prices are directly regulated.

Implication 3. We should not cut programs that benefit poor children or their parents

A number of articles in this volume highlight the important and growing body of evidence showing that elements of our safety net and social insurance system represent crucial investments in people's future lives. For example, Currie and Duque (this volume) cite studies showing that children covered by Medicaid early in life or in utero experience greater academic success and go on to have higher earnings and better health as adults. Schanzenbach (this volume) reviews evidence showing that early life exposure to the Supplemental Nutrition Assistance Program (SNAP) is associated with better health and economic security in adulthood. Collinson, Ellen, and Ludwig (this volume) discuss research suggesting that children who stay longer in public housing see higher earnings and lower rates of incarceration as adults. Hotz and Wiswall (this volume) cite a number of studies that find that high-quality preschool has beneficial long-term effects on education, employment, health, and criminal outcomes. Collectively, this body of research demonstrates that many of these programs do much more than provide immediate relief to hardship: they yield positive payoffs for years to come.

Paired with the considerations discussed earlier, this evidence makes a powerful case for not cutting or, better yet, providing more support for programs that benefit poor children and their parents. These investments enhance earnings growth in parts of the distribution that have seen only limited growth in recent decades and, in turn, relieve financial struggles and more general hardship. Just as important are the potential benefits for the broader economy and society. Higher incomes and more financial stability at the household level may make the macroeconomy more resilient to shocks and less prone to downturns. A more productive workforce means higher potential output and higher tax revenues, which should help to relieve fiscal challenges. Budget pressures may also be eased by lower future spending on safety net programs and fewer funds directed toward crime prevention and incarceration.

Implication 4: We should change safety net and social insurance programs so as to provide stronger incentives for work (or smaller disincentives)

A return to the rapid growth rates of labor supply seen in the latter decades of the 1900s is not in the cards given both that the ongoing retirement of the Baby Boom generation is substantially weighing on labor force growth and that we are highly unlikely to see another huge surge of women into the labor force. However, participation rates for working-age men and women in the United States lag those of many other high-income countries (Bown and Freund 2019), suggesting that we can do significantly better. And we should try to do better given the important role that labor force participation plays in fostering individual economic security and our nation's productive capacity. Reforms to our safety net and social insurance programs could help. The arguments for such changes go beyond their substantive effect on labor supply, as they would also create more political support for safety net and social insurance programs by reducing the unfairness that some perceive in allowing people to collect government benefits without working.

Most of the articles in this volume include discussion of the evidence on how their respective programs influence labor supply. Some highlight successes. For example, Haskins and Weidinger (this volume) show pronounced increases in the labor force participation rates of single mothers—and, in particular, never-married single mothers—in the mid- and late 1990s that they argue are probably linked to the work requirements associated with the Temporary Assistance for Needy Families (TANF) program that replaced traditional welfare in 1996. Hoynes (this volume) points to a body of work showing that the Earned Income Tax Credit (EITC) has a significant positive effect on the labor force participation of single women with children (although research also suggests that the EITC leads to small reductions in the employment of married women—as expected given that these women are likely to be in households with income in the phase-out region for the credit). Hotz and Wiswall (this volume) cite a number of articles suggesting that programs that provide or subsidize child care have some degree of positive effect on maternal labor supply.[6]

At the same time, most of the articles also acknowledge that features of their respective programs can provide disincentives for work—by reducing the need to earn money and, often, lowering the return to work by reducing benefits as income rises. The evidence is complicated and mixed in many cases. While some authors conclude that the effects are likely to be modest, others are more concerned about disincentive effects. For example, Maestas (this volume) highlights widespread and long-standing concerns about various negative effects of the Social Security Disability Insurance (SSDI) program on labor supply.[7]

In any event, a number of the articles argue that there is scope for reducing the disincentive effects of safety net and social insurance programs or changing the programs in other ways that would encourage labor force participation. For example, Maestas (this volume) proposes reforms to SSDI that would allow applicants to stay in the labor force longer, better identify their available work capacity, and encourage them to make use of this capacity. Hoynes (this volume) suggests expanding the EITC to childless workers, which could be particularly fruitful given both the demonstrated effectiveness of the program in encouraging labor supply and the fact that the decline in working-age male participation has been concentrated among low-skill men. Daly and Duggan (this volume) argue that we should speed up the Supplemental Security Income (SSI) application process so that applicants who are ultimately rejected suffer less skills atrophy and also introduce partial disability benefits for those on the margin of qualifying so that they can make use of any work capacity they might have.

Implication 5: Any reshaping of our safety net and social programs needs to take into account their role as potential stabilizers to the macroeconomy during recessions

The constraints on countercyclical monetary policy discussed above mean that fiscal policy will have to play a larger role in stabilizing the economy than it has in the past. But, as also discussed above, discretionary fiscal policy faces both substantive limitations (because of lags) and potential political limitations (because politicians may resist undertaking it). These two considerations suggest that we would be well served by putting more automatic fiscal stabilizers in place.

Many of the programs covered by this volume tend to expand and provide more benefits to individuals and families when the economy is weak and incomes are lower. For example, Bitler and Hoynes (2016) highlight the substantial support provided to U.S. households during the Great Recession by unemployment insurance, the EITC, SNAP, and TANF. In general, the safety net and social insurance programs not only relieve hardship for those who suffer most during recessions but also provide meaningful fiscal stimulus that helps the economy to normalize more quickly. Indeed, the programs can be particularly powerful tools for boosting aggregate demand because they put money into the hands of individuals who are likely to be stretched very thin and, in turn, have high spending propensities.

The role that our existing safety net and social insurance programs play as automatic stabilizers is not as high as it could be. One of the reasons that the set of programs highlighted by Bitler and Hoynes (2016) provided as much support as it did during the Great Recession is that unemployment insurance, the EITC, SNAP, and TANF were temporarily expanded by the ARRA. The ARRA also temporarily increased the share of Medicaid expenses paid by the federal government, which provided relief to state budgets and, in turn, supported the economy by reducing the cutbacks that states would otherwise need to make in other spending.

Several recent academic articles propose automatic expansions to safety net programs in response to the concern that future policy-makers may not always be willing to make (or may be slow to make) discretionary changes in fiscal policy to increase the size or generosity of these programs. von Wachter (this volume) suggests adding a trigger-based federally financed emergency unemployment compensation system that would automatically and quickly expand the unemployment insurance program when the economy weakens. Similarly, Hoynes (this volume) and Schanzenbach (this volume) propose automatically increasing the maximum SNAP benefit; and Fiedler, Furman, and Powell (2019) propose automatically increasing the federal share of Medicaid expenditures when the unemployment rate climbs above a certain threshold. Hoynes and Schanzenbach (2019) also point out that work requirements can diminish the automatic stabilizing properties of safety programs since jobs are particularly hard to come by when the economy is weak; policy-makers should be mindful of this consideration when reforming these programs.

Implication 6: Replacing our current set of safety net and social insurance programs with a universal basic income (UBI) system is not desirable

Because the other articles in this volume cover individual programs in specific areas, they do not delve into whether our entitlement system *as a whole* should be fundamentally changed. But it is worth considering whether macroeconomic developments warrant replacing our current programs with a UBI system. In its simplest form, a UBI provides a sizable regular cash payment to all individuals regardless of need.[8] Advocates of switching to a UBI system often point to the potential for rapid technological change to cause wide-scale and permanent destruction of jobs as a reason to make this change. Others support moving to UBI because they see our current set of programs as being overly complicated, administratively burdensome, and featuring too many disincentives for work and saving.

There would be a number of drawbacks to replacing our current system of safety net and social insurance programs with a UBI system. To start, the switch would have high fiscal costs. Hoynes and Rothstein (2019) estimate that a "pure" UBI of $12,000 per adult would cost $3 trillion, compared with a cost of $2.3 trillion for the existing set of safety net and social insurance programs (including Social Security and the big health care programs). Thus, the switch would materially increase the size of our tax and transfer system. Moving to UBI would provide a large downward redistribution of income relative to the current system, but with a much larger share of transfers going to childless, nonelderly, nondisabled households who are less vulnerable than the population being supported by our current set of programs. Indeed, payments to elderly and disabled households would be substantially lower than they are now. A further complication is that a UBI system alone does not provide certain important forms of insurance—most notably, insurance to cover large health care and long-term care expenses. Retaining such insurance would limit the potential streamlining associated with overhauling the system as it would mean either keeping parts of our existing health programs or requiring individuals to purchase health insurance through regulated insurance markets like those established under the Affordable Care Act. Finally, the politics of a UBI system are complicated. On one hand, switching to UBI would reduce the stigma that may accompany using our current set of safety net programs. On the other hand, having a UBI system is likely to incite fairness concerns—indeed, a basic income program piloted in Finland in the mid-2010s was reportedly controversial on the grounds that beneficiaries were getting "money for nothing" (*Reuters* 2019).

Historically, periods of new general-purpose technologies have caused only temporary displacement, with workers ultimately reallocated to new and better-paying jobs. One cannot say for sure that this pattern will repeat in the current episode given the potential rapid pace and large scope of disruption related to innovations like artificial intelligence and machine learning. Indeed, research already attributes a substantial part of growing income inequality to automation having reduced demand for middle-skill workers (Acemoglu and Autor 2011). Even if the future disruption is larger than usual, switching to a UBI system does not seem like the right solution because it would not address the fundamental problem of workers lacking the skills to complement new technologies. A targeted approach of making investments that enhance education and skills for young people and displaced workers—through both our existing set of entitlement programs and other government policies—would be a better path.[9]

Conclusion

We need to consider broader economic conditions and how they are evolving over time as we think through any restructuring of our system of safety net and social insurance programs. Rising government debt, slower macroeconomic growth, limited tools to fight recessions, greater income inequality, and household financial struggles create constraints but also opportunities as we go about reforming these programs. Fixing the financing of Social Security and curbing growth in government health care spending will be essential given fiscal challenges. Greater investment in poor children and more encouragement of work would not only relieve the hardship associated with limited income growth and other financial challenges but also create better social dynamics and raise macroeconomic growth. Strengthening the automatic fiscal stabilizer dimensions of entitlement programs can help to shorten future recessions and reduce their negative consequences. The articles in this volume will be extremely helpful as we go about reforming individual safety net and social insurance programs along these lines.

Notes

1. Rachel and Summers (2019) discuss the factors that may be behind the decline in interest rates and go on to estimate that "neutral" real interest rates declined by at least 3 percentage points between 1980 and 2018.

2. Taxes and government transfer payments offset some of these disparities, but the differences in after-tax-and-transfer income are still notable, with growth of 219 percent for the top 1 percent, 78 percent for others in the top quintile, 52 percent for the next three quintiles, and 65 percent for the bottom quintile.

3. There are pockets of concern. Most notably, student loan defaults increased sharply following the financial crisis and remained high throughout the 2010s. A growing literature shows that student loan repayment problems have been concentrated among borrowers who attended certain schools that consistently delivered low value to their students, many of which are in the for-profit sector (see, for example, Chou, Looney, and Watson 2017).

4. Brown, Dynan, and Figinski (forthcoming) use accumulated wealth and other variables to project the likelihood of different types of hardship in old age (such as poverty, food insecurity, and being on Medicaid) and find that individuals nearing retirement in the mid-2010s are more likely to experience hardship in old age than those nearing retirement in the mid-1990s.

5. The issue is not one of federal health care costs growing faster than private-sector costs but, rather, health care costs throughout the system generally growing faster than GDP.

6. As already noted, many of the articles that discuss programs that represent long-term investments in children highlight positive long-run labor supply effects.

7. von Wachter (this volume) points to a "long and ongoing" literature finding that more generous unemployment insurance leads unemployed workers to stay out of the workforce for a longer time, but it is unclear that such effects lower an individual's likelihood of participating over the longer run.

8. See Kearney and Mogstad (2019) for a summary of the variants on this idea that have been proposed, such as UBI systems that phase out benefits slowly as earnings rise.

9. If we truly see a "robot apocalypse" whereby most jobs disappear, the important issue will be who owns the robots and the income that the robots generate. One way to create more widespread ownership of capital is to strengthen policies that encourage low- and middle-income workers to participate in retirement savings plans, such as the "automatic IRA" program proposed by Gale et al. (2009).

References

Acemoglu, Daron, and David Autor. 2011. Skills, tasks and technologies: Implications for employment and earnings. In *Handbook of labor economics*, vol. 4B, eds. Orley Ashenfelter and David Card, 1043–1171. Amsterdam: Elsevier.

Bernanke, Ben. 2017. Monetary policy in a new era. Draft conference paper for the Peterson Institute of International Economics Conference on Rethinking Macroeconomic Policy, October. Available from https://www.brookings.edu/wp- content/uploads/2017/10/bernanke_rethinking_macro_final.pdf.

Bitler, Marianne, and Hilary Hoynes. 2016. The more things change, the more they stay the same? The safety net and poverty in the Great Recession. *Journal of Labor Economics* 34 (S1): S403–44.

Black, Sandra, and Wilson Powell. 10 July 2017. Where have all the (male) workers gone? *EconoFact*.

Blanchard, Olivier. 2019. Public debt and low interest rates. Presidential address at the 2019 American Economic Association annual meeting. Available from https://www.aeaweb.org/aea/2019conference/program/pdf/14020_paper_etZgfbDr.pdf.

Blinder, Alan S., and Mark Zandi. 2015. The financial crisis: Lessons for the next one. Policy Futures Paper, Center on Budget and Policy Priorities, Washington, DC.

Board of Governors of the Federal Reserve System. 2019. *Report on the economic well-being of U.S. households in 2018*. Available from https://www.federalreserve.gov/publications/files/2018-report-economic-well-being-us- households-201905.pdf.

Bown, Chad, and Caroline Freund. 2019. The problem of U.S. labor force participation. PIIE Working Paper 19-1, The Peterson Institute for International Economics, Washington, DC.

Brown, Jason, Karen Dynan, and Theodore Figinski. Forthcoming. The risk of financial hardship in retirement: A cohort analysis. In *Remaking retirement: Debt in an aging economy*, eds. Olivia S. Mitchell and Annamaria Lusardi. Oxford: Oxford University Press.

Case, Ann, and Angus Deaton. 2017. Mortality and morbidity in the 21st century. *Brookings Papers on Economic Activity*, Fall: 397–476.

Chetty, Raj, Nathaniel Hendren, Patrick Kline, and Emmanuel Saez. 2014. Where is the land of opportunity? The geography of intergenerational mobility in the United States. *Quarterly Journal of Economics* 129 (4): 1553–1623.

Chou, Tiffany, Adam Looney, and Tara Watson. 2017. Measuring loan outcomes at postsecondary institutions: Cohort repayment rates as an indicator of student success and institutional accountability. NBER Working Paper 23118, National Bureau of Economic Research, Cambridge, MA.

Congressional Budget Office. 2007. *The 2007 long-term budget outlook*. Available from https://www.cbo .gov/sites/default/files/110th-congress-2007-2008/reports/12-13-ltbo.pdf.

Congressional Budget Office. 2019a. *The distribution of household income, 2016* [along with the additional data for researchers file]. July. Available from https://www.cbo.gov/publication/55413.

Congressional Budget Office. 2019b. *The 2019 long-term budget outlook*. June. Available from https:// www.cbo.gov/system/files/2019-06/55331-LTBO-2.pdf.

Davis, Steven J., and Till von Wachter. 2011. Recessions and the costs of job loss. *Brookings Papers on Economic Activity* Fall:1–55.

Elmendorf, Douglas W. 2018. What is wrong with U.S. health care and how can we fix it? Remarks delivered at Princeton University. Available from https://www.hks.harvard.edu/sites/default/files/ Dean%27s%20Office/what_is_wrong_wit h_us_health_care_and_how_can_we_fix_it.pdf.

Elmendorf, Douglas W., and Louise M. Sheiner. 2017. Federal budget policy with an aging population and persistently low interest rates. *Journal of Economic Perspectives* 31 (3): 175–94.

Fiedler, Matthew, Jason Furman, and Wilson Powell III. 2019. Increasing federal support for state Medicaid and CHIP programs in response to economic downturns. In *Recession ready: Fiscal policies to stabilize the American economy*, eds. Heather Boushey, Ryan Nunn, and Jay Shambaugh. Washington, DC: The Hamilton Project and Washington Center for Equitable Growth.

Furman, Jason. 2018. The fiscal response to the Great Recession: Steps taken, paths rejected, and lessons for next time. Discussion draft for Brookings Institution conference on Responding to the Global Financial Crisis. Available from https://www.brookings.edu/wp-content/uploads/2018/08/12-Fiscal-Policy-Prelim-Disc- Draft-2018.09.11.pdf.

Gale, William G., J. Mark Iwry, David C. John, and Lina Walker. 2009. *Automatic: Changing the way America saves*. Washington, DC: Brookings Institution.

Hoynes, Hilary W., Douglas L. Miller, and Jessamyn Schaller. 2012. Who suffers during recessions? *Journal of Economic Perspectives* 26 (3): 27–48.

Hoynes, Hilary W., and Jesse Rothstein. 2019. Universal basic income in the U.S. and advanced countries. NBER Working Paper 25538, National Bureau of Economic Research, Cambridge, MA.

Hoynes, Hilary W., and Diane Schanzenbach. 2019. Strengthening SNAP as an automatic stabilizer. In *Recession ready: Fiscal policies to stabilize the American economy*, eds. Heather Boushey, Ryan Nunn, and Jay Shambaugh. Washington, DC: The Hamilton Project and Washington Center for Equitable Growth.

Kearney, Melissa S. 2014. Income inequality in the United States. Testimony before the Joint Economic Committee of the U.S. Congress. January. Available from https://www.brookings.edu/wp-content/ uploads/2016/06/16-income-inequality-in- america-kearney-1.pdf.

Kearney, Melissa S., and Magne Mogstad. 2019. *Universal basic income (UBI) as a policy response to current challenges*. Washington, DC: Brookings Institution. Available from https://www.brookings.edu/ research/universal-basic-income-as-a-policy-response-to-current-challenges/.

Krugman, Paul. 29 April 2015. The case for cuts was a lie. Why does Britain still believe it? The austerity delusion. *The Guardian*.

Laubach, Thomas, and John C. Williams. 2016. Measuring the natural rate of interest redux. *Business Economics* 51 (2): 57–67.

Lusardi, Annamaria, Peter Tufano, and Daniel Schneider. 2011. Financially fragile households: Evidence and implications. *Brookings Papers on Economic Activity*, Spring: 83–134.

National Academies of Sciences, Engineering, and Medicine. 2015. *The growing gap in life expectancy by income: Implications for federal programs and policy responses*. Washington, DC: The National Academies Press.

Papanicolas, Irene, Liana R. Woskie, and Ashish K. Jha. 2018. Health care spending in the United States and other high-income countries. *JAMA* 319 (10): 1024–39.

Rachel, Lukasz, and Lawrence H. Summers. 2019. Public boost and private drag: Government policy and the equilibrium real interest rate in advanced economies. Conference draft for the Brookings Papers on Economic Activity, Spring.

Reuters. 9 February 2019. Finland's basic income trial boosts happiness, but not employment.

Summers, Lawrence H. March/April 2016. The age of secular stagnation. *Foreign Affairs*.

Survey of Professional Forecasters. 2019. First quarter 2019 survey. Available from https://www .philadelphiafed.org/research-and-data/real-time-center/survey-of- professional-forecasters/2019/ survq119.

Yagan, Danny. 2019. Employment hysteresis from the Great Recession. *Journal of Political Economy* 127 (5): 2505–58.